# LIVES, LIES AND THE
# IRAN-CONTRA AFFAIR

# LIVES, LIES AND THE IRAN-CONTRA AFFAIR

*ANN WROE*

*I.B. Tauris & Co Ltd*
*Publishers*
*London · New York*

To my parents

Published in an updated
paperback edition in 1992 by
I.B. Tauris & Co Ltd
45 Bloomsbury Square
London WC1A 2HY

175 Fifth Avenue
New York
NY 10010

In the United States of America
and Canada distributed by
St Martin's Press
175 Fifth Avenue
New York
NY 10010

A CIP record for this book is available from the British Library


Library of Congress Catalog Card Number: 91–65138
A full CIP record is available from the Library of Congress

ISBN 1–85043–558–8 pbk

Printed in Great Britain by
WBC Print Ltd., Unit 8, Waterton Industrial Estate, Bridgend.

# Contents

# Introduction

THIS book was written in an attempt to sum up, and make sense of, the Iran-contra affair. The scandal had been dogging me and bothering me for four years, and the best way to clear it out of my head seemed to be to write about it. It seems only courteous, nevertheless, to apologize to Americans who think it is none of my business. To study the scandal as a 'Brit' is a presumption. My defence is that I covered it, on and off, from the time it broke; that it is a story large enough and intriguing enough, it seems to me, for a number of books, although it has produced very few; and that an effort to treat Iran-contra in terms of universal and timeless issues, rather than contemporary American ones, perhaps provides an excuse for the presence of a foreigner.

This is not a comprehensive account of the scandal. First, I wouldn't dare; second, the logistical sub-details — of all the various arms shipments, and how the money shifted around — quickly get extremely tedious, even for aficionados. It is a personal view from a particular angle, with all the omissions and quirks that that implies. This was a scandal that I sometimes found shocking but more often simply fascinating; perhaps we Europeans are less easily offended, and more cynical, about the deeply anti-democratic ploys that go on beneath the surface of ostensibly democratic governments. I found it foolish, sad, irresponsible and inevitable; and, above all, the perfect scandal for our morally ambiguous and mixed up times. It raised all over again, in a very peculiar contemporary case, the issues of ends and means, right and wrong, obedience and conscience, truth and lies; and left them for people to sort out. Often, they could not do so. Much of America was appalled by Iran-contra, but much of the country saw nothing wrong with it; and a sort of moral fault-line developed (the phrase comes from *Time*), down which the scandal eventually seemed to disappear.

It is the moral and ethical side of Iran-contra, then, that is covered in the pages that follow. It is not done chronologically; the narrative jumps about, following the various themes ('duty', say, or 'lying') through multiple layers of events. At this point, therefore, it seems wise to take the reader through a short chronological account of the business, so that he has something to cling to in the chapters ahead.

The Iran-contra affair was not one affair, but two. Both were features of Ronald Reagan's second term, which begin in effect with his landslide re-election in November 1984; and both could be taken as outgrowths of hubris, of a general feeling that anything was both possible and permissible. The first 'affair' was the Reagan administration's covert programme of arms sales to Iran in exchange, it was hoped, for American and other Western hostages held in Lebanon by the terrorist group Hizbollah. This covert programme originated in Israel, and was brought to America's attention in the summer of 1985. The Americans were cautious; but in July Reagan authorized contacts with Iran, and in August he agreed to replenish the weapons Israel was about to send there. On August 20th 1985, 96 TOW missiles were shipped to Iran. No hostages were released; but on September 14th 408 TOWs were shipped by Israel, and on the 15th one American hostage, the Rev Benjamin Weir, was set free.

The Americans were still feeling their way; but on November 17th they were called in to help with another Israeli shipment, this time of Hawk missiles, which had been held up in Portugal. The National Security Council procured an aircraft from the CIA and unblocked the shipment; the procedure, as a covert action, had to be hastily legalized afterwards. The logistical horrors of this shipment encouraged the Americans to start dealing with Iran direct, not through Israel, although Israel continued to serve as a cover. A proper finding authorizing the arms shipments (but concealing, as much as possible, the fact that this was a swap of arms for hostages) was signed by Reagan on January 17th 1986.

From then on the programme was America's responsibility; and it became a saga of hopeless negotiations and failed expectations. On

February 19th, 500 TOWs went to Iran; no hostages were released. A second shipment of 500 TOWs went on February 27th; again, failure. On May 23rd an American delegation led by a former national security advisor, Robert McFarlane, took the considerable risk of going to Tehran to talk with the Iranians directly; they took some Hawk parts with them. No hostages came out, and the Americans were bitterly disappointed; but the contacts continued, and on July 26th the release of a Catholic priest, Father Lawrence Jenco, convinced them that they should perhaps carry on despite the odds. More missiles were sent in August and October and on November 2nd another hostage, David Jacobsen, was released. The next day an account of McFarlane's trip to Tehran appeared in a Beirut magazine, and the story was blown.

The Iran operation caused consternation for three reasons. First, America had gone round the backs of its allies, sending arms to Iran even though its public policy ('Operation Staunch') was not to supply weapons to any regime sponsoring terror. Second, the administration had gone round the back of Congress; it had never informed the Intelligence Committees about the scheme, even though they were supposed to be told 'in a timely manner' of covert operations. Third, arms-for-hostages was simply a bad idea, running completely counter to the western consensus that deals should not be struck with hostage-takers. Nonetheless, the furore over the Iran arms shipments might have died down in a month or so (many other western countries had struck their own deals, after all), had it not been improbably tied in with the administration's most controversial piece of foreign policy, support for the contra rebels in Nicaragua. On November 22nd 1986, in the middle of a fact-finding inquiry into the arms sales to Iran, a memorandum was discovered mentioning the use of profits from the arms sales for the contras; and the furore became a full-blown scandal, whose reverberations continue to this day.

The second 'affair', then, was another covert operation, that to supply equipment and weapons to the contras. To support the contras had been public administration policy since 1981, when Reagan came into office. But a majority in Congress did not agree with it, and from 1982 onwards a series of restrictive laws, the Boland amendments, were put through Congress in an attempt to shut down the war in Nicaragua. For a time these were narrow and specific, and the administration, determined as it was to keep the contras going, could easily scramble round them; but in October 1984 the 'full' version of Boland passed, prohibiting the spending of any appropriated money on the rebels. This took the Defence Department and the CIA out of the picture; but it appeared to leave a loophole for the National Security Council, as part of the President's staff, and through the NSC an extremely complicated system of private cut-outs was set up to get the contras arms. This arrangement, of an extremely ramshackle and obvious kind, lasted until August 1986, when Congress passed a $100m package of military and humanitarian aid for the rebels; and all the time it lasted, the NSC denied that it was doing anything outside the strictures of Boland. The lies began to fall apart, as they were bound to, on October 6th, when one of the 'private' resupply aircraft was shot down over Nicaragua, and a White House telephone number was found in somebody's pocket.

The existence of this operation could hardly have come as a surprise to people with their eyes open; but the discovery of the memorandum linking it to Iran suddenly diverted attention away from arms-for-hostages. The question at the heart of the scandal became whether the President had known about the diversion of Iran arms money to the contras: an essentially petty question that, as it turned out, nobody was ever able to answer. (I cannot answer it, either.) The question of how far President and cabinet had guided and prodded the two operations in general was the more interesting one; but Congress seemed to withdraw from that, as if it did not have the stomach to pursue it. In the course of 1987 there were extensive inquiries, taking of depositions, and public hearings; in 1989 and 1990 there were trials; but much of the scandal remained mysterious to most people. In part, this was because the inquiries were conducted with so narrow and distorted a focus; they came to seem irrelevant. In part, it was because the affair was so complicated, and some of the essential strands were presumed to have been lost when the NSC operations managers resorted to wholesale shredding in October and November 1986. Much of the evidence, too, was kept back on grounds of national security; and for these reasons, although the affair touched and damaged Ronald Reagan in the last two years of his presidency, it could not shake him. Iran-contra was left as a scandal whose natural constitutional denouement — the fall of the man at the top — had never happened, and whose true nature would possibly never be known.

Because of this unfinished quality, writers have naturally hesitated (as I have) to lift their pens. We are aware that some of the T's are not crossed and not all the I's are dotted. Some of the cases are still on appeal in the courts; convictions have been overturned. The special prosecutor had not yet packed his bags, and there may be more surprises. On the other hand, the accounts of the affair are growing fainter and fainter; the shape of the scandal (in Reagan's careless words, 'a covert action that was taken at my behest')[1] has been plain for some time; and certain aspects of the affair are already as well documented as any investigator could wish for. It is possible now to get the whole mess into perspective, and to try to sum it up a bit.

Iran-contra was a constitutional brawl: the rights of the executive (particularly in foreign policy) were pitched against the prerogatives of Congress. It was also a political tussle, and it divided the country along predictable political lines: conservatives broadly supporting the players, liberals and moderates against them. And it was, not least, a classic tale of corruption: of good ends (as many saw them) scuttled by bad means, and of decent men persuaded into lying and self-delusion. Senator Daniel Inouye put it well at the start of the public hearings, in May 1987.

> The story is both sad and sordid; it is filled with inconsistencies and often unexplainable conduct. None of the participants emerges unblemished. People of great character and ability holding positions of trust and authority in our government were drawn into a web of deception and despair.[2]

This book is precisely a study of that: of how, in one extraordinary case, men conducted themselves, and how they felt they should have done; how they dealt with the dilemmas they encountered, between policy and conscience and orders and causes (if, indeed, they saw dilemmas there at all); how they justified what they did, and how they failed to; when, and why, they lied; whether they were playthings of fate, or responsible for their own actions; and how they deceived themselves. When they were questioned afterwards, it was often difficult to tie the players down to dates or times or actions; but they freely gave away their moral and political philosophies with almost every word they spoke.

By 'political philosophy', I do not mean party affiliation. As it happened, these people were conservative Republicans; but in some of their approaches to some of the moral issues discussed, they might have been liberal Democrats. Or they might have been civil servants in ancient Athens; for in this particular field, not much has changed. My own training was as a medieval historian. Pulled into Iran-contra as a journalist, I stayed there foraging among the documents as in my college days; and it was only after the book emerged that I realized it followed almost exactly the shape of my old doctoral thesis on the political attitudes of lesser officials in fourteenth-century France.

The 'players' referred to above are principally the three architects of the scandal: Robert ('Bud') McFarlane, John Poindexter and Oliver North. I call them 'architects' with a purpose. Architects design buildings, but they work to a commission; the need and idea for the building are someone else's. Architects also delegate the roughest work, the brick-and-mortar laying (though North did quite a lot of that, such as negotiating with the Iranians); and when the building is done, and is an eyesore, the architect carries the blame for it. So it was with these three, and so it largely remains. They were not the *primum mobile* of the scandal, but they were the men in charge of the operations: the managers, the action officers, and thus the men round whom the moral questions gathered.

I have not talked to these men. In part, this is my training; both as an historian and a journalist, it is the written accounts (preferably on oath) that I tend to look at, and there was certainly no shortage of those. But North and Poindexter, in any case, have never given interviews on the subject, and presumably will not until all the legal procedures are over. I toyed with the idea of approaching them for a while (as a foreigner, what danger could I be?), but then gave up. All I can offer at first hand is an exchange of a dozen words with North, from which I carried away an impression of irrepressible energy wound up tight as a spring; and (perhaps not insignificant) an exchange of even fewer words with Reagan, before he became president, in which he seemed already to be crumbling away with age, leathery and brown as an old doll.

It was McFarlane, Reagan's third national security advisor, who initially allowed the Israelis to get their toehold into American policy towards Iran. ('It was Bud's idea', as Don Regan, the chief of staff, said later; 'you have a lousy idea, you get lousy results.'[3]) It was also McFarlane who was entrusted by the president to keep the contras together 'body and soul', despite what Congress might have to say about it. He was a particularly difficult man to read; Caspar Weinberger, the secretary of defence, said he always found it hard to tell where he stood on anything. He served as national security advisor for two years before resigning, in November 1985, in misery, frustration and exhaustion. His training was essentially military, in the Marines. In civilian life he kept the clenched at-attention face, the stiff back and the mercilessly tortured syntax of a soldier not at ease with what was required of him. He had been raised by an aunt in a small town in Texas, and his background was one of strict Methodist decency and frugality: qualities he retained in public service. His most painful moment in office seemed to come when he was accused of an unlikely affair with a reporter; his most notable outbursts of temper came whenever he was accused of trying to be a second Henry Kissinger, a lesser one, and failing.

McFarlane was succeeded as national security advisor by Poindexter, who was expected to make no waves at all. He was a closed book, even to his secretary ('The Admiral', she admitted, 'was not a very social bird'[4]); a man who would take care to keep the office door closed, even when all he was doing was eating a punctilious breakfast from a tray; a man who, when asked by the apoplectic Regan what the hell was going on, paused to dab his mouth with his napkin before replying;[5] a man who said 'I don't recall' or some variant of it, 184 times when he was called to account before Congress. For his trial, in 1990, he grew a jolly moustache and sported a range of flat caps; but during his twelve months of power he appeared, by contrast, a man of unrelenting remoteness and austerity, characterized by his bald head, his pipe and his coldly staring bifocals. Raised in small-town Indiana, he had risen to the highest echelons of the Navy and had won golden opinions for his efficiency, memory and uprightness; but his medals had been won for shuffling paper, not in combat. At the NSC he kept his careful ways. His desk was always tidy, and he made little lists marked with square boxes to be ticked when jobs were done. Poindexter wished always to be private, to hold things close, to be unremarkable. There was no question of his wearing his uniform at the hearings, as North did; and the fact of his extraordinary intellect seemed only to embarrass him.

Under Poindexter, as under McFarlane before him, the Iran and contra 'accounts' were handled by North: a Marine Corps major, later lieutenant colonel, seconded to the NSC for a term of years that kept being extended. North was an altogether different figure, neither tortured nor secret. Born in 1943, raised in upstate New York, he was the son of a soldier and a teacher. He was a slight, boyish man, but with the solidity and handsome battered face of a boxer; and he rose to prominence by eagerness, prostrating work and a willingness to stroke his superiors. Friends used to complain that whenever they took group photographs he would always find his way to the front, pulling a face or waving; and so it has seemed with this book. By putting himself in the middle of every morally vexed situation, North naturally comes to centre-stage; chief volunteer, fall guy, spokesman for the cause and, not infrequently, chief victim of his own machinations.

He was also 'an altar and throne man all the way', as his friend Pat Buchanan described him; a romantic, an instinctive obeyer of orders, and a born-again Catholic whose faith gave a particular poignancy to the grubby dealings in which he involved himself. North, in some ways, was a man of almost impossible moral rigidity — apparently untempted, for example, by his gorgeous secretary — but in other ways, such as the uses of lying, he seemed to have no moral compass at all. He was not quite the type of Graham Greene's Alden Pyle, 'impregnably armoured in his good intentions and his ignorance', for by all accounts he was shrewd, and no innocent. But his notebooks of his doings at the NSC, full of arms and dollars and middlemen, also included one phrase, ringed so that he would remember it: 'For Him, With Him'.[6]

These paradoxes lead on to a final point. A book of this kind inevitably makes moral judgements, both about policies and people. Policies I take as fair game; people I have tried to treat gently. From my safe position a long way away, with no burning political commitment of my own, it is easy enough to hope that I would always behave impeccably; but I doubt it. If the pressure was on me, if it was my cause that was at stake, what would I do? I do not know; and it is precisely because these questions of 'right' behaviour are so vexed that I have wanted to write about them. Had the main players in Iran-contra been bad men, their part in these 'ignominious episodes' (McFarlane's phrase)[7] would not have held much interest. But the scandal was characterized, as well as by wholesale deception, by a certain striving-to-be-good; and in this lies both the oddity of it and, perhaps, some of its importance.

# PART I

## Pictures on a Screen

We live in a world of perceptions, not reality.
>                              North PROF note to Poindexter, 15.7.86

I find much of what I've heard is implausible. Perhaps
I'll come to the conclusion [that] . . . that is because it was
real.
>                              Senator William Cohen, hearings, 30.7.87

Even as the operations were in the making, between 1984 and 1986,
they were dogged by an air of unreality and self-delusion. They were
secret, but not professionally so. They were policy, but of a highly
odd and experimental kind. Large numbers of people had wind of
them, indeed opposed them, but did not wish to admit that they
even knew what was going on. From the very beginning, therefore,
witnesses to the operations and players within them suspended their
disbelief. In this cloudy world, where so little seemed dependable or
real, moral values were frequently suspended too. This chapter
investigates how that world appeared to the players and the lookers
on, both at the time and afterwards.

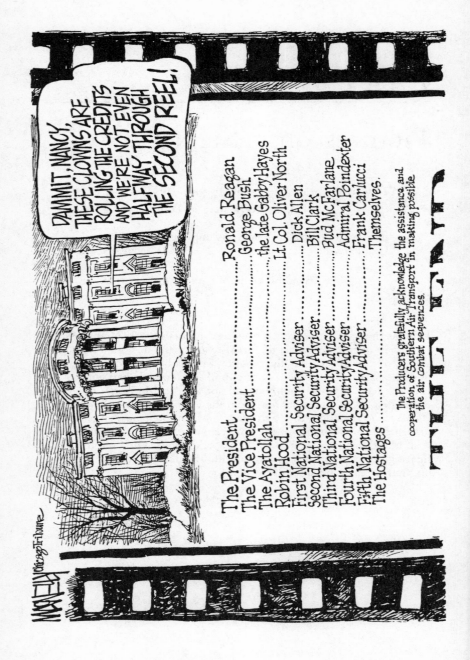

# Chapter 1

# The Politics of Illusion

TWO illusions lay at the heart of Iran-contra. The first was that the Iran of Ayatollah Khomeini could, in some sort, be reasonably dealt with; the second was that a band of rag-tag guerrillas, the Nicaraguan contras, could save the West from Communism. Both illusions were shattered in ways that underlined how fragile and ramshackle the policies were, and they were shattered within a month of each other. A supply aircraft, carrying weapons to the contras, was shot down by the Sandinistas at the beginning of October 1986; and on November 3rd a Lebanese magazine, *Al-Shiraa*, broke the story of American dealings with Iran. Once they were revealed, it seemed extraordinary that either operation should have borne the stamp of the American government; they seemed to be bad dreams. But that same quality, of political self-delusion, was also clear as they were in the making.

*Al-Shiraa's* was a small piece, about the clandestine visit by McFarlane to Tehran in May. McFarlane was then no longer in government; he travelled to Iran on Reagan's orders, accompanied by North, Amiram Nir of Israel and half a pallet of missile parts that he hoped to exchange for hostages. The trip was to become the epitome of the affair: misconceived, well-meaning, disastrous, courageous, deceptive and surreal. The group had false Irish passports. A copy of McFarlane's was produced by the Speaker of

3

the Iranian parliament, Ali Akbar Rafsanjani, at a public news conference in January 1987; it was displayed by a man with short, dirty fingernails beside a spray of plastic flowers. Beneath the unmistakably hangdog face of the former national security advisor was his Irish alias, Sean Devlin; born in Dublin, 14th August 1937; colour of eyes, hazel ('cnodhonna' in the Gaelic). Rafsanjani displayed this more in mystification than anger, as if the purpose of McFarlane's mission was still unknown to him.

Indeed, when the party had arrived at the bleak airport in Tehran in the middle of Ramadan, hoping to find a government delegation of equal weight, nobody was there to meet them. It emerged afterwards that nobody in Iran had known who McFarlane/Devlin was.[1] 'It may be best for us', McFarlane reported back at the time, 'to try to picture what it would be like if after nuclear attack, a surviving Tartar became Vice-President; a recent grad student became Secretary of State; and a bookie became the interlocutor for all discourse with foreign countries.'[2] An expatriate Iranian satirist, Hadi Khorsandi, later claimed in fun to have had the ear of Rafsanjani, who told him that his discussions with McFarlane 'were meant only for him to practise the English language . . . all the contacts he had had with Americans over the past year had been made for the purpose of learning irregular verbs.'[3]

McFarlane was said to have taken a cake and a Bible on the trip. There was no Bible except North's own, which the pilot with some surprise spotted him carrying onto the plane;[4] an official Bible, autographed by Reagan, went on a trip in October. But there was a key-shaped chocolate cake — a 'joke' between North and the Iranian middleman, Manucher Ghorbanifar,[5] ordered by North from a kosher bakery in Israel — and a pair of Colt pistols in a presentation box. The cake and the Bible were linked ever after with McFarlane, although neither was even his idea. Whatever larger and higher purposes the trip may have had, they were subsumed in circus. McFarlane knew it, and resented it. He was reduced to saying stiffly to one interviewer: 'Simply put, there was a cake on the mission. I didn't buy it, bake it, cook it, eat it, present it, or otherwise get involved with it.'[6] He had little chance; the Revolutionary Guards at the airport, famished by Ramadan, took it away and ate it.

As North later described the first approaches to the Iran idea, Israeli officials talking to Americans in the spring and summer of 1985, it was a 'philosophy' rather than an operation.[7] The philosophy presupposed, first, that the Iranian regime contained officials of reason and moderation with whom America could do business, and that these officials would intercede with the terrorist Hizbollah to release the American hostages they held in Beirut. Yet nobody knew for certain who these moderates (sometimes called 'pragmatists') were; or, if they existed, how much influence they had. 'Are there any pragmatists in Iran?' asked Clair George, the CIA's deputy director of operations, putting the question rhetorically; 'Does anyone play the piano in the Fiji Islands? Yes, somewhere.'[8]

The man who organized the aircraft to get 1,000 TOWs* to Israel in February 1986 (and 500 TOWs from there to Tehran) thought that 'if the government wanted to establish relations and there were modernists, we should do what we could to assist.'[9] Modernists and moderates were probably as numerous as one another, as Charlie Allen of the CIA reported to Casey as late as November 1986. He had notionally divided up the Iranian government into a fanatic wing, an extremely fanatic wing, a bridge group and a 'right-wing group' that leaned towards the West. But it was not this group, as Allen knew, with which America had been dealing. At best, he knew of only one moderate who was waiting to meet some senior American somewhere in the 'foggy' councils of Tehran.[10] Michael Ledeen, an academic and consultant who did much to promote the Iran venture, took heart from the fact that when an arms shipment went disastrously wrong, in November 1985, the Iranians still gave the crew caviar on their flight out of Iran.[11] But the reality was stated by Nir to George Bush, quite plainly, in July 1986: 'We are dealing with the most radical elements . . . we've learned they can deliver and the moderates can't.'[12]

The American policy also assumed that if TOWs were bartered for lives, as North put it,[13] the transaction could be passed off as something other than ransom, neatly tied up without the stakes being raised. George Cave, who went on the Tehran trip to translate, was soon disabused of that. Cave was older than the rest of the party, and the only one with knowledge of Iran; he also suffered from a bad back, and must have landed with a fierce combination of jet-lag, suspicion and pain. At the very first meeting in the Tehran Hilton, renamed the Independence, one of the Iranians ('a rug merchant') complained that the spare parts the Americans had brought were second-hand. Cave replied, furious, 'You know you weren't supposed to unload them until after the hostages showed up.' The Iranian snapped back: 'You've only brought a very small amount of spare parts.'

'Well, that's all we could fit on the airplane.'

'Well, it didn't take up hardly any space.'

* A shoulder-fired anti-tank missile.

'Yes, but we could only take a certain amount of weight.'

And so on and so on. Cave later discovered that the box of parts had not been opened at all; another conversation premised on something that had not occurred, designed to raise both the bidding and the temperature, and a chimera.[14]

A political gamble was taken too: that if hostages were released, Americans would not greatly mind what the price or the means had been. This might have been the case in France or West Germany; but, as the administration rapidly found out, it was not the case in the United States.

Some sensed the danger early. Caspar Weinberger, the secretary of defence — a small, determined, beaky man, best-known for cutting any budget but his own — first heard of a possible Iranian operation on June 18th, 1985. It came in a memorandum with a covering letter from McFarlane; the premise was that unless the United States changed its policies towards Iran, America's position in Tehran would never improve. The regime was highly unstable and about to fall; conservatives inside it might be cultivated and, as a sign of good faith ('bona fides'), they might be sold arms. Weinberger believed none of that. He was less bothered by the thought of arms sales, however, than by what he saw as the fundamental unreality of the proposal. There was nobody in a position of power in Iran, he believed, but 'irrational lunatics', with whom 'we didn't have the slightest possibility of getting any kind of an improved relationship'.[15] He passed the memo on, as requested, but scribbled in the margin: 'Almost too absurd to comment on. It's like asking Gadhafi over to Washington for a cosy chat.'[16]

So absurd was the idea to Weinberger that he seems never to have understood the hold it acquired over other people, including the President. Although Weinberger opposed it, he did not often do so with force: partly because, it seemed to him, nobody was foolish enough to propose it with much vehemence. George Shultz, the bluff and portly secretary of state, evidently thought much the same. He had received word of the Iran scheme in a stream-of-consciousness memo from McFarlane, delivered to 'Secretary Shultz personally and to no other for him', aboard his aircraft on July 13th, 1985. McFarlane, having spelled out with caution the Israeli arguments and the Iranian blandishments, admitted that 'the concept raises a number of imponderable questions', including 'where this might lead in terms of our being asked to up the ante on more and more arms and where that could conceivably lead . . . Clearly that is a loser.' 'George', he concluded, 'I cannot judge the equities on this. We need to think about it. But I don't think we should tarry.' Despite that dazzling contradiction, typical of the affair, Shultz said he agreed with him. There could be 'a tentative show of interest . . . I do not think we could justify turning our backs.' There were certainly 'imponderables', however, and Shultz had a shrewd solution for those: 'Given the nature of this matter, I am inclined to think it should be managed by you personally.'[17]

Yet it was not simply a matter of proposing; the policy was soon enough carried out. Arms were shipped by Israel with American acquiescence in August and September 1985, and the Israeli stocks replaced. ('The people who sold the soap for us want to replenish their supply' came the typically slippery message to McFarlane; his secretary described how, when such messages came, he would look at her with a puzzled expression.)[18] But as a result of the September shipment one hostage, Benjamin Weir, came out, and from then on American misgivings were countered by another thought: the scheme had worked. In all, three hostages — Weir, Lawrence Jenco and David Jacobsen — were successfully traded for arms. Three more — Joseph Cicippio, Edward Tracy and Frank Reed — were seized in 1986 by kidnappers newly alerted to their value in Hawks* and TOWs, giving a net result of zero. The releases, however, were crucial. They saved the scheme from being dismissed as nonsense.

Heartened by the sight of Weir standing beside Reagan on the South Lawn, the administration allowed itself to be drawn further into the Israeli-Iranian manoeuvres. In November 1985, arms were sent with American participation. That shipment was a classic of incompetence. North called it 'a bit of a horror story' and, for once, he understated:[19] it went wrong from start to finish, and ended with the wrong missiles, still with their Israeli markings, piled on the ground in Tehran.

The story of the operation, in all its farcical mystery, was best told by the officers and crew of the CIA proprietary airline called in to help on November 22nd.[20] Three flights had to be made to fly missiles into Tehran. The air branch officer thought it all 'very nebulous. Based on my experience, I thought it would go away overnight. They usually do.' This one did not. The captain did not know what the craft was carrying, though that was not unusual, and the line was under contract partly for its discretion. 'It is sort of like a tramp freighter, sort of plodding round from point to point', said the air branch officer; 'and you don't ask too many questions when you are doing this.' At most, they might enquire whether the cargo was dynamite or something explosive, 'but then you have to worry about thunderstorms, you know.'

* A tripod-fired anti-aircraft missile.

The pieces, 80 of them, were an odd shape, and difficult to load. The crew grumbled about them. They heard at first that these were industrial spare parts, then medical equipment, then mining equipment, then oil-drilling gear. The cargo had no manifest in any case, so there was no telling what the stuff was. It was simply described as 'sensitive'. The pilot thought the size of the gray-green boxes, 'seven metres long and one meter wide' was familiar, somehow; but 'as long as you don't open the boxes, you don't know what you have . . . it is blessed by the government when it is being loaded, so I couldn't care less what it is.' One of the crew, having his wits about him, joked that whatever was in the boxes should probably be fired into Iran, not sent; the project officer thought he might well be right.

The aircraft was American-registered, anyway; it could not fly into Tehran. The Israeli contact, Al Schwimmer, offered to paint on a new registration and forge some new papers, but was politely turned down. Schwimmer then suggested formation flying with two 707s, one hiding behind the other to conceal its American colours. 'I told him you have to be kidding', the project manager remembered. 'I can't fly a 707 formation flying down to Tehran, you know, I mean . . . the longer it went on the more I had the feeling I am dealing here with lunatics.'

When the aircraft took off, at last, with a mere 18 missiles, no clearance had been given for overflights between Tel Aviv and Tehran. The pilot, with no diplomatic clearance number, made one up; air-traffic control did not believe him, but he managed to weave his way towards Iran even as he argued with them. For crossing the border into Iran, he had a code ('I am coming for Mustafa'), but no-one asked for it; and so they landed in Tehran. While the aircraft was unloaded the crew was spirited away by car through the back roads of the airport by a civilian with a machine-gun, who took them to the old Sheraton Hotel and offered them cakes and coffee. The crew had done wonders, but back in Washington the project officer was furious. He had never, he wrote to his superiors, seen an operation so badly planned or so amateurishly organized; 'at the CIA, we really do run a better show than that.' But then, of course, it had not been the CIA in charge of 'the show'. It had been the NSC.

The Americans (and North in particular, who had been pitched by McFarlane into handling the Washington end) had stumbled into the operation before they were ready, either practically or legally, to handle it. A presidential authorization for a covert operation, a 'mini-finding', was rushed out at the end of November, so secretly that hardly anyone knew of it; this made good what had happened already, which was not supposed to have happened at all. On December 7th too, when the matter was raised at a meeting of the President and principals, the operation was presented by McFarlane as essentially prospective, something that had not happened yet; but the purpose of the meeting was also to justify policy after the fact. Half the people there did not know that. Those who did kept quiet. Don Regan, the blustering ex-Wall Street chief of staff, had attended the crucial meetings of the previous August and September; but he had apparently spent the September meeting more bothered by McFarlane's pronunciation of 'bona fides' as 'bonerfydies' than by anything he picked up about weapons shipments. (As 'an old Latin scholar', he was appalled that people could mangle words that way.[21]) On December 7th, it was Reagan's particularly flashy plaid jacket that distracted him.[22]

Weinberger found himself, allegedly to his surprise, arguing against the policy again. McFarlane said he had made contact, through the Israelis, with a group of Iranians who seemed 'different'. Not different at all, countered Weinberger: still fanatically anti-American and virulently anti-western; America could not do any business with them. McFarlane did not argue back to any degree. As Weinberger complained, 'He was very, very close-to-the-vest type of approach in almost everything.'[23] The President, sitting with his feet up beside the coffee table, also did not say much. When he did, he seemed to agree with Weinberger and Shultz. Weinberger told his deputy, after the meeting, that he thought the initiative had been 'strangled in its cradle'; his deputy noted later that Weinberger 'also believed that nothing was really dead in Washington'.[24] And so it turned out. The decision had come down in favour of illusion: the President's dream of triumphant new diplomacy and the hostages home. There was even a business fantasy, probably injected in the President's ear by Don Regan after the others had left. 'In my other capacity as head of Merill Lynch, I opened an office in Tehran . . . during the 70s . . . and I thought that that country had quite a future.'[25]

Once the policy was authorized, in a proper finding of January 17th 1986, Weinberger and Shultz both let it go. They hoped to be spared the details. In large part, they were; the government now stood back from the operation, and the 'private' middlemen and cut-outs took charge of it. But on January 22nd Shultz got word of the latest version: 'a proposal by Lieutenant-Colonel North to seek the help of the Pope and Cardinal O'Connor, and to trade some Shia prisoners held by General Lahad in South Lebanon.'[26] This, according to White House officials later, was North's 'pipe-dream', proof that he lived 'in a Peter Pan world'.[27] Shultz treated it accordingly. A week later, however, Charlie Allen of the CIA sat down with an undercover agent in North's office to hear North read from his notebook

> A very detailed schedule, starting one date after another . . . And that schedule . . . later became a printed schedule and he had a very finely developed scenario where eventually a certain amount of equipment, particularly TOW missiles, would be sent to Iran, [and] hostages would be released . . . At some point Ayatollah Khomeini would step down. And I recall that I laughed aloud at that stage and I believe [the agent] joined me in that.
> We didn't think that was terribly plausible, but he was quite serious.[28]

Ledeen said he would remember 'to his dying day' these entertaining sorts of discussions, the search for a 'magical simultaneity' in horribly complex events: aircraft full of missiles entering Iranian airspace, money at that moment jumping by electronic transfer into the right account, hostages at that moment sprung from their prisons, 'and all kinds of things of this nature'.[29] North found a similarly cynical audience among the Iranians, too. For them, the discussions were basic business; they wanted 'every missile known to man or beast', Ledeen said, or at least everything they could find in a catalogue.[30] For America, the talks were high diplomacy. The terms of reference were diametrically opposed; in more sober moments, even North would agree that the meetings might represent 'only a limited, momentary, tactical coincidence of interests.'[31] Yet the parties continued to keep sitting down together in hotel rooms across Europe and America, resuming their dialogue of the deaf.

A decision was also taken, early on, to deal through a middleman who was a fabricator. Manucher Ghorbanifar, alias Ashgari, alias Nicholas Kralis, alias Nick the Greek, familiarly known as 'Roddi', was a shrewd, extravagant businessman, the Iranian director of Star Shipping, a joint Iranian-Israeli concern 'with heavy intelligence overtones', as Cave put it.[32] He was a charming, thick-bearded man with faintly hooded eyes; he came with Israeli recommendations, 'the best thing since bagels',[33] and had, at some time past, worked with the CIA. The arrangement had been terminated. As Clair George recalled, a 'burn notice' had been issued, advising members of the agency to have no truck with him. When listening to Ghorbanifar, as a CIA man reported in December 1985, it was 'extremely difficult to separate the good from the bad information.'[34]

Ghorbanifar claimed to be intimate with the government of Iran, close enough to know that a 'terrorist war' would ensue unless the United States reached a rapid agreement cemented with arms. He claimed to have links with Gadhafi, and inside knowledge about Libyan and Syrian backing for terrorists. Ledeen, with no trace of irony, thought him 'altogether too good to be true . . . he magically appears . . . I do not believe that things like that normally happen in a lifetime.'[35] 'This', he told McFarlane in July 1985, as the Ghorbanifar-engineered arms deals began to gel, 'is the real thing.'[36]

The real thing, subjected to a polygraph test, showed deception on every question except his name and nationality.[37] On the other hand, Iran was not an area the CIA knew much about. Lacking reliable counter-sources, the Americans had to rely on the world as constructed by Manucher Ghorbanifar. A rich flavour of the exchange comes from a tape recording of Charlie Allen, his CIA 'minder', and Ledeen talking to Ghorbanifar on January 25th, four days before North had read out his grand scenario for the end of the regime.

*Ghorbanifar*: Here is where they have to pay us. I mean to our organization. Why we, we need this money, we need for the bringing of reform in Iran. To help Ollie for his costing in South America (*laughter*) and, to rout all terrorism network in Europe and in Iran.

*Allen*: Yeah . . . I have some, some fresh fruits. I'll get some grapes if I may. That my, my little daughter and I eat grapes a lot. Apple will be good too. Thank you, Ghor.

*Ghorbanifar*: Here. (*sound of pounding*) . . . If you agree with this operation . . . the new terms he was ready to pay $10m cash and all these things. You remember I gave Ollie to tell you the new terms of . . .

*Allen*: He didn't tell me this.

*Ghorbanifar*: He forgotten it?

*Allen*: Yeah. I'll, I'll check.

*Ghorbanifar*: Yes. The general new terms he, agreed to pay $10m in cash now. Besides for 10m barrels of oil two, two below the market.

*Allen*: How, how much in oil?

*Ghorbanifar*: 10m barrels. Two dollars below the market price

. . . and it turns out that we agreed that we do the whole operation for him in the United States . . . and he will supply another $10m for this start for bombing and, uh, assassinate in US.

*Ledeen*: You said bomb and assassinate in the United States? Can we go to the State Department first? (*laughter*) Listen, I'll give you some offices on the sixth floor. (*laughter*)

*Allen*: This has got to be a long-term plan. We have to go over our plan. If we enter this relationship to work with you . . . trying to find a way to bring back . . . the kind of government that you want then we have to establish . . . basic rules of order.

*Ghorbanifar* . . . This is going to work very well. But the step is this step now . . . You know the Khomeini has decided to step down . . . on the 11th of February. And to, to resign and to bring the new leader in charge to settle for a time. You know, he wants everything be fixed when he dies . . . These are the most sensitive days in our history. Where are our friends American? And we need a lot of stuffs. (*laughs*)[38]

'There were no illusions', wrote Casey later, referring to the overture to Iran;[39] but there were many. Not least, the CIA was induced to help before it realized that the man with whom it would be dealing was one it had already discarded. 'We never played with a full deck', complained Clair George. 'I'm running around saying hey, here is my burn notice, this guy is a loser, and Christ, he is working with the government of Israel, he had already arranged a flight — it's sort of would you please get out of the way.'[40]

Even when the Ghorbanifar channel was closed down and a new one found, in mid-1986, negotiations seldom rose above the level of the fortune teller and the bazaar. Hakim, left behind in Frankfurt in October to arrange some sort of deal, ended up with a promise of 1½ (sic) hostages in exchange for 1,500 TOWs and pressure for the release of 17 terrorists held in Kuwait.[41] The exchange was approved by Poindexter, apparently after informing the President. By then, the initiative with Iran had snapped any moorings in the real world. The Americans knew they were being led a dance, but the urge to rescue hostages — premised on high emotion and some amount of electoral calculation — drove the policy forward.

In these circumstances, the oddest schemes found some sort of currency. North apparently devised, and the attorney general approved, a scheme to ransom two hostages for $2.2m in bribes; extra hostages could probably be bribed free, North believed, for $1m each.[42] The bribes were to be paid in instalments through two narcotics agents, men from the Drug Enforcement Administration, seconded to the NSC for the purpose. Meanwhile, the hostages were to be transferred to a safe house in Cyprus and then spirited away by sea. North wanted them taken on 'his ship', the *Erria*, a Danish freighter, for which several starring roles were intended, but the DEA men were scathing: the *Erria* was 'a filthy boat, filthy . . . a potato boat', and 'an old tub that couldn't do 10 knots'.[43] Ross Perot, a Texas billionaire, advanced $1m as a down-payment, but no hostages appeared off Cyprus where Secord was waiting for them. Perot was furious; instead of chasing chimeras, his money could have been earning interest in the bank.[44]

Another scheme, devised by the FBI and the CIA and co-ordinated by a counter-terrorism group headed by North, actually involved the disintegration of money. A bribe of many millions of dollars was to be paid for a hostage, Peter Kilburn, by giving the captors a suitcase full of chemically treated bills; after a few days, the bills would moulder away. The plot was not quite foolproof. The captors were demanding the money in small-denomination bills, so huge numbers of notes had to be treated. Besides, it took time to get the formula right; one dose began to work on the notes after only 24 hours. In the end, the notes were still being painstakingly dipped and dried when Kilburn was killed, apparently in revenge for America's raid on Libya in April 1986.[45] Another failure, but it is hard not to appreciate the subtlety of the thought behind it: if the cash paid as ransom disintegrates, there is no cash paid as ransom.

This was the Iran operation in a nutshell. A policy that could not work was presented as one that could, and a scheme that stood American policy on its head was elaborately argued to be otherwise. To the end — or at least to his testimony in Poindexter's trial, in 1990 — Reagan maintained he did not believe that he had been trading arms for hostages.[46] As the Iranians quickly discovered, there was always someone willing to be duped. From the Reagan administration's first decision to listen to what the Israelis were saying, the Iran-contra affair had found its firm foundation in political and diplomatic illusion.

If the Iran operation took predicates that were illusory — in sum, that arms could be bartered for hostages with an enemy regime, and it would not look like that — the operation to support the Nicaraguan contras had an equally doubtful premise. This nasty, foundering covert war was supposed, by itself, to bring down the Sandinista regime and save the hemisphere from Communism. The contras had been supported, through the CIA, since 1981; in 1984, in order to get round the Boland amendments (which forbade the administration to spend appropriated money on the contras) management of the war was brought into an office on the third floor of a building beside the White House.

McFarlane did not think of this as war management: it was a matter of encouragement, 'smoke and mirrors'.[47] North, at the public hearings, denied that he ran a war from his desk,[48] but he told his aide Craig Coy that he was doing so in so many words. (Coy was puzzled, reflecting that there was 'a whole Pentagon' to do things like that.)[49] Clair George, listing the things that had to be done — finding private money, transferring it out of the country, buying arms, shipping them, procuring boats and aircraft — noted that North had been obliged to do all this 'with a gum band and some balsa wood'. It was, he said, 'the most complex foreign policy I have ever beheld';[50] and if the impossible quickly went embarrassingly wrong, nobody should have been surprised.

This was, of course, a covert operation (of which North, in McFarlane's words, was the 'visible sign').[51] American diplomats remained in Managua, providing an illusion of reasonable discourse. The private money and foreign contributions were handled by a network of cut-outs and dummy companies so complicated that even North had trouble keeping track of it. But for all the cover, this was an operation that was sometimes surprisingly visible, and visible as a shambles. From the hub of the operation, the Ilopango Air Base in El Salvador, creaking aircraft flew supplies to the contras' northern front billetted in Honduras. CIA officers at the air base knew the aircraft were not theirs. They also knew they were not connected with the humanitarian assistance programme (NHAO) that was eventually run for the contras by the State Department, since those aircraft were 'beautiful brand-new L–100s, the most beautifully painted things'.[52] Still, the limping aircraft, which were assumed to be carrying arms, were not challenged. They were objects of interest, to a degree even their crews did not understand.

One kicker-out-of-loads, Iain Crawford, enlisted for the effort by his mother-in-law and obediently incurious about the cargo he was handling, remembered how the crew camped one night at Ilopango, cooking a barbecue beside the crates of plastic explosives; and a group of men approached them, led by 'Ambassador Duemling of the State Department', and winked at what they were doing.[53] The CIA man at the airport said he did not see any winking going on; but the NHAO humanitarian flights, of which Duemling was in charge, routinely allowed '10% lethal'.[54] Illusion was paramount here, too.

The contras' southern front, a struggling enterprise sheltered by a reluctant Costa Rica, was even more ramshackle. Supply flights had to be made at night; the aircraft had no radar or proper navigation equipment, could not get information even about the weather, and had to find drop zones in thick jungle by the light or smoke of bonfires. Often they could not find them at all. The flavour of this front was best given in the imperfect English of the 'military commission' which tried to examine its chances in 1984: 'The intent of an irregular operation having characteristics of heterodox struggle and design, prevented because of its audacity and little tangibility, adequate following of the SOUTHERN operation, which is out of the control of the most acute analysis.'[55] To put it mildly.

The supposed hub of this resupply operation was a top-secret overgrown airstrip at Santa Elena, in Costa Rica, said to have been the landing strip for Somoza's aircraft when he stayed at his farm nearby.[56] There was no road for 20 miles, so that fuel would have to be brought in by sea-barge; a quarter of a mile away was a place where turtles came to lay their eggs, as the local CIA man pointed out with gentlest concern.[57] A river ran through it, wearing down the gravel and making mud into which aircraft, especially aircraft loaded with weapons, tended to sink. The first cover story for the airstrip was that a group of businessmen wanted to start up a tourist resort there. The second was that it was a farm, run by Americans, on which various types of crops were being grown experimentally.[58] Peons were even brought in sustain the illusion by prodding at the land, and a bulldozer chugged about. Agricultural details were a nice reciprocal touch: the Hind helicopters, with which the Sandinistas were destroying the contras, had allegedly been shipped in by the Russians in crates labelled 'agricultural produce'.[59]

Joseph Fernandez, the local CIA man, tried not to have too much to do with the local airstrip/farm, once he had helped start it; but the cover was sometimes blown in definitive fashion. One of the 'cattle men' turned up one day at Costa Rica's legitimate airport and had to be rescued by Fernandez: in his cattle-man's briefcase were $5,000 in cash to pay for workers on the strip, a spare cassette from North for Fernandez's KL-43 encrypting device, and brown manila envelopes from the White House containing photographs of Fernandez with Reagan. Happily, no official had thought to open it.[60] The illusion of peaceful agricultural enterprise was also blown by Elliott Abrams, the State Department's Latin America man, in front of Fernandez and two unknowing officers. (Abrams was a young, bright, sharp lawyer, always well-tailored, and with an air of fierce aceticism; he will reappear often in this story as a man trying to keep at the edge of it, and usually succeeding.) On a casual visit to Costa Rica he blurted out the code name of the secret airstrip, Point West, and asked how it was doing. 'Obviously, this was

something that everybody in Washington knew about', said poor
Fernandez, 'and here I was, thinking I had a real secret.'

> I said sir, up until now I thought that in Costa Rica there were
> only four or five people that knew about this place. Now,
> because of your question, these two officers, who had no need to
> know, now know. Oh, he said, I apologize. I'm sorry. [61]

As it went along, the hapless operation was partly sustained by a
propaganda machine in Washington that produced hopeful and
sentimental briefings and films. What the contras could not achieve
in reality, they would seem to achieve on celluloid. This was natural
enough, and the Sandinistas countered with efficient propaganda of
their own; but it increased the element of illusion in the exercise. In
the course of two years North developed his own slide show, part
accurate, part exaggeration, part emotion, and this representation
was the bedrock of the domestic campaign for the contras: the world
in 57 pictures of blurry military bases and Communist commandantes, utterly simple in its division between good and bad, and
curiously believable.[62] At one point, too, the producer David Wolper
was approached to make a film about Central America 'to tell the
story better', but he demurred; he had 'the Statue of Liberty coming
up.'[63] The best idea of all, according to Rob Owen, North's courier
to the contras, came from another film producer, a Mr Spivey.

> He wanted to shoot a mini-series — not only produce but be
> involved in the actual ending.
> *Q.* You mean the end of the story of the resistance in
> Nicaragua?
> *A.* Right.
> *Q.* What was the ending to be?
> *A.* That they would be successful.[64]

When they were asked afterwards, both Owen and North
admitted that they had never imagined 'a victory march down the
streets of Managua'.[65] But the illusion of success within the contras'
reach, a success that was in the world's interests, was fostered most
carefully and covertly. It was not only on Central American airstrips
that winking went on, but all over Washington. Representatives of
foreign governments were persuaded to give large sums to the
contras, but were not asked directly, so the story went, and so were
not solicited. As Senator Cohen put it, a sort of metaphysical
exercise went on 'to define how many foreign leaders can be made to

dance on the head of the President's contra programme without calling it a solicitation'.[66]

Thus Prince Bandar of Saudi Arabia, walking in a garden with McFarlane, could hear — naturally as birdsong — that the contras needed $1m a month; he could pass the word to his uncle, the King; the King could give the money; and Reagan would release the Stinger anti-aircraft missiles needed by Saudi Arabia, not in explicit exchange (nothing so crude), but as a reciprocal gesture of princely generosity. There was, in McFarlane's words, 'no cry for solicitation . . . . and if anyone with any gumption could manage without being led or asked, then a contribution would have been welcome.'[67] Reagan was apparently a master: after a private meeting with King Fahd of Saudi Arabia in 1985 the king doubled his contribution to the contras to $2m a month, the subject never raised. Richard Secord was less adept. Secord was North's operations manager, a stocky ex-general in his early fifties, much decorated, and with a notable bluntness of manner. Trying for a second time to get something out of Prince Bandar, he was told 'You can stop twisting my arm' or, in out-of-hearings language, 'Fuck it, stop pestering me.'[68]

Elliott Abrams, smoother-tongued, entered the dream-world of non-solicitation on August 1986 in Hyde Park, in London. Under the name 'Mr Kenilworth' he walked in the park with General Ibnu, an aide to the Sultan of Brunei. 'He asked me how much money', Abrams testified. 'I said: "Ten million dollars." I tried to explain to him why I thought they should, just because they should be interested in the security of the United States. He said to me "What do we get out of this? What's in it for us?"' Abrams, having mumbled about 'the gratitude of the secretary [of state] and of the President for getting us out of this jam', was asked by Ibnu again: 'But what concrete do we get out of this?' 'You don't get anything concrete out of it,' he replied.[69] Nonetheless, some weeks later, the Sultan promised $10m. It was deposited by mistake — as unreality would have it — in the wrong bank account, and subsequently found its way back to Brunei.

What concrete do we get out of this? Ibnu had asked. But this was not a world of the concrete; it was one of winks, illusions and intimations. As McFarlane so aptly and untruthfully said of the Saudi contribution, 'the concrete character of that is beyond my ken.'[70] According to Judge Abraham Sofaer, Brunei was picked especially because it received no assistance already, and would seem to be returning no favours; it was never intended to get anything beyond appreciation.[71] But few countries were in such neutral condition, and very much later the subtle signs of appreciation became known: extra aid for Guatemala, 'enhanced' military aid for Honduras, a veto of a damaging import-limitation bill for Taiwan, and goodness knows what quiet back-scratching for China and South Africa.

Unacknowledged when it was received, the contra money was also unacknowledged when spent. If the help of foreign governments was even suspected, the rebels might not get money from Congress. As North wrote to Adolfo Calero, the chief contra leader, on May 1st 1986, 'source of funding [this was the Saudi money] must not become known. Congress must believe there continues to be an urgent need for funding.'[72] When the first $1m came in, followed by more, Calero therefore had no idea who it was from, and did not ask. Nor did he make a note of it. He was simply 'happy'. His testimony presented the weird picture of a man receiving weapons and money from nowhere, as if the clouds opened and rained them down, and even rotten service did not inspire his curiosity. 'The service was lousy,' he said of the private resupply, 'but I didn't ask who was providing it . . . This war that I was in, you know, was supposed to be clandestine . . . Sometimes I would purposely not pay attention to detail or to nothing.'[73] It was magical; it was illusory, as indeed was the idea that Calero could save the West with the weapons he was getting. As in Iran, the political imperative in Nicaragua was scarcely more substantial than a dream.

# Chapter 2

# Unseen, Unknown

$\mathrm{F}$ROM their very beginnings therefore, and increasingly as they went on, the Iran and contra policies departed even from the strange norms of covert operations. They were run not by professionals in the CIA, but by amateurs on the NSC staff. They had such unwieldy purposes — restoring relations with Iran, saving the hemisphere from Communism — that technical details, such as finding aircraft that could fly, sometimes went by the board. Most of all, although they were meant to be secret, these were secrets that were fairly indifferently kept; if, indeed, they were kept at all. Those on the sidelines tried not to see them or know about them, but it was difficult. No sound was more typical of Iran-contra than the dropping of a secret, like a stone, into otherwise peaceful conversation; at which the other participants would carefully get up and walk away.

People especially did not wish to know about the administration's private efforts to prop up the contras. Thus during the period of restrictions the contras grew, and occasionally even thrived, apparently on air: or on nothing more than the scattered largesse of rich Americans. Even those on the ground, by their own admission, were puzzled. As the Ambassador to El Salvador said (munitions piled round him), 'I didn't say "Hey, how is all this stuff getting in here?" It's logical that somebody had to bring it in.' There was,

North had told him mysteriously, 'an untold story here,' and Ambassador Corr was quite happy if he never heard it.[1] 'We knew there was another side to the house,' said an NHAO man; 'somebody was doing it.'[2] And theirs not to ask how, or why. In August 1985 *Newsweek* ran an article, marvelling

> The influx of $500,000 to $1m a month — some funnelled through secret bank accounts in Panama and elsewhere — has reportedly helped double the contras' numbers (to more than 16,000 men) and upgrade their arsenal. They now have Soviet-made SAM anti-aircraft rockets and AK-47 automatic rifles, and their air force has grown from one ancient DC-3 transport called the Rusty Pelican to a small fleet of light planes and copters . . . Conservatives have decided to do for the freedom fighters what the American left of the '30s did for the Communists in Spain.[3]

The improvement was considerably overstated (it may, in fact, have come from North, who sometimes leaked to *Newsweek*)[4] but it was remarkable, even so. At the CIA, the Central American officers realized at the beginning of 1985 that something was up: not precisely that the contras had money, but 'Oh my, look at that, they are not starving to death and they are operating.' The officers had been plotting a map, in changing colours, to show how the contras were fading out of Nicaragua; suddenly it reversed its trend, and they were back. It was a 'sliding process' said the CIA man, with the caution expected of his craft: signs of 'activity that reflected money.'[5]

In the vice-president's office too, Sam Watson, George Bush's aide, marvelled at how the contras were doing. Although not yet an impressive fighting force, they were a force, and getting supplies from somewhere. He assumed that someone was contributing; it was 'in the air' and 'in the atmosphere'; but he was too busy to ask questions, and, besides, you never knew what might be 'compartmented or committed or authorized'.[6] Watson's ignorance was widely presumed to extend to his boss, later the President; but Bush seems to have perfected the art of attending meetings, talking to North and even encountering some of the fieldworkers of the operations without ever being tainted by what was occurring. This did not mean he did not know. At Thanksgiving 1985, Bush sent North a postcard thanking him for his work 'with the hostage thing and in Central America' and exhorting him to get some turkey; North read it out at his trial four years later as evidence of approval, but it was all delightfully vague.[7] North remembered, too, how

Shultz had put his arm round him at a party and told him what a remarkable job he had done, keeping the Nicaraguan resistance alive: 'I knew what he meant. He didn't have to say "You did a great job on the L-100 resupply on the night of the 9th of April." He knew, in sufficiently eloquent terms, what I had done.'[8] But North was wrong. Shultz swiftly put out word, through a spokesman, that he had not known at all.[9]

The master-class in knowing and not-knowing was given by William Casey, director of the CIA. Casey had become director in 1981, at the age of 68. An Irish Catholic, raised in New York, he had been a gung-ho member of the OSS during the second world war. He was scholarly, shrewd and literate; but few people entirely trusted the ends to which that scholarship and shrewdness were applied. Physically he was a large, shambling old man, flabby-faced and buck-toothed, with a mumbling fashion of speech. In a sense, therefore, his body provided a cover for the sharpness of his mind, and the cold balefulness of his stare a cover for his crusades. Casey did nothing without reason, and his reason was to keep the world safe from Communists; subsidiary principle was often unnecessary. To many his shrewdest move was to die, of brain cancer and pneumonia, in May 1987, before he had been called on to give an account of the role he had played in the affair. 'Maybe I ought to go have [done] to me what Casey had done,' North told a friend bitterly; 'take my brain out, and leave me alone.' He added: 'If only they knew what old Casey knew.'[10]

Casey knew much; but he was also careful not to know. He kept open a line to North, but made sure that he appeared to have no truck with whatever he was doing. When John Singlaub, a retired military man also engaged in anti-Communist operations, visited Casey in his office while the Boland amendments were in force, he would sometimes — inadvertently — mention Nicaragua. 'He threatened to throw me out of his office,' he remembered. 'I would try to say, You are the chief of intelligence. Aren't you interested in knowing what is happening down there? No! he would shout, and make it clear that we would not discuss it . . . he used an expletive that I have not used, indicating that he did not want me to raise that subject with him.'[11] When Joseph Coors, the beer millionaire, told Casey that he wanted to help the contras, Casey simply said 'Ollie North's the guy to see';[12] even old friends could not drag the secret from him. Strangest of all was the lunch he had with Poindexter on November 22nd, 1986, the ruins of both Iran and contra all around them. Poindexter remembered that Casey invited himself, that they ate sandwiches, and that they discussed what Casey had said in his briefing of Congress the previous day. Both men knew the 'deep,

dark secret' at the heart of the affair, the diversion of funds from the
Iran arms sales to the contras; neither mentioned it. 'It's ironic that
indeed he knew', Poindexter said afterwards. 'I wish I'd known
that.'[13]

Within the agency, too, Casey gave nothing away. In February
1986 a retired CIA agent, asked by North to help him with the
contras, mentioned the request to Casey.

> I said what's Ollie involved in, and he says I don't know and I
> don't want to know.
> *Q.* And then he said?
> *A.* But he's a good guy.
> *Q.* Which you took as encouragement to continue?
> *A.* No.[14]

On Iran — another operation from which the CIA officially kept
its distance — Casey played the same game. Sitting in Casey's office
with a group of people sometime in the autumn of 1985, John
McMahon, his deputy, suddenly said: 'You won't believe what Bud
McFarlane just told me at the White House.' 'What, what?'
chorused the others. 'The Israelis have an operation that involves
the Iranians, which could possibly lead to the release of the
hostages.' Casey said 'Who knows?' Clair George, who recorded the
conversation in his usual bombastic way, noticed a twinkle in
Casey's eye as he said that, and wondered if his leg was being
pulled. Casey went on: 'I don't know what the hell he's talking
about.' Testifying two years later, George thought that meant: 'You
won't tell the CIA; they must not know about it.' At the time,
however, he believed that Casey truly did not know what was going
on.[15]

Other cabinet members made sure they were in the same position.
Shultz, for all his opposition to the Iran operation, merely told
Poindexter not to inform him of details he did not need to know;[16]
and the admiral, needing no encouragement to hold things close,
took that line with other members of the cabinet. Receiving a
recommendation from North before the Tehran trip that he should
arrange a meeting with 'RR, Shultz and Weinberger', Poindexter
tapped back testily: 'I don't want a meeting with RR, Shultz and
Weinberger.'[17] And he seldom did.

What they knew, what they didn't know, and what they did not
wish to know tied people in some terrible knots. The classic remark
came from Abrams at the public hearings: 'I never said I had no
idea about most of the things you said I had no idea about.'[18] As
Noel Koch of the Pentagon described it, talking about Iran:

We could sit in a meeting in the Sit[uation] Room and be discussing these other activities, and fall into almost a kind of, you know, warp in which you wouldn't know whether you were talking — I mean, the use of shorthand and so forth in the discussions you couldn't tell whether we'd suddenly slipped into this question of selling arms to get them back this way or whether we were still discussing the other thing.

And it was the most intricate interweaving of subjects and half-meanings and innuendos and so forth, and it was like something out of a Pirandello play.[19]

At his deposition, North's aide Robert Earl offered a breakdown of those who knew about the Iran operation, those who did not know and those who knew a bit of it, like a game of Chinese boxes. Allen, North, Poindexter and his assistant Paul Thompson were all 'in the box, in the compartment'. And those, he thought, were the only people in the NSC who were fully in it. There were others (such as Howard Teicher, who had gone on the trip to Tehran and had seen the spare parts in the back of the plane) who were 'not in all the boxes within the boxes but some element of the box'. And where did the diversion of funds fit in? 'It may have been the innermost box or it may have overlapped with other sub-boxes, but it was within the compartment, yes.' So people who were generally in the big box knew about it? Not necessarily: 'I don't think I meant that even the people who have no caveats attached implied that they knew absolutely everything in the box.'[20] Everyone had their own small measure of deniability, the lid unopened, the box left locked.

It might have been better, in Poindexter's view, if no one had ever known. Nonetheless, knowledge seeped out; not least because both the Iran and contra operations, however much compartmented and closely held, were run by a man who could not resist talking about them. Numbers of people at North's level at the NSC, the State Department, the CIA and the Defense Department knew that 'Ollie was up to something': something hyperactive, makeshift, slightly off-centre, not to be looked into. 'Everybody had their suspicions about him,' said Jonathan Miller, who worked with him; 'A lot of it you would discount because he had a tendency to engage in rhetorical hyperbole. If I discounted 75% of what he intimated, there was a lot to suspect but it was nothing hard and fast.'[21]

The prize for suspicions that never hardened into knowledge belonged to Craig Coy, North's junior aide. Until the end of May 1986 Coy, like Earl, had no office of his own, and the two men would sit on North's couch. Sometimes he would ask them to leave; more often they stayed, and let the welter of codes and commands and memos and messages accumulate round them.[22] Earl, a classmate of North's from the Naval Academy, was privy to quite a lot, including the diversion. Coy tried to pick up as little as he could, tactful as a secretary. If messages came over the secret encoder about military supplies for the contras, 'I would scan it and pass it on. It was nothing that I was responsible for.'

Q. You were not involved?
A. I was not involved. I knew it was military equipment for Central America, pass it on.[23]

Coy had no idea how far North was involved either, and did not want to know, except on one occasion. He could not help overhearing, in April 1986, that North was about to go to Tehran, and asked Earl about it; considering they were sitting side by side on the sofa, he said, it was bizarre to have one man briefed and the other not. Earl reluctantly asked North to bring Coy 'into the box', and it was the last one he was brought into. He seldom let his curiosity get the better of him again.[24]

Even those who were most curious, or who had bosses who would have been extremely interested to know, forbore to ask North questions. Even as it was, they heard more than they wanted to know. Watson, sniffing the atmosphere from Bush's office, was once teased horribly by North at a meeting. North sat down beside him and whispered, 'Max has shut down the resupply of the pilots.' Watson said he asked him what he was talking about; North brushed him off. 'Don't bother me; it's none of your business.' Watson, wondering whether to pass it on, quickly concluded that North was 'playing a game of being important and secretive', and decided not to bother.[25]

He joined many others. 'I think it is fair to say', mused Abrams, 'that everyone involved in the RIG [the Restricted Inter-agency Group that met regularly to discuss policy in Latin America] knew that Ollie was somehow connected with this but didn't know why . . . I think most of us were careful not to ask.'[26] Abrams himself, North remarked with some heat, did not need to ask; he knew;[27] but at a certain point, knowledge became uncomfortable. Asked by Shultz one day to 'monitor Ollie' (Shultz himself, it should be remembered, not wanting to be too exhaustively informed), Abrams asked North a few cursory questions.[28] Once, apparently unsolicited, North told him that 'there was a big network out there of people and companies and bank accounts.'[29] Abrams, who said he had never heard of such a thing before, asked him no more about them. Why, wondered Senator Rudman at the hearings, had he not taken North

into his office and closed the door and put him up against the wall
and pushed him and pushed him and pushed him? Well, said
Abrams, almost visibly squirming, he was not in his department,
and things are not done that way. Besides, 'with respect, I think
you're playing the movie backwards from the end. You know the
end, and I know the end, now we know what happened, now we
know what I should have done . . . but I was not at the end of the
movie, I was in the middle of the movie and I didn't know the
ending.'[30]

Abrams knew much of the plot, however; it was precisely because
he knew so much that he recognized when to hold back. Besides, he
was not dealing with someone who was altogether cryptic. As a CIA
section chief described the two sides of North,

> One is secret and compartmented, and another is sort of boyish
> and boastful, and it would be in character for him to say, I
> won't be here tomorrow, I will be down south, and then for him
> to say, Yes, it was a quick trip and I flew all night and I came
> back and I haven't slept for 48 hours, always complaining
> about how busy he was and how terribly overworked.
>
> It is from that kind of what the Germans call *fingerspitzen
> Gefühl* — just from the smell of it — that I had a pretty good
> idea that North was spending a lot of his time on Central
> American things.[31]

Even the most secret aspects of those 'Central American things'
seemed to buzz in North's head insisting to be spoken. General
Robert Schweitzer, visiting his office one day to talk broadly about
contras, heard North say, alluding to his pet name for the resupply
operation, 'And then there is, of course, my Project Democracy . . .'
'And his sentence then trailed off', said Schweitzer, 'with a series of
. . . almost visible ellipses, and he didn't finish the thought.'[32] On
the first leg of the flight to Tehran, courtesy of one of the aircraft
that also helped with contra resupply, North told Cave 'This is
Democracy Airlines,' and laughed; Cave had no notion what he
meant.[33] Poindexter remembered a meeting one day in the Oval
Office, discussing sources of contra money, when he had to move
quickly to stop North blurting out that there was money available in
places he knew.[34] It was not the only time Poindexter had to shut
North up: partly because North genuinely did not know how widely
the secret was known, but partly because he could hardly resist it
anyway.

North understood what was expected of people entrusted with
secrets. They were meant not to infect other people with 'unnecessary

knowledge'.[35] On the other hand he was proud of what he was up to, and it was exciting and in a good cause; so he talked about it. At one fairly general meeting in December 1985, with people from the CIA and the FBI and the State Department, he dropped in the passing remark: 'even if the last hostage that came out was traded for 80 Hawk missiles'. The CIA major who heard him was dumbfounded, as were the others; dead silence fell. Carefully, the major turned the conversation to an Iranian editorial he had seen, and they laid down the subject. 'Ollie's talking too much at these meetings,' snapped Charlie Allen later.[36] He did so again not long afterwards, again in front of Allen, mentioning how pleased he was with the mini-finding of December that had retroactively authorized the arms sales. He had taken it to the President, and he had liked it, and he had signed it. All this was highly secret; and North said it not merely to Allen but to Bernard Makowka, a lawyer for the CIA general counsel's office. Makowka, as it happened, had worked on the Finding, but he and North were strangers to each other; he was amazed that 'he would be mentioning something as sensitive as that in this sort of context'. On North went: 'I'm really worried because I have the only copy and it's in my safe, and I could cross the street tomorrow and get run over by a truck and so no-one would ever know. And so if anything happens to me, it's here. I want you to know that.'[37]

Perhaps the clearest demonstration of the need to conceal and the compulsion to reveal, the need to bring the always-denied and never-happening into the light of day, was seen in North's attitude towards the diversion of funds. This, he told Meese in his interview on November 23rd 1986, was something above all he hoped could be kept secret; this, Poindexter had told him, 'had better never come out.'[38] Yet North also thought it was 'a good idea', 'a right idea', 'a neat idea'.[39] When he had told Casey about it, his mentor and guardian and sponsor had supposedly called it 'the ultimate irony'.[40] North found the idea of the Ayatollah unwittingly subsidizing the contras deliciously ironic, and also perhaps trifling by the standards of some of the secrets, still unrevealed, with which he was entrusted. He therefore leaked his deepest, darkest secret, but selectively, to those half-way in the know already; and he made it deliberately dramatic, so that there was still a good chance it would fall within the wide range of hyperbole or blarney that his listeners already allowed for. He would make a casual remark, often to cheer someone up, just a joke really; wait for the penny to drop; relish the reaction (it was always astonishment) — and walk away. Richard Armitage, an assistant defence secretary, heard the tale in mid-November 1986:

I called Ollie on the black phone, the secure phone, to find out what was going on, to fill in my knowledge a little bit more. And I think ... Ollie was concerned that I was very upset about [the Iranian arms deals], and he said basically, Rich, don't worry. It'll all be all right when the Vice President goes to Riyadh to sit down with the Iranians and they find out that our hostages come home, and the Ayatollah is either helping us in Central America or the contras.

... And I said, Ollie, wow. And then he and I stopped the phone conversation.[41]

McFarlane heard the tale on the tarmac at Ben Gurion airport in May 1986, as he and North were returning from their disastrous clandestine trip to Iran. North told him not to be downhearted, 'that the one bright spot is that the government is availing itself of part of the money for application to Central America.'[42] He then walked away, leaving McFarlane stunned, though not stunned enough to report it.[43] Charlie Allen of the CIA did not report it either, for a long time; but he heard about it more than anyone else who was supposed not to know. The first time it came from his charge, Ghorbanifar, thrown out casually, that $25m of the money from the arms sales could go 'to help Ollie in his work for South America [sic].' Allen thought this 'a very ingratiating-type comment' with no substance and no meaning; he did not even make a note of it.[44] Central America was not his patch, anyway.

Having discounted that source, Allen next heard it from the horse's mouth. Discussing with North in September 1986 how the arms-sales creditors could be paid off, he was alarmed to hear him say 'Well, maybe we'll have to take it out of the reserves.' Allen thought the statement 'devastating ... little wheels clicked in my mind, that all my fears were probably true.' Nonetheless, he tried to find some comforting way to explain it: maybe the Israelis had set up some sort of contingency fund. Not until three weeks later did he pass on to colleagues in the CIA, and to Casey, the thought that 'perhaps we are overcharging ... to send money to the contras.'[45] The first reaction of Casey's deputy, Robert Gates, was to laugh, 'because it sounded absurd'.[46] When Gates heard it next, at the end of a three-man lunch with Casey on October 9th (North made 'a cryptic comment about Swiss accounts and the contras'), he took it slightly more seriously, and asked Casey about it. 'And it appeared to me that Casey hadn't even picked up what he had said. He kind of looked at me quizzically and he had either not heard it or it hadn't made any impact on him ... and he basically just kind of waved it off.'[47] No one pursued it.

North once told Secord that he had gone so far as to mention to the President that the Ayatollah was helping the contras. This was not quite a true story, he admitted, just a joke to raise Secord's morale. He had made the remark, or something like it, 'to the back of Admiral Poindexter' as they came out of a meeting with Reagan, and Reagan could not possibly have heard it.[48] But North would doubtless have liked him to; for even Poindexter confessed that he could hardly hold back from revealing, just once, the glorious ruse with which the president's dearest cause was being supported.[49]

North seems to have intimated and exaggerated and hinted because, although he was engaged in secrets, he desperately wanted to be noticed; and part of him, too, needed rescuing. To Clair George (who had been involved in managing the contra operation before the congressional restrictions, and was keeping well clear of it), 'he kept saying I have got to get out of this thing, I have got to get out of this thing. And I kept saying, I don't want to hear about it.'[50] Between those who did not want to hear and those who did not want to know, North was left, as George understood, alone. So, too, was McFarlane, carefully endowed by his cabinet colleagues with the managerial responsibility for both Iran and contras; so, too, was Poindexter.

At some point in February 1986 Poindexter apparently made a decision, crucial to the story, not to tell the President about the plan to divert Iranian arms money to the contras. He did so very quickly, in about five minutes, while North was standing in front of his desk.[51] And he did so, he explained at the hearings, to give the President 'deniability'. This was not 'plausible deniability', the provision of a believable cover for someone who already knew the facts; it was, Poindexter agreed, 'absolute' deniability, 'the ability of the President to deny knowing anything about it, and be very truthful in that process. He didn't know anything about it.'[52]

Nor, by their own account, did dozens of others. They had seen something, they had heard something, they had smelt something, but all those various sensations added up to nothing solid: nothing that was known, for certain.

# Chapter 3

# Secret Agents and
# Mystery Papers

So Iran-contra did not happen much, except to certain people; and even those people often felt caught up in events that were exceptionally odd and different, adventures they might have watched on television, and in which they especially did not expect to find themselves. They were actors in a world of secret agents, codenames and mysterious papers: a place where ordinary values and rules were possibly suspended, although they could never be quite sure of that.

North's principal emissary between the White House and the contras was a brawny and cherubic graduate from Stanford, Robert Owen. Owen had been working for a consulting company in Washington before deciding to devote himself to the contras, sitting at North's feet; despite his deep immersion in murky affairs, he still took a wide-eyed view of the world in which he operated. It was fun, in a way. He found himself walking through Denver Airport one day with a hollowed-out Brazilian hand-grenade fitted with a Zippo lighter, a present from Singlaub to Calero: 'one of the scary things was that I walked right through . . . and I never set off the alarms.'[1] Another day he was sent from Washington to a Chinese vegetable stand on the Lower West Side in Manhattan, where he was told to ask for a person with the code name 'Mooey'; Mooey went behind the counter, rolled up his trouser-leg and pulled out a wad of hundred-dollar bills, which Owen thought 'I had better count anyways.' Having counted them (there were 95), and gone back to Washington, he handed them in a rolled-up newspaper to Secord in the lobby of the Sheraton Carlton hotel.[2] After he had told this tale at the hearings, Representative Tom Foley asked him: 'Those were not normal public actions, were they?'

> *Owen.* Sir, we used to joke that truth is always stranger than fiction. In this case, it is true.
> *Q.* You found yourself somewhat surprised to be in this sort of environment?
> *A.* Quite frankly, when I was approached in the Chinese market, I looked around and wondered where the cameras were. I said, 'This is more a movie set than real life.'[3]

Owen was not alone in treating his escapades as an adventure, half funny and half thrilling. Michael Ledeen was also new to the world of covertly shipping arms. Disapproving as he was, he still seems to have found vicarious excitement in talking weapons. In November 1985, when he had heard there was going to be another Israeli shipment to Iran, he called North. 'How many Hawk missiles can you get into a 707?' he asked him.

> And he said something like twelve and I said, what do you mean, twelve? He said, well, they come in big cases and big wooden boxes and packing and so forth. I said so that's interesting. And I remember saying to Schwimmer at one point, what are you going to do, have a caravan of 707s for those Hawks of yours? And he said no, we'll send a couple of planes. And I remember saying to him, but you can only get twelve Hawks on a 707 . . .
> *Q.* Why did you ask Colonel North how many Hawks can you get in a 707?
> *A.* . . . Just because Hawks were going to go to Iran and I was wondering how many planes it was going to be this time. It had been so exciting the last time with one plane. I wondered how many adventures we were going to have this time.[4]

Albert Hakim wondered too. Hakim was the grand treasurer of 'The Enterprise', the web of companies that lay behind both the Iran and the contra operations. He was an Iranian who had fled Iran but maintained grey connections there; a balding, smooth-skinned, soft-spoken man with brown protruding eyes. He already found the Iran operation bizarre in any number of ways. The government had to 'have participation in it', but it was also structured so that 'the government was not supposed to have participation in it'. Hakim was used to transactions where 'all parameters are not known, you leave it for the times that things are known', but this business proceeded on a plane that was 'intangible'. From time to time he would try to pin Secord down on it, but Secord had no more sense of a plan than he had. 'And he went to the degree of saying, when I pressed him, how are we going to stay in this business; he said, Albert, for all I know right now when I am talking to you, we could be finished with the business; I don't know.'[5]

Just before a meeting with the Iranians in Frankfurt in late February 1986, Hakim was brought in to pretend to be a translator. He took the part with manifest reluctance; he did not want to be recognized by Ghorbanifar. His alias was Ebrahim Ebrahimian, a name variously mis-spelled by the players, which Secord supposed to be Turkish. Deputed to get his own disguise, he went off fuming to a wig shop: 'And the lady started to go through all kinds of salesmanship to sell me the wig and if I wanted to swim, I didn't want to swim, and I'm sitting there knowing that this meeting is going to start very soon and I cannot — lady, let's get on with it, I don't give a damn, just give me a wig.'[6]

The wig he finally chose needed modification by a barber; but he got it done, put on a pair of folding spectacles he carried in his briefcase, and had the satisfaction of astonishing his colleagues when he walked back into the hotel. So convincing was he that Amiram Nir, the Israeli counter-terrorism man — whose presence at the talks was even more risky — decided he should change his hair too. Iranians had more respect for people with graying locks; North, already tipped off by Ghorbanifar, had put more white in his;[7] so Hakim and Nir went back to the shop and had Nir's hair sprayed, Hakim all the while keeping his identity firmly under his wig. 'And that was a challenge,' he recalled, 'to spend 45 minutes with a guy and act like a spy.'[8]

Spies were all around; they were literally in the wiring and the woodwork. If Owen looked round for the cameras, North acted throughout as though he was sure they were there. He was convinced he was being both watched and listened to; by the Russians, if by no-one else. Owen confessed that it became something of a joke to say, at the end of telephone calls, 'Say hello to our friend Ivan.'[9] Around the Old Executive Office Building, where the NSC staff had their offices, North was remembered as a man who seemed always caught up in some dark drama: leaving for the airport, constantly being paged in meetings, 'looking like a ghost' in the corridor. One colleague, Jackie Tillman, got wind one day of a piece of the drama in which North and Owen were engaged; she heard that Owen, standing in the rain outside the White House, had handed $2,000–3,000 in cash to a Meskito Indian leader passing by in a car. Alarmed, she tried to tell Poindexter about it; but she knew there was no point in raising the matter with North.[10] There was a screenplay unfolding, and she, and others, had no more than bit-parts. As Larry Speakes, the president's press spokesman, put it, 'I always had the impression that . . . as [Ollie] flew across the country he could visualize a camera on him, and although nobody knew who he was and his mission was secret, the whole thing was being made into a movie.'[11]

North had charge of several covert operations, many of which are still secret; his brief included counter-terrorism, as well as the sending of arms to Iran and the resupply of the contras. All played directly to his love of the theatrical. The old master-spy, William Casey, was said, not least by North, to have masterminded both the Iran and contra operations, and that may well be true of the broad canvas; but the marks are those of an enthusiastic amateur in espionage, a man who had learnt his craft of secret agent more from the cinema than from the CIA handbook. When Liman, the Senate Counsel at the hearings, suggested that it had been 'on-the-job training', North thought that rather a good description.[12] Equivalent-ranking officers at the CIA knew North had no experience in operations.[13] The chief of the Near East Division had sat him down one day to try to teach him about Iran, but he doubted it had gone in.[14] CIA men looked askance at him, particularly since he dealt directly with the highest officers in the agency, preferably Casey, rather than with them. One agent in North's employ remembered being over at CIA headquarters one day when a call came in to him from North, 'and everybody in the room gave me a dirty look.'[15]

'No-one in the Marine Corps taught me how to run a covert operation' said North, ruefully, at his trial.[16] Untaught, he did what he could; and it seemed to many of his colleagues, professionals or not, that he sometimes played at it, doing the things he thought secret agents did, even when they were unnecessary. Because of his other highly classified projects, his office already contained all the paraphernalia of necessary secrecy: the code-block and buttons on the door, the gaggle of different-coloured telephones, the five-thousand-pound safes, even the tempered glass in the windows, as his lawyer noted at his trial, 'so that enemies of the country can't beam through the windows and pick up the sound'.[17] Merely by shutting his door if it was open, North would add to the intrigue of meetings: 'and when the meeting was over, I still couldn't understand why the door was shut and what the intrigue was' said a visiting official, puzzled; 'it was in my mind's eye a social call.'[18] And sometimes, leaving his office, he would close his door in such a way that there seemed to be something or someone intriguing behind it, as Richard Miller noticed when he went to talk to him about banking for the contras; it was deliberately stage-like, impressive.[19] Inside the sanctum, Miller was once made to sit down with the words 'Let me show you how a covert operation is set up.' Earl brought in a yellow legal pad with a number of acronyms on it in boxes, and North put it down on the table; at that point, his secure telephone went off, and he had to ask Miller to leave. Miller never did find out how to set up a covert operation.[20]

Spooks in films could pass unrecognized through airports, and North sometimes gave out instructions that if he was spotted at such-and-such a place, he should not be acknowledged.[21] He once told Earl delightedly that he had spotted Abrams at an airport but Abrams (perceptiveness not his strong suit) had not spotted him, and that 'his tradecraft of observing was better than Elliott's.'[22] Secret agents carried gadgets with which they could speak to headquarters from the most unlikely places; once, at a party, North was said to have produced a scrambler-telephone from his briefcase, together with a half-eaten sandwich, and to have gone out into the garden to dial the house.[23] Owen, Calero and various agents would meet him in Lafayette Park, opposite the White House, to avoid checking into the OEOB, and pieces of paper would pass between them. North also managed to slip a piece of paper ('Next time you are in Washington please contact me, my name is Oliver North') into the hand of Alfonso Robelo, a contra leader, in a reception line; Robelo then had the problem of transferring it invisibly to his pocket.[24]

A favourite North place for secret conversations was the Old Brogue Country Inn in Great Falls, Virginia, not far from where he lived. This was a pub with an Irish band, but North, who had Irish blood, may not have chosen it out of sentiment; the music was so loud that it frequently, and perhaps providentially, drowned out the conversation. One agent went there with Allen, following him blindly 'away from Langley and way out into the woods' to talk about finding the hostages. When they arrived the place was empty — it was early evening — except for 'two street toughs in camel-hair coats' sitting at a table; 'and they were fairly easy to distinguish, and I think we walked up and asked them if they were —— and ——, and they said yes.' When the two sides had carefully sounded each other out, and all parties had ordered two rounds of drinks, they had what the agent called 'a very in-depth substantive discussion about very sensitive material', which grew louder and louder as the band did; in the end they could scarcely hear each other when they leaned across the table and shouted.[25] One of the 'street toughs', actually a DEA man, later wondered what the point of it all had been. 'It was a Friday night. We couldn't discuss anything in the place. What we went out there for I haven't the slightest idea.'[26]

Another agent was recruited to the effort in Charlie's Restaurant in Washington, where he arranged to sit at the bar with two packets of cigarettes in front of him, so that Secord and North could recognize who he was.[27] Genuine covert work, perhaps; but not without an element of cinema.

At the hearings, North hotly denied that there was any element of play involved. His elaborate codes, for instance, were not some joke or 'some childish code from *Captain Midnight*. We were talking on open telephone lines.'[28] He told Calero he ought to find himself a code-name — a suggestion Calero virtually ignored — because 'the Soviets listen to everything on the east coast'.[29] Codes were certainly necessary; but North's more experienced colleagues knew they were not necessary to the degree he insisted upon. One set used in hostage negotiations, rapidly superseded by another set, listed the names of English towns and counties: Gloucestershire (United States), Warwick (Cuba), Norfolk (Iran) and Sevenoaks (Jerusalem). Washington was Ladbrooke, but it was also, in the same list, Cleveland and Canada[30]: the multiplication of codes suggesting either that they were readily broken, or that people were changing them more or less as they fancied.

Poindexter, although he had cautioned North not to 'talk in plain language'[31], confessed that he had never used the three-by-five cards covered with codes that North had given him; he just carried them in his briefcase. 'Who wrote Sampson Secord?' Liman asked. 'I did,' he admitted. 'Did you think of Secord as Sampson?' 'No, not really — what are you calling him?'[32] Even Owen, adventurer as he was, thought the codes a bit of a waste of time. 'We always tried to talk somewhat in codes,' he said, remembering Calero talking to North about arms on a pay-phone from San Francisco, 'so whoever was listening wouldn't quite be able to understand it; but if they had any common sense, they probably could.'[33] The last flourish on codes belonged to George Cave, translating again at a September meeting with the Iranians in Washington, who ended his memorandum of record thus.

US PARTICIPANTS: George Cave as 'Colonel Sam O'Neil'
Oliver North as 'Colonel Goode'
Dick Seacord [sic] as 'General Kopp' [sic][34]

The make-believe Goode and O'Neil were not colonels, nor was the make-believe Copp a general; it was a bit of fun.

So it appeared at the public hearings. Noel Koch was the deputy assistant for international security affairs at the Defense Department when North was at the NSC; he had been given a code-name, and it was 'Aaron'. To his embarrassment, the lawyer at the hearings then obliged him to go through a whole code-sheet to get the names into the record, or perhaps just to entertain the audience. Missiles were 'dogs', the airport was 'a swimming pool', Iran was 'apple' (in another code sheet it was 'Tango', as in 'it takes two') Israel was 'banana', the United States was 'orange', hostages were 'zebras'. 'I want you to know we didn't use any of this nonsense', Koch protested between the titters; '. . . you would sort of start down that road and get so self-conscious you couldn't do it.'[35] Maybe he could not; but North's notebooks contain the entry 'IF THESE CONDITIONS ARE ACCEPTABLE TO THE BANANA, THEN ORANGES ARE READY TO PROCEED'.[36]

North usually picked the code names. (An exception was Secord's name, 'Copp', which Secord found 'not in the usual way, looking though the telephone book', but took in a hurry from a thriller he was reading[37]; Gorbanifar, as a result, thought he was Polish.)[38] North's names for himself are revealing. In one cultural set, in which Poindexter was 'Schubert' and Shultz 'Molière', North called himself 'Wagner', invoking the flames of Götterdämmerung.[39] Some letters to Adolfo Calero, the chief contra leader, were signed 'Steelhammer'.[40] His preferred code names, however, show him acting out yet another part, that of an agent for good; even, perhaps, God's agent. In the January 1986 negotiations he was 'Paul'. From time to time he was 'Mr West' (definitely opposed to the East). But the alias he preferred, and for which the State Department gave him his false passport, was William P. Goode. This prompted a famous exchange at the hearings, when John Nields, the House counsel, began to quesion North on a document headed 'from Goode': 'I take it you are Goode?' 'I was very good.'[41]

North himself sometimes forgot who, or which, he was. William Walker, an official from the State Department, remembered seeing him rush to catch a flight to Central America, having just got off a flight from Europe, unkempt, a flight-bag over his shoulder. His name was not on the passenger list. 'Try Goode or something', Walker recalled him saying; 'and I think he even threw out a third name . . . So Ollie had to change his passport and hand up another passport and I remember saying this guy plays in the big leagues.'[42]

Fascination with code names went well beyond operations, reaching even the contra supporters and fund-raisers. If North was running the contra war vicariously ('from my desk'), the smooth organizers of the private pro-contra network and their rich, mostly female, mostly elderly contributors were even further removed. Their contact with war was to sit in the dining room of the Hay Adams Hotel, or the Petroleum Club in Dallas, or by their own swimming pools, sipping on cocktails and going through lists of guns and launchers and grenades. One of the high points in the life of Ellen Garwood, a wealthy Texas widow and author, was the day she sat with Reagan in the Oval Office ('we had Sanka') and told him that he ought to get rid, first, of the Sandinistas, and second of the secretary of state.[43] Barbara Newington from Connecticut remembered shaking hands effusively with Reagan at the beginning and end of her audience, and each of them saying thankyou to the other; but precisely what she was thanking him for, and what he was thanking her for, neither said. (Both subsequently maintained, too, that they did not know.)[44]

North frequently talked to these contributors, whipping them up with his slide show, and they, too, developed a code-name for him. They called him 'Mr Green', a vaguely Marine idea. Carl Channell, the chief fundraiser — a slight, foxy man from West Virginia — admitted it was 'sort of crazy' to call North Mr Green, or 'our special person' or nicknames of other sorts, but his employees 'loved to do that, because that was exciting . . . I know Ellen Garwood loved to call him Mr Green, and when she would write me letters thinking that Mr Green was her real son, I got the impression that she was talking to me on the telephone underneath her bed, about the fun she was having. She always used Mr Green religiously.'[45]

Channell's organization also used a code name for the weapons account; it was 'toys'. Towards 'toys' — principally mortars, grenades and AK47s — the old ladies, among others, donated their savings. Some expressly did not want their money to go for weapons; others were said to be so thrilled that they wanted their names on the missiles.[46] (Ellen Garwood got hers on a helicopter.) One contributor, reckoning that 'his' missile had shot down a Sandinista helicopter, pestered Channell for a piece of the wreckage as a souvenir.[47]

For favoured contributors, the mystique of secret war could be taken further. They were given briefings by North or sometimes by Abrams in the Old Executive Office Building, shown photographs of airports and harbours, and made privy to mysterious movements of Soviet aircraft and ships. 'The contributors we had are all kind of double-O-seven, cloak-and-dagger types', explained Krishna Littledale, one of the enticers of funds; '. . . if you talk very quietly and tell them they can't tell anyone about this conference, they will give you a lot more money.'[48] One contributor, William O'Boyle, was particularly impressed by the covert aura of it all. An oil and gas businessman, down from New York, he was one of Littledale's 'bloody types';[49] so much so that he had celebrated his donation for weapons, to the dismay of Channell's PR lady, by going to the Hay Adams and ordering steak tartare.[50] Channell told him that supporters who gave $300,000 or more could meet Reagan for 15 minutes, and that their visits were not logged on: 'the implication being that this was so secret that the President wanted to keep it so not everybody at the White House knew what was going on.' He also told O'Boyle that he had been 'checked out' with the government computer system to see if he was reputable enough to join the group. 'I don't know whether this was a fund-raising ploy or whether this was for real,' O'Boyle said, 'but I thought it was for real at the time.'[51]

In April 1986 O'Boyle received his true initiation into the covert world. He was entrusted with what he called a 'secret plan'. Wild horses would scarcely drag this plan out of him at the hearings, even though all he had been shown was a wall map of Central America: nothing classified, no black programmes, no code words. It was enough that a government official in the OEOB, with its mock-French, slightly creepy grandeur, right beside the White House, had told him not to tell anybody. The plan turned out to be North's own favoured 'final act' for the contras: that if Congress did not approve any more money for them they would seize a piece of Nicaragua, establish a provisional government and there make a last stand, while the American Navy blockaded the rest of the country.[52] This was the plan which, according to Abrams, was dismissed by the CIA and the Defense Department as 'the craziest idea they had ever heard; totally implausible and not-doable'.[53] But North insisted at the hearings that not everybody had scorned it,[54] and certainly it sounded plausible enough to O'Boyle; it was a state secret, and he had been allowed to share it.

Nevertheless, he felt uneasy. Here he was, a civilian, suddenly being made privy to enormous affairs of state. Possibly World War III was brewing up in Nicaragua — he mentioned that to North, though North doubted it, thought the Russians would never fight for the place — and here was he, O'Boyle, being told about the innermost strategic details. He felt he was exposing himself 'to some danger from hostile forces, one might say, while at the same time having no training or no institutional support . . . I mean, obviously you're playing in a rather . . . or driving in the fast lane when you're doing this sort of thing.'

O'Boyle eventually became so worried by the secret nature of

North's work that he tore out from his diary the corner of a page on which he had written North's name, and threw it away.[55] There was a limit to the amount of drama in which he would involve himself. And he would not be incriminated by a paper; but North was.

Appropriately enough, in this strange world of not-so-covert agents and hackneyed dramatic devices, it was a secret document that gave the game away: a document that was never meant to be there at all. Appropriately, too, the discovery of that document was attended by all sorts of dramatic flourishes. Even the bureaucrats involved took to playing games and devising ruses, for all the world like secret agents themselves.

On November 22nd, 1986, a five-page memorandum turned up that mentioned, at the top of one page, the diversion of funds to the contras. North had written it, apparently sometime in April, and had somehow failed to shred it. It was an office memorandum much like any other, entitled 'Release of American Hostages in Beirut': closely typed in best office prose, and with no cover sheet. (Without a cover sheet, there was no knowing who might have read it or seen it.) The first paragraph on the fifth page read, in part.

The residual funds from this transaction [a proposed April 1986 shipment of 3,000 TOWs and Hawk missile parts to Iran] are allocated as follows . . .

$12m will be used to purchase critically needed supplies for the Nicaraguan Democratic Resistance forces.[56]

The discovery of this memo brought the scandal to a head. Within two days of the discovery that funds had in fact been diverted, Poindexter was obliged to resign; North was fired; and the open-mouthed press descended like locusts. Within ten days, a special prosecutor had been appointed to look into criminal misconduct.

The finders of this bombshell were two Justice Department officials, Brad Reynolds and John Richardson, who had been sent to North's office to look through papers relating to the shipments to Iran.[57] This was their initiation into the NSC world of secrecy, and they entered into it with a will. Sitting at the table in North's office, they communicated by passing notes to each other, even notes that merely inquired when they ought to meet up again. There was always someone at North's desk, they explained; it seemed safer that way.

The memorandum turned up when they were about three folders into the search; North, as it happened, had not arrived yet. Reynolds came across a slim manila folder with the letters 'WH' marked in red ink on the flap. He drew out the document inside, read it through. Under his breath, so that Earl could not hear him, he murmured 'Holy cow!' ('or it may have been a little more graphic').[58] Richardson looked up.

He either kicked me under the table or something and we were sitting across from each other . . . just a foot or two, and he passed it over, directed me to the top paragraph and had an expression of this was a surprising entry. So I read it and I gave a similar look back and I think I probably said something like that didn't happen or something along those lines, that's hard to believe that had happened and passed it back to him and then that was it, we did not discuss it at the time . . . My first impression was this is too spectacular to think it happened.

Nonetheless, it was 'the most interesting' document they had seen. Reynolds had come across two others like it in all respects, but not in the same folder, and not with the incriminating paragraph; that too was odd, in retrospect. So he marked it with a paperclip for copying, put it back in its manila folder, 'wiped off all my fingerprints', and hid it 'out of an abundance of caution' in the stack of other papers to be copied.[59] Good secret-agent tactics. The two men then left the office to lunch, as arranged, with the attorney-general. On the way out they ran into North coming in. 'He said Where are you guys going, have I missed it, or something like that, and we said . . . we were going out and have a bite of lunch.'

At the Old Ebbitt Grill, on K Street east of the White House, the attorney general was waiting. Meese was in his fifties, solid, plump and pink-faced; a California prosecutor who seemed shocked by nothing, a 'taciturney general', as one lawyer described him.[60] He talked about various meetings to do with the Iran inquiry, and the others listened; when he was finished, he asked Reynolds and Richardson whether they had found anything interesting. Reynolds mentioned the memorandum. Meese 'visibly said something like, oh, a curse word', said Richardson (the curse word was variously reported as 'Holy Toledo!', 'Oh, darn' and 'Oh, shit'), 'and sort of squinted his eyes and that sort of thing . . . and [he] said, Be sure you bring a copy of that out when you come.' But it was still 'very much incredible prospect', as Richardson put it; and Reynolds thought that the mention in the same memo of Colonel Ghadaffi's attempt to buy the hostages was just as interesting as what might have gone to the contras. They discussed it, he supposed, for no more than five minutes.[61]

At about 3.30 Reynolds and Richardson went back to North's office. He let them in. The papers lay on the table, as they were, with the addition of some folders from 1985 that North had promised. Richardson said they wanted to make some copies, and he and North and North's aides copied the stack between them. Reynolds was quite sure, however — excess of caution prevailing again — that he purposely kept the diversion memo out of North's hands.[62]

As Reynolds and Richardson worked on, the diversion memo now in duplicate on the table, North wandered about, relaxed and friendly, at least to all appearances. He read the newspaper, commenting aloud on the accuracy or inaccuracy of the stories about himself. He took a call from an Israeli (real secret-agent stuff, this), and they slipped into code, Reynolds thought, after about ten minutes:

> And then all of a sudden he said 'Poindexter' and then said 'I mean Beethoven.' I damn near fell out of the chair and looked at John and go like that and John went like that . . . it was really quite amusing. I mean I assumed he wanted me to know Poindexter's name was Beethoven . . . it didn't just slip out.[63]

North also offered them coffee, 'real strong military coffee', and Richardson went off to brew it with him. At one point North suddenly remarked, 'Well, I'm not worried, soon I am going to be back commanding a Marine battalion. Someone is going to have to take the hit for this.' At another point, he came over and sat down at the table with them. 'All right, fellows,' he said, 'shoot. I'm ready to answer your questions.'[64] Reynolds, perhaps a little taken aback by all the dramatic military talk, explained that it was Meese, not themselves, who would talk to him.

Meese did in fact call while they were there, to set up an interview with North for the next day, Sunday: the interview in which he was to be confronted with the memorandum. He asked if it could be arranged for the morning. North, wanting to go to church, deferred it. The interview was set, the browsing went on, and sometime after six everybody left. Richardson drove to his 'one-room place' in McLean with the photocopied papers, including the rogue memorandum, locked in the boot of his car; took them out, put them under the bed 'within arm's reach' (as secret agents would) and went uneasily to sleep. So the day ended.

The next day, at two o'clock, everyone assembled at the Justice Department. Meese began the interview with his usual little speech underlining the importance of telling the truth, not putting a good spin on anything to protect the President. They then worked slowly through the chronology, all the parties sitting informally round a small table; so informal, in the mythology, that the subsequent TV docudrama put Meese in a startling pink-and-lavender tracksuit, drinking coffee from a mug. According to Richardson, there had been no discussion of tactics beforehand. Meese had simply said, 'All right, we want to go through the 1985 shipment . . . well, how the initiative began . . . then talk to him about this memo of the diversion of funds.' 'But it was very obvious to me once he began the questioning what he was doing,' said Richardson. 'He had been a prosecutor for eight years.'[65]

The form, in fact, was one beloved of prosecutors both on the screen and in literature. This was precisely the way in which Inspector Porfiry in Dostoevsky's *Crime and Punishment* homed in on the culprit Raskolnikov, a man who was also damned by a paper: an article he had written for the *Periodical Magazine*, months before, offering justifications for certain sorts of crimes. Meese even resembled Porfiry, aimiable and unhurried, 'his fat, round little figure . . . rebounding from every wall and corner' as he strolled up and down the room. Like Meese, Porfiry was most fascinated by the final part of Raskolnikov's paper, in which 'you hint . . . at the existence of certain people who . . . are, as it were, above the law.' Like North, Raskolnikov was appalled that such a small thing, so long ago, so distorted by his interrogator, should have incriminated him.

When Meese handed North the memorandum, he at first showed no surprise. He looked at it for a moment. A few questions about general financial transactions were asked and answered, and Meese then pointed out the paragraph about the diversion. Reynolds remembered 'a noticeable change' in North's demeanour: his answers became halting.[66] Richardson recalled him saying 'You found this in my files?'[67] Meese said, 'Yes. Did this take place?' Charles Cooper, also there for the Justice Department, remembered that North paused for a moment, silent, before he responded. He said yes. 'And you could see him sort of recline back in the chair . . . he was visibly surprised.'[68]

That night, North telephoned Poindexter to tell him the memo had been found. Already the story was becoming melodrama. North said he had spent 'all day' with the attorney-general, explaining 'everything'. Poindexter, weary, did not really want to know and had no memory of the memo at all; he told him he would see him at the office in the morning.[69] On that morning, North dropped by Paul Thompson's office, beside Poindexter's, to tell him the gist of his conversation with Meese, 'that it did not go well'. The drama was then relayed in detail:

> He spent like four hours or something with the attorney general and with these three other staff over there . . . and they spent most of the time talking about all aspects of the Iran initiative and so forth, and then at the very end Meese pulled out that April memo . . . and said, 'what about this?' And North said, 'Oh geez, I didn't realise you had that,' or, 'I don't know where that came from' . . .
> *Q.* Did he tell you that he had told the attorney general about the diversion of money?
> *A.* . . . He was more interested in telling me about the tactics of the attorney general.[70]

North told the story to Bob Earl, too, to whom he was closer, and with whom the story could slip still more bonds with the world of facts. There were several people present at the interview, he told him, and 'at least one of them was an FBI agent.' When, at the end of two hours, they finally showed him the document and he acknowledged what had happened, 'there was a sigh from the assembled people.' At the end, everything explained in detail, North turned to the attorney general and said 'Since you haven't read me my rights, does this count?'[71]

The mystery paper had brought the ceiling down; on the telephone to McFarlane two days later, when he had been fired, North's only explanation was 'I missed one.'[72] How he had missed it, on its own in its disctinctive folder, no-one understood. Nobody understood, either, how it had come to be there at all. Poindexter said he had told North repeatedly not to put anything in writing about the transfer of funds to the contras.[73] North, uncharacteristically, disobeyed. He wrote not one memo about it but, by his estimate, as many as five,[74] and sent them up the line. He never got one back with a check-mark, but he kept copies in his office until, in October 1986, he started to destroy documents to cover his tracks. On November 21st he told Poindexter, who was advising him that the Justice Department 'fact-finding mission' was about to descend on his office, that he had got rid of them all. 'Don't worry,' he said; 'those documents are gone.'[75]

But he was wrong; there was one left. By Poindexter's trial, in 1990, he thought he must have told the admiral that: he was going to destroy that one, and then they would really all be gone. That one paper had to be left, for it could not have turned up otherwise. Indeed, just before his interview with Meese, he had dropped in to see McFarlane in his office precisely, McFarlane thought, to agonize over the fact that the diversion was a matter of record: 'I put it in a memo to the Admiral.'[76] Yet North said he did not remember that conversation, either at the hearings or later; nor did he remember the memo in question, or not with any conviction. This was a memorandum that seemed to have taken on a life of its own: now here, now there, now one, now several, now alone, now gone, now lurking. 'And you destroyed it, didn't you?' asked Poindexter's prosecutor.

*A.* Yes, I think so.
*Q.* You thought that by doing that you had wiped out every document that existed that would reflect [the diversion], didn't you?
*A.* I thought I had, yes.
*Q.* But one shows up later, doesn't it?
*A.* Yes.[77]

When it turned up, it was both horrible and useful; a mind-boggling twist to the Iran story (Pelion piled on Ossa, indeed), but also a magnificent diversion from the Iranian debacle to the Nicaraguan controversy, from approved policy to possibly freelance meanderings, and from Reagan to North. That, indeed, was how Reagan himself seemed to see it. Apprised of the memo, Iran went completely out of his mind.

> My memory of Mr Meese's participation was when, after all of that thing had broken, that he was the one who located a piece of paper in some office that indicated that there was additional money. And . . . his participation was as attorney general in case there was something untoward that was waiting there to haunt us. And that was where I got the knowledge about the extra money, and that is the only thing that I remember about from him.[78]

By itself, the 'diversion memorandum' — soon to be 'Exhibit 1' in the congressional inquiries — dictated the shape of the subsequent investigation. Nothing became more important than whether the President had added his approval to this 'very strange' piece of paper, as Poindexter called it: a memorandum Poindexter said he had never seen before, and which Thompson found him reading the next morning over breakfast.[79] And yet the memorandum was almost pure hypothesis. The transaction described in it had never occurred,[80] though smaller versions had. The scheme had been aborted, like many such schemes, despite their minute and endless delineation; the $12m had neither been generated nor shifted to the contras. In that narrow sense, Reagan was right when he insisted at his testimony, as on every previous occasion, that 'no-one has proven to me that there was a diversion.'[81]

North himself seemed to take it almost lightly. The Case of the Mystery Memo had become, within a day, a little drama he could act out for his colleagues. He had planned for it; it had been expected;[82] it was just another episode of the unreal bureaucratic adventures in which he seemed to picture himself. 'I am, indeed, a Marine officer in real life,' North had told an audience of contra supporters in Nashville in May 1986, 'and Washington is not real life . . . it is not the real world, but a veritable vacuum.'[83] Real life, North's listeners could learn by inference, was the hour of crisis or the field of battle. During his description of the interception of the terrorists who had seized the cruise ship *Achille Lauro* in October 1985 — his best moment at the NSC, and his fiercest crisis — North, who hardly ever used the word 'real', suddenly peppered his account with it. 'Very, very real time intelligence', 'very real courage', 'the very very real direct and immediate assistance of the government of Israel'.[84] Reality was to be up against the enemy and the clock, with lives at stake. Reality was quick and did not brook negotiation; in 'that sad swamp on the Potomac', as North later liked to call Washington, reality passed over like a flare of marsh gas, too swift for most of the inhabitants to catch.

That North should have been caught by a memorandum, one of the common plants of the swamp, was especially ironic. Memoranda made concrete and factual — real, as the world understands it — operations that were often meant to stay in the world of abstraction; schemes that Congress, and most members of the government, were not supposed to have the slightest inkling of. But North's memoranda were also aspirations, plans, dreams and imaginings, as much as schedules of facts. McFarlane talked of a 'Rabelasian cast to messages' and of 'the creation of romantic kinds of activities'; he had four or five years' experience, he noted wearily, 'of reading things which I knew not to be compatible with the realities of things.'[85] The typical North memo, according to General Galvin, implied that 'a whole lot more is going to happen that was really intended to happen in there';[86] a colleague said they were North's equivalent of a Potemkin Village,[87] set down in unreal Washington.

This was also the reality of the covert world, fuelled by information others did not know relayed by carriers whose real identity was hidden; a world of secret agents, mystery papers, dreadful imaginings and improbable suspicions. It was a world that would never solidify, would never be understood, unless it was named; as philosophers knew, only the naming of an object could make it real. Yet several weeks into the scandal, the *New Yorker* complained that the mess had so far mocked all attempts to baptize it.[88] The *New Republic* ran a competition, won by 'Iranamok', and bravely stuck with it when nobody followed.[89] (Runners-up included 'Contraversions', 'Ronnybrook' and, with a nod to Hitchcock, 'North by Mideast'.) *The Economist* introduced 'Iragua', which lasted a fortnight. Some thought the scandal might have done better, in terms of audience ratings, if the name had not been the leaden 'Iran-contra affair' but something with panache, cloak-and-dagger stuff. But such a name never appeared, perhaps for the reason the *New Yorker* itself suggested: you cannot fix labels on a world of shadows.

# Chapter 4

# The Scandal as Cinema

IT was Hollywood, aptly enough, that came to the rescue of those who wanted to pin the scandal down. Many of the players, as we have seen, had been wandering already in a nether world of two-dimensional heroes, villains, adventurers and fall-guys. When the scandal broke the media too placed them there, confirming how odd and ungraspable it all was; confirming, too, that this was not just a political morass, but cinema, and fun. Had not Reagan told North, when he called him after he was fired, that it would all make a great movie one day?[1]

The Lebanese press had obligingly produced a comic version of McFarlane; but the film versions of both Reagan and North were also set as early as November 1986, and did not much change thereafter. Reagan, largely as the result of a disastrous speech 'explaining' the Iran operation on November 13th and an even more discombobulated press conference on the 19th, became the Man Who Was Not All There; the very man, in fact, whom he himself had played in his Hollywood B-movie days, Drake McHugh in *King's Row*. McHugh, waking from an operation in which he has lost his legs, asks 'Where's the rest of me?' Reagan had already used the phrase (he was ever good at self-deprecation) as the title of his campaign biography. Now, with Iran-contra, it summoned up the snoozing president; a leader who, despite all appearances, put no more of his substance into government than the man behind the curtain in *The Wizard of Oz*.

Although on every side people tried to raise the old Watergate question, 'What did the President know and when did he know it?', it seemed curiously flabby and unsatisfactory; as Elizabeth Drew wrote in the *New Yorker*, 'When one talks about what Reagan "knew", one could be dealing in metaphysics.'[2] It seemed that not only the president, but the whole country, might have been in some delightful lotus-sleep for the past few years. When the White House lawyer first tried to debrief Reagan on what he knew of the affair, the president was said to have told him stories of Hollywood; when journalists badgered him about the deals he had half-wittingly struck with Israel and Iran in August 1985, he replied amiably: 'Everybody that can remember what they were doing on August 8th 1985, raise your hand.'[3]

If Reagan was the Great Delegator, the sleeping man with his hand in the jelly beans, North was quickly characterized as the secret agent. For some days after the scandal broke, the press could find out nothing about him. The *New Yorker* of November 24th lamented that the NSC would not reveal even the age or the precise employment of this man, 'who seems to be called on to act as a secret surrogate for something like the entire United States government'. Nor did they know what he looked like. The press had been given nothing but 'blurry, distorted photographs culled from television shots of occasions in the past at which North happened to be present'; at best, ABC News had shown 'pictures of the back of a man's head that may or may not have been North's as the man got into an Embassy car in Cyprus on the occasion of the homeward flight of one of the hostages'.[4] Again and again the film was aired: into the car, back turned, head forward on arms.

Even on such slim sightings, however, the cinematic myths began to gather round North. 'A 20th century Paladin', cried *US News World Report*, a magazine that seldom let itself get too excited; 'He stands alone as the sacrificed knight in the Iran-arms gambit, a true believer steeled and scarred by a lifetime of have-gun-will-travel missions.' His colleagues at the NSC, John Lang continued, had given him the nickname 'Knight Rider', after the television hero ['one man and his machine, dedicated to the righting of wrongs'], for his disappearances to confer with the contras.[5] *Insight*, a conservative magazine, began its December analysis of the debacle with the litany from the television series *Mission Impossible*: 'Should you or any member of the I[mpossible] M[issions] force be caught or killed, the Secretary will disavow any knowledge of your actions. Good luck, Jim' — and noted that the luck of the 'real-life Jim', North, appeared to have run out.[6] Even Shirley Christian's relatively cosy interview with North for the *New York Times* on December 1st — an interview that gained in suspiciousness and oddity because it was the last North gave for two years — plunged suddenly into an action-man world. 'In the midst of the conversation at his house in the wooded hills of Northern Virginia', she recorded, 'a neighbour's horse came galloping down the road, riderless. The colonel ran out into the road, blocked the animal's path and guided it into his own yard, where his children calmed it.'[7]

North was also said, early on, to have worked out of the basement of the White House. Evil things crawled out of basements, and plots were hatched there by the half-crazed. Cartoonists showed the White House half-askew on this basement, noxious odours rising from the grates, while the President snoozed upstairs. After the Tower Report was published in February 1987, and the PROF notes revealed that had passed by computer between the characters, the basement became home to a band of five-o'clock-shadowed Boy Scouts delighting in their own secrecy.[8] In vain did North point out that he had worked, always, on the third floor of the Old Executive Office Building ('the only third-floor basement in Washington').[9] Long after the hearings, even after the trials, 'the White House basement' remained the place where the awful miasma had started.

By mid-December, with the scandal in the news barely a month, a Hollywood producer, Jay Weston, already had his eyes on it. He announced that he wanted to make a biopic of North, with Mel Gibson or Treat Williams in the title role. It could be a movie; it could be a television series. 'It's almost impossible to sell anything to do with politics', said Mr Weston, barely containing his excitement; 'but North touches a deep wellspring in the American spirit. You think "my country right or wrong", but you never know until you've done it.' Several titles had already occurred to him: 'American Hero Gone Wrong', 'The Flawed Hero', perhaps 'Carrying Patriotism Too Far'. Irving Lazar, a literary agent, also made North an offer before the year was out, estimating he could sell his story for $5m. 'North is right out of John le Carré', he said; 'one of those fascinating mystery people you don't meet in life or in government.'[10] Not often, anyway.

North's screen persona, which appeared suddenly to seize the country by the throat when he testified on television in July 1987, had therefore been set at least seven months before. When he testified, he had already been characterized as Batman and Superman and, most frequently, Rambo (but 'a Rambo with all his clothes on', as *The Spectator* put it);[11] he had been a composite Clint Eastwood type, part-lonesome cowboy, part Dirty Harry; he had been James Bond and James Dean, 'the rebel with a cause'.[12] This was, in all probability, the first scandal to be shaped to such a degree by references learned from the screen. The effect was to make Iran-contra only half serious, and only half real.

The public hearings in the spring and summer of 1987 were, of course, stern stuff: the required full-scale inquisition and explanation. But they were also billed, in America, as 'Ollie's Follies', in Europe as 'the latest American soap opera'. One particular missing element had been provided in March with the emergence of North's secretary, Fawn Hall. Fawn was an unlikely combination of the *femme fatale* and the dutiful organizer, a well-brought-up girl from the Virginia suburbs who was also a part-time model. She had long legs and a mane of blonde hair; as she laboured at her typewriter on classified memoranda she drew into North's office a little stream of besotted admirers, and she was to be spotted after the scandal broke driving round Washington in her red sports car (FAWN 1), blowing smoke out of the windows.

The discovery of Fawn turned the story from an impenetrable imbroglio into a juicy tale, and set the appetite for whatever show, or film, could be made of it. 'Almost all of human drama is there', cried the London *Daily Express*,

> except for one thing. SEX. Enter, stage right, the beautiful Fawn . . . Now for the book, the film, the mini-series, Irangate II, Irangate on Ice and so on and so forth! Who better to play Colonel North than North himself? And who better to play Ronald Reagan than that old B-movie actor, the president? They could always write his lines on his shirt-cuff.[13]

An absurdly large raft of congressmen and senators was set to question the witnesses, sitting on a specially constructed double dais draped with burgundy cloth; none wished to drop out of the committees and forfeit a screen appearance.[14] Witnesses beneath the principals were picked for their ability to present a simple, and therefore televisually satisfying, picture of the case. In *Time* magazine on the eve of the hearings Walter Shapiro offered advice for congressmen wishing to become stars, as Sam Ervin had at the Watergate hearings: they should play to the cameras, should not be afraid to wear their hearts on their sleeves, and should never make the mistake of reading their questions.[15] This advice was taken most seriously. On the day itself, Norman Mailer, then a juror at the Cannes film festival, was asked what he thought of the movies on offer. 'Movies?' he replied, 'What movies? I've been watching General Secord on CNN in my hotel room. It's as addictive as cartoons. I may never see another movie for the duration.'[16]

Secord, indeed, opened boldly. So too did John Nields and Arthur Liman, the two star congressional lawyers. The *Guardian* reporter praised their 'soft man/hard man routine: Nields offers the witness a comfortable chair and a cigarette, Liman slaps him round the face and kicks the chair out from underneath him.'[17] The show, however, went up and down. It was often tedious; and for every senator disposed to find it fun, there was another whose face would be set in grim outrage. Several were undecided. Near the end of Hakim's disturbing testimony — bakhshish, back-scratching, dedicated bank accounts — Senator Trible of Virginia said he found it 'part James Bond and part Jimmy Durante, and it would be very laughable, but for the consequences for people and policy.'[18] Senator Inouye was sterner: he realized that ordinary citizens thought Hakim's testimony 'fascinating and exotic', and chuckled at it, but he himself found it 'rather sad . . . to say it is stranger than fiction is an understatement.'[19] It was only when Fawn Hall testified, flicking back her hair in a fetching manner, that Inouye joined in the spirit of the proceedings, holding a piece of paper over his eyes to see her better in the glare of the television lights.

By then, the cinematic apogee of the hearings was near. It was midsummer, and hot. After Fawn Hall, a break was arranged before the second act in which, after excursions by a few minor players, North was to appear. The witnesses immediately before him painted a picture of an elaborate liar, one whose testimony could probably not be trusted under oath, and of a petty thief who bought lingerie, so it appeared, with money meant for the contras; some committee members considered him such a 'wacko', in the patois, that his testimony would be next to useless. The word favoured by headline-writers was 'tarnished', although any lustre North had had in the media was not much more than the borrowed glow of stars whom he superficially resembled. Moreover the *Washington Post*, having taken the lustre away, was plainly only waiting to give it back again. 'Comes now the star performance', began the lead editorial on July 7th, the day North began to testify, before a word was spoken. And it was right.

For six days North passionately defended everything he had done, right and wrong alike. Everywhere, his testimony was a 'show': one that played in dentists' surgeries to relieve the pain of extraction, in bars to give a purpose to drinking, in aeroplanes criss-crossing the country, and in television stores to crowds of people pressing against the windows. A salesman at the Crazy Eddie appliance store on

West 45th Street, in Manhattan, said he had not seen so many people intent on a show since the Mets had played the Houston Astros in the sixth game of the playoff for the National League pennant, and even then they had not stood so close up to the screen.[20]

By chance, North's testimony coincided with the Oscar nominations; he was popularly nominated, and pranksters turned Hollywood's hillside sign into 'Ollywood' in the second week of the hearings. The testimony also coincided with the British release of Commander Bond's latest venture, *The Living Daylights*; in one of the nicest reversals of reality, some reviewers compared Bond to North, rather than vice-versa. North himself was compared to Burt Lancaster, Jimmy Stewart, Charlton Heston, John Wayne, Lilian Gish, Groucho Marx, Steve Martin and 'all the Barrymores put together'; his performance was the most stirring and patriotic display Congressman Hyde had seen 'since the first time I saw Jimmy Cagney singing "Yankee Doodle Dandy"'.[21] By the second day, more viewers were watching North than were watching the daytime soap operas, *As the World Turns* and *General Hospital*. On the third day, the three networks abandoned the soap operas altogether.

By the end of his testimony, North had become a haircut, a logo for T-shirts, a doll, a cocktail, a hero sandwich ('red-blooded American beef, a little bologna, shredded lettuce, Swiss cheese'), a hamburger ('secret sauce from an old Iranian recipe') and a design for boxer shorts; vigils were held for him, and the hamlet of Ollie, Iowa (population 230) was besieged with fascinated enquiries. North-for-President T-shirts were presented by members of the congressional panels to each other, and everyone laughed sportingly.

Quite why 'Olliemania' happened as it did, and with such intensity, confounded almost everyone. Part of it was simple force of personality, buttressed by a Marine uniform; part of it was expectation, a slow series of teasing appearances and an avalanche of peculiar facts, built up over many months. Part of it, some writers supposed, was a longing for heroes in an age without them, for cleavers of Gordian knots (as the *Wall Street Journal* called North) possessed of simple and shining certitudes;[22] at the end of North's testimony even Inouye concluded that he had become another man destined for some piece of important marble in Washington, alongside Lincoln.[23] On the other hand, the 'hero' label seemed a red herring, something the media themselves had dreamed up. An ABC poll of July 12th asked whether North was 'hero, villain or victim', as though those three possibilities encompassed all he was; or as though, indeed, they were mutually exclusive.[24]

Caught up in the performance, few people seemed to wonder

whether what they were hearing was an accurate account of the affair. Few, indeed, seemed to be listening for sense at all. Having waited so long to hear from the 'one man' who knew what had happened, when he appeared they could do nothing but gaze on him; having made him into a celluloid star, there was no reason at this point to spoil it, and make him real. For its issue of August 3rd *The New Republic* hired David Denby, the film critic of *New York* magazine, to look at the cinematic qualities of North's face. After wandering over the 'handsome' mouth and the 'bad-boy's' ears and the hair ('a masterpiece'), Danby concluded that North was a type of composite mythological figure, ready to step into a set constructed from '200 years of American archetypes and 50 years of the cinema'. Small wonder that people were star-struck by this 'deeply anti-democratic mind';[25] or that even the most serious commentators, like William Safire, could not resist having cracks at the screenplay.[26]

The nickname 'Ollie', in itself, had much to do with the way the scandal was treated. Could anything be serious that had at its centre this lovable, rogueish, bumbling figure ('That's another fine mess you've got us into, Ollie')? As Gore Vidal pointed out in *Newsweek*, 'Like Tom [Sawyer], Ollie is essentially fictional.'[27] Even after North's sentencing, the blundering charmer now a felon, both *Time* and *Newsweek* called him 'Ollie' on their covers. To ask 'Should Ollie go to Jail?' seemed automatically to suggest the answer no: soap-opera heroes, diminutives, household names could no more be put behind bars than Ronnie could.

North himself seemed to know how he might go over, if not precisely the scale of it. Asked by Congressman Jenkins whether he could persuade his superiors, simply because of his eloquence, to run against the wishes of the Cabinet, North replied 'I have no doubt about that.' Within a minute or so he modified his cocksureness — 'The good Lord gives us all certain gifts' — but not much.[28] This was not, after all, a secret agent blinking as he was flushed into the light, as the *New Yorker* said it had supposed. This was a man who understood the uses of spotlights. Carl Channell could never forget the first North briefing he saw, one of his contra slide shows in the White House. He was not mad about slide shows himself, it was a wet day, the rich contributors had to be helped in with their umbrellas; he was sceptical that North could do anything arresting. But 'the room was very dark and Colonel North was sort of spotlighted because he was very close to the slides.' And at the end, when they flipped on the lights, 'everyone was just riveted to him. And I decided it was a successful briefing, you know. I mean, this had really worked.'[29]

To those who actually sat in the hearing room, it was difficult to grasp the degree to which cinema had taken over. Before the double dais sat a small, slight, unimpressive man who frequently could not recall, sometimes could not hear and peered at the briefing books through wire-rimmed glasses. The screen, however, romanced him, and the screen ruled. Photographers even took pictures of banks of screens, each flickering with North's identical face. These had a being and authority of their own, like the sets seen by the French philosopher Jean Baudrillard left playing in deserted motels off highways in the west. You would no more turn them off than you would extinguish life. This was the sign, the image, the real thing.

Yet when, after Poindexter's first day of testimony, the story-line reached its conclusion — no, the president had not been told of the diversion of funds to the contras — viewers fell away. As cartoonists had predicted, there was no 'Poiniemania': no vogue for the admiral's sempiternal pipes or balding head, but a sobering up, like a sluice with cold water. Poindexter's expression all through his testimony was one of mystification, shrouded in patient smoke, as if he really could not think why all these people wanted to ply him with questions. When he had finished the hearings quickly wound up with no incisive questioning of the last three witnesses, Shultz, Weinberger and Meese, although their tales would have been worth hearing; the committees, after all, had contracted to finish by early August, whether or not the full story had been told. By then, Iran-contra was no longer a good movie, even if the livelier parts had been preserved on the videotapes that were hastily rushed out. It had become an older, slower, more exacting entertainment, if indeed it was still entertainment of any sort: no longer *Mission Impossible* but, as Senator Warren Rudman put it, 'like sitting on a winter night in New Hampshire with a blizzard raging outside and reading a Robert Ludlum novel'.[30]

If Iran-contra had lodged in the nation's mind at all, it was in terms of North and his testimony: that piece of film everyone had seen and talked about, like the shooting of JR in *Dallas* or the opening on *Geraldo* of Al Capone's secret vault. As the search began in January 1989 for 12 people who had never watched his testimony to sit as a jury at North's trial, one cartoonist imagined it would have to be composed of *mujahedin* from Afghanistan; a satirist announced that the first two jurors selected were Hsing-Hsing and Ling-Ling, the pandas from Washington Zoo. The 12 jurors who eventually emerged, acquitting themselves both responsibly and wisely, were mocked all through the trial for their necessary ignorance. When the hearings came on, they explained, they would run upstairs and lock the door, or try to switch channels, or read the comics, or tidy the house. One elderly juror, whose house had burned down eight months before North appeared, said she tuned in a little to the hearings as she tried to sort everything out, but 'it was just like I was focussing on "The Three Stooges" or something.'[31] And there was perhaps not so much to laugh at in that; for by North's trial, two and a half years after the breaking of the scandal, the overwhelming majority of Americans had come to feel much the same way.

The trial had been supposed to provide a dramatic climax of sorts. At least it was in a courtroom, where in *Perry Mason* or *LA Law* the witnesses cracked and the truth came out; at least it might sort out whether the central figure was hero or villain, and point to how far up the culpability went. Yet, perhaps because it was not televised, it produced mighty little stir. On the first day of jury selection, the *Washington Post's* man was disappointed. Despite the 'fine cast of characters ... assembled for a morality play, even a tragedy, that once promised to rival the Watergate scandal', only twelve people sat in the public seats. The star, too, appeared to have gone. North had now retired from the Marines and, in his blue suit and 'rather bright' red tie, he seemed to have shrunk, becoming 'forlorn' and 'pathetic'.[32] The great storm of Irangate, as *Le Monde* lamented, had blown itself out; there remained nothing but 'a draught or two, like memories, blowing from time to time across the praetorium.'[33]

The jury deliberations in April coincided with the showing of a real CBS television drama — *Guts and Glory: The Rise and Fall of Oliver North*. Sequestered that weekend in sealed hotel rooms, without television, the jurors themselves could not enjoy it; but the trial judge comforted the prosecutor, who was growing anxious about the delay, with the thought that he could watch it if he wanted, to pass the time.[34] The film's director and producer promoted it as a serious and responsible piece of work. He had even provided, as an antagonist to North, a fictional member of the NSC, 'Aaron Sykes', whose job it was to give flesh and voice to those invisible and voiceless colleagues who had presumably tried to dissuade North from what he was doing: to appear, as the Laws appeared to Socrates, 'humming in his ears', about the offence he would cause to country, friends and laws if he did what seemed to him the right thing. Sykes was, the director confessed, a dramatic device, but the story could not be properly told without one.[35] It was crucial to the development of the plot to have a character — in this case balding, in a mackintosh — who would defend the prerogatives of Congress, rehearse the finer points of democracy and say, in answer to North's ringing endorsement of the theory that the end justified the means, 'But that's not what America is all about, Colonel.'

In this case, as in others, television docudrama set itself up as the tidier and balancer of history. No story without Sykes; but with Sykes, in real life, probably no story. And whichever way it went, in any event, the public did not greatly want to know. On the first night, most of them were watching *Bionic Showdown: The Bionic Woman Meets the Six-Million Dollar Man* on a rival channel. They were content to leave North, for good or bad, as they already knew him. They were also content to leave the whole affair as far as they knew it, understood it or had allocated the blame for it. Had they not, after all, watched the movie already?

Iran-contra, however, had always had another star, a more retiring one; and he had not given anything like a full performance yet. An appearance by Reagan, *Le Monde* suggested, might still save the show, even two and a half years after it had started. But Reagan did not appear at North's trial, much as North and his lawyers tried; he did not appear until Poindexter's, in the spring of 1990. As he gave his evidence for videotape, 'genial and twinkly, relaxed in the red eye of the TV camera', as *Newsweek* described him, reporters noted that in an adjacent courtroom Stevie Wonder was appearing in a case about the authorship of a song, and that across the street another crew was filming an episode of *thirtysomething*.[36] It was back to show business, as if the scandal had ever really left it.

Reagan's testimony was indeed a dramatic summation of sorts, and the most bizarre of all. Here was the scandal seen through the eyes of an old man, its central figure, but now powerless, toothless and thoughtless; easily tired, and probably over-cautioned on the dangers of speaking in courtrooms. The videotape was appropriately blurry, like the man; the stuffing had gone out of him. And really, he said, the Iran and contra operations had not been central to his life. There had been so many meetings; 80 a day, someone had told him. There had been so many pieces of paper; 50 million at least, someone else had told him, generated during his eight years as President.[37] When he talked of the hostages or the contras something of the old fire returned, together with the old emotional lines from cabinet meetings and television speeches. But of the policies themselves — in other words, of the 'affairs' — he remembered almost nothing. Gamely, his questioners tried to encourage him. Perhaps he remembered the meeting about Iran in August 1985 when he was in the hospital, or the decision to assist the shipment in November, taken 'in the bedroom of the little guest house' in Geneva? No, nothing; or else the memory of a meeting, 'but I can't recall what the outcome was or what we were discussing.'[38] All he could remember was that TOWs were shipped at some point; that 'the price asked for the military was twelve million two';[39] that the aircraft could turn round and abort the delivery if the hostages were not released, which he thought was 'a most unusual thing';[40] and that it was definitely not 'the Khomeini' with whom he had been doing business.[41] He added, alarmingly, of the November shipment: 'I know that that is in my memory that I had heard of France being connected with such a thing.'[42]

With contra policy, matters became vaguer still. Reagan was shown a picture of Calero meeting him in the Oval Office; he did not know who he was.[43] Bursting to help the freedom fighters, he was reduced, he said, to lecturing his staff on staying inside the law. As for the matter of the diversion of funds, he still believed that there had never been such a thing. He had appointed the Tower Commission, he said, specifically to find out whether money had been generated from the arms sales beyond the 'twelve million two', and, if so, who had done it; but no one had come back with an answer. He was still waiting.[44]

Refusing to credit that story, he was obviously not much moved by the excitements that flowed from it. He had not read the Tower Commission's report, evidently; did not know that McFarlane had pleaded guilty to misdemeanours;[45] did not know the substance of the charges against Poindexter;[46] had not altered in any particular the mythology created when the edifice had first crashed down, in November 1986. Wrapped up in his agreeably muddled versions of events, he might have been speaking from Mars: and with this last screen show, this cinematic oddity, the scandal sank away.

# PART II

# Just Cause and Holy War

> David said to his brothers when they challenged his right
> and ability to fight Goliath: 'Is there not a just cause?' I
> will ask all of you, is there not a just cause?
>
> Robert Owen, Hearings, 19. 5. 87

Extraordinary as the two operations were, they were propelled along by the belief of many players — both principals and walkers-on — that the ends were just. However dark the operations seemed, or however wrong they went, they could be proclaimed as something good; even, at times, as something holy. The unabashed commercial instincts of several of the players were mitigated, as they believed, by the noble purposes that went along with them. Conversely, there was not much high-mindedness that went unmixed with greed. This chapter examines those purposes, both high and low.

# Chapter 5

# Flag, Country, Cause

MORE than any other scandal in recent years, Iran-contra was posited on patriotism. Secord was a patriot, North reassured Owen when Owen began to have his doubts.[1] Hakim was a patriot.[2] Aid for the Southern Front was coming from 'private patriotic Americans', or 'the good Americans',[3] some of whom, on giving more than $100,000, received a mahogany box with the Stars and Stripes folded inside it.[4] The whole contra operation was 'for God and Country', Owen said North told him in the beginning;[5] at its end, it had all still been done 'in the best interests of the United States of America'.[6] Herblock, the *Washington Post*'s cartoonist, took to drawing the principals wrapped entirely in the flag, only their boots showing.

Even after his indictment — perhaps particularly after it — North held his press conferences beside the flag, gave his lectures (on God and country) against flags 900 feet square, and was photographed for *Life* magazine guarding the flag, gazing heavenwards, under a sky ferocious with lightning and clouds.[7] Nor was this simply patriotism *post hoc*. Ghorbanifar remembered how sometimes, driving with him in Europe, North would catch sight of Old Glory: 'and when he sees the American flag you can see the change in his eyes. It is a mystical experience for him. He becomes like a tiger, his eyes glistening.'[8] Emerson noticed this propensity of flags to make ordinary people 'poets and mystics', to set off a tingle in the blood; and flags were festooned round Iran-contra like bunting, exceedingly hard to disentangle.

Brought to trial, the players could not believe that their love for their country had caused them to commit crimes; and the light penalties handed down to all these men, with only Poindexter receiving a jail sentence, suggested that the judges, to some degree, accepted patriotism in mitigation. Perhaps these really were 'men who had high purposes',[9] as North described McFarlane and Poindexter, men who 'were trying their level best to make this world a better place.'[10] Remarkably, the first sighting of Dr Johnson's 'Patriotism is the last refuge of a scoundrel' was in *The New Republic* in March1989;[11] by which time such a bedrock of well-meaning patriotism had been wedged under the case that it proved difficult, if not impossible, to shift.

'Operations in the national interest' was a favourite phrase; good and sharp, and carrying the implication that if you needed to know what the national interest was, you did not deserve to be told. 'The national interest' was also a rebuff to congressmen, who could not afford to be critical of it, even when they already knew it as grounds to keep them in the dark. Few ever defined this amorphous thing, or scrutinized it. Although all kinds of questions were asked about the means of these operations, the ends were usually accepted as 'worthy'. During the hearings political protests, as such, were most gentle: one patriot inquiring after the patriotism of another. At the end of Owen's testimony, Senator Inouye said he had received the impression that to be against the President's policy in Central America was to be 'less than patriotic'. No sir, said Owen.

> It is my belief that the people who are willing to put their lives on the line, we, are patriotic. That does not mean to say those who are against the President's policy are any less patriotic . . . Sir, you are a great American. And I fully believe that.
>
> *Inouye*: I just wanted the record to be clear, because somehow I felt like something less than a patriot all day long.[12]

At best, it could be agreed that some people defined the national interest one way and some defined it another way, and each side was equally well-meaning; only some had pushed their patriotism beyond the law, so keen were they, while others had stopped and thought.

Just as few tried to grapple with 'the national interest', so nobody defined — let alone sought to question — 'high purposes'. High purpose was something that could be recognized in someone, like a gleam in the eye or a tone of voice; it meant that even when that person dabbled in something doubtful, they undoubtedly had good reason for doing so. Since McFarlane was an honourable man, North was not unduly worried when he asked him to alter official documents; and when McFarlane sat down at North's computer on November 18th to type in 'additional input that was radically different from the truth', North still considered he must have had 'a darn good reason for not putting the straight story out'.[13] Similarly Fawn Hall, asked by North to alter memoranda to conceal his work for the contras, remembered feeling uneasy: 'but I believe in Colonel North, and I know that there must have been a good reason why he was asking me to do this, and I — I did as I was told.'[14] Considering his love for the country, her queasiness had to be ignored.

The key word was 'belief'. Belief in each other, however little was really known about that other, and belief in the cause, however nebulously described. One visit to North's office, and the man from the Drug Enforcement Administration — no soft touch — was convinced that the wild plan to ransom the hostages was a moral imperative. 'I believed in what I was doing,' he told the lawyers, smarting at the implication that maybe he didn't; 'Once I talked to Ollie the first or second time, man I believed.'[15] Secord and Hakim told Secord's lawyer that they thought they were doing 'the Lord's work'.[16] Even Casey, according to Bob Woodward's highly contentious description of his last days, answered Woodward's query about the propriety of the diversion to the contras with the remark — uttered not once, but twice — 'I believed.'[17]

'This is also a story of courage and compassion' said Owen, objecting to the fact that Inouye had called it 'sad and sordid': 'caring and sharing' — 'of doing what is right, and dying for a cause'.[18] The wonder of this, the danger and seduction of it, were well caught by William Safire in a piece in the *New York Times*, written while Fawn Hall was testifying. Safire too had worked in the OEOB for a while, as a speechwriter. 'Speechwriters never make it to secret agent.' he observed, perhaps wistfully,

> but I know the feeling of being a member of a brave band of right-minded guys and gals, charged with responsibility no outsider can imagine, working all hours, with bright minds often in good-looking heads, growing ever more contemptuous of the villainous obstructers out there with little faith, less vision and a paucity of patriotism.

It stirs the youthful soul and warps the impressionable mind.

What begins in justifiable enthusiasm for a good end (stopping Communist penetration of this hemisphere is a good end) can easily overlook the need to proceed by ponderously lawful means.

At this point, the tight little band — loving the cause, loving this country, loving each other, loving every exhausting, exhilarating moment — is in desperate need of a boss with a large wet blanket.[19]

But there was no large wet blanket to be had. McFarlane, former boss, eagerly kept contact with the cause on his home computer, aching to be part of it again: North, in reply, urged him to 'keep the faith'.[20] Both Ghorbanifar and Hakim, expecting to find in North the usual grey apparatchik, were amazed at the world of fervour in which they found themselves. 'I saw a man dissipating so much affection for his country and his associates', said Hakim, struggling to explain to a New York lawyer his bad case of 'love at first sight', 'that the radiation of that love — it really immediately penetrated through my system.'[21] Far from wet blankets, even the most shrewdly commercial member of the Enterprise was touched, at least for a time, by unworldly enthusiasms.

Like all fighters in tight little bands, the players in Iran-contra often felt that they were not understood: *nos contra mundum.* 'My part in this was easy compared to his', North tapped out one night to McFarlane, talking about Poindexter's handling of the pre-Tehran manoeuvrings; 'I only had to deal with our enemies. He had to deal with the cabinet.'[22] The enemy in the contra case was supposed to be the Sandinistas; but North's enemies were evidently domestic, political and unarmed, except with bothersome statutes. In the eyes of the principals, Congress and the prying media had already lost Vietnam; now, with their spineless voting first for and then against aid to the contras, they were in the process of losing Nicaragua, too. Men fighting in the field depended on the votes of men splitting straws in Washington.

In public, McFarlane and North often gave the impression of patient negotiation with politicians who did not take their view on the contras. There was a certain amount of talking, since congressional votes on the contras were so finely balanced; but in private this was war. The more North built up the contras in secret, the more he fretted that liberal Democrats in Congress ('Kerry, Barnes, Harkin *et al.*')[23] would become too inquisitive. McFarlane once discovered a good way to kill curiosity, like the cat. When Michael Barnes of Maryland, in the summer and autumn of 1985, made a series of discursive investigations into whatever North might be doing, McFarlane gathered in a large stack of papers, many of them germane, and invited Barnes into his office. Would he care to look at them? he asked. Barnes, who had no staff with him and not enough time, demurred. He never got the chance again.[24]

Owen came up with an interesting interpretation. The resupply effort was probably kept secret from Congress and the public precisely because it was just;[25] the general run of men could not be trusted with fine things. Equally, the Iranian operation could not be explained because, in its respectable long-term aims, it was complicated; and most people would doubtless insist, as they did, that it was just a piece of barter. Among those who could not be trusted were colleagues even closer to home, right inside the NSC, who believed in presenting the President with 'ranges of options' for his policies in Iran or Central America. The President might not want them, but sense, and democracy, required it; so while part of the NSC was on fire with the President's wishes, another part was turning out position papers of a hopeless and reasonable kind. Constantine Menges, who shared the Central American account, constantly elbowing and shoving, with North, remembered unsettling conversations with him. He himself, by his own self-justifying account, was giving the President the facts and pointing out the alternatives; North, speaking the language of military tactics, was for 'boxing him in so there's only one way he can go — the right way.'[26] Right against wrong.

The bureaucracy was wise to balk, if only to protect itself; the NSC, after all, was not meant to be caught up actively with either hostages or contras, and it was difficult to keep crusades covert. Poindexter tried, more than once, to take North off the contra account, but North fought back with all the tactics — bureaucratic manoeuvres, leaks to the press, heartbreaking petitions — of which he was capable. In one long PROF note, written in response to goodness-knows-what upbraiding from Poindexter, he offered to move on, since Poindexter evidently thought him 'too emotionally involved . . . to be objective.' North knew 'in my heart', that this was not so, but the note from start to finish was an admission of total emotional entanglement in a cause. It ended: 'Nonetheless, I consider myself to have been blessed to have had the chance to so serve for as long as I did.'[27] Poindexter (one can almost imagine the slow shaking of the head, the sigh through the pipe stem) wrote back: 'Now you are getting emotional again.'[28] And kept him on.

The emotion was predicated on one particular hope: that one day the high purposes would be recognized, and the actors justified. Indeed, they might be honoured. Reagan thought that if the hostages came out, the cabinet *in toto* would be heroes (adding, with prescience, 'If we don't, we will have a significant problem.')[29] North thought Reagan might qualify, like Teddy Roosevelt, for the Nobel Peace Prize for ending the Iran-Iraq War,[30] and that Secord was directly in line to get the Medal of Freedom.[31] When the Iran operation was blown, North was struck by Secord suddenly remarking, in his terse way, 'I don't know why this is the problem that it is. Somebody ought to stand up and acknowledge what we have done because we are on the side of the angels.' North wrote it in his notebook, by that time wearily misspelling it: 'Ultimately on the side of the angles'.[32]

Bob Dutton, the aviation boss of the resupply, would never get a medal, North candidly told him; but one day the President would shake his hand and thank him.[33] As for North, 'he would either go to jail or be decorated', Secord used to say to Hakim;[34] and McFarlane told him — as he sat jet-lagged and exhausted in his office the night after a gruelling Iranian session in Frankfurt — that 'if the world only knew how many times you have kept a semblance of integrity and gumption to US policy, they would make you Secretary of State.'[35] The world could not know, of course. But North had at least a half-promise of another honour: Adolfo Calero revealed that the contras had plans to put up a statue of him in Managua, just as soon as they had won it back from the Sandinistas.[36]

Talk of this sort was mostly to raise morale, as McFarlane was at pains to say when his 'Secretary of State' remark was thrown back at him at the hearings.[37] Yet it also hid a serious point. Whatever their basis in nefarious dealings, misunderstood intelligence, or dreams, noble things were being attempted, and if they came off the world would have cause to be grateful. If the Iranian operation worked, the hostages would be freed, terrorism would cease, Iran and Iraq would make peace (the grand climaxes were often not connected, but somehow self-generating out of the golden atmosphere), and Iran would be secured in the American, rather than the Soviet, camp. If the contra operation worked, Central America would be saved for democracy and Communism stopped at the doorstep of the United States. As North pointed out, these objectives were almost universally wished for. It was simply that most people, while wanting the ends, preferred to walk away from the means: especially when they were distasteful, and most especially when they failed.[38]

The golden objectives were, in fact, unlimited. The Enterprise, that shadowy sump of money, weapons and operatives that lay behind both policies, was intended to operate in other places too, in fact to be 'pulled off the shelf', as North said Casey said,[39] any time it was needed, with Congress kept well in the dark. Hakim said he never knew what it was going to be used for next; on an organisation chart he left a column for Africa, since North had hinted that he might one day do something there too.[40] 'The Enterprise' was a fine label for the monster as far as Hakim was concerned, because it was a business generating a particularly arcane and subtle set of accounts; but for North this was 'Project Democracy', available anywhere and at any time for freedom-fighters of any description.[41] He so detested the word 'Enterprise', with its ring of commerce, that at Poindexter's trial he scolded the prosecutor every time he used it.[42] He was scornful, too, of the humanitarian-aid programme run for the contras by the State Department through the NHAO, which Owen familiarly called the 'no-way, no-how' and the 'no-hope programme';[43] the State Department itself turned up on local code-sheets as 'wimps', the CIA as 'assholes', the portly Shultz as 'Nancy'.[44] No way, no how, no hope had to be countered by a passionate belief in justified struggle.

The contra war struck a particular patriotic chord. It reminded its supporters of America's own struggle in the War of Independence, and this sentimental analogy was drawn again and again. On one side were the Marxist commandantes, puppets of a giant colonizing power, in their camouflage fatigues and their designer sunglasses, carrying foreign ideology like a loathsome bacillus; on the other the indigenous peasants, barefoot, in straw hats, driven to the point of taking up arms. Once more, it was David against Goliath: on the one hand, as Reaganite statistics liked it, 65,000 well-drilled troops, the largest army ever amassed on the soil of Central America; on the other (subtracting the stragglers, the wives, aunts, babies, cousins) about 12,000 simple folk, determined to stop Communism as it seeped outwards towards Honduras, El Salvador and Costa Rica. Calero gave their motto at the hearings, quoting Benjamin Franklin: 'Hostility to tyrants is obedience to God.'[45]

Franklin's name did not appear in isolation. Reagan called the contras 'the moral equivalent of our Founding Fathers'[46], a notable effort to cloak with democratic virtue a body of guerrillas neither democratic nor virtuous. It caught on. Calero mentioned that the American revolutionaries too had front companies like those set up under the Enterprise, established in Europe to take in money from France and Spain.[47] Both he and Owen seized the chance to quote at congressmen the words of Thomas Jefferson: 'I have sworn upon the altar of God eternal hostility against every form of tyranny over the mind of man.' Calero had 'made his Jeffersonian Oath' after studying at Notre Dame, when he became 'a knight in democratic armour, imbued . . . in the ideals of representative government and free enterprise.'[48] Owen made his on a December day in Washington at the Jefferson Memorial, a grim day, when he had discovered that his father was dying: 'And I don't know whether many of you know, but around the ceiling, engraved in the marble, is a statement that was made once . . . and I guess I took that to heart.'[49]

McFarlane took it to heart also, but only up to a point. To support people wanting pluralism and democracy, he explained at the hearings, was 'in keeping with our own history, the roots of our own revolutionary experience'. He then drifted gloomily away, noting that this could not be 'an open-ended matter that you do in an idealistic whim'. You had to be 'circumspect in identifying where such people that are aspiring to democracy . . . are . . . important to us.'[50] Possibly the contras were in that category, but possibly not. By May 1987 McFarlane was describing them to the *Baltimore Sun* as 'incompetent Coca-Cola bottlers and clerks'.[51] They were patriotic, certainly, and 'terribly well-meaning'. But they needed to be 'popular, truly popular, not some CIA-sponsored rag-tag bunch of ne'er-do-wells', he said, getting surprisingly near the bone; they needed to be 'vital' and 'competent'.[52] He had felt misgivings for a while. Why, then, had he not shared them? Because the cause could not be doubted. To cast aspersions on the new revolutionaries was to put his own patriotism in question: 'if I'd done that, Bill Casey, Jeane Kirkpatrick [the Ambassador to the United Nations] and Cap Weinberger would have said I was some kind of a commie.'[53]

So too would North and Owen, to whom the revolutionary parallel opened up all kinds of opportunities. When North tried to set up a tax-exempt corporation to take in contributions to the contras, he thought it should acquire 'a Post Office Box 1776 in Gettysburg, Philadelphia or Yorktown'.[54] Owen wondered whether the contras should change their name to the Revolutionary Contras or the New Revolutionaries; perhaps they could change the name of the cause, too, to 'Revolutionary Counter-Communism', and the leaders of it (same old leaders) could give a press conference in Philadelphia, in front of the Liberty Bell. They could have a country-and-western song, something like *The Ballad of the Green Berets* ('Hokey, but it could sell,' said Owen modestly); and a symbol too, perhaps a torch raised high by a shackled hand, 'like the Statue of Liberty's'.[55]

North had already thrashed out a democratic manifesto for a unified opposition in Nicaragua, the leaders and himself scribbling it out in a cramped hotel room in Miami; at the hearings, he proudly compared it to the sweaty wranglings in Philadelphia over the Constitution. The manifesto was something he had been 'blessed' to work on, 'honoured' to have been asked to help with.[56] It was not mere public relations, but a paper with near-mystical historical antecedents.

The grandest idea of all, however, was never attempted, even though, according to North, Reagan had thought it 'great'. In 1985 a 'smooth man', a 'sophisticated hustler' appeared in Washington and approached North, saying he wanted to do something for the contras. He turned out to be a Hollywood producer. His plan was for the contra leaders to set sail with their manifesto, or a version of it, to Philadelphia from Nicaragua. North would charter a Caribbean cruise ship, the *Sea Goddess*, for half a million dollars; the contra leaders would come on board, declare their independence from the regime in Managua, adopt a constitution and seek recognition from Washington; the ship would then sail up the east coast, turn up the Delaware river and dock in Philadelphia, and cameras would record it all.[57]

There was a snag. The contras, of course, had no constitution. They had their manifesto — 20 pages of it, what Beatrix Potter might have called 'appropriate moral sentiments wrapped up in paper'. But Calero, for all his 'democratic armour', wished more to fight wars than to play at politics; the fragile political coalition of leaders did not survive, and there was no constitutional cruise. The contra cause was fired by reverence, both among the rebel leaders and their American sponsors, for democracy in its raw form, not far from anarchy: for freedom of action and impulse, for the right to take up arms and set up companies, but not for the constraints of legislatures or even, much, for the damp blanket of different opinions. Cloaked with the panoply of democracy, hung about with the flag, the only result was to make the cause look grubbier and smaller.

# Chapter 6

# Justifying Nicaragua

PERHAPS the contra war could not be decked persuasively in red, white and blue; but its sponsors were obliged to justify it somehow. Nicaragua was an American obsession and a dream, a proving-ground for ideology, and had been so for more than a century. There was no need to understand it. Neither Owen nor Dewey Clarridge, the chief CIA man assigned to the contras, spoke Spanish; North knew a bit from school. Nicaragua was one of those places where freedom was 'at risk', together with Afghanistan and Angola and even Poland, and these places made one disparate crusading territory. As one pro-contra advertisement put it, appealing for 53 cents a day to support a mercenary called 'Charley' and his machinegun, 'There is no "country" called Nicaragua, only a nation of people living under a totalitarian regime.'[1]

The scandal's single and notorious poem, read out by Owen as his last word at the hearings, was supposed to be about Nicaragua, but again this was no real country. It was all cause, all justification.

Today on the fertile plains of Central America cattle graze peacefully. On the wooded hills and green valleys, monkeys play, parrots fly by, and songbirds send forth their music that echoes over a troubled land.

In this far corner of the Third World, we have known

darkness and despair that at times seems almost too much to bear . . .

We have held the hands of our gallant fighters and prayed with them and for them as their life's blood seeped slowly into the dark damp earth of the jungle.[2]

And so on. The author was John Hull, a secret sustainer of contras and allegedly a facilitator of drug runs; he kept a ranch on the Costa Rican-Nicaraguan border, where his favourite sport was to shoot alligators from his veranda. No doubt his poem, which congressmen listened to with deepest embarrassment, sounded better late at night, after a beer or two. It was a common enough way to talk about Nicaragua. Ernesto Cardenal, the Nicaraguan minister of culture, also made political use of birdsong and jungle in his poems; it brought out the symbiosis between the land and the cause. There was nothing, even Nature, that did not take a side. 'Armadilloes are very happy with this government,' he wrote, 'Not only humans longed for liberation. / All ecology groaned. The revolution / is also for animals, rivers, lakes and trees.'[3]

In the Nicaraguan setting all motivations became elemental, and their very primitiveness — together with their drama — perhaps commended them to dramatic and imperfectly democratic Americans. But Hull's stumbling poetry suggested that the contra war could also be made transcendent: an ideological and moral imperative, part of the 'manifest destiny' of America to civilize the hemisphere, as earlier adventurers had phrased it, under the eye of God. It had to be made a crusade, and so it was. 'You will win,' Reagan told Calero at a White House reception in March 1986, 'because God is with you.'[4] Calero passed the message on confidently to a rich supporter in the suburbs of New Haven, Connecticut: 'God wants freedom in Nicaragua.'[5]

This, then, was a holy war, with the Antichrist firmly in sight. Owen, feeling at last that he ought to retire from contra matters — but remembering what he had sworn 'on the altar of God' — hoped that he might still be of use to North 'against another group of Godless communists.'[6] Barbara Studeley, a beauty queen and Miami talk-show hostess, began to broker weapons for the contras after receiving 'a commission from God'; the initials of her company, GeoMiliTech, also stood for 'God's Mighty Team'.[7] General Robert Schweitzer, who told this story to the congressional lawyers, was a trifle envious that after 58 years of daily Mass and 'desperate messages to the Almighty' he himself had never been woken up at night 'with lights on the wall' and a vision of saving Nicaragua; he was not sure Ms Studeley had either, but he gave her the benefit of the doubt.[8]

For North, too, Nicaragua was holy. It was Vietnam again; when asked at the hearings what the difference was between the two battlegrounds, he replied 'Ten thousand miles'.[9] Vietnam was the war his classmates presumed he had prayed to go to, in his near-daily Masses at Annapolis, in the uniform of the Marines.[10] In Vietnam, according to his chaplain, he would always put on a crucifix before he went into battle.[11] When fellow platoon-members wondered why they were there, fighting primitive jungle wars nobody at home seemed to care for when men were walking on the moon, North could not understand them. Were they not fighting Communism? Were they not under the Cross? Even when the moral failings of America's Nicaraguan and other campaigns had been laid out before him clearly, many times, his Manichaean view of the world was undisturbed. In his first public speech after he left the Marines, in May 1988, he painted a picture of the people his audience should keep in mind if they were tempted to think that the Soviet Union was changing: children huddled in the Gulags, dock-workers in Poland, and contras. 'Round their necks there is a cross, and in their hearts there is a prayer: "Do not forget us!"'[12]

In North's briefing on the contras, given widely to donors and politicians when he was at the NSC, the emphasis was striking. The last of his slides showed a wooden cross on a grave. 'And when he got to the last slide,' Channell recalled, 'he suddenly became so powerfully emotive it was just like his whole spirit exploded. He became tremendously emotional and . . . compelling in his language . . . about the need to save Latin America, to save freedom, that these people were sacrificing for America and for freedom all over the world.'[13] But this was also the side, North was saying, of God against the Godless. As he explained it at the briefings and again at his trial, three years later, 'The only people in the conflict in Nicaragua that are today buried beneath a cross are those that fight for the resistance. Those that die in the EPS, the Sandinista People's Army, get buried beneath the plain stone slab at a military cemetery. But the resistance buries them beneath a cross.'[14]

'These Catholics, they'd be pretty strong against Communists, wouldn't they?' asks Pyle in *The Quiet American*; and there was a simplistic equation of that sort to be made, too. To Catholics raised in the church immediately after the Second World War, as North was, Communism was the all-too-apparent enemy, the work of the devil. Pius XI had sanctioned for recital after Mass a special prayer to St Michael 'for the conversion of Russia', imploring him to thrust down to hell 'Satan and all wicked spirits who wander through the world for the ruin of souls'. To those who heard and believed that, unvarying in their belief as the years passed, the contra cause was morally obvious. St Michael could not do it on his own.

As Patrick Buchanan, a pugnacious supporter of both North and the contras, described it in his autobiography, the world divided neatly in those years into 'us' and 'them'. Catholics in America were relatively few, often strangers and outsiders, but they possessed the truth. 'Either men are, or they are not, children of God, with immortal souls, destined for eternity, and possessed of God-given rights no government can take away. If they are, Communism is rooted in a lie . . . We were taught that, and we believed that then — and we still do.'[15] Having been taught that, at a time when priests were not disagreed with, it is small wonder that John Kennedy should have involved himself, and thousands after him, in an anti-Communist crusade in Vietnam; that Joseph McCarthy should have conducted his anti-Communist witch-hunts; or that Casey should have made the fight against Communism his life's work, even asking that money should be given after his death not for flowers, but for the contras.

This was, of course, a faction among Catholics, and one that dangerously found itself outnumbered and outmoded as the years went on. More moderate Catholics found these crusades vulgar, intolerant and immoral; they could not understand them, and they in turn were not understood themselves. As Bishop John McGann pointed out boldly at Casey's funeral Mass in May 1987 — the Reagans in the front pew, conservative heavyweights in rank behind, North somewhere — Casey found a 'fundamentally moral purpose' in American actions in the world, specifically against Communism, and particularly in Nicaragua. He simply could not fathom 'the ethical questions raised by me as his bishop'. 'And I'm equally sure,' McGann went on, 'that Bill must have thought us bishops blind to the potential for a Communist threat in this hemisphere . . . Given the world as he saw it, Bill was seeking to do what was best for the United States.'[16]

Indeed he was; for Casey, Nicaragua was the great hemispheric test of the forces of good against the forces of evil. As Reagan put it early in 1985, 'the struggle here is not right versus left; it is right versus wrong.'[17] This was how North presented his case at the public hearings, never doubting. Shadows of it still remained at his trial, two years later; although his lawyer had evidently advised him to tone down the certitude of righteousness, it would slip out. 'Did you think,' his prosecution pressed him, 'that what you were doing, what you were being asked to do or what you had done might be wrong?' North replied, without a second thought, 'Not for one fleeting moment.'[18]

It was in this spirit that he conducted, round the back of the law, the contra operation. His Central American agents and contacts were patted on the back, or sent into the field, with the words '*Vaya con Dios*', (Go with God); Calero remembered that he never left him without them.[19] The call sign North arranged to answer fellow-Catholic Fernandez in Costa Rica ('Force unable find 5 bundles after two-day search. Now do not believe bundles dropped. Force taking heavy casualties, numbers captured rising') was DV, *Dominus Vobiscum*.[20] The contra operations had to be continued, North told his congressional questioners, 'for the love of God and the love of this nation'. This, he wished it to be understood, was a duty to God incumbent on him personally, one that he couched in the words of the Confiteor: 'And I pray to God that you will not stop because of what I have done or what I have failed to do.' If the cause was abandoned — as ultimately it was, not least because of what he had done — he would have 'the greatest burden of all on my soul'.[21]

North also spoke the religious language of evangelicals. Miraculously cured of back pains just before he had joined the NSC, he had joined a charismatic Episcopal congregation, in which he kept the church manners of a Catholic; and where appeals for the contras were concerned he could take either voice, as necessary. At Love Field, a tin-pot airport outside Dallas, very late one night, he made what can only be described as a solicitation by prayer. Channell introduced him to a friend, Ralph Hixon, 'a very devoted Christian', and discreetly left them together to pray; Channell watched a bit through the glass.[22] The substance of the meeting can be gathered from the telegram North sent to Hixon later.

Dear Ralph It was a blessing to have met with you Wednesday night to share a few moments with a fellow Christian who like I has stumbled on the walk.

The cause of the brave men and women who call themselves the Christian guerrillas is just. The sacrifices they are making are crucial to the freedom of millions . . . as is the sacrifice you contemplated. They're in a crucial period and you can help see them safely through it.

Your help is invaluable and timely, may God bless you for your vigilance. God be with you.[23]

Little other evidence existed, besides North's, that the contras thought of themselves as 'the Christian guerrillas'. The only other reference, alarmingly, came in a notorious CIA 'assassination manual' which was distributed to the contras in 1984, in the section on justifications for shooting civilians: 'The commando tried to stop the informant without shooting, because he, like all Christian guerrillas, advocate[s] non-violence . . . to cut down the lives of their Nicaraguan brothers . . . hurts our Christian feelings.'[24] Here the word 'Christian' seemed drained of any meaning at all; but North quoted the passage in mitigation of the manual, as if he for one believed it.

North lent a good deal of encouragement to Thomas Dowling, 'the priest for the contras',[25] who was called in by Calero to say Mass in the camps in Honduras; but Dowling found the contras drifting, rather than committed. When he ministered, there had been no Masses in the camps for a long time; regular priests would not go in. Dowling himself was an irregular, a member of the Old Catholic Church, a splinter group that did not recognize the supremacy of Rome; he was drawn into the cause as a result of saying house Masses for expatriate Nicaraguans in San Francisco.[26] What he noticed in the camps, however, were large numbers of evangelicals, presumably converted by American missionaries while the Catholic priests were away. Ernesto Cardenal, in his poem *The US Congress Approves Contra Aid*, had also noticed an evangelical quirk in a contra raid:

> The cottage destroyed
> by a barrage of grenades and mortars.
> The hamlet desolate.
> When the contras left
> they scattered Christ propaganda.[27]

Individual rebels, talking much later to the American press, would sometimes profess to be 'born again', and this was presumably the hint North was taking. His holy cause was being fought not only under the cross but according to the rules of 'spiritual warfare', the particular battle of charismatics and evangelicals, confident of their closeness to Christ, against the wiles of the devil in the world.

To suggest that there was any prayer on the other side, any divine sheltering or confidence in God, was almost unthinkable. The most effective put-down of North during his testimony came from Senator George Mitchell of Maine, stung by the colonel's constant juxtaposition of God with the contras. He reminded North that it was possible for an American to disagree with him on that particular, 'and still love God, and still love this country just as much as you do'; although He was regularly asked to do so, 'God

does not take sides in American politics.'[28] North listened to this
impassively; when it was over his eyes filled with tears, but these
were not necessarily tears of compunction. Asked in February 1987
what he had to say about the conclusions of the Tower Report, the
first detailed inquiry into the affair, he referred reporters to 'the
eighth Beatitude of Matthew 5': 'Blessed are those who are
persecuted for righteousness' sake, for theirs is the kingdom of
heaven.' There is no knowing what he would have made of
Cardenal's reading of Matthew, somewhat further on.

> And I think of Matthew nineteen verse twelve:
> And there are those who do not marry
> for the sake of the kingdom of heaven, Communism.[29]

Reagan found understanding of the other side every bit as hard.
Channell remembered a curious phone call from him — not an
everyday occurrence, and Channell was on respectful tenterhooks —
in which the president began: 'I just do not understand Tip O'Neill.
I don't know what's wrong with him, why he doesn't see the need to
be supporting the freedom fighters.' Channell countered with
something shocking:

> Mr President, I need to tell you something. Every night Tip
> O'Neill drops by his bed and prays to the same God that you
> do and he prays for the strength that's necessary the next day
> to defeat everything that you believe in. And that's the way he
> is. And you must fight him as an enemy and you must defeat
> him.

'There was this long pause,' Channell remembered. 'And he
ended by saying, Spitz, I just don't understand Tip O'Neill.'[30]
The cause was not only good in itself; it was also a statement of
loyalty. These people had been encouraged to fight by the United
States; by keeping them going, when Congress was keen to abandon
them, at least some Americans were keeping faith. The contras were,
after all, almost neighbours: two hours' flight from the Rio Grande,
virtually knocking at the door. America's loyalty to them was going
to be interpreted, the players insisted, as a token of its loyalty to
allies everywhere: certainly to rebel groups in Asia and Africa,
perhaps even, North thought, to NATO.[31] Besides, the contras were
friends. Even in the formality of the 1984 National Security Planning
Group meeting that started the whole alternative propping-up
programme, the scheme to find alternative money for the contras
was described as 'next steps to keep our friends together'.[32] They

were also children: 'boys and girls', as the boyish Owen called them, 'fighting, bleeding and dying'.[33]

The suggestion of fatherly closeness was essential, even if it seemed awkward and difficult to illustrate. Contra children would come to Washington to be held aloft by Reagan at banquets, the little girls in lipstick and party dresses; North would visit the camps, trying to talk to the children, and taking pictures to keep in a shoe-box in his office. 'No little girls,' said Channell to Richard Miller before another of North's briefings; there were too many children in the slides, and the audiences were 'tigers', preferring 'blood and guts'.[34] For North, however, to be seen among the local people, to be seen to be doing good generally, even if vaguely, was an essential ingredient in a just war. McFarlane, who in his more sober Methodist way felt much the same, tried to explain it at the hearings. North had apparently asked himself whether it was worth it, to die in Vietnam:

And for him, it was an easy determination that, yes, it was, because there were enough daily shows of evidence by the Vietnamese people, young and old, children, others, of their satisfaction that he was there. And yet, that personal justification was in very sharp tension with the reality that we were losing.

Now in the wake of his service there, having to cope with the vivid reminders of how worth it it was and how tragic a loss of life of Vietnamese . . . I believe that he committed himself to assuring that he would never be party to such a thing again if he could prevent it.[35]

'These people were glad I was there,' North would say of his time in Vietnam,[36] in sharp contradistinction to the way most Americans seemed to feel about it. If they were not glad, how could the war be justified? It was North who, by his own account, rushed into Reagan's television room during the evacuation of American students from Grenada in 1983, desperate that the students might forget (on network television) to be grateful for the American invasion that had freed them; when the first student said 'Thank God for America', Reagan hugged him, and told him he ought to have faith.[37] But North still went in fear of ingratitude. He told a friend of a dream he had had, 'a terrible nightmare' — perhaps apocryphal too, but there are no Secret Service logs of dreams — in which America's support of the contras had failed. Nicaragua had become a second Cuba, and the President had ordered an invasion. North, back in the Marines, found himself landing on a beach; there facing him, with a rifle, was Calero. He did not want an American invasion. He wanted Nicaraguans to save their own country.[38]

As it was, however, the administration had taken over responsibility for this war; and it had to work with what it had, making a just cause as best it could. It was not easy. After North became the contras' overseer, in October 1984, he tried, according to Rafael Quintero, to inculcate some honesty into them[39]: taking Calero's brother Mario off the contract for ponchos and boots (the ponchos leaked, anyway) and putting control of the contras' foreign money in the hands of Secord and 'the company'. This particular move towards 'honesty' was seldom so kindly interpreted; but at least it was then Americans, not contras, who could play hard and fast with the money.

North tried, too, to encourage the rebels to fight. That was harder still. The contra leaders, sitting for much of the time in Miami in their well-cut lightweight suits and their gold watches, had purposes in view, some of them not especially noble; the rebels in the field were mostly tired, variously motivated, and confused. Some gave themselves fierce *noms de guerre*, 'Rambo' and 'El Negro', as if their only purpose was fighting for its own sake, though even that purpose was largely wishful thinking; much of their time was spent hanging round in the camps, doing nothing.

North took that badly. He wanted the contras to be seen to be dying for their cause, emphasizing both how desperate it was, and how just. His own grand plan for them, as O'Boyle had heard in his 'secret briefing', was a sort of wholesale, slow martyrdom, based loosely both on the Alamo and on Khe Sanh, a last-ditch stand by Marines in Vietnam. North was proud of his plan; but then he himself, as several associates noticed, seemed to be desperate to die for his country, even in the course of 'Project Democracy' if all else failed.[40] The contra leaders were considerably less keen. North once offered Calero a bullet-proof vest — 'the same sort the President wears' — only to find Calero shocked at the implication that he ought to be looking danger in the face.[41] One of the field commanders, Edgar Chamorro, continually nagged by Fernandez to get into Nicaragua and fight, at last decided to venture 30 metres inside to attack a border post; heavy fire drove him back and, retreating to a pay phone, he called the CIA in Langley, Virginia and asked them to send mortars. The agency did not oblige him.[42]

North tried, for appearances' sake, to present the rebels as an effective force, but he was up against higher-ranking military men who disagreed with him. General Paul Gorman, a friend, actually gave rival briefings explaining how dim the contras' chances were. There was 'enough sentiment', he admitted, 'enough fire . . . to lead people to put their lives and their families on the line for the cause', but the cause was a mess; too many different groups, no means of making political capital out of them, and 'guys running around in the hills . . . illiterate, ignorant campesinos'. North, badly wanting to shut him up, tried to convince him it was otherwise.

> You know, he would keep citing statistics on how their recruiting was going and what they were doing. He had pictures in his office that he would show me of well-equipped armed bands that he said were taken down in the middle of Nicaragua. And I kept telling him, yeah, Oliver, but the day that, you know, some Nicaraguan unity group appears and it's evident that it's got everybody in it . . . that's the day I'll begin to believe that this thing has a future.[43]

North could not convince Gorman; Gorman, equally, could not convince North. 'It was very clear to me,' said the general in the end, 'that Oliver had a thing about the contras.' The 'thing' led him to a certain way of thinking. If the contras could be neither saints nor crack troops, their appeal had to lie in romantic desperation: the 'fact' that they had been forced into exile, like the 'little old lady' with her hair in a bun and her dress 'held together by safety pins and string' whom Owen had met in a camp in Honduras;[44] the 'fact' that the soldiers were without food or uniforms, their hospitals nothing but hen-coops, lacking even mosquito netting; the fact that there was never enough money for anything.

Ghorbanifar and Secord both remembered North at his wits' end, pacing back and forth, describing how the contras were dying; Secord was pestered continually, and admitted that he never sent the rebels 'as much as Ollie thought we should'.[45] Contributors had their hearts broken. At private meetings over meals or in his office North would produce his spiral notebook or pieces of yellow legal paper, asking 'how in God's name we can expect these young men and women to fight against Communism when this is what they're up against', and often breaking into tears.[46] His listeners were drawn in irresistibly. Soft-hearted Mrs Garwood recalled being told at Dallas airport that food procured for the contras was simply rotting in the warehouses, just as the food sent to Ethiopia in the famine had never reached the starving. She gave $2m.[47]

The mythology of this just cause was not inevitably tragic, though usually so. Myths of triumph sprang up too. One concerned the *Monimbo*, a ship carrying a load of rifles from North Korea to the Sandinistas. (Both sides bought weapons wherever they could get them, from the furthest provenance and under the strangest flags.)

North wanted the *Monimbo* seized or sunk; Poindexter wanted 'measures taken to make sure ship does not arrive in Nicaragua'; McFarlane seems to have choked over the legality of piracy, and the ship and the rifles got through.[48] Calero said he had never heard of it, except to read about it: 'Was that the one we were supposed to blow up on the high seas?' It reminded him of another mad suggestion from a man in California, offering the contras $50m if they would go and take over Malta.[49] North, however, maintained that the ship story ended quite differently, even victoriously, with the *Monimbo* 'on its side on the beach'.[50]

There is evidence that the whole Southern Front operation, for which North pushed particularly, was justified in retrospect with successes that were invisible at the time. Even the damp little airstrip at Santa Elena was glorified with hindsight. At North's trial, the prosecutor twitted him with a glowing memorandum he had written to Poindexter, claiming that the airstrip had played 'a vital role' from July 1985 to February 1986. The land for the strip had not even become available, Keker reminded him, until January 1986, and the only aircraft that had ever landed there had stuck in the mud;[51] but North could not be persuaded that his memo was 'incompatible with the realities of things'. In the same way he lauded the pilots, calling them 'some of the bravest people I've ever met in my life',[52] apparently not noticing that much of their fortitude was required simply to fly the shocking aircraft and the hapless missions with which he had entrusted them.[53]

When two of the pilots were eventually, inevitably shot down in October 1986 — their pockets full of incriminating business cards — the resupply operation collapsed. It was technically already unnecessary, for money for both lethal and humanitarian aid had been voted by Congress a matter of days before. The line had been kept open just long enough. So death, too, gilded the operation: the useless martyrs' deaths of the pilots on a scrubby hillside, and the simultaneous death of the whole elaborate scheme. But the cause had been kept going; and that was its own justification.

Indeed, if all else had failed — if the supplies had seldom been delivered on time, if the contras had declined to fight, if the money had gone astray, if the planes had crashed — the cause was still something that was simply right, whatever sort of mess had resulted. 'It is morally the right thing to do,' said McFarlane, dropping it like a swift brick in among the parentheses and qualifications and regrets.[54] 'We believed very much in the significance of what we were doing,' said Secord, leaving for a moment the sticky operational details.[55] North needed no parentheses. 'Thank God' somebody had done something.[56]

Yet even as North spoke, the contras were collapsing under the very impact of his half-secret operations; and by the time of his trial, less than two years later, the new administration had turned its back on them. The contras, demoralized beyond any more fighting, resumed their preferred occupation of lounging in the camps in Honduras, and in June 1990 the war was officially ended. No longer revolutionaries, no longer a just cause — no longer, after all that, a cause at all.

# Chapter 7

# Bartering for Bodies

NICARAGUA, therefore, was the administration's just cause; but so, in its way, was Iran. Although the Iranian operation was stumbled into almost accidentally, even that policy evolved emotional and patriotic selling points as it went along. To those who argued that the policy was deluded, its sponsors could answer that it had good aims in view; indeed, the more glaring the disappointment, the more glowing the colours in which those aims were painted.

Unlike Nicaragua, however, Iran was a relatively cool subject. Poindexter discoursed on it at the hearings, tamping his pipe, with the aid of the sort of brightly-coloured maps usually found in school atlases. Iran was certainly strategically vital, threatened by Russia on its flank; but abstract because it was so many miles away, politically eccentric, and hard to place. Besides, the issues were complicated. Iran had once seized American hostages, and was an enemy; but the American hostages at issue in 1985 and 1986 were held in Lebanon by Hizbollah, a fanatical group merely sympathetic to Iran, and Iran's good offices were necessary to deal with them. Some bile had to be swallowed.

There was also a war on, between Iran and Iraq, in which America was officially neutral. Israel, on the other hand, was eager to restore relations and intelligence contacts with Iran; Israel leaned towards favouring Iran in the war; and what Israel wanted, America rarely resisted. The administration therefore got involved with Iran again not out of conviction, but with a strong prod from Israel, whose emissaries kept turning up in London and Washington with their slightly unnerving proposals for rapprochement.

American policy towards Iran always had two strands. One was a simple urge to get the hostages out. The other was a great plan for improved relations: sometimes going no further than better intelligence on a crucial country, sometimes an all-embracing scheme for encouraging moderate successors to Khomeini and saving the country from the Soviet camp. First hints of that occurred almost casually, when Michael Ledeen, the first American into the swamp, was chatting with 'an intelligence official of a West European country' early in 1985. Ledeen noticed that the official was looking unusually tanned; perhaps he had been skiing? No, said the man, he had got his tan in Iran. The situation there was fluid and interesting; perhaps America should take a look at it.[1] Ledeen agreed, went, and returned converted. America might indeed do something there. Not the first scandal, but perhaps the most comprehensive, provoked by a suntan.

The grandest exposition of the Grand Iranian Design was given on November 14th, 1986, just after the operation had been disclosed. Neil Livingstone, a terrorism expert, was having breakfast with North in the Hay-Adams Hotel, that perpetual nest of intrigue. North, carefully distracting Livingstone from the thought that hostages might have been ransomed for arms, gave him the Whole Picture. The Soviet Union had designs on Iran. To further these designs (primarily, to reach a warm-water port), the Russians had persuaded the Iranians to over-estimate their strength against Iraq. Iran was now in a poor state in the war, and was about to be wiped out as the Russian Army had been at Tannenberg in 1914: a disaster that had led to the rise of the Bolsheviks. Russia's allies within Iran were already preparing to seize power, and delegations from Japan, Saudi Arabia, Turkey, Pakistan — and Israel — had all visited America to implore Reagan to do something. The 'something', after much thought, turned out to be making contact with 'moderate' Iranians and selling them arms in concert with Israel. 'Far from constituting ransom to achieve the freedom of American hostages,' North assured Livingstone over the cooling coffee, 'the military goods provided Iran were part of a rapprochement process designed to deliver Iran from the clutches of the Soviet Union and to block the Soviet drive to the Persian Gulf.'[2]

Nothing much there about hostages at all. Indeed, to the straight Grand Planners (of which North was not one), hostages were better left out of the picture entirely. Ledeen always thought it self-evident that America should re-open contacts with Iran; it could profit from the political fissures there, and could perhaps exploit the chaos that would undoubtedly follow the end of the Ayatollah's rule. What he could not understand, he said, was how this idea got so muddled up with hostages and the necessity to sell arms.[3] Once arms sales were introduced — originally, ingenuously, as a sign of 'good faith' between the countries — there would be no end to the escalation of demands.

With great reluctance, as he maintained, Ledeen carried the message from Israel's prime minister, Shimon Peres, to McFarlane in the summer of 1985, asking him to approve the first shipment of arms from Israel to Iran; McFarlane replied 'Okay, just that one shipment and nothing else', words that soon aquired a hollow, awful sound.[4] Once the hostages were introduced, something even more dangerous happened: the whole bargaining process became emotional, heavily political, and less than sharp. Ghorbanifar told Ledeen that he thought it would be much better to 'leave the hostages aside'.[5] Ledeen agreed, but by that point — in November of 1985 — the operation was out of his hands. When Poindexter somewhat curtly told him so, Ledeen asked if he could still keep the elements of the Grand Plan simmering along. Poindexter gave him a blank stare.[6]

By then, of course, the hostages had become the chief cause. With Reagan, they had been the chief cause all along. He had become president largely because his predecessor and opponent, Jimmy Carter, had failed to resolve a hostage crisis, and he did not forget it. Long-term Iranian strategy never much interested Reagan, North told Meese in November, implying he had sometimes bravely tried to explain it: 'terrible mistake to say RR wanted the strategic relationship b/c RR wanted the hostages.'[7] Colleagues heard that Reagan pestered North about the hostages two or three times a week; McFarlane, probably the transmitter of the pestering, remembered that he would barely open his mouth at the 9.30 briefing before the President would ask, 'Anything new on the hostages?'[8] Noel Koch of the Defence Department came across North one day in the corridor, frazzled; it was the same story. 'He's driving me nuts about it, and he wants them out by Christmas,' North confided. 'Can you do it?' Koch asked. North's answer was a sigh: 'I hope so.'  [9]

Even sanguine members of the Cabinet dreaded the return of the taunting yellow ribbons that were tied to trees in Carter's time, and feared especially the visits of grieving relatives to the White House. Staff members tried to keep them away from the soft-hearted President, consigning them to the Vice-president not because Bush was more callous, North explained, but because it was Reagan who had to make the policy decisions. It was 'an unfair burden on the heart of our President' to look people in the eye and tell them that 'your government can't, try as it would, can't do anything about it.'[10] Reagan had tried to meet the families once or twice, the first time in a school library in Chicago Heights; the relatives furiously demanded help from him, boxing him in with a semi-circle of school chairs. He had come out moved and horrified. As he tried to explain it later, when the ruins of arms-for-hostages were all around him, 'his heart and his best intentions' had ruled him.[11] The most cynical of his detractors did not doubt that; the President had got carried away.

The usefulness of the Grand Plan, even if it had few subscribers, was that it provided a cover. The fate of seven 'Amcits', a Frenchman and two 'Brits' was not compelling enough to be seen to be driving policy; something much more portentous was needed. But neither could the players talk too much about the Grand Plan, for fear of looking like busybodies in another nation's affairs. The solution, as it evolved in practice, was to argue for a sort of grand amalgam, almost a fit of good feeling, in which war would be ended and hostages exchanged and where men would tenderly understand each other. Something of the flavour appears in a cryptic note sent from North to Rafsanjani late in 1986, when Ghorbanifar had been dropped from the equation and replaced by a more promising-seeming young Iranian official, the 'Second Channel'.* North asked the Second Channel to act as his courier 'as a personal favour for the cause we both believe in'; the note was a draft of a speech for Rafsanjani to make to the Iranian parliament. Its contents seem to be lost to history, but one wonderfully inappropriate phrase survives: 'His Holiness the Imam and his Christian peace.'[12]

Indeed, as the operation wore on, badly in need of justification, peace became one of the chief pretexts for it; and not entirely a pretext. 'Sincerely believe that RR can be instrumental in bringing about an end to Iran/Iraq war — a la Roosevelt w/Russo-Japanese War in 1904,' North wrote to Poindexter in September 1986.[13] He was just back from giving the Second Channel a tour of the White House at night, something he often did, and with a proper historical reverence. They had gone all over the place; peeking into the Oval Office (but the little rope was across, Hakim said); stopping on the stairs to look at a picture called *The Canine Cabinet*, in which North

---

* The identity of the Second Channel has been given as Ali Hashemi Bahramani, Rafsanjani's nephew. He is kept as the Second Channel here, for simplicity's sake.

pointed out a drowsing member and said it was Casey[14]; and into the Roosevelt Room, where North showed the young Iranian the Nobel Prize won by Theodore Roosevelt for negotiating peace between the Russians and the Japanese.[15]

Some of this desire for peace seems to have been genuine, and not connected merely with the glory it might bring the President. Poindexter kept in his study a poster with the words 'Blessed are the Peacemakers' though possibly it had been put there by his minister-wife;[16] North was a member of an officers' prayer group that prayed regularly for peace, particularly in the Gulf.[17] 'Any soldier who has ever been in a war,' he said at the hearings, 'truly hopes he will never see one again.'[18] All the same, this concern for peace in one part of the world, or even generally, sat oddly with a hot disposition to war in another. In the middle of the negotiations with the Iranians in October 1986, North mentioned, laughing, that he had managed to talk to the Kuwaiti foreign minister about matters of mutual concern 'in my spare time between blowing up Nicaragua'.[19] By his own accounts, he could hardly keep himself away from the battle lines in Central America. He told his friend Andy Messing — also an *aficionado* of Central American wars — a fantastic tale of piloting a small plane into the battle zone in El Salvador to evacuate two wounded men, almost crash-landing, losing his windshield to a machine-gunner, and all while on a secret trip for the NSC; his face was covered with cuts from the shattered glass.[20] Messing was never able to find out whether the story was true, but the spirit was North all over.

In negotiations with the Iranians, however, North maintained that his enthusiasm for war had no place. The President himself had transmuted it into a grand desire for peace.

That Saturday when [the Iranian contact] was in Washington, I flew up to Camp David to talk to the President, and I showed him the [weapons] list, and he said, 'Why are you thinking so small?' He took the list, that list right there, and he went like this with it — I was sitting across the table — and he said, 'For someone who has seen so much war as you have, North, you should understand that I want to end the war on terms that are acceptable to Iran.

'I don't simply want to help go out and kill more Iranian youngsters. What about the 2 million people without homes? What about the oil industry which is already in ruins? What about the industrial base of Iran which is being destroyed? Stop coming in and looking like a gun merchant.' And he banged on the table. 'I want to end the war!'[21]

Even if this had been so — and Reagan worrying about Iran's industrial base has the true ring of fantasy — the bartering was not to be turned so easily away from war, on either side. The Iranians, concerned by what Reagan seemed to have done with their wish-list of missiles, wanted to be convinced that they had 'something in hand'. The Americans, called on to prove their sincerity, could only do so in terms of the number of Hawks and TOWs that had already been shipped. Poindexter was not too perturbed by this: arms, as he explained, were often 'the currency of any sort of business in the Middle East.'[22] Provision of the means to wage an atrocious war had been agreed on as a sign of good faith. After one sign of good faith the magic was supposed to work, the hostages out, friends all round; but somehow 500 TOWs was not enough, 1,000 TOWs was not enough, a big shipment of Hawk parts was not enough. In March 1986, the Iranians wanted Phoenix missiles; in October they wanted 100 Howitzers plus 500 barrels, for which, as Cave told them, any country in the world would have to open a production line.[23]

To measure sincerity in weapons proved very difficult, and so, from time to time, the American delegation would fall back on the mantra of peace, peace to which only Iraq was the obstacle, peace in which all these obsessions about the latest arms and the best would be redundant. When, in Frankfurt in October, the talks were foundering, North called it 'a great tragedy for those of us who live on this Planet Earth';[24] nothing less than the misalignment of two spheres that had been about to dance in harmonious orbit. At the end of the negotiations, as he prepared to run off to salvage what he could from the wreckage of the crashed aircraft in Nicaragua, North told the Iranians he had failed in his mission 'to start the process of healing between our countries'; the two nations, Iran and America, were about to pass each other like ships in the night.[25] Among themselves, however, as the tape-recorder wound on, the Americans did not talk about peace. They talked about the difficulty of getting food in, when all they could find was Chinese takeaway; about strange knocks at the door of the hotel room, and why the Iranians sometimes left unexpectedly, and who the hell they were really dealing with; about North's pressing need for aspirin; and about getting the hostages out, for which the only foreseeable currency was arms.[26]

The hostages mattered terribly. Although so little was heard from them, those who kept tabs on them were convinced that they were slowly fading away. Occasional letters and photographs would come from Terry Anderson, an AP journalist captured in 1985; the face grew more haggard, the eyes more accusing and staring. Of William Buckley, the CIA station chief in Beirut, his captors sent back videotapes as he died, slowly, of the effects of pulmonary oedema and neglect. North found these 'awful'.[27] Buckley was a man in possession of secrets, and a 400-page confession had allegedly already been extracted from him under torture. When it became apparent that he must be dead, Casey gave orders to recover the body for proper burial; this became another item in the wish-lists exchanged with the Iranians. At almost any cost Casey wanted him back, but this was almost a private, rather than a public, duty. The secrets were probably gone, passed on to the Russians. There remained a duty of compassion to the man.

So it was with the other hostages. None was a security risk; none knew much, or anything, and there was no compelling national interest to be served by rescuing them. The matter boiled down, in part, to simple morality; innocent prisoners ought to be freed. Calero remembered how he and North would discuss the hostages 'continually', and how he himself considered them another sort of liberation struggle, like the contras.[28] He even gave North precious travellers' cheques to ransom them, although the ransom did not work out.[29] But hostage releases were no public crusade. Both obligation and justification were, in the end, private, as it was with Casey and Buckley, or with members of the families for each other. North told his colleagues that the release of the hostages was a personal obligation on himself,[30] and that seemed not to put it too strongly. Fernandez remembered North breaking down as he told him, sitting in a parked car one night, that Buckley was dead;[31] David Jacobsen, the last hostage to be released as a result of the arms transfers, recalled North in tears on the aeroplane to Germany, wishing that the other hostages had been freed with him.[32] To Peggy Say, Anderson's sister, it seemed that some particularly keen sympathy compelled North never to turn down her requests to see him, when all she would do was sit at his desk upbraiding him and complaining and crying; and when all he could do was repeat, cryptically, infuriatingly, that the government was doing everything it could possibly think of.[33]

It fell to North, McFarlane and Poindexter, as also to anyone else roped into the policy, to carry out a private crusade with a crippling double imperative. The whole operation was for Reagan's sake, as well as the hostages'; it was a present for him, preferably one to be delivered by Christmas, or by the State of the Union address in January, or by the elections in November. It was made the more difficult because the Iranians were at one remove from the hostage-takers; even at best, all they could promise was to lean on Hizbollah and ask for a favour. But North himself, on the point of abandoning the operation, begging to be moved on 'to other things', made plain the point of everything that had gone before: 'Wd very much like to give RR two hostages that he can take credit for.'[34]

The compassionate side of the Americans found the Iranian body-bargaining awful. 'Like you and Bud,' North wrote to Poindexter, 'I find the idea of bartering over the lives of these poor men repugnant.'[35] Yet the political imperative made the bargaining essential, indeed urged it on. McFarlane had come back from London in December 1985 disgusted with the bartering, repelled by Ghorbanifar and wanting to abandon the operation. The Tehran trip in May, in which he was humiliated, made him all the more certain that however good the ends, 'this was not the kind of exchange that was proper.'[36] Poindexter, too, occasionally wanted no more of this 'half-delivered, half-released crap.'[37] But neither man could entirely ignore North's fevered memoranda, insisting that without the awful procession of weapons shipments the hostages would die; and both men, while they were in office, had to go each morning to a president who would ask them what they were doing and importune them to try harder.[38] 'I thought we agreed no more after first 500 unless get all captives,' read Alton Keel's notes, quoting Weinberger at the end of the day. 'Just, always came back Pres, he always agreed go ahead,' replied Poindexter.[39]

At times, when they were tired and worn down by Iran's ever-escalating requests, the Americans were ready to promise almost anything to get the hostages out. In pursuit of the end, any means could be tried. North said he would have offered the Iranians a free trip to Disneyland or a ride on the space shuttle;[40] George Cave, the interpreter, offered to send the Second Channel to Miami Beach.[41] The Iranians, of course, had little interest in vacations, but North could also make them wonderful offers in the currency they understood, TOWs: 'If you get the hostages out, we'll send you a million of them.'[42] Extravagance grew as hope faded, and soon every offer or deal, in whatever currency, was fantastical. Left to themselves in Mainz, the four Americans consulted. 'Ollie,' Hakim said, 'if you get the hostages out, how many shish would you be prepared to eat?' (Clearly, as Frankfurt overdid the Chinese, Mainz overdid the kebabs.) 'I'd eat shish till the cows come home', North answered.[43] Told by Secord that the Second Channel was going to solve the hostage problem, 'but we don't know how,' North replied, 'I don't care how, right now.' 'I don't care how either,'[44] said Secord. But no one had any suggestions; almost everything had been tried, or asked for, or abandoned.

Part of the difficulty was that the cause, so sentimentally longed for, could not be expressed in sentimental terms. The President's desires, which weighed so heavily on the negotiators, could not be admitted except in code. 'The head of our company is most displeased with Mr Goode and me,' Cave said in June, talking on the telephone to an Iranian who was unenthusiastic about weapons prices that had been marked up 300%; 'He said if they don't want to deal, break it off.'[45] By October, the patience of the CEO was clearly exhausted. If the effort failed, Secord explained to the Iranians, Hakim, 'the interpreter', would be shot, 'because somebody had to go.' He and North would be lucky: 'They won't shoot us. We'll just go to jail.'

*North*: Fired.
*Secord*. The President may shoot North.[46]

The hostages, too, could not be described in sentimental terms. They were a mere handful of men, hardly worth worrying about. Around 52,000 people had died in car crashes in America in 1985, North pointed out, and 130,000 had died of lung cancer; in perspective, the hostages were nothing.[47] Why not let them out? What face could possibly be lost by Iran, doing so small a thing? The hostages were 'this hurdle', 'this obstacle lying in the road', a dark huddle of rags in the foreground of a vista of peace. They were something that had to be removed, like flammable rubbish, so that the president could be 'fireproofed' from the fury of his own people when news of the secret contacts with Iran hit the newspapers.[48] Cave, on the telephone again, called the hostages 'the four boxes'.[49] They were also less than that, ciphers, as in a famous North equation of December 1985.

H-hr: 1 707 w/300 TOWS — 1 AMCIT*
H+10 hrs: 1 707 (same a/c) w/300 TOWS — 1 AMCIT
H+16 hrs: 1 747 w/50 HAWKS & 400 TOWS — 2 AMCITS
H+24 hrs: 1 747 w 2000 TOWS — French Hostage. [50]

The front of indifference was hard to keep up. The 'fundamental perpetual change in the world'[51] that North insisted the Americans were aiming for was tied, in fact, to a general and international release of hostages, and the Iranians knew it. 'You say you're here to discuss something very big and important,' said one in Frankfurt; 'but when I read everything . . . the focus and the only thing that is being discussed is the issue of the hostages.'[52] In Mainz, the same perceptive man offered to go back to Tehran with news of what 'the real motivation' was, and clear up both the confusion among the

* Hostage-hour: 1 707 with 300 TOWs — 1 American citizen

Iranians and the various 'different thoughts' in the minds of the Americans.[53] Different thoughts, but one thought: Secord would suddenly explode to the interpreter, 'He's still not talking about the god-damned hostage thing!';[54] or, in North's exasperated words, 'if we're really sincere about this whole friggin' thing . . . they ought to be exercising every possible amount of leverage they've got to get those people out.'[55]

The Americans had offered arms, and they had offered peace, in an attempt to salvage something from 'this whole friggin' thing'. There was another gambit too: to raise the Iran operation on to an altogether different plane, to make it a sort of crusade, as Nicaragua was. In the same memorandum of April 1986 that eventually brought down the whole house of cards — the memorandum that mentioned the diversion of funds to the contras — an extraordinary phrase appeared: 'The Iranians have been told that our presence in Iran is "a holy commitment".'[56]

Whether those words were pronounced or not, something like them was. Because the Iranians represented a theocracy, because they argued that their revolution was 'totally depending on God'[57] and that the Americans, opposing them, were the Great Satan, the American negotiators did their best to answer them in kind. Secord remembered how they would get 'sermonized', and how 'we had a lot to live down before we could do business.'[58] Part of the business was to build on Iranian fears of Russia, but even that would draw forth rich theological arguments. Sitting in the dreary Independence Hotel in Tehran late at night, McFarlane fuming in his room, the rest of the party had got on to a conversation about radars. But there was no point in merely comparing weapons, said the Iranian advisor on foreign affairs:

> The will of the Iranian people is greater than the Soviet people. I myself have a sister with two sons who were martyred in the war . . . Martyrdom [*shehadat*] is great. We congratulate the family of martyrs with congratulations and sorrow. During Ramadan we ask God to let us be a martyr if we are to die. Ramadan is the night of fate and power.[59]

At first, the Americans did not try too hard to meet the Iranians on this uncomfortable holy turf. To listen to 'a load of shit on *shehadat*', as Cave called it, was part of the side-business of negotiating;[60] the Americans would do their best to try to steer their interlocutors back to the subjects at hand. Only North, according to his notebooks, tried to counter in Tehran with something similar: 'Because I am a Christian, I understand and believe that when one dies in faith he will spend eternity in a far better place.'[61] But the atmosphere then was too cool for much of that sort of talk.

Circumstances changed at the end of the summer of 1986, when matters, and men, were becoming desperate, and when North also seemed to think he had found a soulmate in the 'brave young soldier'[62] who was the Second Channel. On his first visit to Washington in September, the Second Channel demonstrated his piety by asking for a rug to pray on on the Friday evening; Craig Coy, wonderingly, lent him his gym towel. (Coy remarked afterwards that he had become 'quite a good distance runner' since his towel was knelt on.)[63] Yet the Second Channel's devotion also seemed to have substance. He noted that the taking of hostages was utterly banned by a *fatwa* of the Ayatollah, and was contrary to the Shia religion. 'From the standpoint of humanity,' he said, Iran was even a little sympathetic towards the United States. North took his cue. Placing his office Bible on the negotiating table, he said solemnly: 'The President strongly believes in the words of the Holy Book as do you. He believes deeply in the teachings of the God of Abraham. Thus, he is very popular here and should be popular in the world of Islam.'[64]

North also said that biblical verses were brought up in conversation, though they do not seem to have made it onto the surreptitious tape. One was the passage from the fifteenth chapter of Genesis in which Abraham cut up a heifer, a goat and a ram and laid them out at the Lord's command, driving the vultures away, falling at last into a deep sleep with 'a horror of great darkness'. 'And it came to pass, that when the sun went down, and it was dark, behold a smoking furnace, and a burning lamp that passed between those pieces'; and Abraham in his dream heard that his seed would rule over 'the Kenites, and the Kenizzites, and the Kadmonites, and the Hittites, and the Perizzites, and the Rephaims, and the Amorites, and the Canaanites, and the Girgashites, and the Jebusites.'[65] He was to be, in fact, the common progenitor of Jews, Muslims and Christians, as North explained in a note to Reagan later. The passage was not some ghastly simile of war or territorial domination (though heaven knows what the Iranians would have made of it), but just a pictorial explanation of the passage North said he read them next, from the third chapter of Galatians: 'Know ye therefore that they which are of faith, the same are the children of Abraham.'

The Iranians, not to mention the other Americans, heard these things with some astonishment. Secord thought it was good, it was trumping them. After all they had been force-fed about the godliness of the Khomeini regime, here was Reagan as a 'man of God'

(North's words), who had gone away for a 'whole weekend' to pray about the Frankfurt meeting and had come up all by himself with an inscription for a Bible to be given to the Iranians.[66] Secord's outfit, in fact, purchased the Bible, and there was a bit of a quiz round the office ('ask the secretary') to find a fitting inscription for it.[67] But North had one up his sleeve already, right there in the next verse of Galatians, soon to become exceedingly well known in the loopy, spidery hand of the President.

> And the Scripture, forseeing that God would justify the Gentiles
> by faith, preached the gospel beforehand to Abraham, saying,
> 'All the nations shall be blessed in you.'[68]

'This is a promise that God gave to Abraham,' North said Reagan had told him, in the slightly hectoring tone he always had in the North dreams; 'Who am I to say that we should not do this?'[69]
The religious element was a ploy, as was everything else. Both sides had an incentive, when negotiating, to link God to their endeavours, and both fell out of godliness fairly quickly once the talks broke up: North desperate to eat and to get more tape for 'the freakin' machine', the Iranians telephoning round to try to get call-girls to come out to their hotel.[70] Yet even on the tapes of the talks, considerably less gilded than the memoranda, it let in a little light for a moment. And, as Secord noted, it kept the Iranians confused. During one of the breaks in the Washington meetings, one of the heads of the Iranian delegation took Secord aside and asked, in Secord's words, 'What's with this guy North? We just left a country full of mullahs, and what do I find here but another goddamn mullah.'[71] North reported back that the line was working; the Second Channel had noted to Cave 'that RR being a man of God had removed the only argument they had — that Allah was on their side.'[72]
A strong religious element also naturally coloured the hostage story. Two of the captives, Lawrence Jenco and Benjamin Weir, were clergymen (Jenco a Catholic priest, Weir a Presbyterian minister); Terry Waite, a lay advisor to the Archbishop of Canterbury, was trying to organize their release until he himself was kidnapped in 1987. North worked with Waite, helping him with transport, using him as a cover, to an extent that is still not public. He also worked with the Cardinal Archbishop of New York, John O'Connor, in ways that are still not known; his notebooks are full of calls to and from the archbishop's office. On occasion he tried to recruit the Pope into his efforts, and the Americans in general could never understand why the Pope-like Ayatollah ('His Holiness the

Imam') could not, with a snap of his fingers, get the hostages released. America might be a superpower, as the Iranians kept saying, but Iran — as Hakim put it — was a 'super religious power',[73] one that might easily find the pretext of some religious occasion to persuade Hizbollah to set the captives free.

All the Bible readings, therefore, the quotations and claims and aspirations, could be seen as part of the religious boilerplate current in the Middle East: as current as lists of arms. But North also had his 'personal obligation'. Release of the hostages, he jotted down in his notebooks, was 'the greatest Christian task'.[74] God was not brought into his messages about Nicaragua, the burning public crusade; but the release of the hostages was evidently something that needed frequent and private intercession, by Poindexter and McFarlane too, at the least. Even complete outsiders such as Pat Robertson, an evangelical minister with no security clearance, were asked by North to pray for him because he was going to Beirut to get the hostages out.[75] 'Pray to God that this works,' he told Charlie Allen in an update of the latest equation from the White House Situation Room.[76] 'Lord willing,' Shultz would sign on to the operation; 'with the grace of God' the hostages would be home by the summer.[77] The Iranians had to keep their part of the various bargains, and both sides had to keep to punishingly complicated timetables; after everything possible had been organized, the rest had to be put in God's hands.

It is suggestive that North, in his weary notes, was never quite sure that the Lord would help. Perhaps His seal of approval was never quite so firmly over this operation as it was over the contras; perhaps that was why he needed to be importuned. The one time North thought He had really come through ('Thank God — He answers prayers'),[78] was a cruel tease. In exchange for most of a shipment of Hawk parts worth $6.5m, no hostages appeared; and the hopelessness of the enterprise was laid out as clearly as if a hand had drawn it in the heavens. Indeed, as even North acknowledged at the end, it was an operation that was damned.[79]

# Chapter 8

# Bakhshish

THE noble sentiments that were used to justify both the Iran and the contra operations did not exist alone. These might be just causes or holy wars, but nothing merely human could remain so pure for long; and these particular operations, so clumsily entered into and with such a grubby array of assistants, had a well-established dark side even in their beginnings. Like yin and yang, black and white, 'high purposes' co-existed with the urge to make money. Much of the exotic flavour of the scandal was summed up in one word, 'bakhshish'.

Almost every player thought that every other player was on the take, and everyone as vehemently denied it. Michael Ledeen, suspected by both Nir and North of taking a commission on the arms sales, said he had actually insisted that nobody in the first channel to Iran should do any such thing; the arms business being what it was, they could all be 'like Caesar's wife' and still be accused of pocketing part of the proceeds.[1] The enormous mark-ups on the prices of weapons sold to Iran, attributed mostly to Ghorbanifar, in fact came mostly from the NSC, where North produced a new price list on 'a little pink card'[2] to justify mark-ups of about 600%, creating a slush fund for the contras.

The source of all the trouble in the affair, and the reason the whole thing came to light, was money. Everyone was stashing it

95

away for purposes of their own; and whether these were noble or ignoble, dinners or jewels or cars or crusades, disgruntled creditors or outraged Iranians, or both, were bound to put an end to it. All through the summer of 1986 they grumbled, and Ghorbanifar entreated with tears on the telephone to his contact in the CIA, Charlie Allen, that he could not possibly pay the amounts he was being asked for.[3] In October one creditor, Roy Furmark, complained directly to Casey, and the gaffe was blown. No more fleecing of the Iranians for anyone.

North insisted that he did not go into either operation 'to make anyone rich';[4] and he also did not believe, when asked, that Secord was making any money out of what he was doing. 'Dick is losing a lot of money,' he would say, presumably having the word from Dick;[5] but he did not need to be out of pocket long. Both operations afforded a chance, at the least, to stack up profits. Richard Miller, Channell's co-fund-raiser for the contras and North's contribution-handler, asked North in 1985 whether his organization might take 10% out of 'the stream of money'; and 'I remember him saying specifically that that was reasonable, that most of the people involved in this were getting anything from 20% to 30%.'[6] Secord's markup for the contra armaments was an average 38% over the cost price.[7]

In his dealings with Iran, Ghorbanifar maintained that he charged a mark-up of 'only' 60%.[8] On one shipment of Hawk spare parts worth $2m, he charged the Iranians $8m. 'So, he's a businessman,' was Secord's reaction to that.[9] A businessman himself, why should he object? Of another Iranian who made a habit of telephoning on open lines, worrying about his money, Secord remarked: 'We have no objection to businessmen making money. That's good. We don't care about that. It's not important to us.'[10] Perhaps it should have been; for private profiteering — from Ghorbanifar's suspected millions to Secord's own relatively modest $1.5m, red Porsche, Piper Cub aircraft and trip to a health farm — tarnished and belittled the 'noble' ends both men were supposed to be serving. It took little — in North's case, the mere suspicion that he had bought groceries and a second-hand van with money meant for the contras — to turn a great crusade into a tawdry trip to the fair.

As it happened, both Secord and Ghorbanifar — each as distasteful to the other — were equally adept at combining their motivations. They loved their respective countries, seriously. And they did not mean to be out of pocket over it. The question most asked about Secord, both before and after he testified, was whether the blunt ex-general was a patriot or a profiteer; but as the editors of

*The New Republic* pointed out, the very construction of the Enterprise — backed by the weight of the government, no more accountable to Congress than a private citizen — allowed him to pose as whichever he liked.[11] Asked by Nields whether he was acting in the national interest or for himself, Secord replied, rather plaintively, 'Can't I have two purposes?'[12]

Nobody, he went on, undertook these missions for compensation alone. The large sums of money that sat under his and Hakim's control in Geneva were there, he said, for several good purposes, including insurance, insisted upon by the Israelis; money for Ghorbanifar, in case he needed repaying in a hurry; and an operational fund, necessary both to keep the whole thing ticking over and to leap to whatever covert adventure North might dream up next.[13] After the first diversion, in February 1986, of Iranian arms money into the Enterprise account, there was $2.6m 'surplus' in the bank; after the May trip to Tehran there was about $10.8m. North wanted it sent to the contras. That, Secord insisted, would have been ridiculous: 'we could never get away with that. We had to keep sufficient revenues in these accounts to stay fluid so that we could go on to the next operation.'[14] With Secord, there were not 'causes'; there were operations, jobs to be done, money to be made, with luck.

On the last score, the contra resupply operation hardly qualified. It was never going to make money. At the Miami meeting in July 1985 where control of the funds was removed from the contra leaders, Secord was horrified to hear that the whole mess, 'screwed up like Hogan's goat', was being dumped in his lap.[15] Hakim, too, was appalled at the thought of sending money to such a slapdash operation; indeed, said Secord, he never wanted to do it, and in any case he hardly knew where Nicaragua was. 'Don't get involved, don't get involved,' cried his business partners, two old CIA hands on the muddy fringes of things. 'It will be nothing but misery. There's no money to be made there.' Secord, according to himself, said he knew there was no money to be made there, 'but that's not the point. Shit, the whole thing is going down the tubes.'[16]

Secord maintained that he never — despite his markups — tried to make any money out of the airlift operation. He was trying to do a vital job and get out of it as soon as he could.[17] When he got out of it, he intended to take the aircraft (paid for by donors) and the portable assets, or sell them for a good price, because those were 'the Company's'; indeed, he thought they were all the Company could usefully salvage.[18] He told Calero that he was making no profit, just helping the movement. Calero took him at his word; when he found hotel bills and air fares being added to the shipment costs of his weapons he was actually grateful, assuming that the Enterprise —

having taken the trouble to itemize — was not also adding on a general markup to cover salaries and expenses.[19] Secord would have thought the gratitude in order. He was only taking on these loss-making contras, he explained to a colleague, because he was sure of a long-term fortune in Iran.[20]

This mix of sharp business and shrewd philanthropy was Ghorbanifar's motivation too. His patriotism, which was effusive, went hand in hand with a frightening, slippery enthusiasm for handling money. Whether he did so profitably or not the Americans were scarcely able to tell, but he was a nightmare to deal with, 'always claim[ing] to be borrowing and then getting paid in part and rolling debts forward and raising costs and it is very, very confusing,' as North sighed.[21] In January 1986, Ghorbanifar told Charlie Allen that 'he and his organization' would carry out anti-terrorist operations for the CIA for free; but once they had done so convincingly — say, 'saving the life of the Crown Prince of Bahrain' — they would expect to gather in millions of dollars.[22] On the other hand, as he also told Allen, he was not like Jacob Nimrodi, the Israeli middleman who was trying to edge him 'out of the business'.

> You know, he loves money. And you know this man dies for money . . . In one bank I have account. I have only there four hundred thousand dollars. In that bank, he has there, in the same offices with my friend, he has seventy-five million dollars.
> *Allen*: Gosh. He has seventy-five million?
> *G*: In the name of his daughter, has twenty-five.
> *A*: Hard to believe. Jacob Nimrodi?
> *G*: In this bank he is good, I think, for at least hundred million dollars.[23]

There were money-grubbers and money-grubbers, and Ghorbanifar was far from being in the first rank, in his own opinion. His business, important as it was, was always presented as a sideline to his real desire, which was to guide Iran's future policies towards America and away from Russia. In his view, the hostages were better out of the equation; but since America insisted, a sort of closeness could be achieved between the nations by paying ransom for the Americans held in Beirut and channelling the payment through himself as a middleman. Ledeen, who thought Ghorbanifar 'a good fellow and a lot of fun',[24] found nothing shocking in that. If this ever-charming and exasperating Iranian could deliver the goods, it would be irresponsible of the Americans not to use him. 'Why should we be concerned,' he asked, 'about his private moral standards or business activities? The question that had to be answered was not "Who is he?" but rather, "What can he do?"[25]

Even with strong stomachs, however, it was hard to deal with Ghorbanifar. 'Export-import in Paris' was the nearest Charlie Allen could get to identifying his precise line of work, but 'Ghorba's group' seemed to be up to other things as well, according to a note in Allen's files: dealing in false passports (Turkish, Moroccan, Greek, Portuguese, or Irish, like McFarlane's); printing Saudi Arabian rials for the Haj; negotiating with the IRA for bombs, passports and booby traps. One Ghorbanifar speciality, offered to the Americans when they went to Tehran, were British passports with driving licences, $10,000 apiece.[26] A conversation with him was a roller-coaster of banks, debts, curious demands, importuning creditors, and the nagging notion that it was all being done for America's benefit, not his own. 'I will take the money . . . we spend the money for you. What, who got the money? Who got the money?'[27]

Increasingly, the Americans tried to wriggle out of giving any money to Ghorbanifar; and he began to realize which way the wind was blowing. In the end the Americans wished to be rid of Ghorbanifar mostly to keep him quiet, for his cries of indebtedness were dangerously loud. In the summer of 1986 they turned with great relief to the Second Channel, but relief was premature. Ghorbanifar was not to be shut off just like that. Supposing that he had lost his business with America before he had recovered his money ($10m–11m, by his own estimate), he was noisier than ever. To cut Ghorbanifar out, North told Allen one night in his office, he would have to raise a minimum of $4m.[28]

Besides, mysterious bargaining by no means disappeared with a more personable set of Iranians. Business-talk was so dominant that the Iranians were perplexed when the conversation strayed away from it. Was it not the matter at hand? They even joked about it, and the Americans laughed, grim as it was. At Mainz in October 1986, the Second Channel told a story: the Iranian government had had a spy in the Tehran meeting with McFarlane. North, disbelieving, wondered who.

*Hakim*: [Deleted] says if you want to hear the rest of the story, you'll have to give him 250 more TOWs. (*More laughter*)
*North*: Quite a story-teller. Where's the phone?
*Secord*: Tell him I have the police right outside.[29]

To deal with one merchant was difficult enough; but in this business there were many. They seemed to come out of the woodwork. North could not keep track of them at all, though Secord and Hakim could. One emerged at Mainz who stood to make a commission of $1,200 on every TOW shipped.[30] Another popped up there too, knocking at the door of the hotel room in the middle of discussions, a contact of a man Hakim said was 'running the show'.

> *North*: Who the fuck is that?
> *Hakim*: Okay, I'm glad you asked. His last name is [deleted]. He owns this shipping company, he's the only guy in town — in Tehran — who can still provide women, wine, and dancing and opium. He provides money . . . he is there now.[31]

From this sort of thing there was no escape. Not even pious references to Abraham could avoid it, for Abraham was, above all, a consummate bargainer with God. The very chapter of Genesis that North said he quoted to the Iranians, in which Abraham heard of the people his seed would rule over, began with the Lord saying 'I am thy shield, and thy exceedingly great reward'; to which Abraham replied: 'Lord God, what wilt thou give me?'[32] Three chapters on the two bargained again (Abraham in wheedling and nauseating style) over the destruction of Sodom and Gomorrah. What if the Lord found 50 righteous men in Sodom? Forty-five? Forty? Thirty? Twenty?[33] Ten? The wearing insistence on the bargain, even as God's side of it was steadily undercut, was not so far from what was heard in the huddles of Brussels and Frankfurt and Mainz. The Americans may have needed to demur, to find some sort of higher justification for it, but the Iranians had no such qualms. Business was business.

On the American side, Hakim had no qualms either. As an Iranian, and as a businessman, his motivation was simple. His native country was an 'attractive' market, it was neglected and misunderstood, and he could 'make a bundle' there, probably $15 billion a year.[34] Whatever North and Secord thought they were, Hakim was a businessman, whose business it was to make money. This is not to say that he could not sometimes dress it up in high purpose. 'The country needed me,' he told Liman at the hearings. 'I was helping out. I made my resources available, all of my resources available to the country.'

> *Liman*: Are you saying, Mr Hakim, that among your resources were TOW missiles?[35]

Charlie Allen was worried about Hakim. He told North he seemed 'one cut above Ghorbanifar';[36] indeed, talking to Hakim one day about what could be done about Ghorbanifar, he was startled to get the reply, *tout court*, 'We'll buy him off.'[37] North, also concerned with buying Ghorbanifar off, managed to overlook that element. He told Allen, with some passion, that he shouldn't criticize Hakim because he didn't know him ('You're right, I don't know him,' Allen said obligingly);[38] he told George Cave that Hakim desperately wanted to make amends for a shady past and become an American citizen. His motives, he said, were as patriotic as the next man's.[39] His colleagues, unconvinced, backed down.

Yet Hakim never hid what he wanted. When he was brought into the negotiations with Iran, his tailored wig on his head, he pleaded not to have to discuss politics. He was a businessman.[40] At a meeting with Cave and an Iranian in July 1986 he spent a lot of time explaining that he wanted, as a cover, to set up a legitimate business with Iran. He could sell medicines, for example, at cost or on credit with up to a year to pay if he could get something out of it; one pallet of medicines was actually sent as a sample. They could deal in oil, perhaps, or rice. The Iranian told him frankly that he would not do this for nothing; Hakim promised him a good commission, and told Cave he was going to pursue these avenues no matter what else the Americans decided. 'I never, never made it a secret,' he said, 'that there is a profit motivation there.'[41]

For such a man, the contra operation was a nightmare. Here was a scheme that would never, it seemed, make money. 'To me it was written off,' he explained. 'Anything that went to anything in my mind as a businessman, I wrote it off. I did not ever at any time took [sic] the attitude that anything that was invested . . . in Nicaragua could have a return.'[42] Why he got involved in it in the first place was difficult to say, and he was never completely clear about it. But the American government, through Secord, seemed to want his help; indeed, the President himself, so Secord said, was asking for it; and it was not certain, at the beginning, that there would never be anything in it for Hakim. Secord was holding out slim possibilities.

I asked him how long this is going to last. He said that I really don't know. I questioned him what impact and effect this was going to have on our business, are we going to be still able to — able to follow up on our business? He said, what do you mean? I said, well, I am a business man, and I have no doubt in my mind that I am willing to help the government, but I would like to see what is going to happen to our business. He said, well, we are going to go into this as private businessmen. I said, well, then I have no problem. It is beautiful. I will help out and make money; why not?[43]

Hakim's enthusiasm was soon dashed. There was some profit to be made but, as Secord explained to him, the contra war was an area in which there was simply not much money.[44] Secord himself was going to look at the weapons transactions case by case, set the prices and determine the commission, which was to be split between himself, Hakim and the shipper. He did not think the market would bear much. Subsequent mark-ups suggest that he was not too tender-hearted, but by the end of the operation Hakim and a third partner, Tom Clines, were frustrated. Since the current shipment of arms (which was stranded in the Mediterranean, the ship having been boarded and searched) appeared to be the last to the contras, the two decided to maximize their profit on it. The arms had been purchased for $1.7m; Hakim and Clines took a commission of $861,000, or about 50%, claiming that their work on the shipment had required extra effort, down-payments and possible disbursements for storage.[45]

To Hakim, however, this was not greed. He was running a company, however ramshackle it was; and his first assumption was that the money in the Enterprise accounts was private. Secord had told him it was.[46] Besides, he had taken the risks himself and made the commitments, often reluctantly. If he had taken the risk, he should reap the reward. As the profits from the Iran arms sales came in, at first trifling, then large, the partners in the Enterprise would argue over the proper destination of the money. North always wanted 'too much money for the contras', Hakim complained. Then he would suddenly ask for heaven knows what — a ship, aircraft, Motorola radios.[47] Secord wanted to be 'operational', but also wanted to be sure the reserve was fat first; and Hakim wanted the accounts built up as private funds, not something that had to be drained down at the beck and call of the government. On the other hand, he was not sure whether he could use the money entirely as he liked:

> To the extent that I thought that sooner or later I would be entitled to some income from my efforts for this covert activity, I thought we were free to do what we wanted. But I never felt free to completely use all the money . . .
> *Nields*: You couldn't use all of the money.
> *Hakim*. I did not feel free. Technically, I could. I'm saying, you asked me a question, if I felt free. You are talking about my conscience, my frame of mind when you say free. [48]

The reservation presumably being, as Nields reminded him sharply, that if he and Secord used all their money for profit-making schemes, North might stop using them as intermediaries. Hakim acknowledged that, in part.

You are asking me my frame of mind. And I told you earlier that I would not in any way kill the —
Q.The goose that laid the golden egg.
A. Thank you.[49]

Money brought obligations, too; obligations to give, and obligations to take. People ought to take what they deserved, Hakim said, just as Secord should have taken his share of the profits. If people worked hard, they were entitled to a cut. Large causes needed employees who were happy and motivated to work; besides, Hakim's generosity would do something to justify his eventual profits to himself. In his own company, Stanford Technology USA, he had sometimes gifted stock to the employees or shared the profits with them, believing that 'the key employees of the company should have financial motivation.'[50] The Enterprise, though it was different in so many ways, sloppy and badly constructed, could still be run financially according to the rules of Hakim.

Round about the time of the trip to Tehran, 'a very, very, touching and sensitive [time] for us because we were all in such a frame of mind that we may lose our boys in one of these events',[51] Hakim became worried about North. He was fretting that he was neglecting his children and could not pay for their education, that his marriage was breaking up. Hakim wanted, by his own account, to help him out, put some money aside for him. This was the way he described it to Secord: 'We have done this for the contras, why can't we do it for him?' Secord, always 'icy-faced' when Hakim spun out these questionable schemes, saw through it at once. 'What do you mean?' he asked. 'You are out of your mind.' When he saw he could not put him off setting up a North fund, he at least made him reduce it to $200,000, not $500,000; and they did not discuss it again. North, however, took the kind offer at face value. Hakim did not tell him about the 'Bellybutton' account, set aside for him, in so many words; 'however, I did tell him that Ollie, we're one family, any one of us who would stay alive would look after your family. I don't want you to worry about that. And tears came to his eyes. So to mine. And living that, tears come to my eyes again.'[52]

There was of course a purpose in caring, a pupose in creating these ties of 'family' knotted up with dollars. When Liman suggested that it was an effort to compromise North, to get leverage over him so that he would continue to lend his official weight to the scheme that was to enrich Hakim, Hakim was indignant. 'No, that is not the spirit,' he said. 'That is not the spirit.'[53] But it was close to the spirit: 'It was a plan that tried to save their marriage and get the kid to go to school, prime the pipe, if you will, to get it going.'[54] On another occasion, he described the scheme as a wheel: North could set it in motion, or he could decide not to set it in motion.[55] In the event, North's knowledge of the scheme was never proven, and he never revolved the wheel. But Hakim saw nothing wrong with the principle. 'I respect my own ideal and my own ethics,' he explained to the congressional lawyers; 'I have a different attitude to these things.'[56]

He had learned it, he said, as a child. '[We say] if you drink this water, I am going to give you this coffee . . . So, the structure of the mind as a child is that there is always a give and a take, there is always a trade.'[57] In dealing with Iranian grown-ups — when, he admitted, 'a certain type of slickness' was required[58] — a trade had to be established, a basis for trust. Both parties had to understand what was in it for them. This was 'entitlement to bahkshish'; and bahkshish, as Hakim explained, trying to smooth over the sneering tone with which the lawyers pronounced it, 'really has a very positive ring. Bakhshish is a donation for religious reasons.'[59]

Even Hakim, then, had his holy cause. He had a crowd of people whose services he was using to make his future 'bundle' in Iran, and to all he owed rewards. It was inescapable; it even, at times, turned nasty. Numbers of Iranians had helped Hakim to get the Second Channel going. They stayed at the edges of meetings between Iranian and American officials, usually in different rooms or different hotels, but once the meetings were over they would descend on Hakim, calling him up, badgering him, getting him to their rooms in the evening, demanding 'when, how much, how they are going to be compensated'. For Hakim, the official negotiations took on an urgency quite beyond the issue of hostages or grand strategy: the issue of a hundred shadowy and grasping hands. 'I am being harrassed by these people,' he explained, 'and I have to come in and I cannot tell especially the Americans, "Hey, guys, my life is at stake."'[60]

One incident especially bothered him, and he hoped it would impress his listeners. It had happened in Frankfurt in February 1986, when he was still wearing his wig and still going under the alias of the President's translator. A man collared him in the corridor as one of the meetings finished, and took him to one side. 'Brother Abe,' he whispered. 'Let's sit down, see if we can strike a deal. Go and whisper into the ear of the President of the United

States and get him to take care of the Volkswagens [Phoenix missiles] right away.' Hakim understood that he was meant to offer the President a bribe. This gentleman, he added quickly, was not at all the type of person they had eventually come to deal with in the Second Channel. No, the gentleman in the corridor was simply typical of the people who waited for him in corridors all over Europe, hoping for good news.[61]

Much of Hakim's forward planning revolved round keeping these people sweet. He maintained a reserve of $2m 'for payments to Iranian officials'.[62] If he died in harness, Secord was given power under a fiduciary agreement to distribute it for him; but North (who was to be allowed eventual control of the Enterprise) was not also given control of the bakhshish fund, because it was 'not proper'.[63] Hakim was not particularly troubled by the thought that there might not be enough money left to continue the work of the Enterprise, 'this strange animal'; but he was exceedingly worried that his payments, the guarantee of mutual trust, would not be made to those who had helped him. Alongside the public causes of great moment, 'all these politicians, military guys, intelligence guys sitting there', was 'a little business guy'[64] whose chief concern it was to pay back debts incurred by him on his own behalf on his way to a private fortune in Iran.

In October 1986, at Frankfurt, the little business guy was left in charge of negotiations with Iran. North had been called back to Washington to deal with the exposure of the resupply in Nicaragua. He left in a flat spin, asking Hakim to do what he could to scrape an agreement from the talks, which were foundering; but emphasizing that he had been given a list of seven points 'by the President', and that those were all he himself was prepared to negotiate.[65] Hakim did not think much of the list, nor indeed of North's approach to negotiations in general. North was always trying to build a long-term relationship, so it seemed to Hakim, in a pressure cooker. Slowness was necessary, and patience; and once the whirlwind was out of the door Hakim sat down to negotiate as a businessman should.

When he was left alone, he told the hearings, 'the only thing that did not cross my mind was financial benefit, and the only thing I was working on was the interests of the United States.'[66] If that was so, he made a strange choice of negotiating partner. According to him, there had only ever been one man on the Iranian side worth talking to. This was 'the real McCoy, the engine, the heart of this'. McFarlane and the others called him 'the Monster'. They did not want to listen to him because, in Hakim's words, 'he called a spade a spade': that is, he talked weapons-trading, rather than the platitudes the Americans preferred.[67] The Americans gone — to all intents and purposes — he and Hakim sat down together.

*Liman.* And did he see you as a businessman?
*Hakim.* Very much so. And he also knew that I have no interest to continue to act as a diplomat or politician. He knew that well.
*Liman.* He understood that your interest was to get the door open to Japan — to Iran and make some money?
*Hakim.* I would be delighted to accept a mission to open the door to Japan, sir. (*Laughter*)
*Liman.* To Iran.
*Hakim.* Yes, sir.
*Liman.* And to make some money?
*Hakim.* Yes, sir.[68]

The two worked through the night, 'adding verbiage to the seven points of Ollie', or, in Hakim's more velvety description, '[making] the position of the US side more flexible and more critical, or rather less committal.' In particular, 'they said that the money would be paid to Albert Hakim. And in paren[these]s that says, by the way, the payment for the shipment of 500 TOWs through the Second Channel, they gave me a blank check. They signed it, I filled in the check.'

The hostages were in their proper place in this agreement. They were Item 4, after the schedule for the shipment of TOWs and Hakim's pallet of free medicines thrown in as a sweetener; and they were treated like any other divisible commodity. The Iranians were stipulating the release of one hostage, the Americans were holding out for two: so 'I came up with a solution — why don't we cut in the middle, just negotiating, and a half.' North, apprised of the new list by unsecure telephone as he landed, exhausted, in Washington, naturally did not understand. When the Solomonic Hakim proudly mentioned his one-and-a-half hostages — one released, one to be tried for, the best he could get — North merely asked him whether he had been drinking.[69]

Although the nine points were a political and diplomatic disgrace, the Americans were desperate. The elections were close, and here at least was hope of something; so Poindexter and Reagan approved them. Hakim, for his part, seemed quite cheerful. He knew, and he thought the Iranians knew, that he had no power to bind the United States.[70] From his own commercial point of view he had drawn up a good agreement. It was also an agreement, extraordinary as it seems, that mitigated his eventual sentence in court; for, disgraceful as it was, it had still got a hostage out, and Judge Gesell thought that ought to be remembered. There was nothing so bad in Iran-contra, it seemed, that it could not somehow contain something good; and as frequently vice-versa.

Besides, as Liman pointed out at the hearings, Hakim had played Secretary of State for a day. No, better than that, countered Hakim; he had achieved more than the Secretary of State. It was no fun to have that job; to get things done in the world, better to be a businessman.[71] Having seen too many negotiations wrecked by intemperate political or emotional desires, Hakim was genuinely anxious to give the United States the benefit of his business sense. Go slowly, establish trust, give something, take something, secure everything with rewards. Far from being bothered by the privatization of foreign policy, Hakim thought the United States would do well to act like a private individual; indeed, like himself.

It was not only with the Iranians, besides, that favours ruled. Every cause pusued covertly acquires its hangers-on: the limpets who 'facilitate' a drop of weapons, or the flight of an aircraft, or the passing of information, and who in return demand favours for themselves. The contra operation too was one in which some people expected to 'make a bundle', however Hakim might sniff at it; the small fry clustered in their wake. As well as Secord and the highly-motivated Singlaub, there were at least half a dozen other arms suppliers on the scene. One, Mario del Amico, was setting up an 'arms supermarket'. He spread the rumour, which Secord's operators maintained was false, that Secord was buying grenades for three dollars apiece and selling them for nine.[72] Crescencio Arcos, acting as doorman for the Ambassador to El Salvador, was surprised to find disreputable types dropping in to describe how corrupt Secord was, and to demand a share of his business. Most worrying was when Felix Rodriguez, an experienced agent, tried to take 'Secord's' aircraft away and assume control over the resupply, apparently out of an excess of high principle. Arcos could not tell who was principled and who was not, but in that business he assumed the worst.[73]

Plainly, the contras bought weapons from anyone and without guile. North and Secord took control of the large foreign contributions away from Calero precisely, so they said, to discourage the purveyors of junk and the hangers-on, but they were undeterred. Calero still had some money (and he, after all, was not bothered by the source of that, as long as it came); he was the man who would run the government and distribute the winnings, presumably, when victory was declared; he would be in charge of the internal market in arms; and out of his dining-room in Miami, in which the dealers sat convivially with him, he was still directing the war.[74] 'Calero is the strong man, and the only one who counts', wrote Rob Owen to North, the courier reporting. 'If members of the USG[overnment] think they control Calero, they also have another thing [sic] coming.'[75]

Owen saw the contras more often, and more clearly, than most; when he ran the envelópes of money down from North to Calero, he took in what else was happening. 'They are not first-rate people,' he wrote of the men around Calero, those whom he most trusted. 'In fact, they are liars, and greed-and-power motivated. They are not the people to rebuild a new Nicaragua ... THIS WAR HAS BECOME A BUSINESS TO MANY OF THEM: THERE IS STILL A BELIEF THAT THE MARINES ARE GOING TO HAVE TO INVADE, SO LET'S GET SET SO WE WILL AUTOMATICALLY BE THE ONES PUT INTO POWER.'[76]

Calero could not be detached from his sidekicks, especially not from his brother Mario, the loose cannon in charge of procurement. They were, as Owen saw, his security; to threaten them was to threaten him. Even the man Calero chose to be military commander in the south was also, according to Owen, someone who 'drinks a fair amount and may surround himself with people who are in the war not only to fight, but to make money.'[77] Meanwhile, cash was also being siphoned off between the NHAO humanitarian aid programme, for which Owen was nominally working, and the suppliers of goods to the contras. Calero apparently told Arcos and the Ambassador that there was a profit of 37%, jigged up by the black-market exchange rate between the local currency and dollars.[78] 'He is splitting this 50–50 with Aquiles Marin, and AC's share is going to the war effort', Owen reported to North. 'Would you by chance know who Aquiles Marin is?' Owen had tracked down Adolfo and Mario's bank accounts, at Lloyd's Bank International in Switzerland; overcome with impatience and distrust, he thought that Lloyd's was probably an invention too.[79]

According to Owen, John Hull was a particular magnet for the facilitators and the hangers-on. They came in swarms to his ranch on the Nicaraguan/Costa Rican border: drug-handlers, weapons-suppliers, mercenaries, people from *Soldier of Fortune* magazine wanting action shots of the war. Hull received them as if he was running a tourist motel, his wife and the maid endlessly making up sandwiches.[80] 'Boy, do I ever get the crazies,' was Hull's remark; but with some hangers-on, scarcely more reputable than others, he associated regularly and freely. Owen remembered several meetings, either at Calero's house or at 'Howard Johnson's contra discounts'[81] in Miami, which Hull attended along with various commercial limpets and self-ordained guerrillas. Tom Posey was there, a renegade member of the United States National Guard who wished to take his 'missionary-mercenaries' down to Costa Rica for a bit of contra-training and fighting. Representatives of different contra factions would be there, offering to sell various sorts of arms to Calero. One 'Colonel Flacko' would be there: 'back in business . . . in New Orleans, and working on some new scams' as Owen reported to North; probably trying with his buddy Tieador to get the Miskito Indians to take control of a working gold mine on the Atlantic coast.[82] 'Too many people,' Owen sighed, 'have learned to make a good living off of the war.'[83]

The main congressional hearings did not investigate any connection between contra resupply flights and drug runs, but it is clear from incidental evidence — including Owen's memos and North's diaries — that drug distributors and weapons-droppers regularly tripped over each other. They occasionally shared the same aircraft, guns going down and drugs up; sometimes the crates of weapons and the sacks of white powder were stacked beside each other at the same jungle airstrip.[84] The networks through which the contra crusade operated after 1984 had been largely established before it. To disentangle the drug thread from the weapons thread, to find 'untainted' aircraft and different flight paths through the mountains, to recruit innocent individuals conveniently running ranches near the border, would have been difficult enough without urgency. But the Americans ('United Statesians', as some folk more accurately put it[85]), were always in a hurry, in Central America just as in Iran: tearing along, they could not stop to be fussy.

Owen would occasionally make a mild complaint to North ('DC 109 used for flight was also used for drug runs, and part of the crew had criminal records. Nice group the Boys choose'[86]), and North said he passed the evidence along;[87] but there is no evidence that this was ever acted on. It was not exactly collaboration; most commonly, it was the turning of a blind eye. In the worst case, General Noriega of Panama, apparently deep in the drugs trade, was allowed to carry on unmolested in exchange for support for the contras, including training, sabotage and the offer of assassinations; North arranged the contacts on the administration's behalf. While Noriega was helping, in 1985, American aid to Panama increased by almost 500%.

If the cause was advanced, the secondary businesses and sidelines of the helpers would not be interfered with, no matter how repellent. Any man was an ally who placed himself on the right side of the ideological divide. Conversely, as Noriega found when the United States invaded and toppled him in 1989, any ally was expendable once the cause had evaporated. The Bush administration turned on Noriega with all the righteous wrath of a Puritan called to account by a harlot, and the military strike against him was given the name it needed: Operation Just Cause.

# PART III

## Obedience

> If the Commander in Chief tells this lieutenant colonel to
> go stand in the corner and sit on his head, I will do so.
>
> North, hearings, 9.7.87

> We are not here as weak and feeble creatures but as sons
> and daughters of Adam — capable of affecting our own
> fate.
>
> North, *Life* magazine, December 1988

The motives behind Iran-contra may have been many and various,
and a weird blend of the rotten and the transcendent; but if the affair
was founded on any one precept, fuelled by any one idea, it was
obedience. Both operations were acts of obedience to presidential
wishes, and those wishes carried the weight of orders: they were not,
in general, to be questioned. This chapter investigates the notions of
obedience, service and duty; the idea of lawful orders; the precise
way in which orders were handed down and understood; and, in the
end, the players' ideas of individual responsibility for the mess in
which they found themselves.

© Vint Lawrence 1987

# Chapter 9

# Soldiers and Servants

THE main players in Iran-contra were soldiers who happened, also, to be presidential servants; and the primary impulse of Iran-contra was nothing more than to do what had been asked. Obedience was as natural as breathing. The closest historical parallel to the case that cartoonists and columnists could find was that of Henry II demanding the murder of Thomas à Becket, not with a proper order, for that was unnecessary, but almost on a whim: and off the knights galloped into the dark, Sir John with his sword, Sir Bud with his cake, Sir Ollie with his crusader's cross, gone almost before he knew it, to do what would make the king happy.

Questioned about the military side of it, the players sometimes failed to understand. When Representative Dante Fascell raised the point with McFarlane, wondering what these men barely out of uniform, or still technically in it, were doing chatting to each other on restricted computer networks, McFarlane could not see the problem; he was just like any other outside consultant to the government.[1] Poindexter, too, professed to be able to treat the post of national security advisor as 'essentially a political position', one for which he had chosen for a time to leave the Navy behind. 'I always felt,' he explained,

that I had two commissions . . . not only as a naval officer, as a

115

flight officer, an admiral in the Navy, but I also had a commission as assistant to the president. I always tried to keep the two positions, in my mind at least, separate.[2]

Even his political position, however, had military overtones. 'I think that it's always the responsibility of a staff officer to protect their leader,' he said, 'and certainly in this case, where the leader is the Commander-in-Chief.'[3] McFarlane, at the hearings, spoke words almost identical to these;[4] and it was not so far from that to North's formulation, when Liman asked him whether part of his 'mission' was to shield those who gave him his orders: 'That is the part of any subordinate. Every centurion had a group of shields out in front of him, a hundred of them.'[5]

Hakim, for one, never doubted that he was dealing with soldiers. 'General Secord was born a general and will die a general,' he explained; 'Generals have a special way of thinking. If you deal with them long enough, you learn how to deal with them . . . I understood his psychology.'[6] But he did not understand it that well. Secord did not talk much, and he was still wavering between making a bundle with Hakim and going back into the government.[7] Sometimes, when Hakim came up with a good scheme for a partnership, he would simply give him an icy glare. At another point, 'in one of his moods', he would suddenly forswear his profits from the various transactions, leaving Hakim stupefied.[8] He did the same in public at the hearings, saying the surplus from the arms sales could go, as far as he was concerned, into the William J. Casey Memorial Fund for the contras.[9]

Secord also seemed possessed of some grim understanding of his purpose: certain things had to be done, others were not to be contemplated, because this was work carried out at the behest of the President. North too, who at every turn thought of himself and talked of himself as a soldier, clung rigidly to his presidential orders whenever he had them 'in specific'. 'That's the President's list,' he told Hakim as he rushed away from Frankfurt in October 1986, leaving the list in Hakim's hands; 'That's all he authorized . . . And there's no way on God's green earth I'm going to violate my instructions.'[10] McFarlane too, facing the dismal collapse of the talks in Tehran, refused to compromise his orders: not, however, with the tact of a diplomat, but with the furious stubbornness of a Marine.[11]

For all the principal players, such thinking belonged to a life (North's 'real life') that they had left behind with some reluctance. Poindexter had been an assistant to three Navy secretaries, and had commanded a guided missile cruiser; McFarlane, North and Secord had served in southeast Asia, doing their best in accordance with their orders, but had come back to find their service dismissed or disapproved of. Vietnam or Laos was not something they discussed much, even among themselves. North's lawyer, with whom he spent most of his time after November 1986, was surprised that he could never draw him to talk about it. He simply never broached the subject. At one point in the long preparations for the trial Sullivan asked North to bring in his combat awards, the official citations for his Silver Star and two Bronze Stars. North demurred, and seemed to be resisting. In the end, when Sullivan lost his temper, he produced them: green and covered with mildew because he had kept them in the basement.[12]

If the Vietnam war had been dishonourable, perhaps it needed to be fought again. Perhaps this time it could be efficient, triumphant, honourable and without the press, for the press, with luck, would never know until the end of it. 'This country fought a guerrilla war,' said North, 'one in which I had served, and we lost . . . we won all the battles and lost the war . . . I would also point out that we didn't lose the war in Vietnam. We lost the war right here in this city.'[13]

McFarlane agreed. He had been involved in Vietnam, by curious coincidence, at the very beginning and the very end; the fact that he had 'landed with the first and [been] responsible for the ignominious pull-out of the last' continued to haunt him.[14] Indeed, it was McFarlane's hints and remarks that lawyers used to draw such statements out of North, for he still would not volunteer them. Even Poindexter was drawn out in this fashion to admit that the unfinished business — the unfinished service — in Vietnam had changed the way he and his colleagues had approached their work in government. 'I think it had an impact,' he said drily. 'I think it had an impact on a lot of people . . . I think I was that way, I think Bud was that way, Ollie was that way, the President [never a combat officer] was that way. We didn't want to desert the contras . . . On the national security policymaking, not just within the administration but within Congress . . . Vietnam played a very big role both ways.'[15]

Not only had the service of the players been dishonoured — so that it remained to be done, or at least made up for — but their military lives had been sidetracked by entering the government bureaucracy. McFarlane had retired as a lieutenant-colonel to join the NSC; North had left Quantico, where he had been training Marines, to go on attachment to the White House; Poindexter had come out of the Navy, although he was in line to command the Sixth Fleet. None saw much glitter in a White House posting ('The glamour wears off very fast,' as Poindexter put it)[16] and none was entirely happy at a desk. McFarlane was said to be bitter that his switch to civilian service had put him out of the running for promotion in the Marines, and he would warn North not to be caught the same way.[17]

North himself was fretful, torn between the Marine he was and the super-bureaucrat he was becoming. In January 1984 he was offered a chance to go for a year to the Naval War College, another rung up the ladder towards a command. Secord, called in to help him decide, said it would hurt his career to stay at the NSC; North countered that his work was too important to leave.[18] In the event, McFarlane — despite his qualms about soldiers staying too long behind desks — intervened on North's behalf, and he stayed on.[19] While at the NSC, he was promoted from major to lieutenant-colonel; it was McFarlane, in his office, who pinned his own oak leaves on North's collar and recited the oath from memory.[20] The two may not have talked much about Vietnam, but they talked about getting a command. McFarlane realized North's chances were not the best; he was 40% disabled from war wounds, had been in hospital briefly for 'emotional distress', and would probably have been invalided out, McFarlane thought, if the Disability Review Board had ever managed to get its hands on him.[21] He still believed, however, that leading a battalion was the only thing North wanted to do in life. He used to rag him about getting desk jobs, which would have taken him out of the service for years, and said he did it to make him furious: North wanted to be leading men.[22]

In 1984 he should have returned to the Corps, civilian assignments being for no longer than three years; but several White House officials and cabinet officers, perhaps less ignorant of his uses than they later became, begged his Marine superiors to let him stay, and the assignment ran on and on. In May 1986 he appeared, at last, to get his chance of a posting. New orders came for North to go to Camp LeJeune, North Carolina, where he would get a battalion to command: the Second Marine Division. It was on a plate, but he did not want it. Just at that moment he was being threatened by a terrorist, Abu Nidal, as in reprisal for the bombing of Tripoli in April; to accept a permanent change of station looked like running away.

He could not contest the order, he knew. He asked Poindexter or Reagan to do it for him 'if it is indeed what you want,' adding, 'I am here to serve you and the President, so direct.'[23] But he desperately wanted not to leave. Life at the NSC was every bit as thrilling, for a soldier, as life in charge of a battalion. A friend invited to his office for a heart-to-heart on Marine postings noted with amazement that North had pictures on his wall of himself with contra commandos, and a street map of Managua: 'normal nonsense of broad-based arrows, grade attacks, that sort of thing.' Not once, but twice, North mentioned that 'we were going to be in Managua by Christmas.'[24] Casey, in fact, had said to him — the problem laid, as North problems were so often laid, at the old master's feet — 'There are more important things than being the battalion commander.'[25]

McFarlane, while at the NSC and in charge of North, maintained a civilian veneer. Once outside it, he and North egged each other on in the language of soldiers. 'Roger Ollie, well done,' tapped McFarlane into his home PROF machine, a machine he should not still have had; 'Bravo Zulu'; 'No sweat, GI'.[26] 'Roger: Any time John,' he told Poindexter in October 1986, meaning that he was ready at any time to go back to Tehran, despite what had happened before;[27] and he offered, 'with my knowledge of artillery', to track down mortars for the contras.[28] A curious PROF note passed between him and North in the summer of 1986, when McFarlane suggested that North should leave the NSC, take a holiday and join him at the Centre for Strategic and International Studies, where he was teaching. They would then work together 'to build up the clandestine capability that is so much needed here and there'. The posting was civilian, but the work had overtones of military missions; North even said he liked the idea of it.[29] McFarlane, for his part, although he said the whole scheme was a joke, was evidently pleased to bring into his pedestrian desk job a thread of covert operations and the fighting life.

North was supposed, by this stage, to have become a bureaucrat. Although he was on active duty and paid as a Marine, he had been, as Commandant Kelley said, 'cut loose' from the Corps for the time of his assignment. He had no duty to report back to Kelley, indeed it would have been unethical to do so;[30] his chain of command now went up through bureaucrats to the President who remained, as before, Commander-in-Chief. At the NSC North wore civilian clothes and virtually kept no rank, except in formal listings and in the directory; he was 'Ollie' or 'North', or by his own appellation, sometimes, 'Dr North at the White House' — no soldier he.[31] His hair grew long, relatively, and he took to name-dropping. Yet he clung on to remnants of his military life. A uniform hung in his office,[32] and he wore his full dress blues — complete with his medals on their ribbons — at black-tie parties and diplomatic dinners, sometimes to general astonishment.[33] His office was littered with books on military subjects;[34] large maps of his areas of operation, Nicaragua and the Bekaa Valley, were on the walls. On a window sill by his desk was a North Korean army hat with a red star, like a prize scalp;[35] and he drank from a canteen that had been shot off his hip in Vietnam — the ultimate affectation, some colleagues thought —

the sort of mouth-puckering coffee he had learned to make in the Corps.[36]

The difference between this artificially constructed soldiers' world and the world of other government servants — lawyers, civilian advisors, most of the NSC staff — was summed up in a formulation at the top of the PROF notes and memoranda that the principals sent so ceaselessly to each other. John Nields, the House counsel, a man whose shaggy hair and rounded shoulders proclaimed him to be in the opposite camp, turned up one of these during North's testimony, 'Exhibit 18'.

*Nields.* That is a chronology that bears the date and time of November 17, 1986, 2000 — which I take it is 8:00 pm.
*North.* Twenty hundred —
*Nields.* I'm sorry, twenty hundred.
*North.* Military time.[37]

Two months earlier, the imperturbable Poindexter has made the same point in his deposition to Arthur Liman, counsel for the Senate.

*Liman.* Where it says, '1000, 17 January 86, is that your handwriting? Page 3?
*Poindexter.* Yes. That's 10 hundred. In other words —
*Liman.* That's the hour?
*Poindexter.* That's the hour.[38]

The President was the commander-in-chief; and he was also an irresisitible civilian employer, a charming and shrewd old man to whom the players felt an overpowering loyalty. Reagan was 'our boss';[39] they were his staff and his servants, political appointees serving at his pleasure. Their jobs depended on his say-so; and therefore, when they served or protected him, they were also to some degree serving or protecting themselves, making sure they continued to bask in the sun of his approval. This natural symbiosis was not brought out until Poindexter's trial, in which the defendant was presented by his lawyer as a tireless and selfless presidential workhorse. Not as selfless as all that, retorted the prosecution: as the President went, so went his servant.

Servant and lord were therefore one, and not merely in the cold eyes of the court. The principals of Iran-contra approached their role with an extraordinary degree of fervour, subordinating their ambitions and desires to Reagan's as if it were a sin to think differently. Shortly after the roof fell in, Patrick Buchanan — the President's communications director — spoke for all soldier-servants, berating those who had 'headed for the tall grass' when the scandal broke. Cowardice, or criticism, or second thoughts were not in order. Were these not men who owed everything they had — preferment, power, influence — to the President's generosity? Did they not owe him thanks? 'And when a mob shows up in the yard, howling that the head of the household be produced, the sons do not force the Old Man to sit down at a table and write up a list of his "mistakes". You start firing from the upper floors.'[40]

From day to day, the circumstances of service were less dramatic; but they were no less eager or solicitous. Like a good servant — indeed, like a discreet butler — McFarlane in the summer of 1984 secreted a note for the President in his 9.30 briefing book to let him know that the Saudis had agreed to contribute $1m a month to keep the contras going to the end of the year: 'and after that meeting was over, I was called to come back and pick up the note card which, as I recall it, expressed the President's satisfaction and pleasure that this had occurred.'[41] Poindexter, who liked the subtlety of that gesture of McFarlane's,[42] also made an art of pleasing the President, knowing what he wanted to hear. This was not a man who wanted to see the nuts and bolts; he had 'a limited amount of time to focus';[43] and every day Poindexter would make 'judgment calls', a term of some art and craft for him, as to what the President should be told about the implementation of his orders. He would brief him carefully about the secret Costa Rican airstrip[44] and the state of the contras in the field ('Sixty days' stock after 31st March'; '30 days' ammo left'),[45] without getting into the level of detail where the President would either yawn or become implicated; and then he would leave him with the briefing book, in case he wished to know more.

When North came up with his proposal to divert money from the Iran arms sales to the contras, therefore, the same tactful servant apparently decided that he did not need to seek his master's approval. Policy details, after all, had to be 'serious and feasible' to be 'elevated' to him,[46] and perhaps the diversion — so often viewed as implausible, or a joke — did not fit the requirement. Or perhaps it was not 'presidential', just as the contra resupply in general was 'not vice-presidential material', just 'bits and pieces' to Don Gregg, George Bush's national security advisor.[47] It was either too hot politically, or beneath his notice, or both, with the strong suspicion that superiors were being saved from shame by their habit of turning away from the bothersome details of getting what they wanted.

Poindexter nonetheless concluded that the diversion was 'within the general charge' that Reagan had given him; that 'I understood the way he thought about issues . . . and that if I had asked him, I felt confident that he would approve it.'[48] Five and a half years of reading Reagan's mind — a mind shrewder and more decisive, in his experience, than many supposed — had taught Poindexter, as he thought, to understand it. It had taught him, too, to be sensitive to the merest hints of presidential desires, the most outlandish suggestions, just in case they could be gratified. In May 1986, in the midst of trying to get the latest contra-aid vote through Congress, Reagan greeted Poindexter one day, with a remark as brusque as a gunshot: 'I am really serious. If we can't move the contra package before June 9th, I want to figure out a way to take action unilaterally to provide assistance.' Poindexter had never heard that formulation before, but he did not doubt what it meant. Unilaterally, Liman asked him later, presumably implied without congressional approval.

A. That is what I was conveying.
Q. And that the President would be exercising his constitutional prerogatives?
A. That is correct.[49]

Poindexter recalled, too, the meeting of December 7th 1985 when the decision was taken to continue with arms to Iran, risky as it was on every count. The arguments and counter-arguments were put forward; 'and the President listened to all this very carefully, and at the end of the discussion, at least the first round, he sat back and he said something . . . to the effect that "I don't feel we can leave any stone unturned in trying to get the hostages back."'[50] And that was that. There was a duty to be ready, willing and eager; and so it went, conversely, that there was a duty not to put dampeners on the President's hopes, and especially never to tell him that what he wanted could not be done.

Reagan himself, however innocent he may appear to have been in matters of arms control or welfare policy, understood precisely the alternatives to taking difficult matters through Congress, and the usefulness of servants public and private. Private contributors to the contras he treated as friends and agents. Rather than promoting a national or even a party campaign, they were the President's own helpers. As Carl Channell liked to say, they were few and select; as Reagan liked to say, when he was alone with Poindexter, they were the modern equivalent of the Lincoln Brigade or the Lafayette Escadrille, private individuals supporting the President's foreign wars.[51] Channell, attending a reception for several dozen of them at the White House, was impressed to see the President address them by their first names; Poindexter would get 'little debriefs' from him about what Tom or Joe had said to him at these meetings,[52] and in the letters that went out afterwards, over the signatures of Reagan or North, the contributors were praised as 'patriots . . . carrying out the President's policy'.[53] Nelson Bunker Hunt, the oil and silver billionaire, called to the White House one day to be thanked for helping, gave Reagan the benefit of his knowledge of Libya: 'I told him that if he sent a couple companies of Marines along, or Army along with the bombers, I think everybody in Libya would have jumped on the bandwagon.' Having said that, he regretted it as soon as he left; Libya was 'sort of water over the dam', and he could have more usefully advised him about Nicaragua.[54]

President and government, of course, were not coterminous; indeed, they were almost opposites. The President was an individual who might choose to involve himself abroad with volatility and passion, while the government lumbered doggedly and cautiously behind him. Talking one day to Owen, North made it clear that Owen was in no sense an agent of the government. He was like 'one of FDR's representatives who was a private citizen yet did things in a private way for the President.'

Q. Diplomat without portfolio?
A. Yes, not being a representative of the United States government.[55]

In his own testimony, North was exceedingly specific about the President's prerogatives. Reagan was 'the person charged with making and carrying out the foreign policy of this country', and he did so virtually as a private man. Being already elected by the people, and being trusted by them to act 'with a good purpose and good intent', he had no need to keep going back to the people to explain that 'I, the President, am carrying out the following secret operations.' He carried them out, revealing and explaining them 'in a timely manner'; that is, when he was good and ready, like an eighteenth-century potentate. And his agents, his 'personal arm', his 'staff', his 'servants', were always there in some guise to assist him. He could do what he wanted with them.[56]

It was traditional anyway, North thought, for presidents to get frustrated with bureaucrats, with 'their lack of urgency; 'and I'm not sure that you will ever find a president who is unwilling [sic] to wait so long that he doesn't draw things in closer to himself.' If the President wished to carry out covert operations with unappropriated moneys he had — at least as North read the precedents — a free hand.[57] And he might send his emissaries out 'anywhere in the world, to talk to anybody about anything'. Liman prodded him, and found he meant it: literally anybody, literally anything. 'Absolutely no problem *whatsoever*.'[58]

North longed to please Reagan, even unadvisedly: to show him pictures of the air drops into Nicaragua, to drag into the Oval Office by their elbows agents and ministers who had been helping, to get the hostages 'all standing in front of the White House wrapped in a ribbon'.[59] If there were presidential letters to be carried to Margaret Thatcher asking for Blowpipe missiles, or to hostages as they came out of their captivity, North pleaded to be allowed to take them.[60] One of his Academy teachers had warned him that at the White House he would need to be clear-headed, keep his values straight, 'because it is hard to tell the President of the United States his fly is open'. But the President's desires were like oxygen to North; they were everything, the only thing, he had worked for. A revealing little exchange occurred at Poindexter's trial:

> *Webb*: Colonel North, you were heavily involved both in the support of the contras and in the Iranian initiative, were you not?
> *A*. Yes.
> *Q*. These were important projects to you, weren't they?
> *A*. I thought they were to the President.
> *Q*. Well, they were important projects to the President, that is true. Were they also important projects to you?
> *A*. Yes.[61]

The role of the servant was not always acknowledged, nor compensated with thanks. Poindexter thought the President 'was clearly aware that Colonel North was the primary staff officer on the NSC for the democratic resistance', and that he would 'see his face' in any meeting to do with Central America,[62] but that was the extent of it. He also told Reagan, *a propos* of Iran, that Secord was 'a great patriot; it's too bad we can't recognize all that he has done', while confessing that the President knew neither who Secord was nor what the dickens he was doing.[63] And that, to Poindexter, was right; staff officers and agents were there to do their work, not to ingratiate themselves, particularly not to fish for approval. Wasn't he ever tempted, Liman asked him, to share with the President the rich irony that Khomeini was bailing out the contras? Take it one step further up the line, since he and North so enjoyed thinking about it that way? The answer came back without adornment.

*A*. No.
*Q*. You never had any temptation to say to the President that we got the Ayatollah to pay for the contras?
*A* Mr Liman, that's not my style to — I really am a very low-profile person. I don't feel that I need a lot of acknowledgement in order to get any sort of psychic income.[64]

North's 'psychic income' was not helped by acknowledgements either. He thought the President knew, in general; and if he did not know the details of his own and other people's service in his cause, then he ought to. North even thought the President should be sent the photo album of the resupply during the hearings (covered with fingerprint powder as it was), because 'it's important that the President know that good men gave inordinate amounts of time, and some gave their lives, to support that activity.'[65] He had had the idea of telling Reagan something along those lines when Buzz Sawyer was killed in October 1986 in the crash of the aircraft; he asked Owen, a friend of Sawyer's, to write a memo about what kind of man Sawyer was. Owen wondered what he could possibly want to do with it. 'I just might show it to the President,' North replied, and Owen naturally understood why: 'to show the President what a great American Buzz Sawyer was.'[66]

To his subordinates, therefore, North seemed to be an intimate; dashing into the Oval Office with this and that exciting news, sharing a laugh. Colleagues were told, until it became an exasperation and a joke, that North had 'just spoken with our boss'; docile congregations of evangelical ministers or Methodist women were told that North had come hot from one of his presidential debriefings. As far as can be gathered from the evidence, he was the junior man who sat at the back of the room, worshipping.[67] Reagan was his 'leader' in a strangely off-key sense, a sort of amiable *caudillo* who was soft as butter but, when necessary, sharp and requiring to be saluted. And North did salute. One of the most extraordinary word-pictures of the hearings came when Secord described how on November 25th 1986 he and North had huddled in a hotel room in Tyson's Corner, a soulless development of malls and offices just outside Washington. North had been fired that day, and the two men were bleakly commiserating. Then the telephone rang.

There were two phone calls that came in for Colonel North. One call was from the President. I didn't realize it was the

President for a few seconds until I saw him stand up at attention. He is a good Marine, you know.

And he said, Yes, Mr President. Yes, Mr President. Thank you very much, Mr President.

And then he said that I am just sorry it had to end this way; I was trying to serve you the best way I knew how, Mr President. I said, Let me have the phone, but it was too late. He hung up. I wasn't quick enough.[68]

Secord had intended to give the President his piece, explaining how he and the others had 'worked like dogs' at his behest, carrying out what he had been told were the President's desires. He was a servant too, but not to the degree that he would allow himself to be kicked about because of a political embarrassment. 'It's been suggested that I write a book,' he said bitterly in an interview later 'It's called *If the Government Calls Again, Let the Phone Ring*.'[69] North, however, was not in a mood to carp, even within hours of being fired. If his boss wished it, his servant would happily accept obliteration. In one code-sheet for the Iran operation, after all, North had given himself the name Uriah:[70] the poor cuckolded dupe sent by King David with a letter asking that he should be put 'in the forefront of the hottest battle, and retire ye from him, that he may be smitten, and die'. Over-extravagant, undoubtedly; but also simply something servants and followers did. 'It's too bad Reagan is so old,' ran a remark attributed to North by a startled colleague. 'It's good to die with our leaders.'[71]

How much was reciprocated, how much was true, may never be known for certain. In December 1986 the President's spokesman, apparently having totted up the entries in the log-book, announced that North had met Reagan 'less than 20 times' in the last two years of his service, and always in a company of people.[72] 'Everything that I could say mainly about Oliver North,' said Reagan at his testimony in February 1990,

> was things that I've heard. We did not meet frequently or anything of that kind, nor do I remember ever having a single meeting with him, as has been hinted at times by others . . . no.[73]

Don Regan, the chief of staff, speaking also for Reagan, maintained that North was 'a virtual stranger to both of us'; he had talked to him once, he believed, on the telephone.[74] On the other hand, Reagan liked to have soldiers round him, and during his two terms about a third of the NSC staff were military men, an extraordinarily high proportion. He was also said, by Casey, to have picked North out specifically for the job of sustaining the contras once Congress had voted against them.[75] North told one of his resupply contacts, in a famous remark he later denied, that the liberals in Congress could not touch him 'because the old man loves my ass'.[76] The old man was also said to call North 'my Marine',[77] appropriately possessive, as if he could be kept in a pocket and sent out, wound up tight with a key, whenever the President wanted fetching and carrying done. But that little snippet too may have come from North, and not from the man he so desired to approve of the boldness of his service.

In some circles, a curious mysticism clung round the figure of Reagan. North was not alone in feeling it. One of the background themes of Iran-contra was an almost Hegelian intensity of purpose. The national task was a moral cause, because the state itself was the manifestation of the divine will on earth; the monarch, or president (why quibble?) was an actual symbol of God's will working in the world. In another of his Iranian code-sheets North called the President 'Joshua', the bold prophet whose trumpets brought down the walls of Jericho.[78] That was why an aide's only duty was to obey the ruler; and why (the ends being so transcendent) the means did not matter much. The American version of Hegelianism had its homelier touches; what was more remarkable was that, at the end of the 1980s, an American administration should have harboured the shade of Hegel at all.

Reagan himself, by several accounts, fantasized about his role as a holy man, chosen by God to re-establish a God-fearing America serenely prepared for Armageddon, which might come at any moment.[79] Something of this fantastical spirit seemed to touch the star contributors to the contra cause when they came, in their reverent groups, to the White House. They had done the President's bidding, they knew, giving to a cause that was 'very dear to his heart'; now they were to be admitted, for ten or fifteen minutes, to the Presence. They would stand 'hand in hand and heart in heart with me to have your private moment alone suspended forever in time with the President,'[80] as one fundraiser wrote to a contributor. Barbara Newington, who gave generously and was therefore afforded her glorious moment in November 1985, made use of it to tell Reagan 'that I thought he had brought God back to the White House. And he said, "I've been talking to Him a lot lately, and I intend to take him to the [Geneva] summit with me."'[81]

McFarlane and Poindexter, not to mention Secord, might have found this a bit much. Other servants, however, took it in their stride. Another story, perhaps apocryphal, perhaps a North story (the two categories ever hard to disentangle), was designed to show that God's instructions came into the White House via Cabinet meetings, too, and were relayed to the staff. At a session in the White House, North's bleeper (always going off) went off; Reagan looked round the table, wondering who could be calling, since everyone of consequence was present. He concluded: 'Must be God for you, Ollie.'[82]

God, the common good, the President, the nation, the Commander-in-Chief; all these sources of orders, all overlapping, yet all tending in the same direction: get the hostages out, keep the contras alive. The mission was mystical as well as practical. On July 16th 1985, thick in the contra operation and with the first stirrings of the Iran operation just being heard in Washington, North jotted down some notes of a conversation with Admiral Arthur Moreau. Precisely what they refer to is a mystery, but the precepts might have applied to almost any of the tasks he was engaged in.

 — Steady Unrelenting Pressure
 — Same as w/. . .
   Children, Dogs, Commies
 ● Great Strength required
 ● Unrelenting
 ● Steadfastness
 ● Rise Above the 'grass'

 — Isiah (sic) 6:8 [83]

The 'grass' appeared to be a reference to Isaiah 40:6, 'All flesh is grass.' As for Isaiah 6:8, that was the moment when the prophet, having seen the Lord enthroned and surrounded by adoring angels, is touched on the lips with a live coal and purged of his sin: 'Also I heard the voice of the Lord, saying, Whom shall I send, and who will go for us? Then I said, Here am I; send me!'

# Chapter 10

# Lawful Orders

AS soldiers and servants, therefore, McFarlane and North had set off on the ill-fated trip to Tehran. Both thought of it as a mission. 'I did it because I was asked to do it,' McFarlane told his congressional questioners, having run through several more nebulous reasons for accepting; 'I have been doing that for 30 years.'[1] He had been given his presidential orders, 'four pages of typed instructions called "terms of reference"':[2] and these he would stick to, no matter what happened.

Extra advice had been passed on to North by Casey, the old expert at going behind enemy lines: he should take care to see that if he was captured, as Buckley had been, he gave nothing away. Apparently, both men carried suicide pills. Cave remembered North saying how risky the trip was, how 'maybe we should take an LT', though Cave himself was not bothered; if he were captured, he was going to become a mullah.[3] But the soldiers, with professional pride, made sure they carried their pills. 'I was confident I had the means at hand to foreclose my being exploited for intelligence,' said McFarlane in his complicated way.[4] North put it more dramatically, ever-willing to announce his willingness to die: 'I took with me the means by which I could take my own life'.[5]

Events soon revealed that they did not have the same understanding of their orders. McFarlane thought he should follow instructions

129

to the letter, even if he risked disappointment. North thought he should get the President what he wanted. The worst disagreement of the trip occurred when McFarlane was woken by North on the last day to find an aircraft on its way to Tehran with more American weapons; North had summoned the second aircraft pre-emptively, as arranged beforehand, on the supposition that all the hostages just might come out. Still groggy, McFarlane flew at North; he accused him of insubordination and ordered him to turn the aircraft round. North did so. In retrospect, however, McFarlane did not blame him. It was the sort of thing he would have expected 'an aggressive young officer' to do.[6]

These were men in suits — by then considerably travel-worn and care-stained suits, crushed in an aircraft alongside pallets of weapons parts, probably sticky with watermelon and the Iranian home cooking Ghorbanifar's mother had given them, the only food they could find when they got to Tehran.[7] They carried briefcases. Yet even as late as Poindexter's trial, in 1990, North still instinctively referred to himself as the 'staff officer' on the Tehran trip, causing the judge to intervene in some puzzlement. The NSC was a civilian agency, wasn't it? It wasn't military? North took some time to give an unequivocal 'No'.[8]

As for McFarlane, not even the news of the diversion of money to the contras, which slipped out on the way home, could ruffle his military-style single-mindedness. Hadn't he thought to tell the President this bit of information? asked Liman. Hadn't he thought to wonder whether North had approval to do it, or how exactly the money could be 'applied to Central America'? To each the answer was no. McFarlane never doubted that North must have had approval to do it, if he had done it; and in any case,

> I was operating, Mr Liman, under the context of a request to return and carry out a mission in government as someone who was not in the government, who had no authority to know nor need to know matters beyond what it required to carry out my mission.[9]

McFarlane's was indeed something like a real mission, something he had been called back from private life to do: dangerous, but glorious if successful. Secord, too, was called back by North at Casey's suggestion to serve his country in these odd short-term ways, ready to undertake his 'mission' in the hope that it would not last long.[10] As for North, he made a mission even of things he had omitted to do. When Liman asked him why he had not asked Poindexter why the diversion had apparently never been discussed with the President, North said simply: 'First of all, I'm not in the habit of questioning my superiors. If he deemed it not to be necessary to ask the president, I saluted smartly and charged up the hill. That's what lieutenant-colonels are supposed to do.'[11]

At this point, the congressman's question to McFarlane bore repeating: 'Just what were you guys doing with the government?' To charge up hills, to turn orders into missions, was not the way civil government worked. This was a purely military ethic; it belonged on the battlefield, not in politics, even if politics sometimes seemed as bloody and as savage. A mission was in the nature of a challenge or a dare; once picked up, the actor's commitment was total, the legalities and proprieties usually unquestioned. The end, not the means. Few words describe Iran-contra better than those of A.H. Clough, quoted at the beginning of Graham Greene's *The Quiet American*:

> I do not like being moved: for the will is excited, and action
> Is a most dangerous thing; I tremble for something factitious,
> Some malpractice of heart and illegitimate process;
> We're so prone to these things, with our terrible notions of
> duty.

That 'terrible notion' had been spelt out clearly for McFarlane, North and Poindexter at Annapolis. They had been given a pamphlet called *A Message to Garcia*, containing a moral tale from the time of President McKinley. McKinley wished to get a message to a rebel leader called Garcia, somewhere in the jungles of Cuba. A man called Rowan volunteered to go. He strapped the letter over his heart, and by some means — nobody knew how — eventually delivered it. Whatever the means were, the passage continued, they could not matter less:

> My heart goes out to the man who . . . when given a letter for
> Garcia, quietly takes the missive without asking any idiotic
> questions, and with no lurking intention of chucking it in the
> nearest sewer, or of doing aught else but deliver it . . . The
> world cries out for such. He is needed, and needed badly; the
> man who can carry a message to Garcia![12]

The chief players in Iran-contra, however, were not soldiers for the moment. They were in sensitive political positions in democracies. To other military men, though not to the rowdier junior officers, the whole affair was deeply troubling. The Navy took Poindexter back afterwards, at a lesser rank, and the Marines took

North, giving him a desk job; General Kelley testified for him at his trial, and other commanders wrote to the court on his behalf. To take back 'their wounded' was the least the services could do, but they kept it fairly quiet. These officers, after all, while still on active duty, had offended against the Constitution; they had deceived Congress, and their fellows; they had tried to cover up what they had done by shredding and lying, and at every turn they had cited orders.

Worst of all, in the eyes of many serving men, North had put on his uniform — which he had not worn at the NSC — to take the Fifth Amendment, an action that was generally thought cowardly and against the nation's interests. It was not much better that he wore it at the hearings, where he admitted how much he had lied. North appeared to be hiding behind his soldierly status, using it as a defence, implying in almost as many words that soldiers were helpless to do anything but obey.

On the other hand, the players' actions raised questions that had few easy answers. In January 1988, a year after the affair had surfaced, a conference for servicemen on 'professional ethics' was held at the National Defence University,[13] the college where North had hoped to spend a quiet sabbatical year after he had left the White House. The interest in ethics was a direct result of the affair; military commanders had assumed they taught it as part of their courses, but evidently not well enough. In particular, when a military officer was assigned to a political post for which his training had not prepared him, how should he conduct himself? The soldiers mulled it over. One speaker at the conference, a Marine, suggested they should keep in mind that they were first of all servants of the Constitution and the American people. An easy answer, and an old one: the foundation of obedience, as Aquinas defined it, was not the will of the sovereign but the common good, which the sovereign also served. On the other hand, if the ruler served it, and if his authority derived from a pledge to act responsibly and morally, superior and common good became in some sense the same animal, and both required obeying and defending.

At the hearings, Poindexter and Senator George Mitchell had a good tussle over that. Mitchell reminded Poindexter that despite the combination, in the person of the President, of the duties of the chief of state and the executive head of government, officials had to realize 'that their first loyalty is not to any person and not to any office', but to the Constitution. Poindexter politely disabused him. The President had taken an oath to support and defend the Constitution, and the job of the NSC staff was to assist him in doing just that. 'And I don't think that my expression of the loyalty of the NSC staff

to the President in any way abrogates the responsibilities that I took
. . . to support and defend the Constitution of the United States.'[14]

It could be argued, and was by some, that North had upheld the
general principle while falling down in the particular; that, as one
general put it, 'setting aside his situational ethics, he adhered to the
core values of the corps.'[15] But apart from defending the
Constitution in the abstract, there was the pressing question of
defending it in practice: reconciling a superior's orders with the law
of the land. This, too, mightily bothered soldier-philosophers in the
wake of the scandal. The Naval Academy had set the ground rules,
simply enough.

> Juniors are required to obey lawful orders of seniors smartly
> and without question. An expressed wish or request of a senior
> to a junior is tantamount to an order if the request or wish is
> lawful.[16]

At the hearings Senator Inouye, himself a much-decorated
military man, reminded North both of this and of the Uniform Code
of Military Justice, which went further: not only did the orders have
to be lawful but, if they were unlawful, members of the military had
an obligation to disobey them. Inouye then drew the irresistible, and
notorious, parallel: this was the same principle America had applied,
and had proposed should be applied internationally, at the
Nuremberg trials.[17] At this point North's lawyer cut him off,
outraged at the implication that his client, like some Nazi
stormtrooper, subsumed the workings of his conscience to the notion
of obedience to the Leader. But what had been claimed at
Nuremberg, monstrous crimes aside? That the defendants had been
under obligation to obey the Fuhrer, had no inkling the orders were
criminal, had even thought them in the best interests of the country.

> *Q.* Is it fair to say to you that under the obligation of your oath
> as a professional soldier, you did acknowledge carrying out
> criminal orders?
> *General Wilhelm Keitel*: One can hardly put it that way. What
> should be said is that the type of government we had at the
> time, and the authority of the head of state, permitted such
> legislative power that the executive organs were not conscious
> of carrying out illegal orders . . . Consequently, I did not
> consider that I was acting criminally.[18]

The duty of obedience was clear; the fathoming or discovery of
what might be unlawful, in the climate of the snapped heel and the

swift salute, was almost heretical. Besides, if a man stopped to think, he had not obeyed an order 'smartly and without question'. At some point — presumably in the margin of minutes between receiving an order and signing it or doing it — the soldier was supposed to run it past his conscience. But missions, North implied, were thrown in his direction, and he simply caught them and ran. 'You got the ball, go on with it,' was how he described the contra resupply;[19] and of Iran: 'Here, fix it and the thing is already on fire and they throw the bag to you.'[20] 'The thought never crossed my mind,' said Poindexter, asked why he had not gone to Meese to get a proper ruling on the legality of secretly helping the contras. 'In carrying out my duties, I simply didn't think about them in terms of going to Ed and asking for a legal opinion.'[21]

Nonetheless North hoped, as the Nuremberg defendants hoped, that simple obedience would not be held against him. He had not known, he said, that the orders were illegal; coming as they did from the superiors he was bound to obey, he had assumed they would not be criminal; indeed, he had supposed that they would be for the country's good. Unquestioning obedience, in this view, was Cicero's *perfectum officium*, absolute duty, one that required no sort of justification, because it was right. North's public, at first, found this idea compelling in its bravado; immediately after his testimony a large majority of Americans, 60% to 31%, thought he was 'right to follow orders without question, even though they may have been illegal or unethical.'[22]

Naval tradition, besides, stayed firmly on the side of snapping to. And it went further than *A Message to Garcia*. Directly after 'The Order' in the Academy handbook came a suggested answer to the dilemma of whether to think or whether to act: Admiral Hopwood's *The Laws of the Navy*, recommended as 'contain[ing] words of wisdom which few of you will appreciate now'.

> Can'st follow the track of the dolphin
> Or tell where the sea swallows roam,
> Where Leviathan taketh his pastime,
> What ocean he calleth his home?
>
> Even so with the words of thy seniors,
> And the orders those words shall convey;
> Every law is naught beside this one —
> 'Thou shalt not criticize but obey!'
>
> Saith the wise, 'How may I know their purpose?'
> Then acts without wherefore or why.

Stays the fool but one moment to question,
And the chance of his life passeth by.

. . .

Now these are the laws of the Navy
And many and mighty are they
But the hull and the deck and the keel
And the truck of the law is — OBEY.[23]

North brought Admiral Hopwood's sentiments whole and entire
into his trial. When McFarlane had asked him to alter six
contentious memos, he explained, all of which showed him getting
more involved in contra tactics than he should have been, 'I said
"Aye-aye Sir", which is what a Marine says.'[24] Keker, his
prosecutor, was much bothered by the 'Aye-aye Sir'. As a Marine
himself, he wished to stress that Marines did not simply salute and
obey. They thought a bit. Keker then dragged North through the
idea of 'lawful orders' as if through a strange forest, full of half-
threatening and half-familiar trees.

*Q*: [At the Naval Academy] they didn't just say you have to
follow orders, they said you have to follow all lawful orders.
Was that your training at the Naval Academy?
*A*: It's not only my training at the Naval Academy, it's my
training as a Marine. All Marines are taught the same
thing . . .
*Q*: And you learn what they mean by lawful and unlawful
orders?
*A*: Well, one is supposed to make a judgment as to whether or
not an order is lawful or unlawful, certainly.
*Q*: And . . . if you're worried that an order is unlawful you're
trained in what to do about it, you either go outside the chain
of command to the next person up or you go to somebody on
the side of the chain of command, for example, chaplains . . .
*A*: Sure.
*Q*: Okay. And . . . they taught courses about World War II
when a lot of German officers at the end of the war would come
and say, Yes, I committed all kinds of crimes but I was ordered
to do it. You were trained that that wasn't a defense, right? It
had to be lawful orders . . .
*A*: I don't believe I ever received an unlawful order.[25]

No more did Poindexter. Like North, he had studied the Uniform

Code and knew the rules, but unlawful orders remained in the realm of curious theory. He had never given one, never heard one: 'Frankly, the issue has never come up in my experience.'[26] If he met one, he supposed that 'I would go back to my superior and tell him my problem . . . see what he directed,' the implication being that if the superior gave the order a second time, he would snap to.[27] And the diversion order to North? 'There was no doubt in my mind but what it was lawful.' Had he ever had occasion to question the legality of a order from the President? 'No occasion.'[28]

Those who gave the orders were, as far as anyone could see, men of integrity and decency. This was crucial. As North described it, he had joined the NSC as a staff member under people eminently qualified to direct him: McFarlane, 'who devoted nearly 30 years of his life to public service', Poindexter, 'a distinguished naval officer' and Casey, 'a war veteran of heroic proportions'.[29] His authority to act, he explained, flowed from these superiors, and their authority to order him flowed from the President. As for that ultimate source, North concurred with Poindexter's formulation: 'Nobody thought in terms of illegalities. I thought I was carrying out, you know, the President's objective.'[30] No reason why he should have thought to disobey.

But trials tease out the petty details, and Keker dwelt lovingly on the fact that the order from McFarlane to North in August 1985, to alter the crucial contra documents, had initially been disregarded. This was an order that seemed self-evidently illegal, to alter finished documents and, in doing so, to lie; but this was not North's reason for resisting it. He had let it slip because 'It didn't make a whole lot of sense'; if he altered a few memos about sinking ships and getting private money, there were still plenty of other incriminating papers about. So he made his protest; agreed that he would do it, all the same; taped the list of documents to be altered to the side of his computer terminal; and then, as Keker put it, 'You went off and disobeyed a direct order, of course, which is what you did, right? You just went off and didn't do it'.

> *A*: I did not get it done then, no . . . I didn't consider it to be disobeying an order. I just didn't get to it . . . and it didn't make a lot of sense.[31]

Here was a scrap of daylight. An order had been thought about, and had been resisted. Keker pressed on.

> *Q*. If an order doesn't make a lot of sense or if you think there's something wrong with an order, did you in your capacity at the

National Security Council think you had a right to question it, raise it again, fight against it, or disobey it? Did you think those were all options for orders that didn't make any sense?

A. I didn't think I had a right to disobey an order. I didn't think the order was unlawful . . . Mr McFarlane was a Cabinet officer. He was 100 steps from the President of the United States.[32]

And therefore North had obeyed him in the end. Even when McFarlane had become no more than 'civilian, retired lieutenant-colonel, professor at SCIS, Robert McFarlane', as Keker acidly described him,[33] the order still kept its hold on North, and a year later — when it was renewed — he got round to doing what he had been told. Actively to disobey an order was something he had never done 'in the 23 years that I have been in the uniformed services of the United States of America'.[34] And was not such obedience a virtue, to be proud of?

In these respects, North and Poindexter seemed to have uncovered a clash between private and public duty that was not quite allowed for in the Honor Concept or in 'Reef Points'; but these were meant to cover every possible eventuality, every 'situation' that could arise. Were the principles deficient, or the men? At the 1988 conference on ethics most officers determined, in the end, that the men were; but few felt secure enough to pass judgment on what they had done. Here, after all, had been the very models of Marine and Naval officers, much decorated, winners of the highest encomiums from their superiors; and also reported to be conscientious, and to think sometimes. Although something had clearly gone wrong, no officer present could feel confident that he, in their shoes, would not have blurred the issues in much the same way. They might have thought more, perhaps. But few could have made Aquinas's useful distinction between the will of the sovereign and the common good, which was not a matter much raised in mess-halls; few could have distinguished plainly, in most of the examples at hand, the legal from the illegal orders; and even fewer would have thought, at the end of the day, of withholding their obedience.

# Chapter 11

# Chains of Command

So the orders originated and were obeyed. But the process was seldom direct, master instructing servant. Orders moved downwards in a succession of steps, solidifying as they went down, gathering details, and sometimes — though not as often as the administration claimed — taking unexpected turns. At the end of the day, the executed action could sometimes be said to bear little resemblance to the order that had been given. Much of the 'scandal' of Iran-contra turned on whether the players really were, in some respects, freelancing, or whether they had proper authorization. It turned, too, on how deliberately vague the authorization was in the first place, and how it was read by the rather over-eager souls to whom it was entrusted.

The 'chain of command' was a concept to which the NSC staff in particular paid elaborate service. It was not, as McFarlane explained to the judge at North's trial, purely 'a military thing';[1] it meant that a man took his orders from his immediate boss, whether he was an officer or not. Nonetheless, it is doubtful whether the principals would have set such store by it if they had not been soldiers. This was a corner of the bureaucracy, after all, where military formalities were still observed even in the chit-chat, at least according to North: where McFarlane was called 'McFarlane' to his face, and Poindexter 'Admiral'.[2]

The chain, however, contained 'some latitude', as both McFarlane and Poindexter admitted.[3] Reagan's orders to the National Security Advisor would be disputed by, say, the Secretaries of State and Defense; between President and National Security Advisor, therefore, the chain of command was already distorted, having to bend round the substantial figures of people in the Cabinet. In the lower reaches, it became more sinuous still. The NSC staff directory for 1986 showed North as the deputy director of political-military affairs. Above him were four men whose names have not gone down in history, all parallel directors. Above them was Don Fortier, the deputy national security advisor, and above him Poindexter. For the first half of 1986 Fortier was often ill and absent, and in the summer he died; but in any case, as Poindexter confessed, that particular chain of command did not mean much. North in fact reported 'directly to him' whenever his projects were sensitive, just as he had done to McFarlane, 'and it was understood by the intervening people in the chain of command.'[4]

This 'direct access' meant, first, that North stood a better chance of getting through the meticulously closed door and into Poindexter's office, a sort of smoky sanctum, where he sometimes had Bach playing;[5] second, that the two could communicate directly by computer, with no-one else eavesdropping. Poindexter, who prided himself on his aptitude for hacking, set up a file called 'Private Blank Check' (the name, he confessed, was unfortunate[6]), on which North could send him messages that needed to stay secret. North sent quantities, and on the basis of these also sent dozens of memoranda ('Top Secret/Sensitive') directly to Poindexter for transmission to the President.

In effect, then, the chain of command that the three main players recognized went from Reagan to McFarlane to North or from Reagan to Poindexter to North, with intermediate fillers who were sometimes informed, sometimes not. Ray Burghardt, the NSC's special assistant for Latin America, was one such filler; he thought that North worked for him, 'but he is a little hard to hold down, and he does other things, and therefore it is sort of overlapping unclear relationship with me and him, but I am really his boss.' North denied this with feeling. 'Hell, no. I have got a whole platter full of things, and even when I am involved in Central America, it has got to do with my other matter. It really isn't sort of under Ray Burghardt.'[7] And it really wasn't. Poindexter confessed that he could, probably should, have promoted North, perhaps to special assistant to the President, but that his apparent position as a deputy in one among several directorates effectively 'gave him more flexibility to do the job he did,'[8] and disguised his importance. It would have disguised it still better had North himself not so loved to boast about the shortness of the chain of command he followed: one from which even Poindexter and McFarlane sometimes disappeared, while Reagan dropped the words of commission directly into his ear.

Lower down than North, the flow of orders became more tangled still. The power of the White House still travelled down the chain of command; but it now reached people who were not in government, the outsiders involved in implementing the President's policies, who did not regard themselves as anyone's servants. CIA officers and assorted bureaucrats realized, with some surprise, that Secord seemed to have the President's stamp of approval; he turned up one day in the White House Situation Room, conclusive proof to Clair George that he must know 'somebody somewhere'.[9] Yet Secord, although he was acting generally 'at the President's behest', did not consider that he took orders from anyone. He was a commercial cut-out; within that unlovely definition, he ran his own affairs.

If North gave Secord an instruction he did not like — such as the order in August 1986 to conduct 'emergency recall' of crews from the airbase in El Salvador — he simply ignored it.[10] If North told him to put the Enterprise money to some particular use, he might or he mightn't. 'Well, who was in charge?' asked Nields, as North pussyfooted round the idea that a major-general might 'respond to his direction'; was it the government official over the non-government man, or the general over the colonel? North replied that he had asked Secord to do things, and he had done them; but when Nields asked him whether he, North, representing the government, had kept control over the contra operation, North could only say 'I tried to.'[11] Calero, too, fiercely objected to the idea that the contras were in any sense 'guided or directed' by American government officials. He considered the opinions of the Washington apparatchiks, and if he didn't wish to do what they said, he wouldn't. He also remarked — a remark that was rich in unintended irony — that the contras had 'never taken any action on account of intelligence from North'.[12]

These men were in no way dazzled by North and his position at the NSC; but others were. Those who worked for North were given to understand that they were carrying out the President's wishes directly. 'My impression from the very beginning,' Hakim told Liman, 'was that the President of the United States was supporting this mission, it was cleared with him. And in my mind, I didn't go further than the President's authorities and I didn't judge the policy of the President.'[13] Dutton thought, correctly, that the contra operation could not have worked at all — intermingling as it did with the State Department, with ambassadors and with the Justice

Department — unless North was acting 'with the highest authority'.[14] As for Owen, although North insisted that his courier could have told him to 'go stuff it'[15] every time he asked him to carry 'down South' the maps and money and suggestions and lists, he did not sound terribly inclined to do so: 'When I walked into the Old Executive Office Building, which is right next door to the White House, and I talked with a man who . . . is a US government representative who works, I knew, very closely with the national security advisors, I believed that that was good enough for me.'[16]

One of the most striking aspects of the affair was the way that North — a lieutenant colonel — could apparently call up three-star generals, ask for TOW missiles, and get them. As he himself admitted, he would have needed a lot more than 'oak leaves on his collar'[17] to summon up TOWs in the normal run of events. A recurring theme of North's fantasy stories was the rebuke from an outraged senior officer round whom he had run in some daring fashion: from Shultz ('Son, don't you ever dare to get involved in diplomatic matters again')[18], or from Admiral Crowe of the Joint Chiefs of Staff ('Young man, you'd better watch your step')[19]. But as one of Weinberger's deputies explained it, it was not the rank of the staffer that counted; it was the trust that he spoke 'for people who are superior'.[20] The generals therefore snapped to, knowing that even if the order apparently came from North, the ultimate source was Reagan (or 'on high', as one staffer put it).[21] If the generals or the Secretary wished to question it or confirm it directly, they could; in nine times out of ten, however, the request was taken on trust.

Lewis Tambs, the ambassador to Costa Rica, also testified to the magnetic pull of the White House chain of command. Tambs was a dignified and bluntly-spoken man, a former admiral, a scholar and later a teacher of history; in July 1985, as he left to take up his post, North 'instructed' him to open up the contras' southern front from Costa Rica. Tambs's usual chain of command was through the State Department. 'I assume,' he told the hearings, 'that [North] was speaking for people in higher authority.' It was not quite as forceful as an order, anyway; but in any event, 'when you take the king's shilling [a startling reference to his appointment by the President], you do the king's bidding.'[22]

Tambs had not asked North where he, in turn, got his orders. 'If a superior officer gives me an order, I don't ask him whether he has checked with his superiors.' And he had not questioned the legality of the order; if everyone did that, government would be unable to function. 'You'd make a hell of a good corporal!' cried Representative Jack Brooks of Texas, and Tambs seemed to take it as a compliment.[23] Senator Mitchell reminded him that he knew about unlawful orders, and had admitted that there were circumstances in which orders had to be disobeyed; he had used the word 'immoral'. Wasn't the order to open up the southern front a case in point? Tambs thought not.[24] In fact, according to Owen, Tambs thought of it virtually in terms of moral obligation: 'He did not say that the President told him to open the southern front, but being appointed by the President, that was the job he felt he had to do.'[25] At times like this the chain of command virtually disappeared, and instinct took over.

Thus the chain progressed: neither straight nor simple, but still with a certain consistency to it. The Presidential wish was (or was assumed to be) at the top, permeating downwards. This was probably true even of the most notable aberration in the whole command structure, North's relationship with Casey.

The lively consultation between these two, a good generation apart, appeared to go off at a startling tangent. Casey was a member of the NSC, but in no official sense connected with the staff. He became involved with North, first and foremost, because North had become the point of contact with Casey's beloved contras, the rebels whom the old man was obliged to leave alone; and second because in the Iran operation, as Poindexter explained it, 'I really always did view the implementation of the Finding as Bill Casey's responsibility, and . . . I wanted the project run the way he wanted to run it. If we wanted to continue to use Ollie North on my staff as a significant player, that was fine; and Bill chose to run it that way. I agreed with him.'[26]

Dozens of meetings were clocked on between the 'significant player' and the Director of Central Intelligence. Deputies below Casey disagreed about the degree of closeness between them. Clair George thought Casey 'loved him', doers and believers both;[27] John McMahon, who was not aware of any meetings, could not imagine 'why Casey would bother talking with North when he could talk to anyone else he wanted to.'[28] At any event, they seem to have talked at least once a week, on the telephone, in Casey's house that overflowed with books and *objets d'art*, in cars and in aeroplanes. Casey conveniently maintained an office in the OEOB, round the corner from North's. There they would sit, North the eager listener and student-at-the-feet, Casey the wise man speaking in mumbles, in his rumpled suits and food-stained ties.

The contacts were not secret. All manner of casual callers to North's office would hear him talking to Casey on the telephone, and would sometimes get a tidbit thrown in their direction — 'Bill's doing so-and-so' — a remark of no more deference, one visitor thought, than as if they had been discussing picking up the cleaning.[29] Poindexter actively wanted Casey and North to meet and talk often.[30] McFarlane knew they met about once a week, not an unusual amount; North would report the session and sometimes — though not frequently — tell him what they had talked about.[31] But McFarlane was suspicious. It appeared that Casey might be cutting him out; if North was operating under Casey's aegis, it might explain why certain things had been done that seemed, to him, out of line.[32] Poindexter, too, noticed incidents that suggested an unadvised closeness between North and the director. Casey called him one day, demanding that North should be careful 'in talking to people about things they shouldn't know about';[33] later a note went out under 'Private Blank Check' ordering North to speak to nobody else, including Casey, about 'any of your operational roles'.[34] The order, North protested, was impossible to adhere to.

> I went over to see [Poindexter] to, first of all, reassure him that, one, I would follow his instructions in every case but that I wanted . . . a release on the issue of talking to Director Casey . . . it was absolutely essential that I be able to get his advice since he was the expert on covert operations and I certainly was not.[35]

The contacts continued. As far as both McFarlane and Poindexter were aware at the time, the chain of command was still intact; whatever was passing between Casey and North was probably not orders issued from superior to subordinate. At the hearings, North himself was categorical about it. Casey was 'a teacher, or a philosophical mentor'; North 'communed' with him, taking his advice and seeking his guidance.[36] That was not at all the same, he thought, as taking orders. Casey was on first-name terms with him; North, for his part, called him 'Mr Director'.[37] But that was to his face; behind his back he referred to him as 'the old man',[38] a tag confusingly identical to Reagan's, as if these two old men really were interchangeable, or versions of each other.

So, at the hearings, Casey was 'a personal friend'.[39] By North's trial, however — the trial at which he was the staff man following orders — it was in North's interests to make the relationship decidedly more hierarchical. Casey was not 'a friend or a buddy or anything like that'; he was 'the kind of person who obviously had the command of what was going on around him and was . . . carrying out the directives of the President. I believe [the relationship] was one of subordinate to a superior.'[40]

Whatever it was, what North received from Casey — according to him — was nothing less than the structure of his efforts. He asked

Casey at the beginning of his Nicaraguan work which of the contra leaders he should talk to, not knowing which to trust; Casey put him on to Calero.[41] It was Casey who told him to keep a proper account of the stream of contra money that flowed, in fits and starts, through his office; a good accountant, he even gave him a ledger, and later advised him to shred it when things got difficult.[42] When the Enterprise was set up to manage the contra resupply, Casey recommended the use of Secord,[43] and as the Saudi money began to flow it went not directly to the contras but into a special bank account; and this too was Casey's idea, according to North, 'to force a unity on the rebels'. At this point in North's trial, Keker became exasperated with the Casey this and the Casey that. It seemed to him that North was hiding behind a ghost.

*Q.* And the late William Casey thought that was a good plan?
*A.* Yes, sir, the late William Casey did, and if the late William Casey, God rest his soul, were here he'd be here to testify about it.
*Q.* You bet he would.[44]

So Casey gave no orders, but on the other hand North did not second-guess his instructions. When Representative Boland asked him whether 'there was ever a time when Director Casey told you to do something that you didn't do it', North could think of only one: 'I didn't get a lawyer soon enough.'[45]

Whatever he had done, on Casey's advice or without it, North was categorical about one particular: everything he had done had been passed by his superiors. On the phone to McFarlane, who had called him in some anguish from London on the evening of the day he was fired, he said: 'You know I would never do anything that wasn't approved.'[46] To Owen he went further, saying on the same day: 'You know, I would never do anything unless I was ordered to or I was under order to do it. I would not do anything on my own.'[47] Both men agreed with him, trying no doubt to be sympathetic, but this was also North's defence under construction. At his trial, asked why his contacts with donors and contra-helpers were scarcely mentioned in his memos to his superiors, North said they must be there somewhere, in the 'literally thousands of pieces of paper that I created', because 'there is absolutely no doubt in my mind that I was fully authorized.'[48] At Poindexter's trial, asked if he had ever done any things he had not told his superiors about, he replied: 'I can't think of any right now.'[49]

There was no doubt at all about the 'thousands of pieces of paper'. The stack of memos produced by North in the course of the two operations, not accounting for those he had shredded, reached higher than his head.[50] Fawn Hall complained that she could never get him away from the computer, tapping out his reports to his superiors.[51] So many memos were sent to Poindexter that in the end they seem to have become a blur; there were conveniently few he could recall in detail. Cave remembered how North would travel with his KL–43, ready to send word of his doings straight back to Washington. 'He would drive me mad with it,' said Cave, 'because I would be hungry as hell, and he would have to go and send a message.'[52]

Nonetheless, there were matters that slipped through. Confident in the ultimate source of his orders, North reported, waited and acted. If necessary, however — so serene was his confidence — he acted first and reported later. Earl, his aide, gave perhaps the best sense of how the process worked in the field.

> There were, it seems to me, occasions in which he was put in a
> position where he was not briefed, that he would have to
> extemporize . . . but . . . my sense is that he would always come
> back and back-brief and say I had to do such and such . . . He
> would dutifully inform the chain of command when he had to
> exceed his brief, if you will.[53]

The idea from which the diversion grew also seemed to be one of those things which were not authorized 'in specific'. After the failed arms shipment of November 1985, $1m dollars remained which Israel did not particularly want back; North told Secord that it should go to the contras. And what, Nields asked, was his authority for that?

> A. Well, I don't know that I actually had any, in specific.
> Q. . . . You had not sought or received any approval from
> people higher in the US government?
> A. I don't know that I did. I am not saying that I didn't. I
> think I may have apprised Admiral Poindexter at some point
> that I had done that, but I did not — I do not have a specific
> recall of that at this point, no.[54]

McFarlane, if he spoke truly, seems to have been dismayed that North interpreted some of his orders so widely. When he told him to keep the contras alive, McFarlane said, he did not mean him to get involved in buying weapons or planning where to drop them, although he might 'understandably' have interpreted it that way;[55] when he gave him permission to go out and make speeches in favour of the contras, he did not mean him to get entangled with Carl Channell and his solicitations. When the southern front came up, McFarlane did not intend his amiable response ('If they can do it, that's fine'), to be interpreted as authorization for North to oversee it; '[It] seems to me a long leap.'[56] On the other hand, he had not forbidden North to do any of these things; and when Liman asked him whether it was true that North, given the ball, would tend to run very far with it, McFarlane agreed with enthusiasm.[57] North was evidently using his own judgment, in good faith McFarlane thought, to decide 'what fell within the scope of the authorities I gave him.'[58] If McFarlane had not been told all the details of operations this was undoubtedly, he thought, because North had any subordinate's instinct to protect the man above him.[59]

The operations, besides, still had their source at the top. The President's wishes were handed down, and they consisted of two simple imperatives: preserve the contras, and make some sort of opening to Iran to get the hostages out. Public or private expression of the President's will was all his aides had to go on; just as Don Regan, when treasury secretary, charted his course on Reagan's vague promise to cut everyone's taxes. The aides were left to their own interpretations.

The Iran operation, for example, began as a tentative series of contacts. These were authorized by Reagan in mid-July 1985, when he was in hospital for a cancer operation; McFarlane remembered him saying 'that yes, there is no harm in listening to the Iranians, and it was a very sensible thing to do.'[60] Sometime in early August Reagan apparently approved an Israeli shipment of arms to Iran, the one that in effect started the whole slide downwards; but he himself said first that he had done it, then that he hadn't. Regan, who seemed to be nudging and correcting, reported that the President was 'upset' to hear that the Israelis had shipped arms, and that McFarlane had explained that they 'had simply taken it upon themselves to do this', quite unauthorized: the first in a long line of accused freelancers. Finally, Reagan said that he simply could not remember whether he had approved or not.[61] But this, perhaps, was not what McFarlane was relying on for his authorization to proceed with Iran. It seemed more important that at the various meetings to discuss the Iran initiative the President was always for it or, at best, non-committal; and that he asked McFarlane every day what news he had on the hostages, as if he already expected the NSC to be turning itself inside out in efforts to release them.

McFarlane also heard directly from Reagan, many times, that he wanted the contras to survive, 'and I translated that expressed wish of the President to Colonel North and others on my staff.' He never heard, in so many words, 'Tell Colonel North that I want him to do this.'[62] Nor did he hear what was to be done. A whole framework of support was mapped out, including approaches to third countries for money. But it was nothing specific, as both McFarlane and Poindexter knew.

*Liman*: Did the President ever designate in words, in substantive words, the NSC to conduct the activities in support of the contras . . . ?
*Poindexter*. I would not characterize it that way at all. As I said, if you take the totality of the President's actions, that was clearly his intent.[63]

Poindexter therefore, knowing what the President wanted done, passed on the orders in his own way when he took over from McFarlane. He did not necessarily specify to North that the President had approved this or that course of action; since he was 'clearly his lawful superior', he knew North would not query it.[64] So North went on, topping up his presumed presidential authorization with the pro-contra speeches Reagan made (some of which North wrote for him); with Reagan pledges, presumably passed through Poindexter and McFarlane, to go back time after time after time to Congress to get the necessary money; with photo opportunities in the Oval Office, the contra leaders chatting amiably to Reagan, North standing behind the furniture; with the President's 'I'm a contra too' T-shirts, and his kissing of small Nicaraguan refugees, and heaven knows what other asides and encouragements. But it is a fair assumption — another assumption — that no more orders came, written or spoken.

To a large degree, then, Poindexter was content to let North roam within the orders, as far as they were orders at all. He saw him as 'the switching point' that made the whole resupply system work in Central America; but 'what he got involved with directly or somebody else did is a little fuzzy in my mind.'[65] So, too, were the authorizations behind it all, both in Nicaragua and in Iran. Did Poindexter approve, Liman asked him, of North using Owen as a courier in Central America? 'In essence I did.'[66] Did he authorize him to approve weapons purchases for the contras and say where contributions should be sent? 'I was aware of it. I agreed with it. I did not have any problem with it.'[67] What about Secord, in his best bustling-general mode at talks with the Iranians in Brussels, committing the United States to war with Russia in defence of Iran? That came under the heading of 'wide latitude'.[68]

Even when the latitude ran directly counter to instructions he had given, Poindexter accepted it graciously. Before the trip to Tehran, he gave a strict ruling that no weapons parts were to be delivered until all the hostages were released. 'You may tell them that the President is getting very annoyed at their continual stalling . . . If they really want to save their asses from the Soviets, they should get on board.'[69] In the event, the party took about a third of the parts with them, so many that North remembered falling over the pallet on the way to the lavatory.[70] Poindexter admitted that he was not particularly happy with the weapons parts going, but it was 'not something that I felt was entirely out of line. I would have preferred it not be that way.'[71]

If Poindexter disapproved of some idea or began to have doubts about an operation (as he did about Iran), North typically went through Casey to try to win his superior over. Poindexter sometimes had blazing arguments with him, from which North departed crestfallen, while Poindexter's secretary quickly passed the admiral a handful of candy, her signal that he needed to be 'sweetened up';[72] but it did not enter North's mind to disobey anything Poindexter had decided. He obeyed him, and he did things on his own within the general authorization he believed he had. Asked whether Poindexter had directly approved something, North was as likely as not to answer 'He never told me not to';[73] to which he added, at the hearings, the look of a child who had been whipped unfairly.

The chain of command, then, was less than rigorous; but it was awkward for North that it was so, both personally and legally. He had to admit that a lot of approval was assumed, including that most crucial instance, presidential approval for the diversion of funds to the contras. Poindexter was somewhat surprised, later, that North should have assumed he had gone to the President about that; he must have been 'thinking more in military terms and not necessarily considering all of the political issues involved, which I felt that I was considering.'[74] McFarlane remembered how, at the end of the day, North was less than happy with the way in which the diversion had been authorized.

> He said, There is one thing that is going to be a problem, and that is . . . the channelling of some profits from the Iran money to the contras.
> And I said, well, that was approved, wasn't it?
> He said, yes, you know I wouldn't do anything that wasn't

approved. I said, well, just lay it out and it will be all right . . .
It isn't you, it is whoever approved it.
Q. Did he say who had approved it?
A. No, he didn't.[75]

It was plain from this little exchange — which North, incidentally, claimed he could not remember at all — that even North's faith in those endless memos, those 'thousands of pieces of paper', was not total. He assumed, when he sent memos up to Poindexter and through him to the President, that what he was proposing was going to be approved; but some of those memos, including the 'five' he said he wrote about the diversion, never came back checked, as far as he remembered. Was he properly authorized, or was he not? When one of these diversion memos was eventually thrust in front of him, by the Attorney General on November 23rd 1986, the only question North could think to ask was whether a cover sheet, which would have shown the routing, had been found on it. No, said Meese; would that show that it had been approved? Yes, North answered; but he did not think it was. Were there other files, he was asked, that might discreetly house Presidential memoranda that had been approved? North said he did not know, but would check.[76] Perhaps somewhere his assumption of Reagan's approval would find some slim thread of supporting evidence; and perhaps not.

He had never needed evidence before. Fawn Hall, after all, said that in four years of working with him she had never seen a disapproved memorandum, although McFarlane queried one;[77] and there was no trickier question or suggestion than one that implied that North's assumptions of approval might be incorrect. When Richard Armitage at the Defense Department told North in September 1986 that 'his ass was way out on a limb' over the Iranian operation, and that Weinberger 'would have thought he was out of his mind with this', he thought North was utterly shocked: all the more shocked, perhaps, because the President wanted it and Weinberger should therefore have been on board, however squirming.[78]

As Clair George expressed the problem, in his inimitable way, 'Oliver North was asked to do the impossible. And who the hell —'

Q. Who asked him?
A. I assume the administration asked him. Who else would have asked him? Now whether Ronald Reagan said 'pal', or Bill Casey said 'buddy', or George Shultz said 'you're going to save the country', I don't know.[79]

North's trial brought out in full the awkwardness of the situation. His lawyers argued that he had relied 'in good faith' on 'a superior's apparent authorization of his actions', but Judge Gesell said this was not good enough. In his two-hour instructions to the jury he pointed out that, first, none of North's superiors could order him to violate the law. Second, authorization itself required 'clear, direct instructions to act at a given time in a given way':

> It must be specific, not simply a general admonition or vague expression of preference . . . A person's general impression that a type of conduct was expected, that it was proper because others were doing the same or that the challenged act would help someone or avoid political consequences doesn't satisfy the defense of authorization.[80]

The appeals court ruled in July 1990 that Gesell had been too particular; he ought to have told the jury to bear in mind 'the instructions, statements and behavior of North's colleagues, whether superiors or not', because these 'surely can affect a defendant's belief that his conduct was lawful.'[81] Back to the Nuremberg defence. But Gesell's skin-tight distinction was exactly the point made by Regan and Meese when the diversion was discovered. It was plainly not authorized, they said, even before they had asked;[82] and its lack of authorization was precisely what made it so awful, so unbearable. Senator Cohen ribbed Regan about this, reminding him that he himself had joked that a 600% mark-up on arms sold to Iran might be another way to balance the budget. Was it really so horrifying, after all? 'It was an unauthorized act,' said Regan sternly; 'that whole idea would have been. . .very, very much contrary to the Ronald Reagan that I knew.'[83]

On this score, Reagan himself never provided much help. Kind words for his aides one day, tending to indicate approval, would as likely as not be taken back the next on the bidding of nervous advisors. The man in whose name both operations were conducted remained oblivious — that is the kindest interpretation — of what he had ever known, let alone what he might have authorized. On March 4th 1987 he told the nation of his 'disappointment' in 'some who served me';[84] in July 1987, while Poindexter was testifying, Reagan answered a reporter's shouted question about the affair with an expansive shrug of the shoulders, a gesture that had become typical: 'I wish someone would tell me.'[85] Here the Becket parallel raised its head again. The king, informed that his knights had murdered the archbishop, said he had been misunderstood, that he had never authorized it; that that was not what he had meant, at all.

In one sense, these statements were pure dissimulation; in another, they reflected the fact that Reagan had always been protected from knowing too much about what his servants were up to. This left the servants painfully and dangerously exposed. When Poindexter agreed on his own initiative to set the diversion going, he realized that he was out on a limb. It was his word against the President's: his assertion that Reagan would have been sure to have approved the diversion, had he known about it, against Reagan's that he would not. Poindexter anticipated the authorization, but there was always the risk — indeed, there was almost the certainty — that if the diversion brought down a political storm it would be seen to be an orphan, unwanted and unprotected, together with most of what the NSC staff had been doing to prop up the contras.

That too, of course, the President did not remember. He told the Tower Commission in January 1987 that 'he did not know the NSC staff was engaged in helping the contras.'[86] When Nields read that flat denial out to North at the hearings, Liman thought he saw North wince. He denied it: 'It may have been that my back hurt.' Liman tried again, reading out the commission's natural conclusion: 'the Board is aware of no evidence to suggest that the President was aware of Lt–Col North's activities.' 'And my answer?' North retorted. The two wrestled for a bit, North and his lawyer consulting and reading the Tower Report 'to make sure it's accurate', Liman indulgently waiting. He tried a third time.

*Q.* Your counsel has asked to read what the Tower Board Report says, and it is in the last paragraph on the page. 'The President told the Board on January 26, 1987, that he did not know that the NSC staff was engaged in helping the contras.' Take that reference.
*A.* I read it.
*Q.* Does that come as a surprise to you?
*A.* Yes.[87]

The blood was out of the stone. Again, it was the servant's word against that of the boss; and if the boss was right, there was no authorization, leaving aside the question of whether what was authorized would have been legal or not. To say the boss was wrong, even to second-guess him, was a breach of loyalty. On the other hand to say he was right, had never known, attended meetings with a paper bag on his head, straightaway tipped the whole affair into the servants' laps. It became — dread and difficult word — their responsibility.

# Chapter 12

# The Men Responsible

RESPONSIBILITY for Iran-contra was one of the great unfixed quantities of the affair. It was passed round like a live coal from hand to hand, now resting with one player, now with another. Sometimes it was borne nobly for a time, until the breath of Congress or the special prosecutor got too hot; in which event it would be shifted upwards, downwards or sideways. Players were patently torn between protecting their superiors, not betraying their subordinates, and covering themselves; and as their accounts of the matter multiplied (accounts with which they had to try and remain consistent), they moved ever more warily through thickets of responsibility, authorization and blame, like scouts in a minefield.

As soldiers, the chief players had been instructed in responsibility, but only up to a point. Trained to take charge of men, they deployed them according to the orders or battle plan of somebody above. Appointed to oversee and carry out policy in the White House, it was not their own policy they were implementing. As Poindexter explained his responsibilities, he had to see that the policy options were laid out before the President and that what the President decided on was done. But Poindexter never decided what that policy should be; and he was aware that if he tried too obviously to take charge of anything, the Departments of State and Defense, at the least, would demand to know why. McFarlane acknowledged the same limitations. Asked if he was 'an active advisor inputting policy recommendations' he replied, dully, that he saw the job 'when I came to it, as a manager, a co-ordinator. That was the largest mission I had.'[1]

The Iran and contra operations, far from being peculiarities, were exaggerated examples of this arrangement at work. The NSC staff was left, deliberately, with almost total responsibility for schemes that originated with presidential approval; schemes that were full of controversy and risk, while Cabinet officers with no need to know tiptoed gratefully away. It was, McFarlane admitted, not the right body to do the jobs assigned; it did them because it was the staff arm, and there was no-one else.[2] McFarlane was not thrilled to have to deal with Iran, no more than North was thrilled to take it over when McFarlane left ('Bud coughed it up somehow,' he sighed to Noel Koch of the Defense Department, 'and shuffled it off to me, and went off to make a living.'[3]) But neither man would have thought of resisting.

Resistance was left to the double-act of Shultz and Weinberger, and even these two pursued it only to the point where they saw that Reagan's mind was set. 'I understood that he was opposed to the plan,' Poindexter said of Shultz, 'that he also understood that the President wanted to go ahead with it, not that he liked that, he accepted it, and he indicated that he didn't particularly want to know the details.'[4] Weinberger put it his way: 'Once authorization is approved, I don't get into the details of the transaction. I don't ask if the planes for Honduras went out last week or anything of that kind. It flows along, along an established normal path.'[5]

Responsibility, therefore, was already something that was being handed round quickly, stuck on to others, claimed in the general and disclaimed in the particular, even before Iran-contra became public. When the scandal broke, it was quickly laid at the feet of the 'action officers': North, Poindexter and, to a lesser degree, McFarlane. They had followed their own bad policies, counter to Reagan's instructions, and therefore could not remain unpunished. A little later, the special prosecutor was brought in to begin his criminal inquiries. But that could not quite be the end of it. North and Poindexter had another clear charge, a duty to their country: they should tell everyone exactly what they had done, quickly and fully. This was all the more clearly their duty because they were military men, who had a particular personal responsibility to protect the nation and obey the law.[6] Yet both men, called to answer questions before congressional committees in December 1986, chose to keep silent. They pleaded the Fifth Amendment against self-incrimination, not

once but continually; before the Senate Intelligence Committee, in
closed session, North was said to have taken the Fifth 50 times.[7]

This was not unreasonable. The charges these men faced were
criminal, and they were wisely instructed by their lawyers to keep
quiet. But the appearance was appalling. As Representative
Hamilton reminded Poindexter, it was the first time an admiral had
taken the Fifth on such an occasion. In North's case, this was the first
time the public noticed both his chestful of medals, and his silence.
He himself, looking, as Mary McGrory put it, like 'an adolescent
who wanted desperately to explain how he had totalled the family
car',[8] seemed to recognize that he was derelict in the duty expected
of soldiers. He wanted to tell the story terribly, he insisted. (He told
friends that he had been prepared to talk up to the last minute and
had prepared 40 pages of testimony, only to be informed by Sullivan
in the car that he had to keep silent.[9]) As a Marine Corps officer, he
told the House Foreign Affairs Committee, he was sworn to uphold
the Constitution. He had tried to do so 'honourably'. But because
there was talk about crimes, 'counsel has advised me that I should
avail myself of the protections provided by that same Constitution
that I have fought to support and defend.'[10] Poindexter, pipe in
hand, made the same point amiably and undramatically.

The committee members were kind. Some, indeed, were unctuous.
They praised both men for their military service and their patriotism
and their medals. Hamilton called Poindexter 'exceedingly honourable'.[11] Even Michael Barnes of Maryland, led a merry dance by the
NSC whenever he had enquired about the contras, pleaded gently
with Poindexter: 'You served our country so well before. You've
never had a time in your career I'm sure, sir, when it was more
important to serve your country . . . The worst thing that could
happen to you [would be] a very short, probably suspended sentence
somewhere.'[12] Robert Dornan of California made the same point to
North with even more kindness and sentimentality: he reminded him
that his role was to serve and protect and take flak from his
superiors, just as as the uncomplaining Tommies did in Kipling's
day. He then applied Kipling directly to the occasion, substituting
'Ollie' for 'Tommy'.

Oh, it's Ollie this and Ollie that and 'Chuck 'im out, the brute!'
But it's 'Saviour of 'is country' when the guns begin to shoot.[13]

North later tried to add his own bit of soldierly rigour to his Fifth-
taking: 'Men have died face-down in the mud all over the world,' he
told reporters on December 18th, 'defending those individual

rights.'[14] In no way, however, could these acts of apparent self-preservation be made to look either responsible or brave. They were incriminating, perhaps; but they also raised the suspicion that responsibility for the scandal might lie somewhere else, somewhere higher. 'Are they teaching this new morality these days at the Naval Academy?' asked William Safire in the *New York Times*. 'Don't give up the rights? . . . By putting personal interest ahead of the needs of his country, [North] undermines military discipline, embarrasses his country and cripples his President. The man who was willing to lay down his life for his country is unwilling to spend a few months in the brig.' Even more dishonour fell on Poindexter, 'who is of an age and rank to recognize the depth of his disservice in evading accountability.'[15]

Some observers took a different slant. They assumed that, by their silence, North and Poindexter were also protecting the President: they were carrying out a personal duty to the Commander-in-chief, whose interests and the nation's were perhaps not perfectly aligned. This was not how the White House saw it. Through the press spokesman came messages that the President wished all his staff to co-operate with any inquiries:[16] they should agree, in other words, to be the culprits. Nancy Reagan, the President's wife, was pleading too, and on December 19th Vice-President Bush made a direct appeal to them: the country could not wait any longer for them to talk and, 'having taken the oath to serve this country', they should know that this 'may summon them to make a great sacrifice.'[17] Still the two men kept silent. The President's orders overshadowed everything they had done; his actions, as well as theirs, were covered by their silence. Besides, as North insisted, they had not heard the command to talk from Reagan directly.[18] They were waiting for him to ask them personally, as good servants should.

For many weeks, therefore — indeed, until July — North made no attempt to tell the story. The Tower Commission produced its picture of a comatose President and his wild aides, and there was no rebuttal. North merely referred ill-equipped reporters to verses of resigned lamentation from the Psalms ('O Lord my God, in thee do I take refuge; save me from all my pursuers, and deliver me.')[19] The few other remarks he tossed to them, out of the windows of his car on raw dark mornings, were often defiant statements of his love for the President; but by his silence he also increasingly implied that responsibility lay with Reagan, and not just with his servants.

Reagan, however, was a man possessed of great charm, guile and good stage-management. Because the authorizations had been so vague, and the President's memory of them so hazy, no allegations of misconduct ever stuck to him convincingly. During the public hearings he went blithely about his business, shrugging and deflecting questions. Lance Morrow, in *Time*, was struck by one particularly cinematic moment: a split-screen image during North's testimony that showed, on one side, Reagan waving and smiling from the door of the presidential aircraft while, on the other, his servant sat under interrogation. One was escaping; one was caught. It was a strange effect, Morrow wrote: 'a kind of moral vanishing'.[20] Some weeks before, Reagan had suddenly admitted that the contra-support plan was 'my idea to begin with',[21] like a man suddenly claiming with pride the paternity of a child he had set out in the cold. The lapse was so uncharacteristic that it never occurred again.

The criminal indictments brought in March 1988 presented a picture of four men — Poindexter, North, Secord and Hakim — acting deviously for their own profit in their own world, sealed off from President and Cabinet. As North's trial showed (in which he spilled the beans on Reagan's efforts to get money from third countries for the contras), the indictments gave a thoroughly distorted picture; and the good servants, faced with them, did not want to be dutiful any more. They wished to shift the blame to someone else, some superior, some orders, anything. Incessantly, self-protectively, North at his trial pushed the responsibility on to McFarlane and Poindexter; McFarlane, by pleading guilty to four counts in which North had been involved, drew North into the blame with him; Poindexter, having no alternative, placed the blame with Reagan. Reagan was forced to testify at Poindexter's trial, and to produce records for him, to 'prove' (though he did not prove it) that everything had been done under the cloak of his authority.

By the end of the trial, with Poindexter convicted on all five charges and sentenced to six months in jail, it was clear that the orgy of finger-pointing had made little difference to where the public assigned the blame for the scandal. It lay with 'Ollie' and the admiral. The administrations of Reagan and Bush, respectively, got what they had hoped for. They had a serious, high-ranking, self-effacing culprit and a theatrical-comical fall guy who continued to travel round the country lecturing on right-wing Godly living; a fall guy who, whether spared criminality or not, would carry the scandal into eternity and, at the same time, make it mediocre. This was, after all, only a middle-ranking aide, an apparatchik; what lasting significance could his foolishness possibly have?

This messy outcome, in which all the players eventually betrayed and informed on each other, was far from what the servants had intended. McFarlane, North and Poindexter had all started with rather noble, self-sacrificing visions of how they would behave when the operations foundered. Each, in his different way and in different particulars, had been preparing to take the blame on his own shoulders, sparing both the President and probably his co-actors. All, in the end, passed it on.

The part of the fall guy was one that North had long and lovingly prepared for. It was to be the ultimate expression of his service. 'When it all came down,' he would uncomplainingly pack his bags. He would take the blame 'for whomever necessary: for the administration, for the President, for however high up the chain they needed someone to say, "There's the guy that did it, and he's gone"'; he would agree to be 'dropped like a hot rock', even though he was not responsible.[22] Keker, at North's trial, stressed that this was in no sense a noble concept:

> It comes from boxing, and it deals with crooked fights. The fall guy is the guy that agrees to fall over and then the fake winner is the guy that is going to be standing up. It is a fix . . . The fall guy is guilty. The winner is guilty, and the people that pay him are guilty. They are all guilty.[23]

Judge Gesell referred to it as one of the 'misconceptions' of martyrdom with which North enflamed the myth of himself; misconceptions he would neither harden, nor honour, by sending him to jail.[24]

McFarlane and Poindexter did not think much of the idea, either; indeed, they found it embarrassing. McFarlane was not sure he had ever heard scapegoat-talk from North.[25] Poindexter had, but not in so many words. He remembered that from time to time North, in a fit of depression, would say 'I can always be sacrificed';[26] but that, he always told him, was a ridiculous and unnecessary thing to say: 'I've been around Washington long enough to know that that sort of thing is just not possible . . . and there was no way that Ollie should or could accept responsibility for all of our operations in support of the President's policy.'[27]

Poindexter seemed to have an inkling of what Keker meant; that to need a fall guy presumed a crime or an illegality, something that had to be speedily covered up for. North simply did not see it that way. Indeed, he seemed to have no specific idea what he was to be the fall guy for, just as Poindexter did not. 'Political controversy' was Poindexter's vague sum of it.[28] Rob Owen, who heard the scapegoat/fall-guy talk many a time ('and Poindexter knows it, and Casey knows it, and I'm willing to act in that capacity'), was told that the scheme would come into operation 'if things went bad', not if things were bad already.[29] Some technical hitch or exposure would put in jeopardy legitimate forms of service, or the public, as anticipated, would not accept them; and the fall guy would be offered up to keep the President safe.

The spear, when it came, was taken quietly enough. To his friends, North simply shrugged his shoulders; he told Mrs Newington that he would have time to fix his roof at last.[30] The only emotion anyone recalled was that, as he told Earl and Coy of his telephone conversation with Reagan, he was banging his hand on the bannister of the spiral staircase that ran between their offices.[31] Yet there had been, it seems, at least a few hours of thought, in which North had weighed up the various duties in his mind. He did so alone in his office a day and a half before he was fired. The memorandum detailing the diversion to the contras had been found in his files, and he had been questioned about it by the Attorney General. It was clear that the game was up.

No-one had come back to me for further questions. I was told that [Meese] had also talked to the President by this point, and it was very clear to me that this was part of pointing the finger at Ollie North and saying he was the only one who knew what was going on, and which I must say was the way it was supposed to be.[32]

He started to gather up documents that he thought would show 'that I had had the authority to do what I had done'[33], and deleted, or made an attempt to delete, the PROF notes in his computer. Other documents he shredded, although much of that had been done already. He was there until 4.50 or so in the morning, at one point setting off the alarm. Much of that time, he said later, was just spent sitting thinking.[34] Two days later, on the Tuesday, just after he had heard from Meese on television that he had been fired and was under criminal investigation, he wrote down in his notebooks a list of his priorities.

1. MY COUNTRY/
2. Presidency
3. Family
4. ~~Others who~~ Hostages
5. ~~Self~~ Others who helped
6. [35]

According to Ledeen and McFarlane, who heard it from North, that list was also the basis of a little speech North gave when he was summoned to see the President, Meese and Don Regan at ten o'clock in the morning on the day he was fired. (None of the Cabinet officers involved was asked about this meeting, and none volunteered knowing anything; committee sources said it had never happened.) 'He had given them a list of his priorities,' said Ledeen, 'in which he thought the most important things were the country, the President, the democratic resistance, the hostages [Ledeen was unsure of the order] '. . . and that he was way down near the bottom of that list, and he would do whatever was necessary.'[36] And what was first? 'My Country.'

Cicero had said that country should be *carissima*, 'the dearest thing in the world'; but he had meant *res publica*, the political state, and North's formulation was closer to *patria*: apolitical, sentimental. To a disinterested observer, it might have suggested that North wanted to help his country more than his President, and tell what he had done. When the soft 'My Country' was set against 'Presidency' — impersonal and institutional — the President appeared to be the loser. Yet for North, the almost mystical America seemed closely bound up with the man who, in person, had 'made America strong again', made it 'stand tall', called it 'the shining city on a hill'. Reagan may have been as much in 'My Country' as he was in 'Presidency': indeed, the oblique sign in the notes suggests that North may have meant to give them equal billing, and then changed his mind.

The core of the dilemma therefore lay, as it had lain before, in the top two items on North''s list. He could do his duty to the country (whose good, an abstraction, was to be found with some exercise of principle and conscience), or he could protect his leader. If Reagan was presumed to be enormously good for America, as North thought he was, then maybe no exercise of conscience was needed. On the other hand, was a man still bound by the same ties of loyalty once his superior had demonstrated that he wished to disown him?

When the President telephoned him on the evening of his firing, he did not say much. (The note of the call was deeply overwritten and underlined in North's notebook, exceptional as it was.) On the one hand, Reagan called North a great American;[37] on the other he said, referring North presumed to the diversion, 'I just didn't know.'[38] Bob Earl thought he remembered North telling him that Reagan had said 'It's important that I not know.'[39] Coy, the other assistant, thought it unlikely, that it sounded 'too much like a Watergate-James Bond kind of thing';[40] North stuck to his version.[41] But whatever the form of words, the message from leader to subordinate was essentially the same: he could not claim to be acting, in that respect at least, according to presidential orders. And he must not have the least idea of claiming such a thing; the implicit instruction, the last in the long line of implicit instructions and desires, was to keep the president protected. Such was the obvious duty of great Americans.

So the blame was apportioned; but by no means all of it was accepted. After his telephone conversation with Reagan, North listed the names of three men who could help him: an organizer for his defence fund, a lobbyist, and a criminal lawyer. Entries for the same day included vigorous attempts to make Israel share in the blame, which were as rigorously rebuffed; they also included the advice, transmitted from Poindexter, to 'put it off on Gorbanifar [sic]'.[42] At the hearings, North tried to explain what had happened. He was still proud of what he had done, he said, still prepared to be the fall guy, but he would not be branded a criminal. As he and Poindexter saw it, their responsibility lay in taking a general and nebulous blame for matters that were still not fully exposed or understood; they would not be linked to particular felonies. 'I am here to tell it all, pleasant and unpleasant,' he told Nields, 'and I am here to accept responsibility for that which I did. I will not accept reponsibility for that which I did not do.' Not even Liman could dislodge him from the general to the particular.

> Q. But Oliver North, I hear you saying that if you weren't on the order for the appointment of an independent counsel, if there was agreement that there was no criminal liability here, people would expect you to come before Congress and say, 'I did it. It's not their fault —'
> A. I did do —
> Q.'I was that loose cannon.'
> A. I did do it. I am not . . . at all ashamed of any of the things that I did. I was given a mission and I tried to carry it out.
> Q. But part of that mission was to shield the others who were giving you the orders.
> A. That is the part of any subordinate.[43]

This was still the fall-guy talking, but there was a change in the air. The scapegoat had revealed himself as a scapegoat, and responsibility was shifted: sharply onwards and upwards.

Poindexter's view of the subject seemed straightforward. He too accepted responsibility — at the crunch — more for the general mess than for the particular act. It was one of the burdens of his rank. When Representative Foley asked him whether his refusal to micromanage his subordinates in fact endowed them with responsibility for their actions, Poindexter was categorical: 'I give them authority. I maintain the responsibility, Mr Foley.'[44]

To Paul Thompson, his aide, chatting to him as he sat 'very tired' in his office on the afternoon of the day he resigned, it seemed clear that the admiral 'had for himself as the naval officer and as the commanding officer of the ship . . . a standard of what we call inescapable responsibility in the Navy, which means you are inescapably responsible for what any member of your staff does.' This sort of block responsibility, however, rose far above specific culpability: Thompson admitted he could not possibly tell, from anything Poindexter said, whether he knew all about the diversion or had merely an inkling of it, like a curious smell in a room.[45]

Poindexter, having no truck with the term 'fall guy', had made a cool and calm decision: 'if the diversion became public, I would have to leave. Simple as that.'[46] The seed of that decision was contained in his action in January or February 1986, when he approved the diversion of funds and apparently resolved that he would not tell the President. In that sense, he made the matter his general responsibility, and did so almost instantly.[47] Poindexter never explained why he did not think it over longer, even merely for an afternoon. He implied that it was unnecessary. It was consistent with policy, he had the authority:

But because it was controversial, and I obviously knew that it would cause a ruckus if it were exposed, I decided to insulate the President from the decision . . . One of my responsibilities was to protect the President.

He added a wistful coda: 'I recognize that it would be a lot easier on me now if I had told him . . . It would now be, you know, his responsibility rather than mine.'[48]

This sort of responsibility protected those above; it was not for those below. Poindexter intended to keep the President out of the diversion; he also hoped, at first, to keep himself at a decent distance from it. When Meese dropped in to his office on November 24th, beginning 'I assume you are aware of the memo we found in Ollie's files,' Poindexter said he was, generally; 'and I told him that I was prepared to resign and that I trusted him to recommend to me the timing of my resignation, and that was . . . essentially the end of the conversation.'[49] On the morning of November 25th, over his neat breakfast tray, he had audience with Don Regan, the man whose desk sported the sign 'The buck doesn't even pause here'.[50] Regan described the occasion.

I went in and . . . said, you know, 'What's going on, John?
What the heck happened here?'

And he was very careful and deliberate. John is a deliberate
man. He adjusted his glasses. He dabbed at his mouth with his
napkin, put it down. He said, 'Well . . . I guess I should have
looked into it more, but I didn't.'

He said, 'I knew that Ollie was up to something.' But he said
'I didn't know what.' And he said, 'I just didn't look into it.'

I said to him, 'Why not? What the hell, you are a vice
admiral. What's going on?' And he said . . . 'Well, that damn
Tip O'Neill . . . the way he's jerking the contras around . . . I
was just so disgusted . . . I didn't want to know what he was
doing.'

Q. You didn't have any discussion with Admiral Poindexter
about any authorization he might have received in connection
with this matter?

A. No . . . I said, 'Well, John, I think when you go in to see the
President at 9.30 you better make sure you have your
resignation with you.'

Q. And what did he say?

A. He said, 'I've been thinking of that . . . I will.'[51]


No-one appeared to question this chain of events. Poindexter
knew about the diversion, and so he would have to go. It was as
natural as breathing. Yet Regan, though he felt 'horror, horror,
sheer horror',[52] was not sure whether or not the diversion was
illegal; even Meese, the Attorney General, did not know; and, as
Reagan put it later, it was certainly not 'contrary to policy'.[53]
Indeed, it might even have been authorized by the President, had
Meese or Regan thought to ask; which they did not. Poindexter
himself felt he had said enough; not being asked about his approval,
he did not care to volunteer it, either to Meese or, later, to Reagan.
'Instinct thought it was better not to at the time,' he explained later;
'I offered to resign, and it wasn't clear whether I would or wouldn't
at that point, and I just decided to be cautious.'[54]

It was also simply easier to pass the blame downwards, especially
on to someone who had been so foolishly eager to assume it; and so,
even after he had resigned, Poindexter continued to propagate the
story he had given to Regan.[55] At his trial, Ellen Glasser of the FBI
revealed that she had gone to talk to Poindexter at his house in
Rockville on November 28th; they had chatted in the living room for
about 15 minutes. When Glasser asked him about the diversion, he
said he had no direct knowledge of that; North was 'committed to

the contra programme and . . . was up to something.' He could have
stopped him, but North was in some respects a free agent: asked if
there were others among the NSC staff raising funds for the contras,
Poindexter replied that North 'could do something like this on his
own.'[56]

By the hearings, eight months later, Poindexter's story had
changed. He was now prepared to take the diversion on himself; by
doing that, he would at least cut off inquiries, and they would go no
further up the chain of command. 'On this whole issue, you know,'
he said, referring to the diversion, in a voice notably calm and
colourless — 'the buck stops here with me.'[57] That remark was
probably the most famous of the affair, the dam that stopped the
flood; one man had finally taken the blame for the most notorious,
though hardly the largest, feature of the scandal, and by popular
extension for the whole extraordinary shebang.

The full consequences of the burden he had shouldered became
obvious only much later, when he was convicted on five counts of
other instances of buck-stopping: preventing Congress, by lying to
members in November 1986, from taking its enquiries to the man
above him. He stood grey-faced as the verdicts were read, rocking
slightly to and fro. He had tried by that stage to pass the buck again,
this time upwards, claiming Reagan's authority for everything
except the diversion; but as a dozen editorial writers pointed out
afterwards, the buck did indeed stop with him, in all likelihood the
highest official to be tried. It was Poindexter, the man who thought
it was foolish to talk about fall guys, who was crowned as 'the
ultimate fall guy' in the pages of *Time* magazine.[58]

What no lawyer could discover, hard as Liman tried, was
precisely why he had decided that the buck stopped there, and had
not told the President. Why had this particular thing seemed such a
'deep, dark secret', in North's phrase, that Poindexter had to take
the responsibility for it entirely upon himself? He himself described it
as 'a very good idea', and, besides, a mere 'implementation' of the
broad policy to get money for the contras from third countries.[59] Not
to tell the President was not only an aberration from his usual
practice but, as Regan put it, 'almost inconceivable' in a man who
was an admiral.[60]

Besides, as Senator Rudman reminded him, the President could
not be so mollycoddled that he lost all sense of his own charges:
'Presidents ought to be allowed to create their own disasters.
Nobody else ought to do it for them.'[61] This was not quite how
Reagan himself saw it. Asked during his testimony whether
Poindexter should have told him of the diversion he replied,
instinctively, 'Yes'; then, turning and winking at Poindexter, he

added 'Unless maybe he thought he was protecting me from something.'[62]

So Poindexter took the responsibility, and the buck stopped with him. Even at the moment he left office, however, his burden was as nebulous as ever. When he went into the Oval Office at 9.30 on November 25th to resign, nothing was said to him about the cause or what he had done. He himself said he was aware (no more) of the diversion. Reagan simply said it was a shame that 'a man with your great naval record should come to this end'; his resignation 'was in the best traditions of the Navy, of the captain accepting responsibility.' The other cabinet members shook his hand and were pleasant. Nobody chastised him.[63] It took about five minutes, and a stray observer in the Oval Office would have known no more about the roots of the scandal after the meeting than he had known before.

Poindexter had not been blamed, and he had taken no blame. To do so would have implied that something wrong had happened, something he should have been ashamed of. But nobody ever said, in so many words, that anything was wrong; and Poindexter himself seemed to feel no compunction for the diversion, beyond the fact that it had been exposed. Like North, he was happy at the hearings to take the rap for actions he was rather proud of; and in the case of the diversion he seemed eventually to be proud not only of the scheme itself, which was ingenious and ironic, but of his own fortitude in risking it, and his daring. If people chose to blame him, it was up to them. It made no difference to his own feelings. Even at his trial he had nothing to say in his own defence; all he offered was a wan and unrepentant smile.

Thus North and Poindexter managed, even at the hearings — even, to some degree, at their trials — to see the operations in a golden light and to take responsibility, insofar as they took it, with some pride. McFarlane did not think that way at all. He felt his responsibility acutely, and he also knew he had failed. When Poindexter and North chose to plead the Fifth Amendment, McFarlane — who seemed then, to be sure, in less imminent danger of criminal prosecution — agreed to talk to congressional investigators, and went on talking. In this, observers agreed, he did his duty, even though his testimonies and depositions and interviews were often internally at odds with each other. McFarlane, because he talked, and because in February 1987 he made an apparent attempt to kill himself with Valium tablets, was widely given credit for his guilt and his conscience. Observing him at the hearings, the man from *Time* was particularly impressed.

He knew he had done wrong, he said. He was sorry. He deserved to be punished. How odd! This kind of guilt, this assuming of moral responsibility for one's actions has all but vanished from public discourse. It is almost as if the closest glimpse the nation got of honor last week came from seeing it in a mirror: a man had acted with dishonor, saw it for what it was and came forth to bear witness that there is still a difference between right and wrong.

If some of the others . . . were to show a similar ability to understand their moral accountability for their actions, perhaps an air of redemption would ensue.[64]

By the end of November 1985, when McFarlane resigned, burned out, from the NSC, he was already full of regrets and misgivings about the Iran operation. He subsequently tried to 'turn it off' after the trip to London in December on which he encountered Ghorbanifar: 'I have a bad feeling about this whole operation,' he confided to Ledeen.[65] But he lacked influence in the councils of state; the operation went on, and he even allowed himself, out of his sense of duty, to get pulled back into it again after he had left the government. About the contras, too, he had his doubts, but did not dare express them. He realized, then — though perhaps more with hindsight than was evident in his PROF notes at the time — that both operations were going bad; but by the time he realized it, the responsibility was out of his hands.

McFarlane often remarked to interviewers later that he wished he had stayed at the NSC. Had he stayed, perhaps the twin disasters would have been averted. This was wishful thinking on a grand scale, for by the time McFarlane left the NSC he was too far locked in with North, with the policies and with his soldierly obligation to the President to do anything but carry on. Most of McFarlane's suggestions to Poindexter afterwards were not to do with altering policies or sounding diplomatic alarms; they were attempts to inject a little more caution by rescuing North, and these too failed.

Indeed, if McFarlane's commitment to the operations had not been so dutiful, it is doubtful whether he would have taken their collapse so badly. He saw the whole affair as a shambles and a disgrace for which he was to blame. His blame, to be sure, was unspecific. There was no one point of detail — even the writing of deceptive letters to Congress, the offence with which he was eventually charged and to which he pleaded guilty — that he would admit as a misdeed perpetrated mainly by himself. In McFarlane's world, the wildly skating North was the man in charge of details; he would cover for him, grimly, as usual.

Yet McFarlane, unlike Poindexter, did not claim to have done anything practical and wise; and unlike North, he took little refuge behind his superiors. On the contrary, he allowed them to take refuge behind him and his unspecific, enormous culpability: his 'inescapably responsible, for my ship and all aboard approach', as Thompson called it, once again.[66] Only once did he try to hive off a portion of the blame on Reagan for the policy of arms-for-hostages, and that was an afterthought. 'I think you know that I feel like I am responsible,' he said he told Meese on November 21st;

> and I am willing to take all of this on my shoulders that is feasible, but I want you to know that the President was foursquare behind this from the very beginning.
>
> There was never a moment's hesitation. He approved this the first time I pitched it to him. It was all right with him whatever the Israelis wanted to do.
>
> He said I know that, Bud. I know very well how he feels about the hostages.[67]

So ended McFarlane's first attempt to shift responsibility upstairs. There was a second, at his testimony, when he mentioned that congressmen who passed so slippery a piece of legislation as Boland 'must accept some of the moral responsibility for the failures that follow.'[68] From then on, he assumed it himself. As Congressman Rodino pointed out, as kindly as he could, McFarlane still seemed to be 'really torn', fighting with himself; he was still not saying it all nor listing what things, specifically, he had done. Back came the all-embracing admission.

> I believe because I was in charge if things happened that were illegal, whether or not I knew about them, I am responsible. And that isn't just a kind of a brush-off, acceptance of the captain of the ship role.
>
> I intend to mean by that the full meaning of the law and punishment by it . . .
>
> I have testified about my trip to Iran and about the errors that I think governed in each one of these situations, errors that were my fault, and I don't know what else I can tell you to make clear that there is nothing that North did for which I don't feel responsible. And I don't know even today what all that is.[69]

The more perceptive of his congressional questioners realized that this sort of thing was a psychological imperative. McFarlane believed he had let both President and country down and, like his erstwhile subordinates, he made no particular distinction between the two; he had failed in his duty, and his overpowering instinct was to make up for it.

> *Senator Sarbanes*: In all of this, who or what are you trying to shield or protect?
> *A.* Very likely myself, my reputation, my own record of performance.
> *Q.* And only that?
> *Q.* Well, I believe, Senator Sarbanes, that President Reagan's motives and direction to his subordinates throughout this entire enterprise has always been in keeping with the law and national values. I don't think he is at fault here and if anybody is, I am.[70]

Congressman Hamilton later tried to dissuade McFarlane from his impulse to 'shoulder great responsibilities'. He reminded him that as national security advisor he had been the President's representative, and had spoken for him; he had been, in effect, Reagan's mouthpiece, or at least had been seen that way. 'When you wrote to the Congress, we accepted your words and your assurances as those of the President . . . and the responsibility must rest with him as well as with you. You cannot, it seems to me, accept responsibility for mistakes, admirable as that may be, and thereby absolve the President.'[71] McFarlane listened glumly, but his mind was set. Provoked unendurably by another questioner a little earlier, he had burst out: 'I deserve responsibility, and I ought to be prosecuted to the full extent of the law and sent away.'[72]

There was a small coda, which McFarlane also mentioned. On one occasion, when he had said publicly that he had erred and was responsible, Reagan had called him. He said 'he didn't feel that way, that he believed he had done the right thing.'[73] This sunny brushing-off of guilt was evidently lost on his listener.

These three men, therefore, imbued with a sense of duty and severely limited, as they believed, in their ability to question, saw their ultimate responsibility in sharply different ways. McFarlane saw it as a doom and a disgrace that he must take on himself and carry away, like some obliging beast of burden, for the good of the country. Poindexter saw it as a simple, undramatic acknowledgement that he had adopted on Reagan's behalf a policy that was risky, and he admitted it as if he still did not know what the fuss was

all about. North, who should have embraced the martyr's crown —
having set himself up for it for so long — in the end went only part-
way. Cartoons of the hearings showed him bravely saluting while
bevies of spears, intended for his chest, ricocheted instead into
McFarlane and Poindexter.

In one particular sense, all three men took a similar line. All
protected 'the old man' until it hurt too much. Most astonishingly,
Congress too adopted this protective mode. Given the chance to go
after Reagan at the hearings, the committees preferred not to. He
was too old. Possibly he had not understood what was happening.
Negligence was not the same as malfeasance. As Seymour Hersh
pointed out in the *New York Times Magazine* as late as April 1990,
Congress had lacked the stomach to bring down another president.
'If you are going to attack the King,' said Hamilton, 'you've got to
kill the King'; but perhaps this time the cold thrust would weaken
America too much, spill too many guts. Liman remarked in a speech
in March 1988 that the decision of North and Poindexter, 'for
whatever reason' not to inculpate Reagan in the diversion was
'morally right'.[74] *Realpolitik* dictated, together with a necessary
deference towards the head of state; and whatever other kinds of
protection Congress disapproved of, with this one it gratefully
concurred, rushing towards it like a mouse that is shown the way out
of a maze.

McFarlane thought he remembered that at least twice, in August
and December 1985, Reagan had said he was 'willing to take the
heat' for making the decision to try and save the hostages; but when
the moment came his servants had no intention of holding his feet to
the fire.[75] Nor did Reagan come close to putting them there. Of the
three formulations he used to apologize to the public for the affair,
all were passive. 'Mistakes were made', 'serious mistakes were
made', 'it was a mistake', said he,[76] always with an air slightly
puzzled and hurt, as if these self-generating mistakes had risen up
and bitten him; as if he had truly never approved, never encouraged,
and never known.

Hakim could not fathom the awful silence that followed Meese's
press conference on November 25th, when the diversion was made
public. Since he thought he had been working on behalf of the
President — going to the White House, taking part in various
meetings, getting his false passport — it seemed to him that the
President should say something finally to his agents, if only, 'Hey,
fellows, you're on your own.'[77] He asked Secord to contact Reagan.
Secord said he had tried and failed; Poindexter himself had rebuffed
him. To his own surprise and horror, a 'wall' had already been built
round the ultimate source of authority.[78]

Instinctive as it may have been, this was a reversal of the normal flow of responsibility and accountability in the military. There, officers were pledged to take care of their men. Indeed, this had been McFarlane's natural instinct in August 1985, when Congress had started to ask questions about North and McFarlane had fielded them himself. North was not a rogue elephant, McFarlane told the *Washington Post* in those days, but 'like a son of mine',[79] a staffer for whom he would willingly go and do something 'not terribly uplifting', such as giving false assurances to Congress.[80] The same instinct was Poindexter's to a degree, as he explained when Thompson asked him why he had never told him about the diversion: 'I intentionally kept you out of this.'[81] And it was North's, who — for all his carelessness on his own account — was careful to keep Owen in one operational compartment only. 'Now aren't you glad you didn't know about Iran?' North asked him at some point after the denouement. Owen replied, with feeling, 'Yes, sir.' [82]

To care more for the lives of subordinates than for one's own was the mark of a good soldier, one committed to his duty. North told Liman that his worst days, far from being those at the end of November 1986, were 'when young Marines died'.[83] The ties of obligation that bound some of the players had to do with lives saved on the battlefield. North had saved William Haskell, who later went on to organize the secret Costa Rican airstrip and who testified for him at his trial;[84] George Cave said he had heard that Secord had saved North, although the when and the how were vague.[85] Instinctively, commanders in battle knew themselves responsible for the weak and the wounded; it was unthinkable that men should be left on the field. In politics, there was seldom such compulsion.

North and Poindexter were popularly pictured in the early days of the scandal as picked bones thrown to the lions or as bodies in the sea. The notion of men thrown over the side was reminiscent of the vision Alexander Haig had seen, writing after his retirement as Reagan's first secretary of state: 'To me, the White House was as mysterious as a ghost ship; you heard the creak of the rigging and the groan of the timbers, and sometimes even glimpsed the crew on deck. But which of the crew had the helm? . . . It was impossible to tell.'[86] And as Reagan shook Poindexter's hand on November 25th, reminding him of the grand tradition of captains going down with the ship, it would have been a brave man who would have inquired who the captain really was.

# PART IV

# What's Right and What's Legal

Creon: And you made free to overstep my law?
Antigone: Because it was not Zeus who ordered it.

Sophocles, *Antigone*, 1. 449

The orders, the lack of orders and the sharing-out of blame became crucial for one reason: the chief players were charged with breaking the law. But which laws, and how? This chapter examines the legal side of Iran-contra: what the players thought about the law in general, how they invoked it, checked it or feared it, and where they thought the edges were; the purview of the law, and whether notions of right and wrong made the law redundant; and lastly the frenzied days of the Attorney General's 'fact-finding mission' in November 1986, an investigation almost as vague about the law as the players themselves.

# Chapter 13

# On the Edge of the Law

THE sentences eventually passed down on the players spoke volumes about the legal ambiguities of the Iran-Contra affair. In March 1989, McFarlane was sentenced to 200 hours of community service and a fine of $200,000 on four counts of lying to Congress. In July 1989, North was sentenced to 1,200 hours of community service and a fine of $150,000 for three felonies: destroying and altering government documents, assisting in the preparation of false chronologies and accepting an illegal gratuity, a security fence at his house. The first conviction was quashed a year later, and the others set aside. In June 1990 Poindexter, judged guilty on all five counts against him, was sentenced to six months in prison.

The cases were bedevilled by three factors, two of them technical. First, much of the evidence needed by both prosecution and defence was proclaimed to be secret, and was judged to have to stay that way. Second, the chief players had been given immunity against the use in court of anything they had said at the public hearings; in effect, the hearings virtually scuppered the trials. The third bedevillment was of a different nature. Outrageous as it seemed, anti-democratic, anti-constitutional and mocking of statutes, Iran-contra was essentially a political scandal. Attempts to make it criminal were not completely hopeless, but the pickings were slim.

The Iran-contra affair had burst on the world as a foreign

policy catastrophe that also, in some indefinable way, smelled bad; something that lawyers should look into as a way to keep the public quiet. The Criminal Division was brought into Meese's inquiry relatively late, and then more out of panic than conviction; certainly North and Poindexter were given time to shred or delete most of what they thought embarrassing. Whether they, or others, also thought it incriminating is a different question. The laws involved in both operations were vague; indeed, some questioned whether laws were flouted at all, or simply exploited to the extent their loopholes allowed. If the latter were true, it could also be argued — with the mirror-thinking characteristic of the whole affair — that the laws had been scrupulously observed even in their violation. You cannot see the size of loopholes if you do not also see, and acknowledge, the law.

Resupply of the contras appeared to run counter to the Boland Amendment, a piece of congressional legislation (technically an addendum to the budget) that assumed, chameleon-like, five different forms between 1982 and 1986. The Iran operation appeared to run counter to the statutory provision that the President should inform the congressional intelligence committees 'in a timely fashion' of covert operations. The true 'crime', which was more in the nature of a general offence, was to scorn the intent of Congress and to demonstrate contempt for what might have been helpful congressional advice; the true felony, of which Poindexter in particular was convicted, was to mislead congressmen in writing and to their faces, an offence as common in Washington as the lobbyist's lunch. Criminal penalties were seldom exacted for that, and none attached either to squeezing round Boland or to rushing out 'mini-Findings' to justify in retrospect arms transfers that had never been reported to Congress. But there was, as Representative Hamilton pointed out, a constitutional requirement that the laws should be faithfully executed;[1] and the unspoken penalty was that the administration had enough rope to hang itself, as it fairly soon did.

The laws being so broad and vague, the players sometimes gave the air of being debonair about them; but there was an edge of anxiety. Owen said North used to joke about who would go to jail first; Owen and a colleague, Jonathan Miller, used to rag each other that they ought to bone up on their chess, so that they could play between the bars.[2] Secord thought North might well end up in prison,[3] and various colleagues kept their distance from him, so they said, for just that reason. 'I don't know what he is doing but it is probably illegal and he is going to jail,' said a CIA man one day, standing well back.[4] One colleague said he saw North pull a paper from his desk, wave it in the air and exclaim: 'This is the law I'm violating, and I could go to jail,'[5]

This, North said, was hogwash.[6] The players did not usually claim, then or later, to be breaking the law; on the contrary, they claimed to be observing it to the letter. At the same time, the law in their eyes was so damaging that to transgress it, in the end, would probably be honourable and right. Channell remembered Bunker Hunt asking North whether, 'if this policy goes down the drain', he was prepared to go to jail for his contra activities, whether he was ready to lie to Congress. 'Oh, yes,' said North to both possibilities, and Hunt chuckled.[7] Convinced that what they were doing was right, the wrath of the law was a detail. According to one story, even Reagan said he was prepared to 'go to Leavenworth' (a maximum-security federal jail) to get the hostages out; he added, looking round with a twinkle at his cabinet, 'But visiting days are Thursdays.'[8]

A line in law, as Justice Wendell Holmes remarked, was always drawn with the understanding that people would go right up to it. Indeed McFarlane implied that if men wanted to do any good in public service, they would have to go so far. 'We want people to come into this government and feel as if they do what they believe is the right thing to do,' he told the hearings, passion again carrying away his syntax; 'they're not going to be scandalized; pretty close to the edge.'[9]

The players in Iran-contra, high and low, had a keen awareness of edges and lines in the abstract, as opposed to their fuzziness over laws in the concrete. 'I think everyone knew we were walking a very fine line,' Owen said.[10] 'I thought Ollie was walking a tight line,' said Channell, 'but I was sure he knew exactly what he was doing.'[11] Nobody quite thought North had crossed over that line, but many pictured him teetering between probity and catastrophe. 'He would say he was always on the edge', Calero said, 'walking a tightrope, or how would I put it — that he was conscious of a law and that he was trying to —

Q. Walk right up to the edge?
A. Yeah.[12]

According to Poindexter the President took risks too, and drew lines. He drew, in fact, what became the baseline of the Iran operation, the very one along which North, McFarlane and Poindexter dipped and swayed: that between giving arms to the hostage-holders, Hizbollah, and giving them to Iran. 'That's a fine line,' admitted Poindexter (a bit too fine for North, for one, and the admiral thought he had trouble with it),[13] 'but he was drawing it.'

*Q*. He also . . . drew a line, didn't he, between selling arms directly to Iran and letting Israel sell them?
*A*. Yes, he did . . . Later we had to fall off of that.[14]

Naturally, the players had a vested interest in claiming that their knowledge of the law was slight; but even allowing for that, a hopeful ignorance permeated both operations. It was assumed that somebody somewhere had checked the legalities, although the players themselves seldom had. As far as the contras went, said Don Regan, he was no lawyer, and he had never thought to investigate whether what the administration was doing was above board or not; 'I left that up to the NSC.'[15] Channell was sure that at the end of the financial year he could take his annual report — weapons lists, tax deductions and all — to a lawyer 'and be sure everything was legal and assure our contributors.' He didn't lose a minute's sleep over it, he said. After all, 'This was the White House. And when we got our report ready . . . all the legal underpinning would be there. It never once occurred to me that it would not be.'[16] Nor did it occur to the President himself: 'I never challenged or questioned what I was told . . . because, not being a lawyer myself, but being surrounded by a number of them in government, I figured that I was hearing the truth when they told me that something could be done and still be exempt.'[17]

To any contra-helper who worried about the law — and most did — North could offer serene assurances. They were not breaking the law; it had all been checked with lawyers. (He had checked it with a lawyer friend, who had asked him one question; to the question he had replied, 'I have not solicited a dime.') 'You're sure all this is legal?' asked Gaston Sigur, the State Department's East Asia hand, as he rather uneasily left a lunch with a Taiwanese official at which he and North had discussed getting arms for the contras. 'Oh absolutely, absolutely,' North replied; 'I wouldn't do anything that wasn't legal.'[18] McFarlane said he usually got 'a pre-emptive explanation' on North's memos — just in case he should suspect otherwise — that what he was doing or proposing was within the law.[19] At the State Department, Abrams too — tiptoeing round the contra operation, knowing 'nothing about nothing', as Congressman Brooks put it[20] — heard about North's lawyers. The thought of them gave him some relief, reinforcing his opinion that nothing wrong was going on anyway, and removing the need to ask questions he did not really want answered. As he himself put it, most succinctly: 'There are things I did not want to know as long as they were legal.'[21]

North himself seems to have relied on one source for his notions of legality: the thoughts of William Casey. Casey, after all, was 'a very,

very, very, very smart New York lawyer' as Liman, another of the breed, encouraged North to admit at the hearings;[22] and whenever he acted as Casey had advised him, 'then it was clearly my understanding that what I was doing was legal.' [23]

In particular, North thought Casey was delighted with the idea of the diversion of funds to the contras.[24] But did that mean it was legal? When Clair George, the CIA operations director, was asked that question, he said at once: 'That is illegal.' Then he corrected himself: 'It is not illegal. It's against the rules of the plans.'[25] Whatever that meant, North seems originally to have presented the scheme to Poindexter as one that was notably legal, as opposed perhaps to other plans that buzzed in his head. 'Admiral,' Poindexter remembered him saying, 'I think I have found a way that we can legally provide some funds to the Democratic Resistance.' Since North was not a lawyer, Poindexter said he took that 'legally' in 'the layman's sense', putting no weight on it, but he was fairly sure that North had said it.[26] It was one of North's preoccupations to find some legal way to channel third-country money to the contras; at one point he had even suggested a finding, but Poindexter wanted no more of those. Here was an alternative, a beguiling sting on the Ayatollah, one only the CIA 'shoe salesmen', as Secord called them, would pour cold water over. 'Against the rules of the plans.'

Perhaps Casey appeared, to North, to have sanctioned the diversion; but the director, shrewd as he was, and aware — as all his chief agents were aware — of the amateurishness and eagerness of North, evidently came to think that the law might have been stepped over. In the summer of 1986 he kept urging North to get a lawyer,[27] partly because the Iranian arms-sales creditors were restless, but also because congressmen were getting curious about the contras. The smart New York lawyer, having convinced and inspired North, seemed in the end to acknowledge that his protégé had gone over the edge before he had been able to stop him.

This innocence about the law — part genuine, part manufactured — was reinforced by another idea: that if the President wanted something done, it was lawful, and legal worries might be academic anyway. As North recorded in his notebooks about the contentious first arms shipment in August 1985, 'RR said OF Course in July — Intent of Pres is important — RR said he would support — 'Mental Finding'.[28] If the President's mere unspoken approval could legalize an action, it followed that men who acted on his assumed approval could not be caught up in illegality, let alone crimes. Richard Beckler, Poindexter's lawyer, put it most forcefully at Poindexter's trial, contending that his client 'did act within the law because he followed the orders of his president, his commander-in-chief.'[29] Moreover, according to Beckler, the President had 'a lawful right and an obligation' to do such things as petition members of the Saudi royal house for money for the contras; and the obligation extended to his servants.[30]

Stanley Sporkin, the CIA general counsel who worked to put Reagan's fiat for the Iran operation retroactively and prospectively into law, was quite categorical. 'You can't straitjacket the President ... If the President calls someone in and says, we have to move today, go out and do it, I think that somebody can be able to go out and do it and then later on you do the paperwork . . .'

*Q.* How long do you think the paperwork should take?
*A.* It shouldn't take long.[31]

Under this interpretation, 'congressional supremacists' (as that self-styled monarchist, Representative Hyde, called them), were powerless to restrict the President. If he wanted to put pressure on his allies to help out with policies too controversial for Americans to agree on, he had every right to do so. If the Findings that allowed the actions he wished to take were not yet drafted, they could be drawn up afterwards; as McFarlane said Meese told him, reinforcing North's notes, 'the President's decision, even though not written, is no less official.'[32]

Although Congress objected heartily to these royalist assumptions, no laws could be invoked against them. What could be invoked, in a frail way, was the idea of courteous consultation. But McFarlane was doubtful even about that: the President was unfortunately forced to behave 'by a rulebook Americans and congressmen and women dictate, which is not adequate to compete with the Soviet Union'; he was 'a product of an electorate that is terribly unrealistic about how he ought to do business'.[33] It might be an idea, he supposed, to put limits on the authority of the NSC staff, 'but I do not think they should extend to an absolute prohibition on the President's being able to use his national security advisor in rare and unusual circumstances that he thought justified.'[34]

Even if crimes somehow resulted from these missions and commissions, the comforting argument ran on, the President would pardon his servants. The law, therefore, could not touch them. They were sure of immunity, or almost sure; it was a twinkle in the President's eye. As Shakespeare's Henry V was told by the good soldier Bates on the field of Agincourt, the rightness or wrongness of the king's course was not to be questioned: 'For we know enough if we know we are the King's subjects. If his cause be wrong, our obedience to the King wipes the crime of it out of us.'[35]

North used to joke with Secord that there was a presidential pardon waiting for him, if the facts came out. Secord tossed that aside: 'I laughed at him and said that's ridiculous. What are you talking about? We have discussed repeatedly no laws are being broken. We are doing everything we can to live within the law';[36] but as quickly as December 1986, North's lawyer was round at the White House applying for one.[37] By that stage, however, pardons were already being quietly ruled out. To pardon the aides would imply that the President was sympathetic, or indulgent, or heaven forbid — involved. To pardon implied, as Secord had realized, that a crime had been committed, and the administration was by no means happy to come to that conclusion yet. To pardon also confirmed, by scuppering the exhaustive and gargantuan legal processes already underway, that the President did not respect the law. Meese remembered 'some jocular conversations about pardons', no more.[38] At Thanksgiving 1987, a year later, Reagan turned to the Presidential turkey, misbehaving in front of the cameras, and quipped 'I'll pardon *him.*'

Constrained by his advisors from issuing pardons, Reagan still allowed his servants touches of presidential grace. He gave it as his opinion, soon after Poindexter and North were indicted, that they were 'not guilty of any lawbreaking or any crime',[39] a statement *ex cathedra* implying, so some thought, that he would protect them from the law if he could. His protection did not go so far as to appear at North's trial, nor to surrender his diaries to lawyers for North or Poindexter, but it went as far as to keep back crucial documents (and therefore jinx the prosecutions) on grounds of national security; and it showed a sympathetic frame of mind, cheerfully oblivious to law, which might have coloured the assumptions his servants gathered in his company. His testimony in 1990 began with a smile and a wink at Poindexter; he stoutly maintained that neither he nor his aides broke any laws, and affirmed that he had always known his aides as honest. Reminded that the law had found McFarlane dishonest, keeping information from Congress, he said, 'I was not aware of that.'[40] Even the joke he had made about lying when McFarlane was convicted ('I've done that myself'[41]) had slipped easily out of his mind.

The will of the ruler, therefore, had the perfume of legality about it. To raise questions was crass; it was a presumption. This was true both of the covert contra crusade, and of the dealings with Iran. Even those who found the Iran operation 'damned outrageous',[42] as Weinberger did, did not, in the end, raise any fundamental questions about its lawfulness;[43] beyond fiddling with the technicalities of arms transfers, there was apparently nothing to be done on the legal side. Yet doubts remained. Noel Koch, who also saw the Iran operation as 'a ransom with no redeeming virtues',[44] but had no idea if it was legal or not, asked Weinberger one day — just joking — whether there was any legal problem with the operation; could anybody go to jail? Weinberger answered, perhaps not joking: 'Yes.'[45] He did not elaborate, and Koch did not take him seriously; he concluded, in fact, that everything was in order, despite what the Secretary had said. Why, 'if what we were doing was illegal . . . and it had all the attendant dangers of doing something illegal . . . he would have said I'm sorry, I can't be a part of this any more and he would have left . . . You know, he became Secretary, put his hand on a Bible, and swore to uphold the laws of the land, and I assumed that was an ironclad guarantee.'[46]

The same point was made about Shultz, and probably impressed itself with similar force on his staff. He hated the Iran operation instinctively, yet the man who had once threatened to resign over White House flight privileges saw no grounds — legal or moral — for resigning over Iran.[47] No more did Regan, who was for getting out of the Iran operation in December 1985 simply because, like Weinberger, he could see it was going nowhere fast.[48] He remembered discussions that the whole November shipment was wrong (wrong sort of missiles, wrong markings on the box), but he never remembered any debate about whether or not it went over the edge of the law.[49]

By that fractious December meeting the law had to some extent been acknowledged and accommodated anyway, if only in retrospect. A shipment of Hawk missiles had already gone from Israel to Iran on November 25th, shipped by Secord. As we have seen, the NSC had needed a bit of help from the CIA in the shape of a proprietary aircraft; the CIA helped, but then recalled that, unlike the NSC, it needed a legal 'Finding' for a covert operation. John McMahon, Casey's deputy, got wind of the slip-up. When Clair George, the operations director, went into the office the following Monday, he found McMahon in an extraordinary rage, demanding to see all the cable traffic that had passed between the CIA and the NSC and the pilots; having read it, he was back again, 'again quite upset and terribly concerned . . . and his remark, which is burned in my mind, was not only did we send the goddam telegrams, but the goddam airplane went in . . . there will be no more activity in support of this without a Finding.'[50]

McMahon was the one who was worried, George thought; that being so, McMahon should be the one to sort the legalities out. He himself, as an operations man, seemed to have a more flexible view. He was privy to most of the strange schemes that had been attempted to get the hostages out, ransoms, bribes and the rest; he was pretty sure that the law had not been broken, but on the other hand, on hostage matters, 'the law is non-existent, basically.' He would 'bend over as far as the law and good sense would allow', but he could cite no law that would stop him, beyond those triggered by the use of congressional money. What, he was asked, if someone offered to bribe the hostages free for $1m apiece: would that require a Finding? George had no idea, and he was not entirely clear on the question of bribery either.

The right answer is, don't pay cash or anything else for hostages. But gee, whiz, is that hard to live up to when it's your emotional problem and not somebody else's.[51]

Into this world, where little was cut and dried and there seemed to be no clear edges drawn, came a quickly written Finding justifying retroactively November 24th's bit of emergency assistance. It was dated November 26th. The CIA was henceforth to be allowed to help all it liked with 'transport, communications and other necessary support' for a trade of arms for hostages with Iran. Similar actions taken already were 'hereby ratified'. In the interests of national security, Congress was not to know (the words were put in the President's mouth) 'until such time as I may direct otherwise'.[52]

Stanley Sporkin, the CIA's chief counsel and the chief drafter of the Finding, was not too troubled by its strange nature. It was usual, he admitted, for Findings to apply to covert actions that had not started yet, but that was 'in the perfect world'. To ratify past actions was not a bad concept in itself, he thought, unless it was abused. He did not think it had been in this case. On the other hand, if he had known that the Finding would earn him his '15 minutes in the sun', as he told the congressmen with a bitter laugh, he would not have done it; and he did not think it would ever be done again.

Sporkin had been called in as a lawyer, and called in in a hurry. The business was ultra-secret, 'to the point where I almost felt I had to . . . do everything personally', but he was not in a position to refuse; as a house lawyer for the CIA, 'you have to take the good as well as everything else that comes along.' He barely knew what the operation was that he was being asked to legalize. Whether it was technically covert or not, whether it even qualified for a Finding or not, he did not try to discover. He had to go from point A to point B, as he explained it, and he was not the sort of lawyer to sit quibbling about what A might be; he proceeded directly to B, which was to get the operation — whatever it was — authorized by the President on a piece of paper.[53]

Brought to birth in this skimpy fashion, the November Finding was treated almost frivolously. 'The mini-Finding, the retroactive Finding, yesterday's Finding, tomorrow's Finding,' George called it; he remembered its several versions, not all of which he ever saw, and supposed he had not done so because 'they didn't think I was the biggest fan in history of all this stuff.'[54] Poindexter was not a fan of the early 'iterations' either.[55] The attempt of November 26th had actually gone to the President and been signed on December 5th, according to Poindexter; but he himself, feeling 'damned annoyed' that he had been pushed into giving the President so flimsy a thing, later tore it in two 'without thinking about it', crumpled it up and put it in his pocket.[56] It had not been fully staffed, he explained; it had been prepared 'unilaterally by the CIA, by people that really didn't understand what our overall objectives were. They had written it in a very narrow way, frankly too colloquially — can we go off the record?'

Well, they wanted some protection.
*Q.* Use initials.
*A.* CYA [Cover your ass]
*Q.* There you go.[57]

This poor little paper put the CIA on the right side of the law, at least for the future (the retroactive part remained murky); but by January 17th a much broader and grander 'expanded' Finding had been prepared, in which the whole geopolitical strategy was laid out as it should be. This had been prepared, once again, by Sporkin with help from North and Meese, and it included a legal way to get the arms to Iran: instead of going through Israel, using Israel's weapons and replenishing, the CIA could purchase arms from the Defense Department under the Economy Act and transfer them to Iran directly. The operation was thus removed from 'the white world', in Richard Armitage's words; they would 'do it black',[58] with no requirement to report to Congress. 'I felt we were on strong legal ground with what we were doing,' Poindexter said, 'and it was consistent with the President's policy. And I simply didn't want any outside interference.'[59] So Reagan signed it.

The next day, January 18th, the NSC staff and the CIA met, and Poindexter handed George the Finding. It was an unpompous, informal session, everyone standing about as George read it. 'And I said, now, are we all aboard here on refraining from reporting it to

Congress, and it was yes.' George recognized the document at once for what it was, 'a quick fix to release the hostages', despite all attempts at grand wrapping. Afterwards North confirmed it as they chatted alone at the table, discussing 'getting TOWs out of Alabama and putting them on planes and sending them to Israel for delivery to Iran'; and George realized that the whole operation, far-fetched or not, now conformed with the law. Nothing could hold it back. Only Congress, which did not know, could object to it on legal grounds; even then, the President could still legally choose the moment at which to bring Congress in. So off went the CIA man (in this case, the acting chief of the Near-East Division) 'to carry on this support as directed by the President of the United States to the National Security Council.'[60]

Almost all the impetus to get legal cover for the Iran operation had come not from the NSC, but from the CIA. Covert operations by the NSC staff, because these were not part of their statutory duties, were covered by no statutory limits; had the CIA not been enlisted to help with the transfer of Hawks in November, the whole Iran operation might have been carried out without Findings. That was the beauty of the NSC, according to McFarlane, in a famous outburst at the hearings; it could operate without restrictions, in the sort of glorious brave rush the government of Israel could show when its citizens were taken hostage somewhere in the world.[61] 'Gumption', a favourite McFarlane word, was what the Israelis had. They were not afraid to use violence if necessary, bribery if necessary. At least they did something. At least they did not stand still, worrying about letting Congress know. The CIA had to do so; and that was why, in both operations, the CIA officers were the men on the sidelines, the bumblers, the 'fools' and 'assholes' as North privately called them.[62] No chance of bursting in on a hijacked aircraft as the Israelis had done at Entebbe, for the agency could not even charter an aircraft in less than two days.[63] It was stultifyingly careful, and all its tracks were marked out with pieces of paper.

As it was, Clair George thought the NSC staff deliberately tried to keep the CIA out of most of the Iran operation, and did so to avoid entanglements with the law. They understood, he thought, that the CIA had to be limited to 'logistical and interpretative' roles; that its members could do little or nothing actively to help get the hostages out, such as actually shipping the missiles or 'hocus-pocussing the money'. 'They tried very hard not to cross that border to get us involved in the illegal side of it,' he said. '[Nobody] ever came to me and said, Oh my God, we are being asked to break the law.' For his part, he had never dashed into Casey's office to say 'Bill, we have got to stop all this stuff.' Yet the very way George talked about it suggested that people were doing things, as they were, right up to the edge of the law, perhaps over it; and though he never made that dash to Casey, he wondered with hindsight whether he should have done.[64]

Casey, on the other hand, raised no apparent objections, and Casey was a master lawyer. As McMahon described him, he was always analysing, working some problem, sharp as a knife; his bumbling and mumbling were deceptive. He would never put himself in a position where 'he would be cross-wise with the law'; 'he might nudge it and push it and stretch it as far as he could,' said McMahon — the law now a sort of putty, or india-rubber — but he would not break it.[65] Although Casey's public reputation, built up on such incidents as the CIA-sponsored mining of Nicaragua's harbours, was as a man who cared little for legal niceties, the reverse seems to have been true; Casey cared a lot for legal niceties, but knew how to use them to his own advantage. The NSC staff, he sometimes implied, did not. According to Bob Woodward's account, Casey told him after the scandal broke that he could not see any American illegalities in it; 'Poindexter just got caught.' Nobody would go to jail 'inside the Beltway'. At that point he hung up, as if exasperated by the absurdity of it all.[66]


If the laws covering the Iran operation were nebulous and shifting, with few men claiming they could tell where the edges were, this was even more true of the operation to prop up the contras. The third, or 'full' version of Boland, passed in October 1984, prohibited the spending of any money on the contras (in effect, banned all operations) by 'all agencies of the government involved in intelligence activities', specifically the CIA and the Defense Department. In August 1985 it was modified, allowing $26m to be obligated for humanitarian aid over the next six months by some agency other than the Pentagon and the CIA; in December it was modified again, allowing exchanges of intelligence between the CIA and the contras and allowing the State Department to solicit money for humanitarian aid from third countries. In October 1986, money was voted for both humanitarian and military aid. The very fact that the law was changed so often, banning help and then allowing it, suggested how loath Congress was to abandon the contras entirely. If Congressman Boland meant, in his 'pretty plain English'[67], as he thought, to stop the contra effort dead, he carried few committed congressmen with him. Moreover, if he meant to stop it dead, every avenue should have been closed off; but there were always men who could argue that the intent of Boland was not to go quite so far.

As Hamilton admitted, 'If we had wanted to be precise we would have been precise. But we drafted it broadly.'[68]

Reagan emphasized in his testimony that 'whatever we did in trying to maintain the existence of the contras' had to be done within the law, and that he was 'always' telling his aides as much.[69] This implied that the aides were forever straying over the edge of it; and in any case he also said, a little later, that he did not think Boland applied to his staff.[70] The wilful confusion was general. North maintained that everything he did in Central America, setting up alternative structures of support, was done in order to comply with Boland, getting the government out of it all;[71] yet he also said, most defiantly, that Boland did not apply to the NSC.[72] McFarlane, under whose aegis the NSC attitude was set, was even more unclear. He had fought against the passage of Boland with the best of them, and when it was imposed he continued to hate it. He could be heard complaining how difficult it was, how detrimental to America's interests.[73] When it was modified, becoming even less straightforward, he candidly admitted — too candidly — 'We were pleased to get more murk.'[74] Yet he maintained through all his testimony that Boland covered the NSC; he said he told his staff, in an almost daily 'litany', that they should consider themselves bound by it.[75] At North's trial he came up with an especially mystifying formula: 'It did [apply], not as a matter of legal proposition or not, but yes, I felt that we were bound by it.'[76] Paul Thompson, Poindexter's aide, drew from this an even cloudier conclusion: the NSC was 'spiritually subject to Boland'.[77] And this was as far from the truth as possible, for while the letter of the law might be kept to — in the most cynically fastidious fashion — the spirit of Boland was being freely broken every hour of the day.

McFarlane may have been glad the law was murky; but he was also troubled, sometimes, by his own inability to know where the edges were. In the autumn of 1984 he thought perhaps he ought to avoid meeting Calero, not because he had analysed the law, but because he 'instinctively' felt it was 'somehow forbidden'. Yet 'the more I thought about it the more I thought, no, that's silly, of course I can do that, and I did do it.'[78] He did it secretly, however, and he required the same of North's contacts with contra leaders ('Exercise absolute stealth. No press awareness of presence in area'), because of 'congressional perceptions'. 'In other words,' North's lawyer went on for him,

What you are saying is that there was no fixed rule; it was a case-by-case analysis, that as it struck you would think like calling it in or out, first base, it's either okay or it's not okay?

*A.* That's right.[79]

A particular case arose in McFarlane's solicitation of Prince Bandar of Saudi Arabia, legal when he first approached him but illegal (Boland shifting continually, like sand) when he wanted the generosity topped up, some months later. Liman grasped his tactics: he could not come right out and say 'I want a contribution', but he could express concern that the contras were running out of money; and if Prince Bandar offered any, McFarlane could say thankyou.

*Q.* And it was that sort of line that you found you had to walk in order to keep the contras going?
*A.* That is correct.[80]

McFarlane worked, by and large, by trying to read the mind of Congress. It seemed to him that by passing the first versions of Boland in September and December 1982 Congress had actually been winking at the administration, doing it a favour. Those versions of the law had banned aid to rebels trying to overthrow the Sandinistas. Perhaps, then, in 'a very surreal interpretation' they could be seen to allow aid to rebels and their supporters who could pretend that they did not want to overthrow them.[81] So the administration pretended. (The contras were less good at it.) When the law went through its various sterner versions the winking remained to some degree, or so McFarlane thought. There was a grounding of cynicism. As Clair George put it, 'What the hell does the law mean if it says we're not allowed to overthrow the government of Nicaragua and yet we're down there making war?'[82] What, indeed?

When asked what the law boiled down to, McFarlane had his answer. The 'central concern' of Congress, he thought, was to stop fund-raising for the contras. 'Marginal activity' was of no consequence, and the congressmen had not meant to put an end to that.[83] Boland would not stop North, for example, if he were visiting the contra camps, from telling the rebels to camouflage their jeeps a bit better.[84] The law meant that the NSC could not raise, seek or handle money for the contras, and within these limits, McFarlane thought, it was implacable. The NSC could make suggestions to the contras, hold their hands, keep up with what they were doing; but it could give them nothing material directly. In that specific sense, everyone had to stay away.

In that specific sense, too, the NSC and the CIA were in the same boat. Casey, so careful about Iran, kept an even more rigorous distance from 'his boys' in Nicaragua. He forbade visitors, often rudely, to raise the subject with him. If they insisted — as Secord insisted on a rare visit — Casey would say, lugubriously, that he would love to help but could do nothing. He asked how much money the contras needed until the end of the summer. Secord said $10m.

[Casey] said, '$10 million, $10 million,' and then he mentioned the country which he thought might be willing to donate this kind of money. But then he said, 'but I can't approach them.' Why, I don't know . . . and he didn't say. But he said that two or three times. And then . . . he looked at me and said, 'but you can.'[85]

But you can. In the pause that followed one might almost hear the sound of illegality, like a fly, buzzing from one man's sleeve to the other's.

Scrupulous himself, Casey also fostered throughout the Agency — at least as far as the Boland Amendments were concerned — an almost fanatical prudishness about the law. This, of course, was how the CIA officers themselves presented it, law-abiding as could be. But it is equally clear that this prudishness did not extend to defending the law, or reporting its possible violation by 'private benefactors'; it meant sliding away, keeping quiet, turning the back, closing the eye. Men like Alan Fiers, the chief of the Central American Task Force, found themselves acquiring sensitivities they had never had: noses for a bad operation, ears for 'shyster alarm bells' and, overall, 'a status of willful ignorance', fearful of disturbance by information from anyone.[86]

Fiers was no hermit. He was often in Washington, went to meetings at the State Department, dropped in on the NSC and often found himself in positions he could hardly back out of, just on the edge of breaking the law. By dint of carefully negotiated agreements with the congressional committees, for example, the CIA was allowed to give advice to the NHAO, which handled the humanitarian aid for the contras out of the State Department. Fiers agreed to interview a supply pilot, Dick Gadd, to see if he was suitable for NHAO flights; Gadd already worked for the Secord operation. As the chief talked to him, he said later, all his sensors began to flash. The alarm bells rang. The more he probed, the more 'mystic' and 'closed-mouth' Gadd became: 'and I smelled that he might be turning into a private benefactor. . .and didn't want to get involved and backed away from it. I did not like what I felt or saw and thought that that was much too close for me.'[87]

This was typical. All of a sudden the scene would become dangerous, as if the ground had cracked underfoot. Sometimes there was no warning at all. If a CIA officer wished to be dogmatic about it, he could break the law merely by attending in good faith a meeting where someone suddenly mentioned contra operations; if he could not get to the door in time (supposing that he would try), he was obliged at least to operate a shutter in his brain. Clair George explained how it worked: 'Ollie would say in a telephone conversation, "Oh, my God, I got to get out of the Central American thing." And I am neither a coward saying "don't you ever say that to me again," or a fool and say "oh, tell me what you're doing," and he never did.'[88]

After a while, Fiers too acquired a proper delicacy, enough to maintain that 'my tack was to play a passive role, to not seek things out and look the other way'.[89] His contacts, too, sometimes showed discretion. North would say, if his questions seemed unwise, 'You don't want to know'; Fiers would answer, part-scornful, part-relieved to be reminded, 'You're right, I don't want to know.'[90] Yet dangerous things happened. One day, at a meeting in the State Department, Fiers saw North pull out pictures of the secret airstrip in Costa Rica and show them round to 'a whole bunch of people'. 'Look at this!' he was saying. 'Isn't this great?' Fiers was appalled; once again he found himself backing away, desperately trying to put at least a mental distance between himself and what was possibly a blazing infraction of the law. Common courtesy got in the way a bit; he actually took the pictures, looked at them, passed them on. He also remembered a mysteriously large amount of what North said about the airstrip, either because he knew already or because, like all forbidden stories, it burned itself into his mind. But he was thinking 'My God, this is dumb'; it was 'like showing pornography in junior high school. It is something you don't want to get caught with in your hands.'[91]

When he was in the field, Fiers seemed to find the law clearer. He knew where the edges were, to a degree that might have been useful to his frequently confused subordinates. He could not approve supply flights to the contras; he could not say 'Drop to' anyone; he could not break up loads, or say who should get what; but he could gently, 'in a generic sense', make suggestions.[92] In the field, there seemed no need to back away from anything; but matters were much more awkward in Washington.

At one nerve-tingling Washington meeting in August 1986 Fiers found himself with Don Gregg, the Vice-President's national security advisor, and several other folk to talk about matters fringing on the resupply of the contras. (Reminded of a similar meeting two years later, when he was up for the post of ambassador to South Korea, Gregg thought it could not possibly have been contras they were talking about; it must have been 'a garbled reference to something like the resupply of the copters'.[93]) Nevertheless, this one sounded like contras to Fiers. He felt horribly uncomfortable; everyone else too, he remembered, was reticent, all 'backing away from this thing, saying "Yes, yes, yes."'[94]

More especially, he was worried that Gregg would mention North, and that somehow this would make his own contacts with North open to public question; more than anything, he wished not to be in a place where he might learn more about what North was doing than was comfortable for him to know. He had no notion whether North was overstepping the law or not; he deliberately kept himself in such a state of ignorance, or so he claimed, that he had no idea of what North was even doing, beyond being a sort of 'second-team quarterback flashing signals'.[95] North sometimes asked him for intelligence. Fiers sometimes gave it, supposing it was for NSC briefings, and sometimes withheld it, suspecting it was going to be passed on to the contras. North seldom specified; it was just that, at times, the station chief 'did not like the feel of it.'[96] Again, those almost super-human sensors, quivering at the least whiff of illegality. Again, too, that awful fear of 'the unknown, that I didn't want to be associated with': the child in the dark forest or, in Fiers's own metaphor, the captain steaming among perilous shoals.[97]

In a sense, Fiers was fortunate. He was usually at one remove from the activities — talking to contributors, mingling with the contra troops, picking up radio signals from pilots — with which he would have dirtied his hands. His officers in the field, on the contrary, had been doing everything required to run a covert war before October 1984, when the most restrictive version of Boland came into force. The order to 'cease and desist' came out at once from headquarters; Fiers remembered that he sat down and wrote the cable as soon as Boland passed.[98] In an instant, the field officers had to drop charge of their unruly band of contras, decline to help them, refuse even to pass information to them. There had been a run-down of sorts, for the CIA had been able to see for a while which way the political wind was blowing; when the order went out the NSC, mostly in the person of North, was waiting in the wings. Nonetheless, the order was hard. This was, after all, a war.

And it was going to be carried on somehow, whatever Congress had decided; the law was going to be picked at for all it was worth. At some point, somebody noticed that the aircraft that went down with NHAO humanitarian supplies were not completely full. What about the space left over, came the innocent inquiry: did it have to be filled only with non-lethal stuff? What, in any case, did lethal or non-lethal mean? Presumably radios were non-lethal; on the other hand, how were signals given to attack targets? A truck carrying wounded soldiers was obviously humanitarian, but what if there were bullets on board? People at the State Department remembered these arguments well, how they went round and round. Elliott Abrams was asked one day by Robert Duemling, the NHAO's director, whether he could pay for wristwatches for the contras: 'And I remember saying, well, you know, unless you have a very large wristwatch and hit somebody with it, it was not lethal aid. This was deadly serious, deadly serious.'[99] In the end, Poindexter said, the line between lethal and non-lethal was 'a real uncertain distinction', indeed 'just a matter of semantics'.[100] In practice, cabinet officers soliciting money from third countries did not make that distinction, as far as he knew; still less, then, were lowly factotums loading up aircraft likely to make it on the ground.

This being so, the question of the partly-empty aircraft was discussed in depth by the CIA and the State Department. They reached a surprising conclusion, at odds with both the letter and the spirit of the law: 'that if there is some small and relatively insignificant space left on an airplane, it is not inconsistent with the law to fill it up, on a space-available basis, with some lethal material.' Back came the innocent query: what did 'space-available' mean? The answer: 'Not more than ten per cent.'[101]

This was not the only perforation of the law. The CIA was also forbidden to do anything to help the 'private benefactors', but this did not stop one officer at the airbase in El Salvador making friends with some of them, inviting them in for a beer or a Coke in his office, and allowing them to glance at the map on his wall, which contained 'little personal marks which only I understood of enemy positions.' 'We were friends,' he explained. 'I mean, I couldn't tell them, you know, stay the heck out of my room.'[102]

Joe Fernandez, in Costa Rica, was one of those who was determined not to give the contras up, whatever the restrictions. He had joined the CIA after a career in the Dade County police department, in Florida; his neat grey hair and pleasant, fatherly face (he had seven children) still suggested the local traffic cop rather than the secret agent. He and North occasionally took family holidays together; when both had become famous (although the charges against Fernandez were eventually dismissed), they went into business together, selling bullet-proof vests to policemen. Fernandez was not a natural lawbreaker, but he had his doubts about Boland. After all, it might not be on the books for long; perhaps in three months, six months, the law would be overturned. He did not think that he, or any of his colleagues, could have survived in their jobs without that hope.[103] So they waited, and tried to keep busy. Fernandez helped set up the secret airstrip; he relayed messages to North about drop zones and movements of troops; he was essential to the survival of the southern front, yet he felt he had to do much of it without letting his superiors know. They would not have wanted to be told.

By his own account, he worried about the law. At times his superiors would tell him to back off from the private benefactors, keep his distance; at others they seemed not to mind what he did. No lawyers were assigned to his station, and what guidance came by cable from lawyers at HQ 'was understandably terse and narrow and did not pretend to address every eventuality.'[104] Accordingly, he came to feel that he was in the middle of a minefield. When an order came down from North about a lethal supply flight in January 1986 ('send the information about where the drop zone is and start a novena'), he said 'Is that legal, Ollie?'.

And he'd say yeah, you are passing information [at that stage something, the only thing, the CIA was allowed to do]. You are just passing information. You are not co-ordinating. You are not running a military operation. You are just passing information; is that clear? You are just passing information. I said, Fine, as long as that's the case, then that's all I need to know.[105]

He was not quite so fine as he sounded. The passing of information came to take up more and more of his time; sometimes he was still trying to do it at two or three in the morning. Occasionally, too, in the heat of the moment, 'information' for North would transmute into military fantasies. 'My objective is creation of 2,500 man force which can strike northwest and link-up with quiche* to form solid southern force . . . realize this is overly ambitious planning but with your help, believe we can bring it off.'[106]

He confessed one day to his division chief — the chief having spotted the KL–43 in his office — that he wondered if there wasn't a better way to do it; the chief said he would check on the law when he got back to Washington. His conclusion was that they had a problem. Fernandez came up with an idea: use a Nicaraguan communicator as a go-between, so that CIA men and 'private patriotic Americans' no longer had to talk direct. The idea did not work, so it was back to Fernandez again, teetering on the edge of the law, with his 'understandings'.[107]

His involvement with the building of the secret airstrip at Santa

---

* Presumably a code-word for a grouping of contras.

Elena had already taken him deep into the question of whether he helped or didn't help, and how much. His role, he decided in that case, was one of passive observation. He would watch the men clearing the piece of land. That was not illegal. Their intentions, of course, might be different, but it was their actions that counted. But he knew, did he not, asked a lawyer at the hearings, that these men were not planting an apple orchard? That they were building an airfield to resupply the contras? Well, yes, said Fernandez:

> That it was an airfield to be used eventually for the contras, yes, that is true, but in and of itself, it wasn't necessarily an illegal or an intelligence activity, by my interpretation.[108]

His interpretation was good for himself, evidently. Others thought it dangerous. In December 1985 he found himself on a hotel veranda with the Central American station chief, and told him how the airstrip was going. Fiers reacted sharply: 'Jesus, Joe, watch what you do. Stay legal. Stay within the bounds.' 'I know what I am doing,' Fernandez answered. 'I have already made my decisions.'[109] Having made them, he did not need always to kowtow to HQ; he could beat his own, sometimes solitary, path through the thickets of the law. On January 12th 1986, for example, he received a cable from his superiors.

> There have been numerous allegations of violations of law by P[rivate] B[enefactor]s. We do not have a firm handle on whether all of the allegations floating around are false, consequently we do not wish to have CIA-provided assistance tied into an entity that may or may not be bad.[110]

Painstakingly, Fernandez explained at the hearings that this was not a message to 'cease and desist'. If his superiors had meant that, they would not have minced words. Instead, they were leaving the decision to him. Headquarters was saying it would be nice if things could be done another way, but 'it is really you haven't done anything wrong. There is nothing basically wrong with what you are doing.'[111] And so he believed. 'Let me make it very clear to you,' he told his questioners: 'to this very moment I never did anything wrong — ever. Maybe I didn't do everything right, but I never did anything wrong.'[112]

That sounded like North-speak, but the two plotters and friends also understood how close they were breezing to the edge of the law; and Fernandez, at least, was worried. Perhaps this was why, when North jotted down in January 1985 a list of things available on site for a family holiday with Fernandez in Costa Rica, the list took a startling turn.

Swimming pool & Beach
Football, softball, Frisbee, books
trivial pursuit
Insect repellent, Suntan lotion
Confessor [113]

# Chapter 14

# Right and Wrong

As Fernandez showed, it was possible to be both uncertain about the law and overpoweringly certain about it; unsure whether it applied to certain people and procedures, and at the same time positive that it was morally and politically wrong. Iran-contra presented the spectacle of people ostensibly very worried about the law, nit-picking it for all it was worth, who were also prepared to skirt it as an article of faith. There were considerations above the law, as Fawn Hall said, most notoriously, at the hearings. There were times when statutes simply had to be overridden or stepped round.

The players did not seem to see much correlation between right action and observance of the law; conversely, they did not see much correlation between breaking the law and acting wrongly. The two codes were poles apart, different worlds. As North put it at his trial, speaking of the lies he had told the House Permanent Select Committee on Intelligence in August 1986: 'I was raised to know the difference between right and wrong. I knew it wasn't right not to tell the truth on those things, but I didn't think it was unlawful.'[1]

During North's testimony Congressman Hyde, one of his most florid supporters, quoted Thomas Jefferson: 'A strict observance of the written laws is doubtless one of the high duties of a good citizen, but it is not the highest. The laws of necessity, of self-preservation, of saving country when in danger are of higher obligation.' In the final congressional report on the scandal, published in November 1987, he took the quotation further: 'To lose our country, by a scrupulous adherence to the written law, would be to lose the law itself . . . thus absurdly sacrificing the end to the means.'[2]

When Reagan startled Poindexter with his idea of 'taking action unilaterally' to help the contras, he had just been reading an anthology by Benjamin Netanyahu, an Israeli expert on counter-terrorism, and in it a striking description of a president's executive power: 'the power to act according to discretion for the public good, without the prescription of law and sometimes even against it'.[3] This too was 'the law of necessity' and it had, where necessary, a political impetus. When Weinberger first warned Reagan about the legal problems attending the Iran operation, Reagan replied simply: 'Well, the American people will never forgive me if I fail to get these hostages out over this legal question.'[4]

Noel Koch put the concept in Pentagon terms.

When you live in this environment after a while you decide that if you're going to do anything in furtherance of your country's interests then you're not going to do it through this damn bureaucracy.

And it doesn't have anything to do with circumventing the law. It has to do with circumventing the absence of leadership and people's willingness to make the goddam thing work.

Koch also acknowledged the inevitable coda.

Once you make that departure from bureaucratic norms, you're in a state of willy-nilly. And so he says I need this done, and this becomes this little band of brothers that are functioning in effect.[5]

Imperatives of action, moral imperatives; sometimes the two were the same thing, and the law had little to do with either. 'Given the lack of alternative,' as North said of the contra resupply, 'I still see it to be within the law.'[6] McFarlane had been told that he was to support the contras 'body and soul', and felt that Reagan had 'a far more liberal interpretation' of what that meant than he did; Poindexter knew that Reagan saw the contra operation as the latest extension of 200 years of American support for 'Simon Bolivar . . . the Polish patriots, the French Resistance and others seeking freedom'.[7] Laws did not enter into it. Where right was concerned, indeed, laws might stand in the way. Losing the war in Vietnam, said McFarlane at the hearings, was 'a matter that was done extremely legally': so legally, that North wanted nothing to do with such a thing ever again.[8] Asked at his trial whether 'moral bells' had gone off in his head as he worked on statements designed to mislead Congress into thinking that the law was being abided by, North retorted: 'It would be improper for me to describe it as a moral bell. I thought it was extraordinarily immoral to have fielded a force, equipped it, trained it, fed it, clothed it, armed it, sent it into combat and then left it in the lurch. I thought that was heinous.'[9]

America, of course, was a nation of laws, not men; the phrase became the theme-tune of the affair. In the final congressional report, the writers of the majority opinion — admitting it was not their job to look into infractions of the law, and devoting no more than ten pages to doing so — could not resist a quotation from *A Man for All Seasons*, Sir Thomas More addressing Roper:

> The law, Roper, the law. I know what's legal, not what's right. And I'll stick to what's legal . . .
> *Roper.* So now you'd give the Devil benefit of law!
> *More.* Yes. What would you do? Cut a great road through the law to get after the Devil?
> *Roper.* I'd cut down every law in England to do that!
> *More.* Oh? And when the last law was down, and the Devil turned round on you — where would you hide, Roper, the laws all being flat? This country's planted thick with laws from coast to coast — Man's law, not God's — and if you cut them down — and you're just the man to do it — d'you really think you could stand upright in the winds that would blow then?[10]

On the other hand, 'the laws of nature and of nature's God', as cited in the Declaration of Independence, were supposed to be the basis of all other laws; and the law of nature seemed to come close to that of the heart (or that of necessity), triumphing over the head and over all pieces of paper. As Patrick Buchanan pointed out in his defence of North and Poindexter, even so eminent a legal scholar as Blackstone had declared that no law had any validity if contrary to the law dictated by God.[11] In the Thomist view, which Buchanan seemed to approve of, the goodness of an act was defined by its objective; to this objective, means were subordinate; if a man's reason for acting was right and good, he was not obliged to side with the law. God, who was less a law-maker than a dispenser of grace, would reward the intention. Even the sinner Augustine had comforted himself with that.

On December 9th 1986, in the *Washington Post*, Buchanan took characteristic aim at the idea that 'we are a nation of laws, and Oliver North broke the law . . . and surely we cannot condone that'.

But we don't know that Ollie North broke the law. What we do know is that those Americans who, a century ago, ran escaped slaves up the Underground Railroad to Canada — they broke the law. We do know that Franklin Roosevelt, who secretly ordered American destroyers to hunt down German submarines in the North Atlantic . . . he broke the law.

And those Americans who ran guns to Palestine in 1947 and 1948 — they broke the law. And they are considered now — and they consider themselves — to be heroes.[12]

Once North was a hero too, on the same contentious principle (calling his indictments 'a badge of honor'), he was asked by *Life* magazine in December 1988 to answer the question 'Why are we here?' He replied that life was a series of 'hard choices between good and evil' through which a man could pick his way 'by using an ethical system not invented by man but by our Creator — a framework of truth and moral guidance through which we can find deliverance from despair.'[13] Undoubtedly, given the chance to make his moral case in a few sentences, North was making it. The creations and constructs of men were deeply imperfect guidelines for behaviour, he was saying, and they might even be irrelevant; it was God who would judge him. Everything had been done in His name, in any case; it been referred to Him, and presumably, even if it went awry, it had been approved of. It was right.

The precepts that mattered, therefore, were not necessarily laid out in statutes devised by congressmen. They also appeared in the Bible that North carried about with him, and kept in the office, and read on aircraft flying to Tehran. A passage at the beginning of Galatians, next to the one so carefully scrutinized in the dealings with the Second Channel, contained some thoughts of St Paul on the law: specifically the Jewish law, specifically a plea for justification by faith rather than works, but not without appeal to those who distrusted certain rules invented by men.

We acknowledge that what makes a man righteous is not obedience to the Law, but faith in Jesus Christ . . . In other words, through the Law I am dead to the Law, so that I can live for God . . . If the Law can justify us, there is no point in the death of Christ.[14]

As if to press the point, North later sat at the defence table with his New Testament in plain view, God's law thrust defiantly in the face of the laws of men. Keker, his prosecutor, was enraged by this presumption of righteousness; in their summations, the two opposing lawyers tried to outdo each other with biblical chapter and verse. The prosecution chose the sternest Old Testament readings, wrath and brimstone, reminding North of the true rigour of the law he was setting against theirs. 'Woe to him who calls good evil and evil good,' said Keker, after Isaiah, referring to North's lies to Congress; and of his penchant for shifting responsibility to his bosses, 'the wicked walk on every side when evil men are exalted.'[15] Sullivan responded with John, chapter 15, verse 13: 'Greater love has no man than he be willing to lay down his life for another.'[16] The all-black jury, supposing they were being pandered to as gospel-loving simpletons, took offence at both sides. But there was a deeper point, closer to St Paul's distinction between the old law and the new order: between the rigid, spiteful morality of Isaiah (doubtless bred out of laws) and the redemptive love of Christ, without boundaries, available even to sinners. 'Ollie North may be going to jail,' the defendant liked to say in the days when his sentence was in doubt, 'but he's not going to go to Hell.'

In the whole of his trial, North could be persuaded to admit only one thing that was wrong, and that was misleading Congress 'face to face' in the summer of 1986. Even this was pulled from him with some difficulty: 'I didn't think it was right. Therefore, it must be wrong.'[17] He had been following conscience all along, as far as he was aware; moral and political action had become, for him, one and the same thing, and even Keker could not succeed in disentangling them.

> *Q.* [McFarlane] is asking you at this point to associate yourself fairly closely with a letter that he is sending to Congress that's about your activities. Any qualms besides political ones by this time?
> *A.* I will go back to what I said earlier. My whole impetus, my whole effort . . . was an effort not to have this whole process laid before the Congress. I tried.
> *Q.* Put aside the politics of it. Any moral qualms, anything tell you from your upbringing, your Naval Academy training, your time in the Marine Corps, Gee, this doesn't seem right; this seems wrong to me?
> *A.* Sure. Absolutely.
> *Q.* Not just politically. I mean morally.
> *A.* Morally.
> *Q.* I am not proud of this?

*A.* I am not proud of this. I am not proud of the fact that [McFarlane] felt he was in that position. I am not proud of the fact that the administration didn't stand up and do what I thought was right politically.[18]

It was Fawn Hall, North's secretary, who finally blurted out to Congress — her artfully wild hair falling round her face — the words that many on the panels had been waiting for: the admission that these people thought the laws were secondary to what they believed in. When North had asked her to alter old memoranda, she had not liked it; the act was not legal and cannot have seemed so, even to a tactful secretary; but 'sometimes you have to go above the written law, I believe.'[19] There it was; she had said it.

She tried to retract at once. 'I don't know . . . Maybe that is not correct. It is not a fair thing to say.'[20] Questioned later by Senator Trible, she admitted that 'we all say things out of emotion that we don't necessarily mean.'

*Q.* You were not suggesting that you were serving some higher good that permitted you to undertake these activities?
*A.* No.[21]

On the other hand, it was not the normal thing a secretary would say. Nor, for that matter, was her apologia at the start of her testimony: 'I would prefer to have remained a relatively obscure but responsible secretary at the National Security Council, doing — as a friend of mine paraphrased Franklin Roosevelt — "the best I know how at the moment, for what is right".'[22] She went on to say she could not do that now; no opportunity, she implied, to work for 'what was right' in the secretarial job she now held in the Pentagon. And if she had immediately regretted her public endorsement of 'going above the law', the principle was evidently still in her mind, deeply embedded.

'Emotion' had caused her to go above the law before, at the end of November 1986, when she had folded up copies of incriminating memoranda left by mistake in the office and tucked them into her skirt and her boots to smuggle them out to North; actions that were justified, she explained later, if it seemed that 'the Soviets and everyone else could read it'; especially if 'the KGB was coming in the door.' Senator Rudman answered, patiently: 'It wasn't the KGB that was coming, Miss Hall. It was the FBI.'[23] Fawn, who had explained that she didn't know 'what's legal and what's not legal',[24] seemed a little stung by this lawyer's rebuke, but in an interview some time later her confidence bubbled out again. There were higher considerations than the law:

> History shows that there have been tons of cases . . . Your wife is about to die and you have to break the law and speed, civil rights; there's all different areas where that's been proven. I believe it was important . . .[25]

So important that she retyped the old memoranda when North asked her to, concealing his illegal excursions for the contras, even though she knew these were 'finished actions already approved';[26] even though she felt she had to turn them over when Craig Coy came past her desk.[27] As she continually said, she 'believed'. She was 'part of the team'.[28]

The other members of the office team, Earl and Coy, took the same line: if an action seemed right, they were not about to query whether it was lawful. When North told Earl in May 1986 that some of the Ayatollah's money was going to support the contras, it did not sound the alarms in Earl's brain that Liman thought it should have.

> *Q.* I assume, Colonel Earl, that if North told you that he was about to do something that you thought was illegal, such as rob a bank to get money for the contras, that you wouldn't just simply write it down in your book.
> *A.* I would not have been a party to something that I knew was illegal, that clearly was illegal to me. I mean, it's my obligation and my duty to not carry out an immoral or illegal order.
> *Q.* And wouldn't you have said to Oliver North, . . . Ollie, there are some limits to what you ought to do for a good cause?
> *A.* Yes, sir. In fact, I guess I prided myself on the devil's advocate role that I felt I could play for him. . . .
> *Q.* And you didn't do it on this?
> *A.* I did not, because I didn't think there was anything wrong with it.[29]

Owen, too, entered enthusiastically into these moral considerations. 'When you talk about integrity, you ask yourself, "Is what I'm doing right, or is it wrong? And if it's really right, then I must do everything in my power to help, and if it's really wrong, then I must oppose it with all of my might."'[30]

If an action was really right, what possible weight could a law have, supposing that it were suddenly raised in opposition? Some congressmen, Hyde first among them, thought Owen was undoubtedly 'answering to a higher call' when he passed money to Miskito

Indian leaders through car windows in the pouring rain, or fetched it from trouser legs in New York; members of the sanctuary movement, or people opposing apartheid, took just the same lofty attitude to the law, and liberals — indeed, almost everyone — approved of them.[31] Most congressmen, however, were suspicious of the Fawn-and-Owen approach. Their words suggested an office atmosphere of high and dangerous dedication, even in the phoning and the filing; they also had the ring of something picked up and repeated as naturally as memos were taken to be typed, and the committees had little doubt whom it had been picked up from. A matter of minutes into North's public testimony, when Inouye had read out yet another request from Sullivan for special treatment, the senator remarked that here, once again, North was suggesting that he was above the law.[32] And indeed, superiority to certain laws was suggested in the very cock of North's chin, but he was not foolish enough to say so in the presence of so many lawyers.

> *Liman*: And you do not share the view that was expressed and retracted by your secretary that sometimes you must rise above the written law?
> *A*. I do not believe in rising above the law at all, and I do not believe that I have ever stated that.
> *Q*. And you haven't.
> *A*. I have not. [33]

More than most, the lives of the main players had been shaped by obedience to rules: rules of highly disciplined households, rules of their churches, rules of the Naval Academy, rules of warfare. In their public lives McFarlane and Poindexter seemed almost unnaturally cautious and hidebound, the last people to be found guilty even of a traffic violation. Michael Ledeen, who had worked with North on the capture of the *Achille Lauro* terrorists, was impressed at how scrupulously he asked for legal advice even at the height of the crisis, double- and triple-checking everything with State Department lawyers.[34] But these were rules North presumably thought right; and in the case of contras and hostages, the idea of 'right' began to raise its head in disregard of laws. It was wrong not to be able to help the contras, as Boland laid down; it was wrong to be unable to use the last ounce of persuasion, or force, to get hostages out. As Noel Koch described it, '[North] had what he felt was a charter, and that is get the hostages back, and whatever other things conduced to that, basically, if he could get away with them . . . He felt that it was necessary to do it.'[35] And the means was to take the operations underground.

Yet could an action possibly be secret, and also be right and good? Wherever the word 'secret' cropped up, so did the suspicion — in small actions or large — that people were doing wrong; that, as St Paul said, 'the things which are done in secret are things that people are ashamed even to speak of.'[36] When Rob Owen heard from a contra fundraiser that his telephone patter included mention of 'secret' briefings at the White House, he went to North to complain: the word 'secret' seemed inappropriate, unethical, and if the press got hold of it they could doubtless make it look bad, too; and North agreed with him.[37]

McFarlane, in his turn, had to justify at the hearings why he had used a secret means — slipping a card into the President's briefing book — to tell him about the Saudi donation to the contras. It wasn't, was it, a lawyer pressed him, because he was trying to conceal something wrong? No, McFarlane explained, there was just 'an interest in minimizing the circle of awareness of that contribution'.[38] To hide something was not wrong, not an admission of having broken some law; it just looked that way. As McFarlane had told the same lawyer earlier that afternoon, 'as a practical matter I have just answered 20 questions in the negative, and the average viewer assumes that anybody who says no that many times in a row must be evil.'[39]

Occasionally the secrecy could be justified, just as covert operations could be justified, by the ends they were meant to serve. A classmate of North's at the Naval Academy had found him one night making for the college office, intending to remove the medical records that declared him too disabled to serve as a Marine. He was breaking the rules and knew it, or he would not have done it under cover of darkness; yet his classmate did not obstruct or report him, because he was doing it to serve his country.[40] This, however, seemed to be the exception that proved the rule. North's worst action in the Iran-contra affair, according to himself — his 'grossest misjudgment I have made in my life'[41] — was also done in secret. After his dismissal he typed a couple of false letters pretending that he had meant to pay for a security fence given him by Secord, against government regulations; but he was too ashamed to type them on one of the children's typewriters at home or in his office at Marine Corps headquarters. Because 'I didn't want anybody at work to see me doing a letter that was dated back in May 1986 in December',[42] he went to a Best's store in Tyson's Corner, where there were typewriters for customers to try, and drafted the letters there, where nobody would see him.

Despite that, North still tried to argue that there was no correlation between secrecy and grubby dealing. At his trial, he protested continually that what he had done in the secret Enterprise was not 'dirty' or 'sinister' or 'wrong'. Marine though he was, he objected fiercely whenever Keker described these doings in the language of the gutter. At one point Keker took him through his titles for the CIA, many and various.

*Q.* And you called the CIA people what?
*A.* Well, it was a profanity that I would choose not to use in the presence of ladies. It was a male-to-male communication between friends. And if you would like to use the word in this courtroom, you may.
*Q.* Is it a word that starts with an A?
*A.* Sure.
*Q.* Okay, is that what you thought of them?
*A.* At that point, yes.[43]

In Mary McGrory's words, North's tone cried out for the addition of 'You cad, sir'.[44] He objected equally to the idea that Mrs Garwood or Mrs Newington had been 'hit up' for money for the contras, which they then 'kicked in'; they had 'chosen to contribute to a cause they believed in'.[45] Crude language cast the activities under a cloud which perhaps, in the general scheme of things, they did not deserve; and whatever the legal dubiousness of the transactions under discussion, Keker's rudeness was more offensive.

Conversely, if shady deals were done in a 'proper' way, perhaps their murkiness could be redeemed somehow by a neat appearance and the right tone of voice. At his deposition, Poindexter was asked about ransoming hostages with private money; he objected to the word. Well, said Liman, you can call it ransom or you can call it a bribe.

*Q.* This tended to be considered a bribe rather than ransom?
*A.* That's exactly right.
*Q.* You felt better when you called it that?
*A.* That's right.[46]

Besides, as North argued, these operations were not as secret as all that. These were activities that were planned, briefed to his superiors. Secret though it might be, he could see 'all over the world' the work Secord was doing: the airstrips, the ships creaking with arms, the SAMs clattering out in their boxes, weapons from hither and yon. The very fact that he could see it, surely, removed the impression that this was anything wrong.[47]

Nonetheless the impression of wrong, like dirt, crept in everywhere. Poindexter admitted that the Finding of January 17th was an attempt to make the Iran operation 'clean', five months after it had started.[48] That effort, as Ledeen pointed out, was probably futile from the outset. Once the scheme was entered into, 'between 100 TOWs and 500 TOWs it wasn't such a big difference, so that one could pretend to having been pure at a hundred and corrupt at 500.'[49] McFarlane acknowledged that the Iranians he had tried to deal with were 'not your normal Western Jeffersonian kinds of persons'.[50] The rules of the game that the world knew were not the American kind, decency and fair play; and although Americans should not sink to the world's level when dealing with 'barbarians' whose 'breath would curl rhino hide',[51] neither should they be 'so flaccid and puritanical as to presume that posturing will achieve our purpose.'[52] As North noted ruefully at the hearings, America could not use Mother Theresa (everyone's favourite symbol of purity) to work the Iranian back-channel; you used whomever you could find.[53] You went on working it, then, not because it was honourable or pleasant, but because it had been successful once or twice.

One retired major, himself involved in trying to find the hostages, attempted to argue North out of the arms sales. Just because arms-for-hostages had worked, it was not necessarily the right thing to do. It was a bad business. The major said as much one day to Charlie Allen, wanting it passed on to North. Allen burst out, 'Goddam it, Ollie knows all this. Just put the words down.' The major did so. Later he met North face-to-face to tell him that the Iran operation could not work, that it encouraged terrorism and was contrary to policy; North made no comment on anything. At one point, he raised his eyebrows.[54] There was always another side to the equation: the thought that, as Noel Koch put it, at the hearings, 'this hostage situation could be resolved rather handily if we chose to do it, but these are not the sort of things we are prepared to do, because we indulge the luxury of pretending we have some higher morality.' He elaborated:

> If you want a more imaginative answer, I would go pay a call on Mr Fadlallah, who is the head of Hizbollah, and I would take him off to a nice warm dry place and I would take off something that is not life-threatening, like a finger, and wrap it in a note to Imad Mughniyah that says, 'There is a lot more where this came from, and I would like to see my hostages in the bar in the Commodore Hotel by Friday . . . and if not, we will be sending some more of this stuff around.'
> *Q.* I assume you hadn't got a legal opinion on that one?

*A.* No.[55]

Koch also supposed that these tasks had been given to 'a lowly lieutenant colonel' precisely because they were not 'neat and clean', and there was no glory in them.[56]

The sense of stain and corruption was even more marked in the contra operation, despite the high talk. Both the CIA and North's own agents thought the resupply was 'tainted' by the end — aircraft, airstrips, sheds, crates, log-books, covered with a sheen of grime.[57] The CIA, offered these assets, would not touch them. At lunch with Casey and Gates on October 9th 1986, after the resupply aircraft had crashed, North took pains to assure them that the CIA was 'completely clean'.[58] He tried, too, to make Owen clean, or in Owen's words 'a little bit more legitimate' by getting him seconded to the NHAO humanitarian aid programme run by the State Department. As Owen said, 'It would be better if I was not trying to hide what I was doing.' His role was still far from pure: he would 'take off my NHAO hat and be Rob Owen private citizen and . . . see that the plane was loaded up with arms';[59] but at least he was not obliged to skulk about all the time.

'If you wanted to do dirty work,' said Bob Earl, who had been in the CIA himself, 'you used dirty people.'[60] You used small-time narcs, ex-CIA men, mercenaries. Don Gregg, hearing about these characters, perhaps encountering some in person, said he began to worry about corruption; he supposed that North, being spread so thin, 'was not in a position to really exercise quality control over what they were doing.'[61]

General Schweitzer, in whom North sometimes confided, expressed surprise that this man, with his 'very finely developed moral sense and conscience' should get so tied up with bad elements; having got involved with arms traders himself, he was not impressed with the idea that men could not work in that business without losing their moral bearings. Schweitzer had talked once to a Dr Cline, who was vaguely connected with the CIA, offering to provide arms where they might be useful. Dr Cline had asked whether he really wanted to be involved in that trade: the people were terrible. 'I can deal with despicable people,' Schweitzer replied. 'I have had to do that before'; he drew the line only at being partners with them. Cline smiled, and said again that there were not many good people in the business. That was why he wanted to get involved, Schweitzer insisted: 'We think we are good people, and we believe we can do this honourably.'[62] North evidently shared that feeling; that, as Neil Livingstone said, 'He could get down and dirty in the trenches and none of it would rub off on him.'[63]

As the tale unfolded, looking decidedly grimy, numbers of people attested that at least North's motives were 'pure'. It was the word they preferred, giving the impression of a man who was nobly or innocently above it all, whatever the appearance. As Meese apparently described it to Reagan on that awful Monday afternoon, November 24th, 'North probably did it for good reasons, or patriotic reasons, whatever was done.'[64] Bush told the *Washington Post* in the aftermath of the hearings that North was 'motivated by high purpose, not any selfishness, not any venality.'[65] After his trial, 64% of Americans pronounced North 'well-meaning but misguided',[66] as if indeed he could not help the company he had kept.

In the *Washington Post* in the first half of August, 1987 — not long after North had testified — a spirited debate occurred between Colman McCarthy and Samuel Ginder over what Aristotle would have made of North and Poindexter, and whether they would have qualified as good or bad by the standards set in the *Ethics*.[67] McCarthy quoted a section on wicked men, whose ignorance about what they should do led them to become immoral; he noticed Aristotle's censure of those who feared nothing at all, becoming rash, and those who took delight in lying. Having started from the supposition of wickedness, his judgments followed accordingly. Ginder, who gave the impression of a closer reading, noted Aristotle's emphasis on 'tough decisions that cannot be made by a set of rules', on the desirability of the mean between extremes and on the importance of 'what lies in the heart': Aristotle believing, like Aquinas later, that the end in view gave the action its essential moral cast. He concluded, no more hitting the mean than McCarthy could, that

> North and Poindexter made their decisions to act as they saw to be the harmony of the whole, the just act. 'In justice is every virtue comprehended.' They made false statements to Congress to uphold their commitments to loyalty and obligation.

Both writers ignored one complicating factor: the moral reversals of the world of covert operations. In this world North suddenly found himself 'a long way from the Marine Corps',[68] and by implication far from honour codes, concepts of integrity, perhaps any kind of high standards. Midshipmen, according to the Annapolis Honor Concept, 'should neither permit nor accept anything that is not just, right and true.'[69] But where were just, right and true when you were sitting opposite Ghorbanifar, or even opposite some over-curious congressman who did not believe in the cause? The answer, according to the Academy rule book, was that the players should

have developed 'a keen sense of integrity that commits you to do
what is right whether your actions are witnessed or not'.[70] Covert or
overt, the same standards applied. Keker, a Marine too, was equally
adamant. Questioning North about his attempts to conceal the
contra operation from Congress, Keker asked him: 'At the Naval
Academy you would be kicked out for this, wouldn't you?' North
answered ruefully.

> In the United States Naval Academy nobody taught me how to
> deal with running a covert operation, Mr Keker. Nobody
> taught me how to run a covert operation in the Marine
> Corps . . .
> *Q.* They do teach you that even warfare, real warfare, not just
> political warfare, but real warfare has rules, right?
> *A.* Yes, Mr Keker, I know that.
> *Q.* And you understood that if real warfare has rules, that
> political warfare has got to have some rules, didn't you? Some
> rules?
> *A.* It would be nice to have seen some of those rules applied
> and I saw very little of it at that point in time.
> *Q.* And since other people didn't apply those rules you weren't
> going to apply any rules, is that right?
> *A.* No, I applied a lot of rules. I tried very hard to live within
> the limits of what I was told to do.[71]

After his testimony in 1987, much of the country still starry-eyed
with the impact of North, Michael Novak, a right-wing columnist
and Catholic theologian, suggested that North had done as well
morally as it was possible to do with a covert operation. Such
operations imposed particular moral restraints 'in addition . . . to
everyday morality', such as the need to keep secrets to save lives,
and the obligation to discern the lesser evil in two bad choices. In
effect, he said, North made a framework for himself in contradistinction to the framework put up by congressional lawyers like Nields,
based merely on the law of the land; and within these limits, of
which North was the sole arbiter, his actions 'by and large' were
legal, moral and right. He 'dramatized the clash between two
antagonistic moral visions', of which one was dull old legal process
and the other a heady and glorious fidelity to 'what he thought was
right'.[72] But this was not North at his trial, nor did it seem true of
him and his superiors as events unfolded. They were in a dirty
world, and knew it; they hoped they could somehow do right, not
wrong, but it was neither glorious nor certain.

In the contra operation, in particular, 'right' conduct was judged by the narrowest of standards. The Boland Amendments, as we have seen, had been boiled down to a technicality: government officials should not handle money for the contras. But this prudishness about money, the players insisted, did not really have anything to do with Boland, that tiresome piece of legislation; it had more to do with some vague, half-remembered code of right behaviour. 'I understood that there were regulations against government officials soliciting,' said North, 'and I tried very, very hard to live with that prescription, not because it was Boland, not because the NSC was in any way obviated from doing what I was doing, but only because someone had told me that a US government official should not, cannot, will not, whatever, solicit.'[73] At his trial, he said he thought he was proscribed because he was a military officer.[74] Poindexter thought McFarlane's worries about solicitation were nothing to do with the Boland amendment, but with something else: 'Now, I don't know exactly what that law is . . . [but] there is other legislation . . .'[75]

Sullivan, however, said there was no law or rule at all.[76] There was simply a conviction that handling money was wrong. Solicitation, too, was shameful not because the law forbade it (although the law, at times, did forbid it), but in itself. It was begging. As Abrams said, although it would have been 'immoral' not to have asked for money from Brunei when the contras were starving, it was 'shameful for the United States to be going round rattling a tin cup . . . it was awful.'[77]

Poindexter was always uneasy, he said, about directly handling money. When he found out that North was keeping cash in his safe, as much as $150,000 in travellers' cheques to meet the occasional expenses of the contras, he ordered him to give it back; there were 'perception problems'. 'I told Colonel North that I didn't think it was a good idea . . . and I prefer that he did not have any cash. At some point after that, he informed me that he had returned the funds . . . I recall at the time being relieved.'[78]

North's safe had a history. When he started at the NSC in 1981 he had found $1,000 in it in a brown envelope: favour-money from Japanese lobbyists, as it turned out, that had been given to Richard Allen, then the national security advisor. North, uncertain what to do with it, took it to his commanding officer in the Marine Corps, General Kelley, to ask his advice.[79] His find plunged Allen into disgrace and forced his resignation. In later years North and Owen used to joke about the money they kept in the same safe, much more of it, and potentially much more damaging if anybody found out.[80] North said he kept immaculate track of it, down to every serial number, in a ledger that Casey had given him;[81] but because he claimed he had destroyed the ledger later, also when Casey advised it, he had no proof of all this carefulness. [82]

During Calero's testimony, it emerged that North himself had signed some of the travellers' cheques for groceries, cigarettes and children's leotards, apparently pocketing the change.[83] This was supposed to be the contras' money, desperately needed. He also bought snow tyres. 'When was the last time it snowed in Nicaragua?' asked Senator Rudman of Calero; 'Sir, it does not snow in Nicaragua,' the contra chief replied.[84] North said he had been reimbursing himself for his own money spent on contra business (the DEA agents he employed did the same, calling it 'adjusted monies'[85]); again, he offered no proof of it. It was his own word on oath, or nothing at all.

At North's trial the prosecutor wondered too how he had been able, suddenly, to find $8,000 for a used van in the summer of 1985, when up until then he used to chase the NSC payments clerk down the hall, hollering to be reimbursed and pleading for his cab fare.[86] 'You had gotten loose at the NSC, hadn't you?' Keker asked him.[87] North denied it flatly, impatiently. He said the money for the van had come from a fund into which he had also dipped for the contras when the stash in his safe had gone: a midshipman's metal box bolted to the floor of his wardrobe, in which by 1985 he had 'about $15,000'. He had built it up from an insurance settlement, he said, and the small change emptied out of his pockets on Friday nights; if Keker did not believe him, he would bring it in and show him. 'The metal box, when you show it to us, is not going to have $15,000 in cash in it, is it?' asked Keker acidly. North said he had no idea how much was in it now.[88]

The story was so incredible that it might, in the endless improbabilities of the case, have turned out to be true; but the prosecution naturally feasted on it. This was a return to the flimsy lies of Tammany Hall, said the prosecution; the hacks of the old Democratic machine in New York, boasting of how they had built up their fortunes by returning deposit bottles or giving up cigarettes. They too had put their savings in 'a little tin box'.[89] The used-car salesman was brought in to testify against North, and did so convincingly. Indeed, in the public esteem, and typical of the propensity of the affair to trivialize itself, North was tarnished more thoroughly by a used-car salesman than by any other charge brought against him. Keker in his summing up called North 'the Joe Isuzu of government', after a used-car salesman well known from television commercials: ever-ready with the tall tales, conning his customers with junk.[90] Yet the charges did not stick at trial. Perhaps the jury simply believed North; or perhaps they also bore in mind the pattern of almost obsessive caution about money shown in their official lives by all three chief players. It was this caution that convinced them they were acting uprightly, even as they went round the law.

Poindexter, and indeed McFarlane, were at several safe steps from the money operations. They kept no stashes in their offices; nor, in general, did they give the sort of contra briefings where money was asked for afterwards. But exceptions occurred. One potential contributor, at least, was briefed on Nicaragua by McFarlane in the White House Situation Room, always an impressive place to be instructed, 'the *sanctum sanctorum* of the White House', as Clair George called it;[91] when the briefing was over, and the contributor wished to know how he could send his money, McFarlane handed over to North, explaining that 'he knew how it could be done.' (This was the same McFarlane, of course, who said repeatedly that North was never to explain such things.) Nothing more about money was said at that meeting, and McFarlane made his getaway.[92]

The year was 1985; then, and later, North did as McFarlane had done, and with the same careful show of rectitude. The line he walked often seemed invisible to others but was, to him, apparently as broad as day. He could not say 'Now Mrs Jones, or Mrs Smith, or Mr So-and-so, would you please give money';[93] but there was nothing to stop him doing it indirectly, going right up to that difficult point in the conversation, and handing over.

There were awkward moments. One was when Joseph Coors came to his office in August 1985, sent by Casey and volunteering $65,000. North talked about the cost of various things and suggested that Coors should sponsor an aircraft, but it was hard to explain to McFarlane and Poindexter that he had not persuaded Coors to give. Both of them grumbled that 'Bill Casey ought not to be doing that', and North said he would tell him: not to be done again.[94] Every contact with potential donors, however, carried a risk of this sort, and North developed his own internal rule, a sort of alarm, to keep himself out of trouble. He would make his case, often going as close to the line as putting down price-lists of weapons among the half-emptied glasses in the English Grill at the Hay-Adams Hotel; he seldom lingered to eat or socialize, beyond the occasional glass of dark beer;[95] when he suspected that the pitch was turning ineluctably towards money, he left, sometimes so abruptly as to seem rude. At the end of his public speeches he could explain himself, say why he couldn't ask. In restaurants he would simply make an excuse, as he did at the dinner with Hunt on the top floor of the glittery Petroleum Club in Dallas, leaving the table 'to look at the stars'.[96] Carl Channell, soft-voiced, soft-lipped, would then make the solicitation.

North did not seem to care much for Channell. He kept his distance and did not return his calls;[97] even more, he tried to avoid explicitly discussing money. To close colleagues like Secord and Ledeen, by contrast, he seemed to be always sighing about his lack of money, the expense of college for his children, where he could find the cash for a new car (the metal box not mentioned); Secord thought he was 'poor as a church mouse' and confided to Hakim, when North was about to be advised on his finances by Hakim's tame Swiss banker, that this would be 'like making chicken soup out of chicken feathers.'[98] With Channell and his colleagues, however, North drew back, perhaps because they were so eager to draw him in. Contributors were brought into his office and their cheques waved under his nose; once, when Barbara Newington sold some of her stock, half a million dollars in certificates was dumped on his desk. He would say, uncomfortably, 'You don't have to show it to me.'[99]

Swept up by the philanthropy of these occasions, and with an important man to cultivate, the fund-raisers began to think they should help him too, but he was not encouraging. Channell wanted to set up a world-wide fund-raising scheme for the contras through a foundation in England, and there were suggestions that it could help North too, perhaps giving his eldest daughter a grant to go to Harvard. The scheme was discussed with North on several occasions; as Dan Conrad, a colleague of Channell's, remembered, 'he didn't warm to the conversation. On any occasion, he didn't warm to it. He kept putting roadblocks in the way.'[100] In the end, North suffered Channell to give him nothing but a briefcase, to replace his own when it fell apart in the street.[101]

He also went for a weekend, with his family, to Barbara Newington's house in Connecticut; but there, again, Channell overstepped some invisible line of propriety. Rich Miller, the man who handled the contra money after it had been solicited — dispensing it from his Cayman Islands account at North's direction, but ensuring that North was never sullied with a cash transfer — remembered how Channell and his hostess went up to North as he sat by the swimming pool on Sunday afternoon, not long awake. 'He asked Colonel North to give Barbara a description of the way things were going on the ground in Nicaragua,' said Miller,

[and] I got the feeling that he was somewhat disturbed by having to do that. He didn't really think that to be the purpose

of his being there. But he agreed to do it, and described to her the general situation on the ground for the resistance fighters.

And Spitz then asked Ollie . . . how much does it cost a month to keep their operation going? And Ollie's response was $2 million. And at that point he was beginning to be agitated, and he simply got up and kind of walked away. It was clear to me that he did not want to be put in the position he had just been put in.

And then Mr Channell asked Barbara Newington to please help. And she agreed.[102]

Deep within the operations, North tried his best — so it appears — not to know what was going on with money. He was often 'shocked' and 'surprised' at the hearings to find that much of the money he had intended to be siphoned to the contras had never got there;[103] in particular, that about $8m from the Iran arms sales was still on deposit in Hakim's bank account. 'I trusted,' he said of Secord, 'that he was an honourable man.'[104] Trustingly, he would get summary sheets of gross expenses of The Enterprise, sent as messages on the KL–43, but had never asked for an accounting sheet on even an annual basis; he relied on Secord's judgment 'to see that these moneys were appropriately allocated'.[105]

Secord, of course, was a friend. But even with men he scarcely knew North took the same line, insisting that he trusted them and did not want an accounting for any of the money he gave them. At the CIA, where covert operations were carried on with appropriated funds, rigorous accounts had to be kept by law; but this private replacement for the CIA was outside the statutes, bound — insofar as it was bound at all — virtually by bonds of honour between the players, like medieval outlaws. As Bob Dylan sang it once, in words that were picked up continually through the affair, 'To live outside the law, you must be honest.'

The DEA agents recruited by North to help ransom the hostages were given large amounts of money: at one time, $200,000 in four manila envelopes. There had already been trouble bringing this across the state line; it lay on the coffee table in North's office, while the agent explained that he would rather not walk it round the city to the DEA safe at two o'clock in the morning. North agreed, and put it in his briefcase.[106] Neither on this occasion, nor on others, was there any talk of receipts. The agent had no idea where the money came from, whether government or private sources; in the end, he supposed that it was CIA money. On the other hand, when you took CIA money you always wrote out a receipt. 'He didn't want anything,' said the agent, in some wonder; 'he didn't want anything written from us.' If the agent found out anything, names, vehicle numbers, that might open up some tunnel into Beirut, he would write them on scraps of paper and pass them to North as they walked in the park; similarly, if he incurred expenses, 'I would sometimes take a little piece of paper and I would say, hey, this is telephone calls, this is laundry, this is the bill.' North took them, but made it clear he did not want them. Once the agent claimed $3,700 for a trip and handed North an itemized bill; North simply said 'No, I believe you.' Sometimes the agent would simply call North to say 'It is about six to eight hundred'; no evidence or receipts at all. 'He wanted it that way,' he explained, haplessly, as the lawyers wondered why on earth there were no vouchers or claim forms.

> I said, do you want to see — he said I don't want to see anything. I trust you. He tried us out, you know, once or twice. After that —
> Q. What do you mean, 'tried you out'?
> A. You know, if you came back with ludicrous things.

The bond of trust had to work both ways, for North's unorthodox sources of money sometimes dried up completely. The agent would come to him to be reimbursed for the hotel or the laundry, and North would say he had no cash. 'I would tell him, hey, look, my American Express is calling me . . . He says I will get it for you as soon as I can. Trust me. He says, I am having a problem . . . I am a little short, trust me.' As the agent recalled, North had stipulated from the start that 'we get the money where we can get it.' No, it was not quite what he would have expected from Uncle Sam; but he trusted North, as requested, and sooner or later the money always came through. In many ways, he thought, it was a breath of fresh air working for North: no forms, no accounting, no red tape, just 'do what you have to do to get the hostages out.' If curious things happened, such as being reimbursed for hostage expenses in Hardee's hamburger restaurant on 18th Street ($7,000 in a yellow envelope inside an accordion folder), 'I didn't even look at him because I trusted him.'[107]

To lawyers who heard this, the chronic lack of accounting suggested clearly that something was wrong. A member of the government was using money for government business, and that money could never be traced or the business checked on. It was irregular; it was possibly illegal. The DEA agent and his colleagues, on the contrary, were confident it was fine. North 'always said it was okay'; and although he never said precisely who had okayed it, it was pretty clear that somebody higher up had done so. The cause was right, besides; they believed in it; and the law was nowhere on the scene. 'Why would I ask a guy working in the White House,' exclaimed one agent in amazement, 'if he's going to get in trouble?'

# Chapter 15

# Criminal Inquiries

WHEN the scandal broke, all these complications — where the edges of the law were, what was right and what wrong — should have been simplified. The amateur lawyers left the scene and the professionals came on, charged with finding out what had happened. Yet the administration's inquiry, such as it was, seemed to be shaped less by concern for laws than by fear of bad appearances. Crimes had been committed perhaps, but that was most unclear, and the administration was hardly keen to incriminate itself; what was imperative was that some sort of legal action should be taken to stem the avalanche of political scandal, and taken quickly. This chapter looks at the 'fact-finding mission' of November 1986 through the experiences of Meese and his deputy, Charles Cooper: two men on the sidelines suddenly brought to the centre of the stage.

The investigation proceeded with extreme slowness, the government's lawyers inching along in the dark. The Iran operation was still going on and was highly compartmentalized and sensitive. Early in November Meese had told Cooper to be prepared to look into the law relating to arms sales to Iran. Nothing specific that he could put a finger on, just the possibility of something 'coming down the pike'; it was an aside in a corridor as they went into a meeting. He told Cooper to limit his staff to one lawyer, just to be safe.[1] Poor Cooper: this turned out to be the grossest underestimate of the work involved.

215

He was a young lawyer, fresh-faced and pug-nosed, with the air at the hearings of an eager southerner suddenly dropped into unbelievable Washington sleaze; like Clark Kent, he would fight it somehow. But Cooper barely had time for the Iran inquiries at the best of times. Other things had to be done that were plainly more important for his legal career, such as 'a very lengthy lecture and article on consent decrees' and 'my first presentation to the President on the question of federalism'.[2] His colleague John McGinnis took on most of the task of searching the statutes on the basis of hints taken out of the newspapers.[3] They had nothing else to go on. 'Kind of groping around,' Cooper called this later; 'it was still an unformed notion that legal issues are raised by this.'[4]

To shape it up a little, he went to have a chat with Poindexter on November 12th. Here he got his first hard lead, a look at the Finding of January 17th, which Thompson produced from 'a hidden place' in his desk. Cooper had never seen a Finding before. He sat reading it while Thompson told him that it had been reviewed for legality by the Attorney General, and passed on. There was a cover memo with the Finding too, and that was useful; it cited an opinion of a former attorney general, comforting to Meese, as to how presidents could legally transfer arms and delay telling Congress; and this set Cooper on the legal trail at last.[5]

He wanted to know a few facts, too. But Thompson was more protective of his facts than he was of the Finding. Proper chronologies were being done, he kept telling Cooper and McGinnis; he would let them know more when he could.[6] Frustrated, Cooper was reduced to noting down 'facts' from the President's highly fantastical television account on November 13th, which he took in out of the corner of his eye while he tried to write his lecture.[7] After a week on the job, he had nothing much to show for it but some copies of the statutes relating to arms sales which he had given to Meese, neatly filed in a three-ring binder.[8] Meese, as John Richardson said, was 'very committed to looking at the law. He doesn't like for you to tell him what it says, he likes to look at the statutes and all that kind of thing.'[9] So he had his statutes, at least.

For his part, Meese was not worried yet about the legal side. He had been party to the debates in January 1986 about the principal Finding that Cooper had just looked at, and seemed to have fairly smartly disposed of quibbles then. Not much had taken up his time except the question of notifying Congress; but if the President transferred arms under the National Security Act, rather than under the Arms Export Control Act, he could delay telling Congress for as long as he liked. Casey had told him that.[10] They had all talked — himself, the President, Poindexter, Casey — about letting Congress know as soon as the hostages were all on the aircraft and out of Lebanon. If, in the event, the moment had never come, that was not their fault. 'Mine was not an in-depth review,' he admitted. 'It was more of a concurrence with the legal analysis done by General Counsel Sporkin.'[11] It was done in a matter of hours, and it was done orally: 'to keep the record clear. There is nothing wrong with that.'[12]

Until about November 20th, Meese maintained, he was not too worried about all this anyway. He did not know about either the November 1985 shipment of Hawks or the mini-Finding that justified it. Justifying something in retrospect, putting it right with the law when the horse was already well out of the barn, seemed to him 'of questionable legality';[13] but that had not been a cloud on the horizon in the first days of his inquiry. Cooper was not so sanguine. As he pursued his researches, the arms sales seemed to be cropping up earlier and earlier. According to a chronology Cooper received from the NSC on November 17th, there had been a transfer of arms to Iran by Israel as early as September 1985, well before the November shipment, and America appeared to have something to do with it. The next day Cooper went to a meeting chaired by the White House lawyer, Peter Wallinson, at which 'no-one knew much about arms sales'; to his horror, all kinds of legal suppositions and possibilities then started to spring to the surface, like bubbles. Iran was a terrorist nation, wasn't it? someone asked. Could anything be shipped there legally, even through intermediaries? Could the President approve the transfer of arms from a 'good' country like Israel to a 'bad' country like Iran? Or might such a transfer possibly be all right if the president personally approved of it when he found out about it afterwards? Cooper listened in confusion; he had no idea.[14]

He was worried now about the mechanics of the transfer of arms, but he had still found nothing that struck him as illegal. Various versions of the NSC chronology came in, some saying that weapons had been shipped in November, some maintaining that it was oil-drilling equipment; Cooper did not pause to think what might be going on there (he never, he admitted, attempted to compare the versions), but mostly passed them over to the overwhelmed McGinnis. Whether it had been Hawks or drilling equipment did not matter so much, he insisted; 'it wouldn't change the character of the event as a covert operation.'[15]

On November 20th, apparently for the first time, Cooper and Meese got together on the project. They both attended a meeting in Poindexter's office at which Casey's testimony to Congress was passed round in draft and debated. Casey, Poindexter and North were there, all strangers to Cooper. The discussion went way over his head; he barely spoke at all, but he noticed with awe how much North seemed to know, and how everyone in the room deferred to him as he 'straightened out' Casey's proposed testimony to Congress about the November Hawk shipment. The straightening out consisted of saying that nobody in the government (as opposed to nobody in the CIA) had known about the November shipment at the time it occurred: the most reassuring of lies. Meese sat quietly and caused no fuss, merely marking the changes on his copy.[16] He and Cooper left the meeting, Cooper remembered, 'with smiles on our faces . . . we were all about a course of action that was entirely proper.'[17] Buoyed up, Meese went off to a dinner at West Point.

While he was there, a call came in from Cooper on the secure line. It was 10 o'clock; Cooper was still at work. He had heard something that suggested to him that Casey's testimony, as amended, was not true; Shultz, for one, had known about the Hawk shipments at the time they occurred. If some people in the government had known about them, there ought to have been a Finding. Legal alarms were now ringing in Cooper's head (he said later that he had heard them faintly that afternoon, too, at the meeting in Poindexter's room); but it is hard to say whether they were sounding in the mind of Meese. He cancelled the next leg of his trip, to Harvard, and came back abruptly to Washington with the order that Casey's testimony was to be changed.[18] It was no clear proof of illegality, however, that had suddenly raised the temperature; it was a horror of inconsistency, of absurdity, and of huge political embarrassment. Intentionally to mislead Congress, as North appeared to be attempting, was a felony, but even at the hearings Meese still seemed to resist the idea that he should have raised legal objections. 'It's an offence to make false statements to Congress, isn't it?' Nields persisted. 'It's a felony, isn't it?' The Attorney General was imperturbable: 'I believe it is, yes.'[19]

In his various testimonies later, Meese implied that he was still bothered mostly about trying to get the facts straight. The story of the November shipment was getting too complicated. Too many people had small pieces of it, and even those small pieces did not fit together. At 11.30 in the morning of Friday 21st he went to see the President, offering to gather up the facts about that pesky shipment if Reagan wanted him to. Still no panic, at least as he retold it later. What he proposed, Meese insisted, was not a legal investigation. It was to be 'an administrative inquiry', an asking-round, for which he gave himself a weekend;[20] and he was to act not as the chief justice officer for the country but as the President's legal advisor, a friendly sort of chap. At the hearings, Representative Jim Courter asked why he hadn't behaved more like one of Agatha Christie's detectives, telling the murder suspects to touch nothing. Meese replied: 'It was not a Hercule Poirot investigation, or an investigation at all really.'[21] Not even that.

On the afternoon of November 21st, the chance to be Hercule Poirot came and went. Meese had an offer from William Webster, the head of the FBI, to bring the bureau into the case. 'Is there anything we can do for you?' Webster said he asked, not pushing; Meese replied, 'Well, I don't know of anything that's criminal at this point; do you?' 'No, not on what I know', said Webster. 'I don't know either.' Both agreed that it was a government administrative matter, probably not criminal; and that presidents, moreover, had been criticized in the past for bringing in the FBI for purely political reasons.[22] Cooper agreed with that. 'I mean,' he asked, 'on what basis would the AG have suggested, Mr President . . . we are going to send in the FBI agents and investigate criminally your White House? We had no basis for such a thing as that.'[23]

They continued to have no basis, for a while. The Attorney General's inquiries were relaxed. Shultz called and offered to talk; Meese fitted him in obligingly, not sure whether or not he wanted to get to a golf game.[24] He called Weinberger, distracted with a sick wife, and determined that the secretary of defence did not know enough about the shipments to warrant a meeting; they could talk about it later.[25] He called Poindexter, and asked him to get all relevant documents out for his aides to review. Saturday morning would do; there was no urgency.[26]

The only worrisome occurrence was his interview with McFarlane on the afternoon of the 21st, in which McFarlane seemed 'reluctant' and 'hesitant', 'not totally forthcoming'. Meese gave him what was to become his stock reminder, that he should not try to protect the President or put a good spin on things,[27] but McFarlane, drawing him aside at the end of the interview, implied that he had already taken the blame on himself for the Iran operation in general and the November shipment in particular; this, despite the fact that 'the President was four-square behind it.' Hearing such nerve-tingling stuff, Meese sought — for his own sake, as much as McFarlane's — to put a comfortable gloss on it. It might help, he said, from a legal point of view, if the President had approved it. It might mean that everything was kosher after all. [28]

Cooper, as usual, was bearing the brunt of the fact-finding mission. He also seemed to be bearing the brunt of the legal anxieties, such as they were. Everything was rushed, telescoped into an impossible span of hours. Cooper meant to be efficient in the weekend interviews, and take notes which he could get typed up afterwards. Instead, 'events kind of swept over me'; he typed up a page and a bit of the interview with McFarlane, getting as far as August 1985, and then abandoned the exercise.[29] He found McFarlane a bit odd, though he was hard-pressed to say why: ill at ease, perhaps. McFarlane's line that he had opposed the arms sales all along, but was happy to take the blame for them, seemed contradictory to Cooper, to say the least. His recollections, too, were flawed 'on a point where it seemed unlikely that recollection would be flawed',[30] and Cooper believed 'silently' that McFarlane knew that he knew that.[31]

As far as the law was concerned, all was still quiet. There were two inconsistent stories, Shultz's and McFarlane's, about what exactly had been shipped to Iran the November before, and who had known about it. McFarlane had said it was oil-drilling equipment, Shultz had maintained it was Hawks; Shultz said McFarlane had told him about it, and McFarlane said nobody knew. Cooper supposed, as Meese did, that this was just a case of faulty memories. With luck, memories might be jogged into synchronization. It was true that a disconcerting number of people seemed to know that the shipment had been Hawks, from the CIA's general counsel to the pilot of the aircraft, who had whispered as much into the ear of a man in the general counsel's office;[32] but Cooper still found that he was not thinking much about the need for a Finding. By lunch on the 22nd nothing had happened, in his mind, to put the legal cat properly among the pigeons.

It was then that Reynolds mentioned the memo he had found diverting money to the contras. This shocked Cooper, perhaps partly because it shocked Meese, a man so placid that Cooper had scarcely ever seen more than 'a flash of irritation' pass across his face.[33] Legally, however, he could not fathom what the diversion memo, or even the fact of a diversion, meant. When he gave his deposition, seven months later, he was still 'not sure I fully appreciate the legal significance of it.'[34] He knew little or nothing about the Boland Amendments. What had struck him, as he supposed it had also struck Meese, was how politically explosive the scheme was. The ramifications would be awful. The headlines could be imagined. Yes, his deposing lawyer agreed, it did look bad. But did Cooper understand why it was bad?

> *Q.* Of course, the political ramifications would only be there if there were possible legal problems, wouldn't that be a fair statement?
> *A.* I don't think so. [35]

Meese, too, maintained that after his initial cursing over the diversion he had pulled himself together quite quickly. All might not be as bad as it seemed. It might not have happened at all. What did they have, exactly? A proposition. If Meese is to be believed — and at this point his story began to stretch credibility — he did not even bother to mention the memo to Casey when he called round to see him at his house that night. They drank beer, and chatted, and Casey's family came in and out.[36] But as to the memo, 'We didn't know if this was a memo, somebody's pipe-dream, a proposal that had been implemented, hadn't been implemented, or anything else. We just had this thing here.' Besides, 'I guess it is just a lawyer's natural instinct not to talk about anything until we had more.'[37] Casey even proposed a bit more, that an associate of his was complaining that some of the money arising from the arms sales — and allegedly owing to creditors — had been diverted to other projects, including the contras. Still Meese went on savouring his beer. 'You don't tell somebody something until you know what it's all about,' he patiently explained to reporters five months later. 'I wanted to find out what North knew before I talked to Casey . . . This was just a common-sense way of approaching it.'[38] So the two canny lawyers sat, each amiably withholding information from the other.

Thus alerted and bothered, but still far from clear on the legal questions, Cooper and Meese set out for their interview with North the next afternoon. North confirmed their fears: he acknowledged that a diversion had happened, certainly once and possibly twice. Meese took the news in his stride, it seemed to Cooper. He did not get angry. No-one 'jumped around the room.'[39] North himself had been rather friendly, even calling Cooper 'Coop', although they had scarcely met;[40] and he had not brought a lawyer with him. Indeed, nobody had even mentioned such a thing. All Reynolds could remember was 'sort of a light banter to the effect, Geez, maybe I would be well advised to . . . To the extent he made any reference, it was as a joke.'[41]

When the memo suggesting the diversion was presented to North, nobody suggested there was any wrongdoing in it. It was North himself who had raised that possibility, describing the diversion as the only 'black' — or maybe 'dark' — element in the affair, and hoping aloud that it could be kept quiet. But how was it black, and how dark? All Cooper could surmise was that the diverted money might have been American money, belonging to the Treasury, 'but that was certainly not the inference that flowed from the facts that [North] related to us naturally.'[42] In fact, he had come away from the interview not knowing whether it was American money, Israeli money, or what it was.

Again, the chief worry was political; indeed, it was almost cosmetic. It was over what it would look like if the *Washington Post*, rather than the President, announced the story of the diversion to the world. Cooper remembered that he and Reynolds and Richardson brainstormed together after the interview, wondering how the administration could go public first and avoid a 'calamity' on a huge scale. The example of Watergate was still vivid in their minds: it was not what officials did that damned them, but their efforts to keep it quiet afterwards.[43]

The three aides passed their 'most enthusiastic, vigorous agreement' about the pre-emptive strike on to Meese, although they hardly thought he needed telling. This was political instinct, 'the facts of life'. And the Attorney General evidently knew. On Monday 24th he went round like a whirlwind, trying to tie things up. 'It was a rather hurried morning,' he admitted later, 'because I was trying to get this done so that I could get over to the White House.'[44] At 7.20 in the morning, Cooper was directed to start looking at the criminal laws. At 10 o'clock Meese talked to McFarlane about the diversion, 'essentially to compare what he knew with what Colonel North had told me': no questions about authorization, or whether the President knew, or who else knew at all, or why McFarlane hadn't divulged this piece of information the Friday before. McFarlane was already concerned about the diversion, even as little as he knew; he had already told North, in front of colleagues, that he had 'a problem', and later said he thought North must have realized, by the end at least, that the diversion was improper; he could not imagine 'this kind of thing being justified in law'.[45] But if he mentioned this in his interview with Meese, he was brief; according to the official chronology, Meese was done with him in two minutes. He showed him no documents, took no notes. 'It appeared that his knowledge was very limited of the whole thing,' he said later. 'It was just limited to what Colonel North had told him on the trip to Tehran.'[46]

Meese then went to announce the diversion to Regan and the President, asking no questions, taking no notes. It was not much more than a head-into-the-office to ask for a little more time for the investigation, just before the President went off to meet the chief of the Zulus. ('I have got a few last-minute things to button up,' Regan remembered Meese kept saying.)[47] At 2 o'clock he went to the President and Regan again; whatever they talked about (Zulus?), nobody remembered any mention of the diversion. At 4.15, again *sans* notebook, he went to talk for the first time to Poindexter. He was brief and informal, not in the least upset; Poindexter, proceeding with caution, said he knew about the diversion 'generally', but had not told the President.

> And then . . . he said I knew when this became public I would probably have to resign, not because there was anything wrong with it, as much as because of the political uproar it would cause.[48]

Meese did not enquire further. Had Poindexter said anything different, he testified later, he would have conducted a formal interview; but he had said what he had said, quickly done. Returning to the Oval Office, Meese told Reagan and Regan that he had finally 'gotten all the pieces'[49] and was 'looking at what applicable criminal laws there might be.' He did not ask Reagan whether anyone had been authorized to carry out the diversion, since it was 'obvious' no-one had. He also did not seem to ask him, then or later, whether he thought it was wrong. It was assumed that it was: 'that it shouldn't have happened, and it especially shouldn't have happened without the President knowing.'[50] So the President's conclusions were made for him.

The rest of Meese's interviews — with the Vice-President, a formality, and with Casey, who told him he had heard of the diversion just that minute from Regan — were handled with dispatch. He took no notes.[51] At the hearings, Senator Mitchell could not believe that the nation's top legal officer should conduct an inquiry that way. 'It may be strange to you,' Meese snapped. 'It may strike you that truth is stranger than fiction. But I take offence at the idea that it's hard to accept.'[52]

In effect, Meese now had his possible crime and his possible criminal. After Sunday's interview with North, all he needed was a little corroboration. McFarlane provided enough to tell the President, Poindexter enough to tell the public. But Poindexter had also implied that there might be nothing wrong, save appearances; and Meese himself, even on that Monday, was far from certain. In the afternoon he asked Cooper to look at the facts again, to determine 'whether there was any basis at all to commence a criminal inquiry and whether there were any possible criminal offences involved, because at that time there did not appear to be any apparent.'[53]

Back at his statutes Cooper, by now bone-weary, tried to get things straight. That evening he and the long-suffering McGinnis went over what McGinnis had turned up during the day, 'things like the Boland Amendment and possible misappropriation to personal use of government money, Anti-Deficiency Act, Neutrality Act . . . a host of things.'[54] Still there was nothing concrete; and when Cooper met the White House counsel on Tuesday 25th to draft, presumptuously, something for Poindexter to say as he resigned, he still could not impute even vicarious law-breaking to the national security advisor. Poindexter needed to go simply to calm things down. 'Doesn't know all details,' ran Cooper's notes: 'but in light of Cong[ression]al — Pres needs new for. policy team. Fresh start.'[55]

Events, however, did not wait on assistant attorneys general looking up the law. Before Cooper had finished or reported back, Meese found himself in the White House press room in front of a baying mob of reporters, trying to explain. It was 12.09 on the Tuesday afternoon, and Meese had not yet consulted properly with anyone from the criminal division. 'All the information is not yet in,' he admitted, eerily echoing Cooper's draft remarks for Poindexter; but 'the President directed that we make this information immediately available to the Congress and to the public through the media this noon.'[56] The sight of the Attorney General holding this press conference — Reagan had slipped out, almost furtively — immediately suggested to reporters the stink of illegality. When Meese mentioned the transfer of arms through Israel, the press started up in chorus: 'Was that legal? Was that legal?' Yes, replied Meese, confidently enough. Another piped up: 'Did what Colonel North do, is that a crime? Will he be prosecuted?' Meese hedged: they were still looking into exactly what North had done. Shouldn't a special prosecutor be appointed to look into it? asked a voice, and this time Meese was categorical: 'No.'

He was on the defensive. Impossible to contemplate that these reporters, completely unversed in law, should have a keener nose for infractions than he had. But it happened again. As he explained that the diversion had occurred 'when the funding was not being provided by the Congress,' another voice chimed in: 'Therefore, it was in violation of the — wasn't it?'

*A.* What?
*Q.* Is this definitely in violation of the law, then?
*A.* That's something we're looking at at the present time because it depends on two things: precisely what was done and precisely who did it . . .
*Q.* What's to prevent an increasingly cynical public from thinking that you went looking for a scapegoat and you came up with this whopper, but it doesn't have a lot to do with the original controversy?
*A.* Well, the only thing I can say is that we have been very careful to lay out the facts for you and for the American public just as rapidly as we've gotten them, much — much different

than we would do in a normal inquiry or investigation when we usually wait until the inquiry is complete.

Difficult, this; to pretend that the inquiry had been thorough, and to admit that it had been fast. In a sense, and probably as the administration had hoped, the reporters were bowled over by the speed of it all, barely knowing what questions to ask. Nevertheless, they seemed to think of angles, some of them simple, that Meese had not much considered yet; and in answering them, alert to the suspicion that he might have been lazy, he was almost brutally categorical. 'How high did this go?' someone asked. Just as high as a lieutenant-colonel and an admiral? Meese replied that they had checked 'rather extensively': no higher than that. And what about the money that was diverted, was it owed to the government? 'No,' said Meese, apparently oblivious to the fact that Cooper and McGinnis, somewhere in the Justice Department, were still struggling with the question. 'It was not owed to the US government . . . it was never United States funds . . . we have no control over that whatsoever.' Why, then, another wondered, was Poindxeter resigning, if criminality was not established? Well, Meese answered, the answer being obvious, he was a distinguished naval officer. Distinguished naval officers did that sort of thing. Mercifully, the reporter did not follow up.[57]

When the President's press man had rescued him, eventually pulling him away, Meese called in Bill Weld from the Criminal Division. He wanted to know, having started up furious investigative hounds in the mind of the press, whether there was any basis for starting a criminal inquiry. By his own account, he was still not sure there was any criminality there. People had 'misused their positions'; there seemed to be (poignant and revealing phrase) 'wrongdoing, at least in the sense of not following the President's directions';[58] but he did not feel he had stumbled on a nest of felons. Weld thought differently. As far as he was concerned, he should have been called in long before. He had asked Reynolds on the Friday, 'with some warmth' (though not, he said, wanting to angle for trade), whether anyone was looking into matters properly. On Monday 24th Meese had telephoned him to say that the reason he had not called in the Criminal Division was not 'negligence or sloppiness'; things were being done that way on purpose. So Weld waited.

When at last, on the Tuesday, he was told to go ahead, he had already taken 'a quick and dirty look' at the statutes covering the transfers to Iran; but the diversion was news to him. It was like a first-year law-school exam question, he remembered: What torts can you find here? The first that occurred to him was 'conspiracy to violate the Boland Amendment', and he wandered on from there: mail fraud, wire fraud, munitions statutes, tax violations, theft of government property.[59] A whole range of things with, as Richardson said, 'no facts to back them up yet'.[60] Later that afternoon he gave the 'laundry list' to Meese, noting that it contained 'several of his least favourite statutes'; he indicated, in Meese's words, that 'while it might be stretching, there were some possible offences' that might involve criminal laws.[61] By December 1st or 2nd, Weld thought he had enough to put in a request for a special prosecutor, and Meese agreed with him. Yet the panic was still essentially political; and at this point faint echoes could be heard of Joseph Heller's *Catch 22*, a book North considered one of his favourites.

> . . .the officer without insignia . . . wrote a word on a page in the folder. 'Chaplain', he continued, looking up, 'we accuse you also of the commission of crimes and infractions we don't even know about yet. Guilty or innocent?'
> 'I don't know, sir. How can I say if you don't tell me what they are?'
> 'How can we tell you if we don't know?'
> 'Guilty,' decided the colonel.
> 'Sure he's guilty,' agreed the major. 'If they're his crimes and infractions, he must have committed them.'[62]

The discovery of possible crime in one sphere, besides, had ruled out the necessity to look for crimes in another. According to one officer at the Justice Department, it was never quite clear what the criminal division had on the arms sales as a whole: 'but the contra memo was the thing that kept jumping up and down like some sort of a jack-in-the-box.'[63] Although Weld insisted that 'no way was I going to look only at the Nicaragua side of the fence,'[64] and although the subsequent hearings and reports picked away at the Iranian arms transfers, for criminal purposes they had no importance; the law was left as unclear as when Cooper had first puzzled over it, the activities merely 'mistaken', or 'foolish'. Indeed, as far as the special prosecutor was concerned, the Iran operation was completely legal. The third part of the first count of the indictment brought against Poindexter, North, Secord and Hakim, conspiracy to defraud, contained a sentence that was almost shocking. It claimed that the defendants had tried to defraud the country

> by deceitfully exploiting for their own purposes and corrupting a United States Government initiative involving the sale of arms to elements in Iran, rather than pursuing solely the

specified governmental objectives of the initiative, including the release of Americans being held hostage in Lebanon.[65]

The side-operations (buying the good ship *Erria*, spending money on ransom schemes) were, by this standard, legal too: 'otherwise lawful, but not within the Iran Finding'.[66] All that was illegal was a conspiracy to defraud the government that probably never occurred, characterized by various petty felonies that did occur. Lawrence Walsh, the special prosecutor, offered no rationale in law for why the Iran operation should suddenly appear scrubbed, tidy and respectable; it appeared to be a gesture of despair. Even the diversion, 'the heart of the case', as Walsh called it, never added up to an illegality. In the context of the indictments, as Gesell stated in the middle of North's trial, 'it was lawful and would be treated as lawful.'[67]

By that stage, the conspiracy charges has been dropped anyway: too complex, too all-embracing, too difficult to prove. Incredible as it seemed, the Iran-contra operations — so wide-ranging, so misconceived and so mocking of the will of Congress — boiled down to nothing but petty felonies: misleading Congress, shredding documents, preparing false chronologies, neglecting to pay for a fence. These were, as Mary McGrory complained, 'the moral equivalent of double parking'.[68] But the wider violations, as Cooper and McGinnis might have warned Walsh, were never sufficiently clear. Appearances were awful; the law trailed cautiously after.

In essence, the legal cast of Iran-contra had been set in those days in November. The administration was in panic, but not about statutes or the breaking of them; it could barely focus sufficiently to notice the smaller laws being broken under its nose. Nobody, for example, seemed to notice shredding of documents going on, or even suspected that anyone would try to cover their tracks that way. 'I mean, I may be too trusting and too naive,' said Cooper, quickly saying it before it was said for him; 'but that is an inconceivable event almost to me.'[69] Meese, apprised much later that North had destroyed documents on the Sunday night after he had interviewed him, thought they were 'probably irrelevant'.[70] Assuming that he was not dealing with criminality, he did not give orders to seal North's office until it was much too late.

The players, too, were extremely debonair about shredding. They had been shredding documents as Meese carried out his inquiry: but were shredding and obstruction of justice really the same thing? Members of the NSC staff were meant to shred secret papers; as North said, 'that's why the Government of the United States gave me a shredder; I mean, I didn't buy it myself.'[71] Shredding was almost a light-hearted occupation. 'Walk out the door, . . . turn the corner, turn on the shredder, drop them in,' as he explained the process. 'It eats them pretty quick.'[72] Turned them into confetti, in fact (breezy, funny stuff), unless you were over-ambitious and jammed up the works, as he and Fawn Hall did on the 21st. 'Did I get them all?' he asked innocently at the hearings, when Nields wondered whether other documents might have escaped his attention.[73] It could not be taken seriously, could not be criminal. The audience laughed with North, after all, as he made these remarks, and not long afterwards an advertisement appeared in a reputable Mexican newspaper: 'Intimus Shredders, as used by Oliver North at the White House.'[74]

McFarlane said he knew well what obstruction of justice was. He had known it equally well in November 21st 1986, sitting beside a worried and pensive North as they drove back downtown from Ledeen's house. North said, according to McFarlane, that there was going to have to be 'a shredding party'.[75] 'And you say that you did not, if I recall, in any way advise Colonel North that that was not the proper thing to do, that that was illegal; is that right?' asked Representative Rodino at the hearings.

*A.* That is right.
*Q.* You were riding with Colonel North at the time. Why did you not, knowing that you were going to see the Attorney General, tell the Attorney General?
*A.* I should have, Mr Chairman . . . I didn't take it as expressive of his intention to carry out a massive obstruction of justice.
    Now, I think I was wrong and I think that I am justifiably wrong about that.[76]

And suddenly the law was clear again. 'As you sit here today,' Senator Mitchell asked him, 'what do you feel the obligation of an American citizen is when he learns that a crime may be about to occur?

*A.* He should seek to prevent it.
*Q.* Did you do so in this case?
*A.* Not well enough.[77]

All three chief players appeared to have lied to Congress, too. But could misleading Congress be a crime, or not telling Congress everything you knew, when half Washington seemed to work that way? When North tried to throw out the charges against him in November 1988, he argued that he had never been formally warned that lying to Congress or destroying official documents was illegal; the judge rebuked him sharply for his cynicism.[78] North seemed to be implying that such behaviour was perfectly normal in government, not possibly criminal because everyone did it; and both jurors and appeal court judges, at least in part, agreed with him. He might really not have known his acts were illegal; or he might have known, but considered that any illegality was bleached out by presidential orders. North certainly seemed unworried on his own account: he told Coy, when offers of lawyers began to come into his office in October or November, that he had no legal problems at all.[79]

Part of the unreality of Iran-contra, therefore, was that the most shocking activities were not crimes; that the crimes, as charged, were actions the players hardly credited they could be brought to book for; and that the impetus to find those crimes, first and foremost, was fear of the wrong sort of story-line at the top of the evening news. The law, which seemed endlessly changeable and pliable while the scandal was in the making, remained as cloudy afterwards; and secondary, as before, to notions of what was necessary, or desirable, or 'right'. Being more or less what men made it, they could break it almost with impunity. And so the world went on.

# PART V

## Lives and Lies

I am but mad north north-west; when the wind is
southerly, I know a hawk from a handsaw.

*Hamlet*, Act II Sc. 2

This above all: to thine own self be true,
And it must follow, as the night the day,
Thou canst not then be false to any man.

*Hamlet*, Act 1, Sc.III*

The law, stretched and glossed as it was, was not the chief casualty
of the Iran-contra affair. That honour fell to the truth, battered
almost out of recognition both before the denouement and after.
Founded on deception, the operations were also concealed by lies;
and to some degree, and for a while, the lies worked. This chapter
considers the world of lies: how they became routine, how they were
justified, how Congress was bamboozled, and how in the end the
tiers of lies collapsed, leaving a dust that may never completely
clear.

* Included in 'Reef Points' for commital to memory by midshipmen

231

# Chapter 16

# The Realm of the Lie

MUCH of Iran-contra seemed improbable; the characters far-fetched, the negotiations ludicrous, the motivations touchingly simple-minded. Yet a great deal of it turned out to be true. This, believe it or not, was the way it had happened; these were the people America had dealt with; these were the subterfuges that had been engaged in. To follow the scandal at all involved a certain suspension of disbelief. It required submersion, too, in the realm of the lie.

Dozens of ways were found to colour the facts, conceal them, deny them, dress them up, water them down, put them in a good light. Policy, as Representative Hamilton put it, was driven by a series of lies.[1] The contra resupply began to raise questions from congressmen in August 1985 and August 1986; the Iran operation was exposed in November 1986. Both were protected with bulwarks of lies. McFarlane and North briefed congressmen, and letters were written, 'explaining' that the NSC had always kept its distance from the contras; Poindexter briefed Congress, and Reagan gave speeches, to give a cosmetic outline of the opening to Iran. These untruths were not always told easily or happily; but they were understood to be essential. The operations were, after all, covert, and their nature — as North explained — therefore lay in lies:

There is great deceit — deception practised in the conduct of covert operations. They are at essence a lie. We make every effort to deceive the enemy as to our intent, our conduct, and to deny the association of the United States with those activities ... and that is not wrong.[2]

The chief players in Iran-contra — none of them trained in covert operations or in the mildest work of secret agents — found themselves in a grey world, so they said, in which lies and double-crossing were the rule. The men in the contra resupply, according to Owen, loved 'Machiavellian politics, lies, deceit and scurrilous rumour';[3] if he disliked it himself, so often being the butt of it, he still faithfully reported it back. As for Iran, the Americans went into the swamp under the tattered wing of that liar *par excellence*, Ghorbanifar, and sat through many a meeting at which it was clear that he had systematically misled both sides. ('Nir [the chief Israeli contact] sort of let that go by the boards as being Iranian business practice,' said George Cave; 'I tried to argue that it is not quite that way.'[4])

Both the Iran and the contra operations were run on networks of informers and sub-informers whose word could not be trusted, but whose stories were accepted because they were the best intelligence to be had. In both operations aircraft flew with their markings painted out, with well-instructed incurious pilots and false manifests. The players themselves, as we have seen, sometimes sported false names, passports and hair, and fabricated press 'guidance' in case they were caught. They worked in compartments, and the compartments were protected with authorized false stories; and the talks with Iran, in particular, were full of statements and promises that were not true. Too hard to call it lying, though, said Cave; that was what Ghorbanifar did. When North did it, misleading the Iranians between mouthfuls of their pistachios, it was much closer to diplomacy.

I wouldn't put it as lying. I think that he was trying to prevent himself ... from having to make any categorical statements that we will or we won't do this ... he was somewhat reluctant to give a total negative reply on anything — he didn't want to cut off the negotiations ... I would say it's Middle East negotiation.[5]

North agreed. He offered tall tales too, about Reagan's private conversations and his 'weekends of prayer', but these were really pleasant deceptions: fuzzy enough to keep the Iranians interested in talking until negotiations reached a higher level, at which point they could be forgotten.[6] ('The objective is to string this out,' as the notes of the planning session read for the talks in Tehran; 'not just a two-hour slam bam, thank you ma'm.'[7])

Sometimes the objective was to keep the Iranians fascinated, or frightened, or on edge. As the American party waited the long hour to be received in Tehran, still on board the stuffy aircraft with the pallet of Hawk parts, they rehearsed under North's direction a briefing they intended to give the Iranians when they got to their hotel. Talking very loudly, hoping an Iranian or two would hear, they said they were worried that the Iranians might not believe the evidence they had of the Soviet invasion plan, and what a pity it was that they could not reveal the name of the Russian who had leaked it to them. North called him 'Vladimir'. He was a major-general (still nice and loud) who had taken part in two of the war games on the invasion of Iran. At this point, Cave snapped open a briefing book to give one of the Iranians a quick glance, and shut it again. It was a good bit of play-acting but, as Cave noted, they never actually performed the part they had rehearsed.[8] Major-General Vladimir was lost in the sweep of events.

The players liked to stress how skilfully they had bamboozled the tricky folk they had to deal with, 'out-frazzling them', as Cave put it.[9] But at the end of the day these ploys and jokes were lies, too; North admitted it. Asked about his little story that Weinberger had told Reagan he would be impeached if 'one more screw' went to Iran without the release of the hostages, North replied, with a hint of a proud smile, 'That is a bald-faced lie, told to the Iranians.' 'Question was, did you say it?' asked Nields. 'I absolutely said it,' said North. 'I said a lot of other things to the Iranians. To get our hostages home . . . . I lied every time I met the Iranians.'[10] And it was lying, surely, that didn't matter; par for the course.

Colleagues were bamboozled too; the web of necessary duplicity was thick. Charlie Allen met an instance of it in September 1986, when Nir was in Washington trying to reactivate the first Iranian channel, the one that featured Ghorbanifar. By this time, Allen was something of an expert in deception. He had been Ghorbanifar's case officer, for his sins, for about eight months, was well aware of his spectacular failures of polygraphs,[11] and could sum him up with ease as a fabricator. The September meeting — Ghorbanifar now the deceived, not the deceiver — was different, and worrying. North had been dealing with the Second Channel, and working to cut Ghorbanifar out, for at least two months. But he had told neither Nir nor Ghorbanifar, and for two or three hours one morning, at CIA headquarters, he went through the motions of discussing the use of the first channel to supply the remaining Hawk parts, as if it was still operational. Allen thought this bizarre. He gave his data, as North asked him to; Earl wrote down the cost of the parts and the packaging; but everyone there, with the exception of Nir (perhaps not even, Allen speculated, with the exception of him), knew that the shipment would never occur. Once or twice, Nir asked North probing questions about 'other contacts'; North deflected them, and carried on with the dissimulation.[12]

Allen could not really work out what was going on. These were people he did not consider sinister, going through some 'artifice' or 'charade'. He did not ask North what was happening, since it was almost a given of the affair that no-one asked North: North knew the truth, and his colleagues did not particularly want the burden — should he have told them — of concealing it for themselves. Had he asked North, North might well have told him it was a sham. When lies were told during negotiations, they were by no means hidden from those who had reason to know. North carried a little tape-recorder in his pocket or in his briefcase, and he or the CIA taped all the talks with the Iranians: 'so that there would never be any doubt in the minds of my superiors as to what I had said, or why I had said it . . . there was no effort whatsoever to deceive anybody in our government from that.'[13]

The fact that these tapes were made, transcribed, the tapes and transcriptions eventually handed over to lawyers, bathed the whole negotiations in a weird glow of honesty; just as, at the hearings, North's plain acknowledgement of lying gave him the allure of an utterly truthful man. The deceptions were up-front, accessible, plain, available. Anybody could hear them. In the same strange way, the fact that North could not find his way round his computer with sufficient skill to delete his private notes to Poindexter gave these notes, when they were recovered and published in full in the Tower Report, a striking openness. The frank deceptions — such as North's claim to have called the President of Costa Rica to choke off a press conference about the secret airstrip, when he had not[14] — seemed almost too candid to be dishonest. Several readers of the Tower Report talked of the principals afterwards not as men but as boys, with a child's propensity — no worse than that — to exaggerate and to fib: the sort of talk that inevitably went with undercover deeds.[15]

Moving in this grey world, men had to lie not simply to operate; they sometimes needed lies, North argued, merely to carry on. Most of his stories and jokes, fantastically apocryphal as they were, may not have been meant to deceive anyone. They smoothed the path a little, raised a smile, made him liked, just as they had done at difficult points in negotiations. North told Secord he had told the

President that the Ayatollah was helping out with the contras because Secord was tired, and needed perking up. 'Why would you joke with him if it wasn't true?' asked the humourless Nields, as if lawyers would never think of such a thing. 'To keep him engaged in the activity,' North answered.[16] All the tales of derring-do — North's escapades in the war zone in El Salvador, his pivotal roles in the invasion of Grenada and the overthrow of Marcos in the Philippines, his trips to Beirut and meetings with the President — were also designed to spur people on, to keep them close to him, to enhance his own importance and advance his causes, which were the President's causes. 'God bless poor Colonel North,' said Clair George, launching into an impersonation: 'Everything was his — "The world is mine, I'm going to see the President, I'm going to see the king, I'm going to fly down to Central America and have a private conference, how would you like some tickets to the Redskins game?"' The deposing lawyer wondered how his colleagues had put up with it.

Q. Here is a guy, he exaggerates, he lies to you, I mean —
A. No, I don't. I think — look, he had to run this whole thing. . . And in order to get it done, you've got to do some slight exaggeration. So Ollie would say, Clair George says this is fine, the President told me that. I don't think that reflects — yeah, I mean if we were all Jesuits it would be sort of difficult to understand.

But on the other hand, if you are operating in Washington and trying to do what he was trying to do, a certain amount of exaggeration is to be expected. Unfortunately when it ends up like this, that it's on record, and you know, I met Mike, and Mike says, I never met him, it's sad.[17]

To this day, the true and false have not been sorted out in North's stories. They may never be; with repetition the stories became true, as stories will. North told some of them on oath, and other witnesses threw cold water over them; the two versions henceforth stood, his extraordinary word against theirs. (Clair George, for example, thoroughly doubted North's story about the suicide pill that Casey had given him before he went to Tehran, claiming (bombast meeting bombast) that the rules for giving out such pills were stricter than those governing nuclear weapons; Casey could not have done it, though he might have given him a bottle of sleeping pills.)[18] Liman concluded of North, when his testimony was over, that if he had gone into Wall Street (Liman's home turf) he would have been 'the biggest producer of bonds ever. And then he would go broke, because he would buy everything he ever sold.'[19] In that sense, Iran-contra could only have happened in the 1980s: a sort of wholesale political junk-bond offering, with no shortage of takers.

Poindexter, ever low-key, admitted that North 'did have a tendency to be a little bit expansive in describing things.' He himself made a habit of reading North's memos through a 'filter', in particular substituting 'I' for the royal 'we' wherever it occurred.[20] 'Romanticism,' McFarlane called it; he had grown used to it, and simply overlooked it in reading.[21] Indeed, several of those who met this hyperbole, even those who were victims of it, admitted that it did not change their perception of North as a fundamentally honest man. Richard Armitage of the Defense Department thought that although North magnified everything, 'in his own mind it wasn't magnified — whatever he was working on was just as he was thinking or saying.'[22] And perhaps it was; in the realm of the lie, lies large and small — lies serious, lies for a joke — quickly became the normal kind of currency.

The word 'lie', however, was not one most of the players accepted for a moment. They eked out the truth, they withheld information, they were 'not sufficiently probing or self-critical' (McFarlane's phrase);[23] but they seldom, by their own admission, lied. An interesting instance occurred in October 1986, when Abrams was asked by a congressional committee about administration support for the contra resupply and replied that there was none. Alan Fiers and Clair George, both of whom knew the reverse to be true, sat beside him in silence. They did not even suppose they were hearing a lie, George said: perhaps Abrams really did not know what was going on. He ought to have telephoned him afterwards, he felt, 'saying "Elliott, if you don't know the way it is, that is not the way it is. I don't know what it is, but you shouldn't run around Washington categorically stating that nobody nowhere at all anywhere in any way is supporting the contras."'[24] But George did not do it, at the time or later; he was too obsessed with making sure that nobody suspected the CIA of helping, and to pull Abrams aside, to point out the error, would raise too many eyebrows. He 'didn't have the guts.' Besides, he hardly knew the man.[25]

Fiers, for his part, was also aware that Abrams's statement was wrong. But he did not want to be the first of the three to break rank and say so, because he was the junior officer. In any case, the question had not been directed to him, 'and for that I was extremely grateful'; it was his business to keep quiet.[26] In Abrams's blanket assertion of innocence they both silently concurred. Both men, thinking about it later, were troubled that they had not spoken out; but it was absolutely not a case of lying. They did not do that sort of thing.[27] No more did Abrams, who described his October statements at the hearings as 'completely honest and completely wrong'.[28]

This was a fairly common formulation. To do something honest and harmless, simply not saying something, or saying it wrong, should not necessarily bring down that terrible charge of lying. McFarlane, accused of lying to Congress about the contras, defended himself indignantly.

> My thinking was that I felt quite passionately about the fact that I had not wilfully lied to people. It's very clear that I had withheld information. Now, the moral turpitude and I don't have a good word for that — the — for me the assertion that I had wilfully lied to somebody is something I just couldn't accept. [29]

Poindexter said the same, mildly objecting to Liman's charge that he had tried to put out a cover-story about Iran in November 1986.

> We wanted to withhold the fact ... of Israel's direct involvement and to put out frankly as little information as we could ... and so to that extent, yes, we were withholding information. But there was never any effort on my part to mislead or deceive anybody.
>
> You know, you or somebody else could interpret withholding information as misleading, but — I guess that's a judgment call. . . I don't view it that way.[30]

The example of Watergate was to hand: there the crime had consisted not in the bugging of the Democratic headquarters, but in the cover-up that followed. The crime was lying; but that was another scandal, long ago. 'I lived through Watergate, John,' McFarlane wrote to Poindexter on November 13th 1986, in perhaps the most poignant note of the whole episode. 'Well-meaning people who were in on the early stages of the communications strategy didn't intend to lie but ultimately came around to it.'[31] Within a few days of that note, McFarlane himself was apparently putting false paragraphs into the official chronologies of the Iran operation. But this was different, he argued. He was trying to lay out the facts; indeed, he had involved himself in the chronology in the first place because he had spotted things that were 'not quite accurate' in it.[32] The intention was not at all to lie, and he did not believe he had ever done so.

Indeed, in Bob Earl's view, this was simply the way the political world worked. He still did not think, in the spring of 1989, that people had lied as the scandal was breaking: 'There was a political situation which I believed was receiving a political solution.'[33] The public, faced with the ubiquity of lies in this case, seemed generally to take Earl's view; though they might be nauseated by the scale and scope of the untruthfulness, they were used to that sort of thing coming out of Washington. What they heard throughout the explanations and hearings and investigations seemed to be the tinny but authentic echo of ordinary Washington talk, and McFarlane confirmed their suspicions. At North's trial, he tried to explain the traditional procedures used by national security advisors to brief Congress: they were not straightforward. Not to tell the truth was not quite a matter of giving 'less than full answers', he told Judge Gesell; not *'per se'*.

> *Gesell*: Well, what do you mean by that? . . . You tell the truth or you don't tell the truth or you put a gloss on it? What are you trying to say?
> *A.* . . . You don't lie. You put your own interpretation on what the truth is.
> *Q.* When you say you put your own interpretation on what the truth is, do you turn night into day?
> *A.* No, certainly not. You present the truth as it best expresses your behaviour.[34]

So there was no such thing as lying; and there was also not much chance of the plain truth emerging. To tell the truth was highly dangerous. Nicaragua was a war, domestic as well as foreign; Iran was a 'high-risk operation' that the CIA, at least, hoped might be over in a few months. The thinking was military, the compartments very small. Participants were served up little pieces of the truth; non-players were expected to know better than to ask for it. And beyond these boxes and compartments and specific anxieties lay a more general danger, 'the nation at risk in a dangerous world'. At the hearings, solemn lectures were given to Congress: if it persisted in this dogged way, trying to nose out the truth under every stone, it would damage the nation's best interests and invite the scorn of its allies. 'In my opinion,' said Secord,

> the whole world is laughing at us. We have been hearing a lot of talk about the cleansing effect of these kinds of hearings. I don't believe that. I don't think it does that. I think it opens up our guts to the rest of the world, they not only don't trust us like they used to, they also laugh at us.[35]

North, still bothered by his friend Ivan, reminded Nields that the hearings were being broadcast in Moscow. If it were possible to insulate them under some sort of giant bubble, he would be only too happy to explain covert operations to the American public. But America was not an hermetic capsule, 'and I'm at a loss as to how we could announce it to the American people and not have the Soviets know about it.'[36] Nields kept pushing: was it not Congress that was the real enemy, and the Russians a pretext? Congress could scuttle both operations, presumably would have done if it could. The Russians were unlikely to have bothered. In the end, North admitted it: 'I didn't want to show Congress a single word on this whole thing.'[37]

One was an enemy as much as the other; and clearly no enemy could be dealt with straightforwardly. War imposed its own rules on combatants, and the first were silence and stealth. Wasn't answering questions from congressional committees, as Liman suggested to Earl, a bit like being under interrogation by enemy forces? Hadn't he and North decided in that circumstance, in 1986, 'to treat it as if it were the North Koreans,' and to lie?[38] Earl found that question tricky in the particulars, but he agreed with the principle. Indeed, at North's trial he defended his lies to the FBI in the spit-and-polish terms of any good soldier instructed in his duty.

Q. You didn't tell the complete truth, is that correct?
A. That's correct, sir. I was still protecting the compartment.
Q. You told them the truth about certain things . . . right?
A. Yes, sir. I told them as much as I felt I could.
Q. And you lied to them about other things, right?
A. That's correct, sir. I maintained the cover story on portions of the operation.
Q. In answer to other questions you did lie, isn't that correct?
A. Yes, sir, I protected certain information.[39]

Soldiers, after all, protected their own side; there was a virtue in that denial or that silence. And this was a paradox, because military men, as others pointed out, were trained not to lie; indeed the training of North and McFarlane and Poindexter was more rigorous, in this respect, than most people's. Well beyond their inculcation as children, they had been indoctrinated as cadets with the Annapolis Honor Concept: trained to be 'truthful, trustworthy, honest and forthright at all times and under all circumstances'.[40] North acknowledged this himself,[41] and it was a point made tellingly by Inouye at the end of North's public testimony. What was the first Honor Concept, 'first, because it's so important, over and above the others'? 'A member of the brigade does not lie, cheat or steal.' What was a lie? 'A deliberate oral or written untruth.' What did 'mislead' or 'deceive' mean? 'A deliberate misrepresentation of a true situation by being untruthful or withholding or omitting or subtly wording information.'[42]

As they listened to this, North and Sullivan could scarcely contain themselves. It was one thing for the Honor Concept, and Inouye, to define lies in the abstract; another entirely, so the players thought, to put them in the context of duty, obedience and other moral imperatives attached to the twin crusades of hostages and contras. When Senator Trible raised the Honor Concept with Poindexter, the admiral was indignant: 'I have always lived by the Honor Concept. I still live that way today. One of the things you also learn at the Naval Academy is the ability to exercise independent judgments that are in the best interests of the United States.'[43]

Perhaps the normal moral injunction against lying, as Representative Cheney suggested during Poindexter's testimony, had to be suspended on occasion: just as the injunction against killing had to be suspended when wars were just. 'There may be times,' he mused, 'when telling truth is more immoral than failing to'.[44] Not necessarily when before a congressional committee, or in November 1986; but Cheney at least accepted the necessity in the abstract. War, or emergency, or exigency, could bring out the lies. This was how North described it too, noting that it was no more pleasant than the other duties of war.

> Please. It was not right. It does not leave me with a good taste in my mouth. I want you to know lying does not come easy to me. I want you to know that it doesn't come easy to anybody, but I think we all had to weigh in the balance the difference between lives and lies. I had to do that on a number of occasions in both these operations, and it is not an easy thing to do . . . I was trying to weigh — and I'm sure that others . . . were trying to weigh in their souls what would happen to those, for example, whom I had sent money to or enticed into this activity or published pamphlets in Managua, or ran radio broadcasts or blew things up or flew airplanes if the American government stood up and announced it.[45]

As the *Washington Post* pointed out, North not only made a heroic act out of admitting his lies to Congress; he also implied there was heroism of a sort in the lies themselves, because telling them had been so hard. War had forced them out of him, and perhaps those cartoonists were not entirely wrong who showed him hung with medals specifically for his deceits. He had emerged as the master of the Patriotic Lie, as Mark Hosenball defined it in the *New Republic*: the cover-up of actions presumed to be right and good, the sort of falsehood that could be promoted (as Fawn Hall also promoted it with her shredding and document-smuggling) with a defiant toss of the head.[46] Keker got hold of this variety at North's trial, calling it the 'flat-out, 100%, old-fashioned American lie'.[47] 'It's almost as though he's a symbol for honesty,' said one mixed-up Kansas Republican; 'People respected the fact that he admitted that he lied and tried to do something.'[48]

When the debate reached the military colleges and academies in the summer of 1987, other soldiers agreed that the line of moral duty was unclear. Was it always wrong for an officer to lie? What if he were under orders to withhold information, to keep quiet, as all the Iran-contra players were, with the order coming directly from the Commander-in-chief? What if the obligation of silence even prevented an officer going to someone outside for moral direction, as General Kelley confirmed that North could not have gone to him with these questions of lying, even if he had wanted to?[49] Since covert operations seemed inevitably to bring so many lies in their wake, should active-duty officers get involved in them at all?

The question at the base of all these — whether it was ever permissible for an officer to lie — was submitted by a reporter to the Joint Chiefs of Staff in July 1987, but they declined to reply.[50] The answer to that precise question did not seem to be in the rule book. Journalists next rounded up what retired officers they could; but for every one who said that it was always wrong to lie, another would say that their job had required North and Poindexter to do so. There was a distinction, said one, between lying 'for oneself' and lying for the government. Another thought that when a soldier moved into a political arena, the Honor Concept ought to be 'reinterpreted'. Perhaps if you could not lie, cheat and steal to just a small degree, you could not function politically at all.[51]

At the 1988 conference on military ethics, one major defined what he called the 'North Doctrine': 'When telling the truth will result in placing lives at risk, do not tell the truth.' Another major responded, mysteriously, that 'the North Doctrine must be rejected as an end which is not normally within the reach of the military professional.'[52] What did that mean? That because so extreme an occurrence did not arise more than occasionally, it did not count? Did 'not within the reach' mean outside the ambit of soldierly good conduct, or merely something that, if a soldier was lucky, he would not need to think about?

Sometimes, the players insisted, there seemed to be simply

nothing else to do; it was the lesser of two bad choices.[53] Abandon friends on the field of battle, as the most sentimental equation put it, or deceive Congress. And this too was not lying; it was 'protecting', the sort of thing soldiers naturally did. When McFarlane dropped into North's office on November 18th to help with the chronologies of the Iran operation, his duty was apparent at once: he should protect the President, whose servant he no longer was. 'I think we all had an instinct,' he said later, 'that the President should not be harmed.'[54] North, cutting and pasting and worrying, kept saying 'The President must not be hurt by this.'[55] He said the same to McFarlane as they rode downtown in McFarlane's car two days later, desperately repeating that 'it not involve the President, that the President be protected.' He meant, as it turned out, covering and shredding for him; but what, Senator Cohen wondered, did McFarlane think he had meant by that?

> *A.* Well, I really believe, sir, that it was a kind of an instinctive statement by a subordinate about what he believed his duty to be. I don't think it was any more conspiratorial than that, that here he was, a lieutenant colonel, talking to someone, me, that he saw as his superior, and he wanted to acknowledge to me . . . that he believed he had an obligation to protect me and the President.[56]

North's own subordinates followed. Chief among Earl's 'multitude of motives' for lying repeatedly to the FBI once North had been dismissed were 'intense personal loyalty to my commander-in-chief and to my chain of command,' a loyalty that he admitted had come out of the Marines.[57] Fawn Hall, with no soldierly experience, automatically slipped into their jargon. 'I don't use the word "cover-up",' she snapped, referring to North's 'shredding party': 'I would use the word "protect".'

> *Rudman.* Who are you protecting it from?
> *A.* I was protecting the initiative.
> *Q.* From whom?
> *A.* From everyone. Because . . . there could be people whose lives could be lost. And I also felt that . . . if this thing breaks out, I mean we're sitting up here talking about all kinds of things. We're revealing sources, we're revealing everything. [58]

This was less a democracy than a state of snoopers and destroyers, and the little band at the NSC prepared to resist them as best it could. Fawn insisted that the atmosphere at the shredding party was not 'lock the doors, pull down the shades', but routine: the pieces fed into the shredder at only a slightly enhanced rate from 'normal' days, her boss going almost insouciantly through his files to pull out this paper or that.[59] But the shredder jammed under the weight of the load; and by the Tuesday following, the 25th, when North had been fired, Fawn entered into her proper dramatic role, the loyal girl of the resistance concealing the facts in her clothes. With the contentious memos carefully hidden ('Tehran minutes in one of the boots . . . and the PROF notes . . . inside the back of my skirt')[60], she got into a waiting car with North and his lawyer, Tom Green. The memos taken out and handed over, she was given her first lesson in dealing with the enemy. 'What would you say if you were asked about the shredding?' Green asked her, no interrogator specified, for they were all around. Fawn answered: 'We shred every day.' 'Good,' he replied. Two days later a telephone call came from a White House lawyer, asking about the shredding. 'We shred every day,' came the practised answer.[61] The lie worked; the enemy retreated.

'There would be lives lost' was the crucial phrase: lives lost by telling the truth. Lives of the hostages, lives of contras, lives of Iranian officials who had dared to meet the representatives of the Great Satan, lives of the kind of men whose lives had already been lost, flying rickety supply aircraft too close to Sandinista guns. To some extent these were certainly men in jeopardy, and some of their names remain blacked out to this day in the depositions and exhibits. The classified papers concerned with the case, in their thousands, presumably contain dozens more, together with the programmes that cannot be talked about, the deals that cannot be revealed, and the numerous top-secret 'projects of the United States and of Israel'.[62] These were what needed protecting, even from the intelligence committees of Congress: with lies, if it came to that.

One exchange between North and Nields, about the chronologies put out in November 1986, is worth quoting at length. North had given his reasons for not telling a straight story: in sum, the protection of the Iran operation and the people involved. Nields then asked him whether there were not 'reasons on the other side'.

A. Would you — would you give me — I don't understand your question about reasons on the other side.
Q. There were reasons — well, I'll give them to you and see if you agree.
     First of all, you put some value, don't you, in the truth?
A. I put great value in the truth. I came here to tell it.

*Q.* So that was — that would be a reason not to put forward this version of the facts?
*A.* The truth would be a reason not to put forward that version of the facts. But ... I put great value on the lives of the American hostages ... I put great value in the possibility — that we could have ended the Iran-Iraq war —
*Q.* We'll get back to that in a minute.
*Sullivan.* Let him finish, counsel.
*A.* — and we had established for the first time a direct contact with people inside Iran who might be able to assist us in a strategic re-opening, and who were at great risk if they were exposed.[63]

And so, yes, I put great value on the truth ... But I also put great value on human life.

Lying, in North's words, became something that 'honorable men' were 'forced to do'. Liman asked: 'Who forced them?' North slid past the question; Liman asked it again. North blamed 'the relationship that exists between the Executive and the Congress on these issues',[64] a lame answer, but more or less repeating McFarlane's view of the world: the two sides simply could not talk straight to each other. It was Congress that had obliged them all to lie, not understanding the urgency and drama of what was going on. Poindexter produced an extraordinary piece of logic: 'We had to misinform Congress because we were using private funds; with appropriated money you have to be truthful.'[65]

Here was truth, then, in all its strangeness and smallness: as little as necessary, and when forced. 'Some sort of cryptic, artful truth' was how Bob Earl described it.[66] Truth was both malleable and friable; you could shape it, and you could split it into little pieces, 'shreds' and 'smidgeons',[67] as Poindexter called them. The admiral had his own semantic way of disbursing truth: chopping logic, defining words, debating concepts, all in a manner which Senator Cohen described as 'summer lightning, just a sort of innocuous illumination'.[68] Poindexter called administration support for the contras a secret activity, but not a covert action; maintained that America had 'acquiesced in' the first shipment to Iran, but had not authorized it.[69] To his mind these were large differences, and also ways out of a corner: a stickler for accuracy, he then appeared to be more intent on truth than his interrogators.

H.L. Mencken, commenting on truth, said it was not 'to be thrown about loosely, like small change; it is something to be cherished and hoarded and disbursed only when absolutely necessary.' Poindexter's view, to put it in its best light, appeared to be similar. The distinction being made here was much the same as Cicero's paraphrase of Diogenes, *Aliud est celare, aliud tacere.*

> At this present moment I am not concealing from you, even if I am not revealing to you, the nature of the gods or the highest good; and to know these secrets would be of much more advantage to you than to know the price of wheat was down. But I am under no obligation to tell you everything that it may be to your interest to be told.[70]

This was precisely the thought behind the decision never to mention the diversion, as North understood it: 'It was never supposed to be revealed and I made no effort to do so.'[71] But for an action officer, the distinction between concealing and not revealing was sometimes trickier to draw. Asked at Poindexter's trial 'What's the difference between you not being able to reveal something and you having to conceal something?' North answered: 'Nothing.'[72]

It all ended up, as he explained, in lies. And at Poindexter's trial, in 1990, North appeared to have some strange things to say about lying. He had not been worried about telling lies to Congress, he said. He had been much more concerned that a cover story agreed with Israel 'for over a year' might be blown, or that part of it 'wouldn't hold water'; he was worried that the lies would be 'futile', that they wouldn't work. Neither prosecutor nor judge could quite believe these answers; they thought perhaps North had misunderstood the question. He was concerned about lies in themselves, wasn't he? North answered yes; but went on to say it was political embarrassment he was afraid of, the act of being caught out in stories inconsistent with stories told before. And when the judge inquired whether he was worried at all about 'deceiving the elected representatives of the American people,' he replied: 'I don't recall that even entering my mind.'[73]

So truth was put in its place: it was merely one of a number of imperatives. Lawyers might put it first, but lawyers — the implication heavy in everything North said — did not work on dangerous secret operations, nor did they understand the risks of open government. The world was very tricky. It was not a place where truth could venture with much safety into the open air. Lies ruled it and with lies the players were going to go.

# Chapter 17

# Questions and Answers

So the lies spread, apparently as natural a part of both operations as the air and the sky. Yet the players argued that there would have been no noticeable lies, no bothersome false confections, if people had not asked questions. The lies began to multiply when Congress and press began to catch glimpses of the operations, and when the administration decided that it had no option but to answer the accusations. Had everyone minded their own business, it might have been all right.

It was Earl, North's deputy, who proved to be expert on the theory of questions and answers. He was a Rhodes scholar, ex-CIA and a Marine; the slippery concepts rolled off his tongue as easily as if he had learned them in boot camp. This is what you did, he told the deposing lawyers, when you were faced with the exposure of something you did not want exposed: the demise of the First Channel, perhaps, or contacts with Iran of any sort at all.

I have, from my own reference, categorized phase one, two and three in this damage control operation from the leak we started with, phase one being no comment/deny, no comment, where possible . . . deny it if there's no other way, but to protect the compartment.

. . . Phase two . . . was briefing of the Congress and

ultimately the people on what could be briefed to them about the compartment, if it became necessary to go from phase one to phase two.

Phase three is . . . termination of the compartment.[1]

'No comment/deny' was thus the administration's tactic of first resort, underpinning both operations. Poindexter acknowledged, however, that it was difficult to invoke convincingly. When he and Nir had met at the beginning of January, 1986, they had discussed what best to do if the Iran operation were exposed, and people began to ask questions. One option was

the US just simply deny it, and for a while that was a working hypothesis, but frankly —
*Liman.* Wasn't very plausible?
*A.* Wasn't very plausible.
*Q.* All right.
*A.* So I never took that part of the plan seriously.[2]

Perhaps he did not, but others did. North's notebooks contain a message in code, passed on presumably to Nir: 'JOSHUA [Reagan] ALSO WANTS BOTH YOUR GOVERNMENT AND OURS TO STAY WITH NO COMMENT IF OPERATION IS DISCLOSED.'[3]

It was imperative not to talk; and indeed the administration was obsessed from top to bottom with the possibility of leaks. 'If I could ever find that bastard who is unnamed administration official,' muttered Reagan in notes of a meeting with congressional leaders on November 25th 1986, 'all sorts of punishment on him.'[4] As for Nicaragua, at the end of the meeting of the National Security Planning Group on June 25th 1984, the crucial meeting on alternative help for the contras that remained secret until North's trial, McFarlane remarked that 'I certainly hope none of this discussion will be made public in any way.' The President chimed in: 'If such a story gets out, we'll all be hanging by our thumbs in front of the White House until we found out who did it.'[5] With that the meeting ended, and the lesson seems to have throbbed in McFarlane's ears.

He never did say go lie to the Congress. He did say, for example, when learning of the contribution of a foreign country that we shouldn't share that with the Congress.

*Keker*. Okay. Did he say to lie about it or just not talk about it?
*A*. He did not say to lie about it. He just said do not share that information . . . I . . . reported to him that no-one knew about this and he made clear to me that no-one should and let's keep it that way.
*Gesell*. So you felt you were acting on President Reagan's instructions in not telling the CIA.
*A*. Yes, sir . . .
*Q*. The President didn't mention the Congress, did he?
*A*. Not *per se*, it was everybody basically. Anybody.[6]

North at his trial remembered 'numerous occasions' when he was told by McFarlane and Poindexter that the President did not want his operational activities revealed, nor the President's own role in the support network, nor the Saudi contribution.[7] The 'circle of awareness', as McFarlane put it, was to be kept as small as possible; and that, in itself, would reduce the need to lie when people began to get curious. By sparing a cabinet member like Shultz too much knowledge, McFarlane gave him 'deniability';[8] he was protected from having to lie if Congress asked him questions, and indeed he appeared at the end of the day as a witness of singular soundness, as much in the dark and outraged by it all as Congress was. Poindexter, too, did his duty by concealing from Casey North's work for the contras (probably to no effect, as it turned out), because 'I didn't want to . . . put him or [the other cabinet officers] in a position of being evasive in terms of answering questions.'[9] And he did it, not least, by apparently keeping the diversion from Reagan, believing that his Commander-in-Chief should be given deniability whether he wanted it or not. With some satisfaction, not untinged with bitterness, Poindexter saw the scheme play itself out in front of him. He believed, he said, that the President would have approved the diversion if he had asked him.

*Q*. But the President, Admiral, has indicated . . . that he would not have authorized it. He said that.
*A*. I understand that he said that, and I would have expected him to say that. That's the whole idea of deniability.[10]

As a congressional lawyer reminded Poindexter, there were two sides to the coin of deniability. Some men were saved from making the choice between having to lie or disclosing the truth, and they were saved by men who took the burden of that choice on themselves.[11] Yet there was a third choice, and one that stopped short of lying: not to say anything at all. People came frequently before the intelligence committees of Congress, Keker reminded North's jury, and would say they were not authorized to answer the questions they were asked: 'And the intelligence committees go, "Fine. We don't need to know. That's fine. Don't tell us the secret."'[12] Keker also suggested another answer, suitable for Marines: 'Leave us alone, get out of here';[13] and implied that the questioners would melt away. But North, for one, had tried this tactic and found it did not work; he had tried it with the contra operation.

In August 1985 and August 1986 Congressmen Hamilton and Barnes sent letters to the White House and the national security advisor, inquiring about the NSC and the contras. Both McFarlane and Poindexter told Reagan about these awkward questions, and apparently received silence back; a response that seemed to be taken to mean that they should somehow keep silent themselves. North said he was prepared to try.[14] When the first letters came in 1985 to McFarlane, he immediately suggested that 'we shouldn't be answering this, that this kind of information is what is properly the prerogative of the White House and the President and we ought to invoke . . . executive privilege.' The NSC's activities, he said rudely, were not a matter for 'congressional intrusion'. McFarlane told him he had to say a bit more than that; so he drafted a page-and-a-half-long letter 'to try not to give a response, to avoid the issues', and then went up to the fifth floor of the Old Executive Office Building, where there was a law library, and burrowed through the books. He was looking for executive privilege. What he found he put in a third paragraph of the reply, as weighty as he could make it: 'The right of the executive to maintain confidentiality of information important to the conduct of our foreign policies must be sustained.'

McFarlane did not let the paragraph in, and the White House lawyer thought the whole approach 'too confrontational'. It was also useless; for all the elaborate covert play, the contra operation was too well known, too explosive, and too obvious. Little bits of it trailed out everywhere, as in the truly secret projects they did not; the widows and the corporate sponsors and the customs handlers and the office colleagues and the sympathetic congressmen — yes, congressmen too — were all privy to pieces of it. If so many people knew, or thought they knew, what was really going on, could a man stand up before members of Congress and say he would not tell them? Another approach had to be found; a subtler way; a lying way. To the inquisitors' version of the truth, which was not wholly true, had to be opposed another version, also not wholly true: the next step into the quagmire.

The next step involved the creation of a cover story. Earl could explain that, too.

> Cover was a consuming concern of this whole enterprise, to protect the cover of this thing . . . there was always a need for cover to explain that which people could see, so that the covert operation would not be blown by the press or somebody else stumbling onto something and not having a plausible explanation to make it go away.[15]

Earl was talking in this case about Iran, an operation that originally had a fairly good cover: the cover of Israel. As Don Regan put it with typical straightforwardness, 'If Israel did it, that's one thing; but if we were to do it, that would be bad and we'd have to be able to deny it.'[16] Israel had begun the arms transfers to Iran in the summer of 1985, and continued to provide the cover up to February or March of 1986, when the Americans decided wholeheartedly to try the scheme for themselves. At the White House meeting of December 7th when the initiative was apparently turned off, then on again, multifarious ways were discussed to handle the arms transfers directly; but 'What about letting Israel do it?' Reagan asked. 'Can't we just go on that way?'[17]

As long as Israel was dabbling in Iran, it seemed safer to hide behind the Star of David. For domestic consumption, the connection with Israel was always to be kept secret: the Finding of January 17th referred to Israel as 'private parties',[18] a cover Reagan tried to keep long after it was blown.[19] Even the trip to Tehran in May was meant to be covered by using two Israeli 707s, as Earl explained, in case somebody should pick up details of the flight plan: 'the fact that it was Israel would help provide protection of the operation, that it didn't automatically point the finger that the United States was doing this. Sure.'[20]

To some degree, Israel was willing to be the explanation; hence the offer of the 707s in May. To some degree, too, America was a cover for Israel, which also could not be seen by its citizens to be dealing with Iran. Clumping about on the scene, the Americans drew the Iranians' attention; the Israelis, meanwhile, pursued a more subtle and different agenda of their own. But Israel would not take responsibility for catastrophes caused by Americans. At that point, the cover collapsed. North and Poindexter tried, once the diversion was out, to pin the blame for it on Nir (and indeed the general notion of creating a slush fund for other projects did seem to originate with Israel, though perhaps not the particular wheeze of sending it to the contras). Back came the chilling reply: 'I cannot back this story.'[21] Covers had their uses, up to a point; but there was always the danger of pushing them a notch too far, revealing them as churlish flesh and blood.

In the contra operation, the 'plausible explanation' was that private individuals were helping the rebels, not the National Security Council. When North was asked where the money was coming from and who was organizing the flights, he would reply 'private patriotic Americans', or alternatively 'the good Americans'. Even McFarlane, implausibly, said he asked that question of him, and heard that answer.[22] Abrams apparently got that sort of drift too; and it became the basis for the most famous recital of the contra cover-story, that given in a television question-and-answer with Rowland Evans and Robert Novak on October 11th 1986. The resupply of the contras, Abrams said, 'was not in any sense a US government operation. None.' ('That would be illegal.') Instead, it was managed by 'some people who were in Air America, which had connections with the CIA in Vietnam, and who were in Vietnam, and who were in the CIA . . . there are a whole bunch of them.' Was there any truth to the rumour, Evans asked him, that they were being paid with Saudi Arabian money? 'As far as I am aware it is just plain false.'[23]

To be quite unequivocal about the general shape of the cover, as Abrams was, was the first key to briefing Congress and the press; the second was to answer with the greatest specificity, even pernicketiness, the questions people subsequently asked. Abrams proved even better at that. The technique reached its apotheosis in a question posed to him in November 1986 about the money he himself had solicited for the contras from Brunei. He was asked whether the rebels had received money 'from Israel or any other mid-Eastern country', a question that was meant to elicit the answer 'Brunei'; Abrams answered 'No', because, as he explained later, 'Brunei is not a Middle Eastern country.' The members had expected him to volunteer the fact that, even if those specific countries had not sent money, other countries had; but Abrams was not volunteering anything. His congressional questioners at the hearings, six months later, got to the heart of the case.

*Q.* In fact, your approach . . . was that unless the senators asked you exactly the right question, using exactly the right words, they weren't going to get the right answer. Wasn't that the approach?
*A.* That's exactly a correct description.[24]

Abrams had also been asked in November whether he had ever discussed 'problems of fund-raising by the contras' with members of the NSC staff. 'Well, yes,' he had answered; then 'No, I can't remember.' He had changed his answer because the senator had asked about fund-raising 'by the contras', and Abrams had only discussed with the NSC fund-raising *for* the contras. He knew exactly what the senator meant; but if Congress could not be absolutely precise, why did it deserve to know?

> *Q*. And so your answer . . . was technically correct, because the Brunei solicitation was not fund-raising by the contras, right?
> *A*. It was technically, yes, it was technically correct.[25]

McFarlane, less gifted with the gab and less alert to lawyers' niceties, was also driven to this route when the rebuffs and straight denials ran out. He was reduced to technical correctness. The first rule was to volunteer no information, to do nothing beyond strictly answering the questions asked. Thus when he was interviewed by Meese on November 21st, McFarlane said nothing about the diversion of funds to the contras. 'As you sit here today, were you trying to hold anything back from Meese?' Liman asked him. 'I don't think so,' McFarlane said; 'he was asking the questions.'

> *Q*. Why didn't you tell him about the diversion?
> *A*. As I say, he was asking the questions.[26]

McFarlane was also asked about soliciting, and the question once asked could not be avoided. He was extraordinarily sure, in his own mind, that he had never solicited Prince Bandar of Saudi Arabia for money for the contras; there had been nothing more than vague mutual commiserations about problems across the globe. When he faced the House Foreign Affairs Committee on December 8th, 1986, he was categorical.

> I did not solicit any country at any time to make contributions to the contras. I have seen the reports that various countries have, Country Two [Saudi Arabia], third countries, and I have no idea of the extent of that or anything else.[27]

This was untrue, but if you picked it apart, as McFarlane suggested later, there was accuracy in it. He had not solicited, or not as far as he believed. He had indeed seen the reports that countries had given money. And he did not, he insisted, know the full extent of what Saudi Arabia had given. 'I was trying to use some tortured language,' he admitted (language, like truth, being infinitely plastic and malleable). 'Inappropriately, I think, but to comment that I did not know the extent. To be technically accurate, I did not and do not today.'[28]

It was not, he confessed, a full account, just as he had not given the House Intelligence Committee a full account of North's exertions for the contras. 'What did the Congress have to do,' pleaded Nields, more in frustration than in anger; 'what did they have to ask you in order for you to tell them what you actually knew?'[29] McFarlane ignored that question as rhetorical, but the answer was clear. Congress had to ask questions that were utterly specific about the activities it was guessing at or half-knew; and as long as it was not specific enough, the administration would keep the upper hand.

When Representatives Hamilton and Barnes sent their letters of inquiry to him in the summer of 1985, McFarlane had taken essentially the same tack. Having decided that North could not simply brush the questions off, he gave him a challenge. He was to try to answer without giving the game away, and also without telling lies. He gave him a bit of guidance on the right sort of things to say, phrases which gave a good impression and were not untrue, and left him to get on with it.

To North, this was 'like throwing gasoline on the fire': the press already having wind of so much of what the NSC was doing, fudging facts would only make things worse, or so he maintained at his trial.[30] McFarlane did not agree; he thought North was exaggerating again. He had not told him to lie. The technique was one he explained in his description of sections of his own reply to Barnes: you did not necessarily give a full and fair summation of the facts, but you nonetheless provided 'administrative information that is true'.[31] This did not amount, McFarlane thought, to deliberately misleading Congress.

Congress, moreover, was not blameless itself. Enough media reports had appeared to tell members the truth if they wished to know it. Some members, such as Henry Hyde and Bill McCollum, had been briefed specifically on contra support from third countries by McFarlane.[32] But, like so many members of the administration, they did not necessarily wish to reveal that they had heard. They did not need to acquiesce so readily, and so gratefully, in the lies the administration told them; and the fact that they did so suggested, to Liman at least, that there was winking and dissimulation going on on that side too.[33] North maintained later that his meeting with Hamilton's committee was mostly meant 'to mollify the ego of Chairman Hamilton', convincing him he had brought the White House to heel over the affair; after which the White House could proceed as normal.[34] Congress was afraid of the responsibility of abandoning the contras; therefore, when it was lied to, as Liman said, 'it could not have been surprised.' McFarlane, though he seemed to Gesell to be choking on semantics, knew exactly what shadow-game he was involved in, and there were two teams.

'Like you,' began North's first draft to Hamilton, 'I was concerned when I saw recent press accounts alleging that National Security Council staff were violating the law and, as a result, I have looked into the matter very carefully.'[35] Was that true? asked Keker. North said yes, he assumed so; he had seen the stacks of documents assembled in McFarlane's office, though perhaps not before he had written the letter. And everyone was certainly concerned, although possibly not for the reasons Hamilton might suppose.

Next sentence, said Keker.

As you know, I and all the NSC staff members have sworn an oath to uphold the law and defend the Constitution and we all take that solemn oath very seriously.

'Was that a true statement when you wrote it?' Keker asked. Sure, said North; it still was. 'Next sentence', said Keker.

The President as well is sworn to uphold the law and at the time the Boland Amendment became law he instructed the staff to be extremely careful to observe and obey the law.

'True?' asked Keker.

Here North said he did not know; he assumed 'that that is the kind of words that I got from Mr McFarlane.' Much later on, Reagan confirmed it; but it did not much matter. All this was McFarlane and North throwing obsequious dust in the eyes of Congress. Tellingly, each sentence of the draft began with a statement that was true; and each led on neatly to an invention, an exaggeration, or, at best, an assumption. As he got the words from McFarlane, however (assuming that is where they all came from), North claimed he did not take them to be lies. Suspending his critical faculties, playing the innocent subordinate to the hilt — as he did throughout his trial — he assumed they were correct, and put them in the letter.

Keker ploughed on.

Okay . . . you go on to say . . . 'I can assure you that the actions of my staff have been fully consistent with both the spirit and the letter of the law.' Now, where did that language come from?
A. I would guess out of my typewriter.

*Q*. Okay. And why did you — It was false, wasn't it?
*A*. No.

North gave his usual reasons. Boland did not allow the CIA or the Defence Department to spend money, and neither had. 'Furthermore,' it did not apply to the NSC. 'Furthermore,' Reagan and McFarlane and Casey had sent him running all over the place, going outside the government to support the contras; he assumed that was 'consistent with the letter and spirit of Boland,' or it was a lot of energy wasted. 'Okay, is any of that in the letter?' Keker asked. Some was, said North; the bit about not spending appropriated money.

The letter went on, in apparent detail, to tell what the NSC had done with and for the contras. Discussions about political unity, in Washington and Managua; advice on not committing atrocities; proposals for a church-mediated dialogue with the Sandinistas; administration of humanitarian aid. All these things had occurred, but as North/McFarlane said, all innocence, 'We did not interpret the Boland restrictions as prohibiting contact with the resistance for these purposes.' And indeed they were right, technically. But all the military activities, the solicitations from third countries, the Southern Front and the airstrip? asked Keker.

You left that part out.
*A*. Yes.
*Q*. Why?
*A*. Because it would have revealed the essence of all that had transpired since Mr McFarlane and the President got the $32m from Saudi Arabia.

The full truth, in other words, had to be kept back, and the little bits of 'technical correctness' allowed through instead. It was hard work, North wanted Keker to understand. Perhaps the letter was not 'adequate'; perhaps it was not 'full in its exposition or its description'; but 'it tried to stick as close as we could to what was the truth without revealing all of what they wanted to know.' North thought it was the best he could do, executive privilege having been thrown out of the window. It was true, or mostly true, as far as it went; and it went no distance at all.

Unfortunately, McFarlane did not leave matters there. He wrote a second draft that was categorical in its denials. Not only had his staff not violated the letter or spirit of Boland, he wrote, but 'I would extend my assurance to the violation of any law.'[36] 'At no time' had the NSC encouraged military activities. Funds had not been solicited, ever, 'either from Americans or from third parties.' McFarlane concluded, unblinking, 'Thank you for this opportunity to clarify what has been a most unfortunate misrepresentation of the facts.'[37]

No point in telling him that the letter was false, North said, admitting that he had not tried to do so; McFarlane was perfectly aware of that.[38] By his own account he made one last appeal for asserting executive privilege, not answering at all. McFarlane said 'Go ahead; give me your edits.' Faced with this catalogue of falsehood, however, all the fight went out of North; his edits came back as little fiddlings with McFarlane's lumpen grammar, improvements to his style. In effect, having entered well and truly into lying, he set about gilding and polishing.

> His original wording was, as I read it, 'This urging against continuing military activities was as close as we ever came to commenting upon or making influence the military aspect of their struggle.' And I tried to convert that into some readable English by saying, 'Our emphasis on a political, rather than a military, solution to the situation was as close as we ever came to influencing the military aspect of their struggle.'
> *Q.* You thought it would be better to tell the Congress —
> *A.* I thought it would be better English.[39]

And so North proceeded through the letter, picking out 'minor little nits', putting in 'fluff'. 'Equally clear' became 'also true'; 'activities in support of' became 'contacts with' (not quite fluff, that one); 'pluralistic' became 'democratic'. The lies stood, set in smoother words. At his trial, Keker bearded him mercilessly for this 'better English'. It was nothing more, or less, than North's last gasp of free-agency. By that stage his argument with McFarlane was lost; his draft letters, according to Vince Cannistraro of the NSC, had been 'modified, changed, redirected, redrafted, *etcetera*', and he had given up complaining; he would play and obey. The letter, he recognized, was 'thoroughly deceptive and false', either concealing what he was doing for the contras or denying it, but his conscience did not appear to prick him.

> First of all, it's not a completely false letter. There are falsehoods in the letter. Second of all, I was uncomfortable principally from the point of view that that kind of answer was going to make things worse . . .
> *Q.* Those sound like political concerns. What I'm —
> *A.* Those were political concerns.[40]

Keker wondered why North was not more troubled; why he had not gone to his Commandant, or to a lawyer, worrying that lies were being laid before Congress. North answered that it had not occurred to him. No law had been broken by that, as far as he knew; McFarlane had presumably checked with a lawyer, anyway, and besides, the President wanted the whole thing kept secret: 'And if that's what the President wanted to tell the Congress he could tell them pretty much what he wanted or not tell them pretty much what he wanted.'[41] Reagan, when asked in February 1990, concurred: shown copies of Poindexter's later letters to Congress, completely predicated on McFarlane's, he remarked 'I am in total agreement. If I had written it myself, I might have used a little profanity.'[42]

Reagan, however, drew the sempiternal distinction: he had not authorized his aides to lie. He simply wanted nothing said; and how they resolved that was up to them. Perhaps they saw no difference. Keker put it to North:

*Q.* Do you see any difference between the President saying . . . that Saudi Arabia contributed 32 million to the contras that may never be revealed and somebody lying about it?
*A.* Yes, there is obviously a difference and I understand it.
*Q.* What's the difference?
*A.* The difference is that one is right and the other one gets you into all kinds of problems, particularly politically.[43]

Indeed, in that August of 1985, the lies were already multiplying. McFarlane had assembled a little pile of documents — six in all — that were 'problematic', as he called them, inconsistent with the sham assurances that had just been given to Congress about the contras. By North's account he showed them to him, saying they needed to be 'fixed' to be consistent; by McFarlane's account North offered voluntarily to make them 'clearer'; either way, both men understood that the record would somehow have to be altered.[44] Late one night, as he was leaving, two pages were put into McFarlane's hand. 'These operations were conducted in response to guidance' had become 'in response to awareness' that the contras had to cut Sandinista supply lines, 'to remove the impression that there had been guidance given by anyone in our government'. On the last page, which North had promised to 'make more clear', 'current arrangements' (that is, Saudi money) had been changed to '*ad hoc*' arrangements, and a sentence about delivery of lethal supplies had been deleted. Well, McFarlane explained later, it had been misleading; it gave the impression that the NSC itself was running the guns into the jungle camps, when it was not. On the other hand, could original documents be altered, just like that? McFarlane took the question to Thompson.

> [I] said, look, if a memorandum contains an error and misrepresents what is true, even though it is a document, an official document, can it be corrected to — or mustn't it be corrected to reflect the truth?

Thompson accepted the question as guileless. You could do it, he replied, but the document had to show it was a re-work; in other words, spill the beans. There could be no simple substitution of one piece of paper for another, and McFarlane, though he was 'kind of torn in my own mind about it', threw North's altered versions away. They were not exactly misleading, he thought, as corrections went. But they did 'remove information'.

Meanwhile, the NSC's misleading letter had been sent back to Congress. On the basis of that letter, McFarlane met the House Intelligence Committee on September 10th, 1985, and falsely reassured them; on the basis of his briefing, North wrote answers to a list of detailed congressional questions. By now, there was no getting round it. These were not careful redactions of the truth, but lies. Although North knew well enough what he had been doing on the Nicaragua front, he dutifully went to McFarlane to get the 'proper' answers, the false answers, that had already been given.[45] So as not 'to create even further problems than we already had', the deception was carefully synchronized with the boss. Had North used his influence to facilitate the movement of supplies to the contras? No. Was it true that tactical advice had gone from North to the contras? 'Patently untrue.'

There was, of course, another option. Gesell noticed it, though North did not.

> *Q.* Colonel North, did you at any time in this process consider in your own mind just not doing it?
> *A.* Doing the memorandum, your honour?
> *Q.* Yes. Saying — just say no, I won't do it.
> *A.* No, I did not.[46]

All he thought he could do to exculpate himself from this blizzard of falsehood was to attach a cover sheet, telling McFarlane that the answers were 'based on your earlier briefing before the committee' and to include a last paragraph on executive privilege. 'Okay, but change the last page of questions and answers,' came back the implacable reply.

*Keker*: At any point . . . did Colonel North express misgivings to you about the statements that you were making to Congress?
*McFarlane*: I think he did occasionally.
*Q.* What did he say?
*A.* I'm not sure. Occasionally he said that's hard to defend, or we're very close to that, or genuine worries.
*Q.* You both knew you were doing something wrong, didn't you?
*A.* I knew I was withholding information.
*Q.* And Colonel North by what he said to you indicated that he knew he was doing something wrong too . . .?
*A.* He was clearly concerned. I made the judgment and I went ahead with it.[47]

And North did as he was told. As he sat in his office one day, labouring over the answers, his colleague Vince Cannistraro dropped by to see him. North showed him some of his replies; Cannistraro put his hand to his nose and gestured to make it grow, like Pinnochio's.[48] Well, North told him, I am not entirely a free agent. 'Is this truthful?' Cannistraro asked him. North, parrying such a straight question, said he thought it was legal.

He seemed to be very concerned about it and . . . I don't recall whether he actually told me this or it was just my general impression, but it seemed to me that his responses were being very narrowly crafted to be precisely correct but maybe not fully truthful. I don't recall that he said to me that he was lying. It was my impression that he was lying, however.[49]

In his own view North was still concealing, rather than lying. Yet this was a distinction more easily maintained on paper than in person. In writing, you could take the time to craft the truth rather carefully. Face to face with colleagues, the convincing answer was to look a man straight in the eye, and lie. McFarlane, with his 'tortured language' that seemed to lay him open as a book, was not good at it; but even he convinced Hamilton when he met the House Intelligence Committee informally on September 10th, and the candid falsehoods uttered then set the administration's tone to the end of the chapter. 'How do you accuse a man of lying,' asked Keker, 'if he looks you in the eye, a respectful person, and tells you that X is Y or yes is no? You don't.'[50]

After the scandal broke, this was something North appeared to be expert at. His expression was singularly straight and clear, his words utterly convincing, as the country discovered at the hearings. 'His spirituality and decency shine from his face', ran one letter to the *New York Times*, 'for truth is a shining pillar against which evil has no defence.'[51] Yet his talent for persuasion was called in relatively late to deal with the inquiries from Congress. Drafting misleading letters in the background, North was not summoned for some time to mislead Congress to its face. Hamilton wanted to talk to him directly in the summer of 1985, and North offered to go; but McFarlane would not let him.[52] Possibly he was afraid that North would try to assert executive privilege again, and tell Congress to get lost; possibly he thought him not skilled enough in the ancient tradition of artful withholding between national security advisors and inquisitive legislators. He was soon to prove that he was.

McFarlane left at the end of 1985, but the structure of denials and false assurances built around the contra operation remained under Poindexter, and now North was the man in charge of it; the man who carried with him the institutional memory of lying. When the congressional questions appeared again the next summer (the contra support operation proceeding as boldly as ever) it was North who was naturally deputed to answer them. It might be helpful, Hamilton told Poindexter, if North were to talk with the House Intelligence Committee in the Situation Room, informally. North's account of what happened there became notorious: there was no better illustration, it seemed, of sheer bravado and lust for lying.

> I will tell you right now, counsel, and all the members here gathered that I misled the Congress. I mis —
> *Nields.* At that meeting?
> *A.* At that meeting.
> *Q.* Face to face?
> *A.* Face to face.
> *Q.* You made false statements to them about your activities in support of the contras?
> *A.* I did. Furthermore, I did so with a purpose, and I did so with the purpose of hopefully avoiding the very kind of thing that we have before us now.[53]

By the time of his trial, with a jail term riding on the charge that he had lied, North did not brag about the meeting any more. He began to cry, explaining that he had known he was doing wrong.[54] Keker asked the jury to ignore these 'crocodile tears',[55] but the jurors let North off. Subordinates all, janitors, housewives and clerks, they were soft-hearted to the dilemmas of a staff man apparently sent to lie for his superiors; and they also accepted, as North had argued, that politicians lied a lot. It might not be proper, but it was almost as common as air, and therefore could not be criminal.

Poindexter, then, was the man in charge of setting up the meeting. He told Hamilton his 'rules of engagement': it should be informal, narrowly focussed, no notes taken. And it should be held in the White House Situation Room, where the NSC had a tactical advantage. He also referred Hamilton back to the letters written by McFarlane, which might 'resolve your doubts'. [56]

Poindexter was well aware that there was a tradition of secrecy surrounding the contra operation; indeed, no man prized secrecy more. He did not also know in detail, he claimed, about the tradition of misleading Congress. When the congressional letters arrived in 1985 he had been temporarily in charge, McFarlane being in California; but he had never seen McFarlane's eventual reply to Hamilton. He had merely been sent a draft for 'review' and 'input', which seemed to have made no impression. At some point the next summer, with the meeting pending, he asked Thompson to dig the letter out for him; Thompson did so, but Poindexter 'never got around to looking at it.' When he finally did, reading the version that was printed in the Tower Report in February 1987, he was surprised. 'I wouldn't have responded the way that Mr McFarlane did', he said. 'I would not have been as categorical . . . I don't know what Bud had in mind.'[57]

Not only did Poindexter not look at McFarlane's letter, but he did not look at the Resolution of Inquiry that was drawn up by Congress detailing the questions that North was likely to be asked. 'I simply didn't get into that level of detail of the issue at that point,' he admitted. Had he done, he thought later, it might have been prudent to sit down with North and give him some instruction on what he was to say to the committee. As it was, he supposed that North, with his 'resourcefulness', could handle it: 'he had been in much tougher situations, I was sure. The analysis as to exactly how he would do it did not enter my mind.' Certainly he did not tell him to lie. He assumed that North would withhold information 'and be evasive, frankly, in answering questions. My objective all along was to withhold from the Congress exactly what the NSC staff was doing.' Most of the stories that were floating round about contra resupply were fanciful, in any case; Poindexter thought North could 'knock those stories down by answering the questions truthfully.'[58]

On the other hand, if North were to be asked a direct question calling for information about a story that was not false, Poindexter did not quite know how he would wriggle round it. How, for example, asked Nields, would he answer the question of whether the contras had received money from any foreign government in 1985 or 1986, when the money had come in secretly from Saudi Arabia? Poindexter went into a little huddle with his lawyer, emerging to say: 'I would have expected him to withhold that information.'

> *Q.* But . . . supposing that question were asked, what should he answer?
> *A.* . . . I don't know.[59]

North told Poindexter, according to his account at both their trials, that to talk to Hamilton was 'not a very good idea', nor helpful; there were certain things he had been told never to reveal. Poindexter, on the telephone, reassured him. The meeting was in the White House after all, 'on our turf'; Hamilton was from Indiana, as Poindexter was; in short, North could handle it.[60] Yet when Owen asked North how he was going to answer the questions, he said he did not know; perhaps he would not have to.[61] The congressmen might cancel the meeting, or perhaps Poindexter would extend a fatherly arm, like McFarlane, and take the burden on himself. Perhaps, too, when he got there (North's last, best hope), 'there would be enough friends of the policy down there to kind of vector the conversation away from the tough issues. And I was wrong.'[62]

Owen had asked North, not long before, how to answer questions from two Republican congressmen on his own account; North had answered, 'Use your best judgment. They are good people.'[63] In his own case, his advice seemed almost impossible to take. Earl found North unusually lacking in certainty in those days, desperate for guidance from his boss. He kept telephoning, trying to get in touch with him.[64] But Poindexter was away on leave, at his cabin on a lake in western Maryland, with a 'very protective outer office',[65] and it seemed to Earl that his leave might not have been coincidental.[66] When it came to the crunch, silence was what Poindexter preferred.

Earl might have tried to give North some advice, as he had done before; but he seems to have watched from afar. He knew there was 'compartmented information that was not to be shared', because the President had said it should not be briefed to Congress. 'How do you respond to a question that refers to that which is in the compartment?' he mused aloud at his deposition. Liman offered some suggestions.

> Well, one way you respond, of course, is by saying, I'm not free to answer that question. That's an option. And another option is to protect the information by lying. That's correct too, right?

*A.* Sure. I mean, I would say a cover story.
*Q.* But a cover story can be a lie, right?
*A.* It can be, or it can be a half-truth, a partial truth, a limited statement that protects. [67]

In the end, this was what North fell back on. By the time of the meeting, according to Poindexter's aides Sable and Pearson, who went with him, he had recovered from his hesitation; he was confident and relaxed, and, turning up last in the packed room, sat down in the chair usually reserved for the President.[68] It was mid-morning; coffees were handed out, and Hamilton remembered doughnuts.[69] It was all informal enough, North implied later, to make his lying of fairly small consequence.[70] He talked for about 15 minutes, including an explanation of 'the United States' legal position . . . under the Boland Amendment', and then answered questions for half an hour. Exactly how he answered is not known in detail, but he denied again that he had given military advice to the contras and gave the impression that he saw Owen only occasionally.[71] Owen asked North how he had dealt with that question shortly afterwards, and appeared relieved to hear the answer;[72] he admitted later that he automatically provided the same sort of cover for North, when people confronted him. ('Do you know Colonel North?' 'I have met him.'[73])

At last the questions seemed to run out; North offered to answer more, but Hamilton and his colleagues pronounced themselves satisfied. They would not need to take the matter further. Poindexter returned to find a note from Pearson summarizing the deceptions, beginning 'Session was success. North's remarks were thorough and convincing.' 'Well done,' he wrote to North. Well done for lying, presumably? asked Liman.

*Poindexter.* That is my note. What well done refers to is not clear.
*Q.* It is not clear to you?
*A.* It is not clear to me . . .
*Q.* What was it that Oliver North had done that was well?
*A.* He had apparently appeared, and had satisfied Chairman Hamilton.[74]

If Poindexter did not know what the note meant, North claimed that he did not have much idea either. He told Poindexter's prosecutor, at first, that he could not remember receiving it at all; then that he had, but that he could not recall 'having any emotion' when he read it.[75] By that stage, every possible permutation had been tried to conceal the truth about support for the contras: denials, refusals to answer, cover stories, statements that were 'technically correct' or 'not untrue'; and unadorned lies. Perhaps, like Hawthorne's Arthur Dimmesdale, North had by then become so fixed in the deceptions that it was better to keep feelings out of it; perhaps, by that stage, he had indeed felt nothing at all.

# Chapter 18

# 'A Damn Good Story'

THE denials superseded, the cover stories crumbling, the 'technically correct' answers no longer satisfactory, the administration was driven at last to try to explain what it had done. The contra operation was never redacted in this fashion, because in a way it was simple enough and the rationale already public. Iran, however, was a far harder policy to explain. Official policy, impressed on allies too, was that there should be no dealings with Iran, no negotiations with terrorists of any stripe, and no ransom arrangements for hostages. All had been ignored, and the first transfers of arms through Israel had not even been sanctioned by law. The administration had to explain why America, not always pulled by Israel, had done these things. It proved to be the hardest story that any of the players had ever attempted to tell.

When the Iranian operation began to come to light, in November 1986, the chief players automatically took the line of denial; or most did. Don Regan, by his own account, was the only man who thought from the start that someone should try to tell the tale. These things could not be kept secret, he kept saying. The cover was blown.[1] On every side, however, people disagreed with him. Regan dated their fascination with denials from November 3rd, when David Jacobsen, the last hostage to be traded for arms, was given a reception in the Rose Garden of the White House. Regan was most struck by what happened next.

[Jacobsen] said in his remarks — he had cautioned the media against discussing this . . . 'For God's sake, don't talk about that . . . You're endangering the lives of people I love. These are my friends.' That made quite an impression on the President. And even though this same day I urged him again to get the story out, he said 'No we can't, Don. We can't endanger those lives.' And he didn't.[2]

On November 4th the President's press man, having asked in all innocence 'What is this story?' was told by Poindexter 'Brush that story off; there is nothing to that.'[3] On the same day, on board the presidential aircraft, Poindexter handed out a written answer to the question of what was going on between America and Iran. It was, Earl remembered, a masterpiece of double-speak, 'very carefully crafted'. For the duration of the arms shipments, Iran had ceased to support terrorist acts against the United States. Poindexter's statement read that as long as the Iranian government continued to sponsor or support acts of terrorism against Americans, America would not sell Iran weapons.[4]

By that stage, however, the canniest denials did not stop the questions coming. 'Mr President,' asked a bold reporter on the 6th, 'do we have a deal going with Iran of some sort?' 'No comment,' said Reagan briskly.

But could I suggest an appeal to all of you with regard to this: that the speculation, the commenting and all, on a story that came out of the Middle East that to us has no foundation — that all of that is making it more difficult for us in our effort to get the other hostages free.[5]

The line of 'No comment' was still holding the next week, when a crisis meeting was held on November 10th to decide what to do. Alton Keel, Poindexter's deputy, remembered feeling optimistic. There was 'excitement' about the contacts with Rafsanjani, about the prospect of stopping terrorism and bringing an end to the war. They had 'a good story'; and as soon as they told the intelligence committees of Congress about it, they would surely understand. The gloomy dissenter was Weinberger: 'I think it is going to be more difficult for Congress to understand.' Regan, too, was finding the story hard to sell. 'If you get into a press conference, you're going to blow the whole thing. So you better not do that. And how about a sanitized TV speech? Well, perhaps we can explain it to the nation.' And Poindexter was worried 'about how much we could say. Geez, if you can't say enough, does that help you or hurt you?'[6]

Perhaps less confident now, Keel scribbled down some notes of what Reagan recommended. It was almost entirely denial, what they had not done.

Don't talk TOWs, don't talk specifics
Basic statement has to come out
not paying ransome [sic]/(not negotiating)
not dealing w/kidnappers/terrorists
avoid specifics, declare consistent w/our policy
can't engage on [sic] speculation

Poindexter reinforced him: 'Say less about what we are doing, more about what we are not doing.' Reagan recapitulated: 'Support Pres's policy but say nothing else.'[7]

North's instinct was to take this line too, and on the 5th he had jotted down the essence in his notebook: 'Actions which may/may not have been taken not material.'[8] Yet he had also been instructed to compile a detailed chronology of the Iran operation, start to finish, 'to get the facts straight'. Everyone was to bring their pieces of recollection to North's office, where the versions would be scissored-and-pasted together. It was a long process, with at least ten people commenting, subbing and interpolating;[9] and while it went on other briefings and statements were given — by Poindexter to Congress, by Reagan to the nation — that had to be as vague, yet as definite, as possible, and point in the same general direction as the big story under construction. The 'sanitized TV speech' had been drafted, in the end, for Reagan to give to the nation on the 13th, and it was extremely reassuring: the charges that America had ransomed hostages for arms, and had undercut its allies, were 'utterly false'.[10]

North's aide, Craig Coy, had looked forward to the speech as his first chance to find out what had been happening; sitting on the sofa in North's office, he had been as oblivious to the real course of events as a mechanic in Albuquerque. He had been told, typically, to stay out of the various draftings; that those were North's job, and it was his to keep the office running; but still he would come downstairs into the office, see people scribbling notes, and read them 'to try to get started, thinking I would finally understand what the heck was going on in the whole thing. So, I would read it for grammatical reasons, see if it made any sense.'[11] He wanted to make sure the sentences had verbs, and McFarlane's style in the drafts for the speech caused him some grief; but 'these charges are utterly false' was a problem of substance. The words were to be read out by Reagan that night, on television.

I viewed it — those things could have been false or not true, but in my mind, when you say the phrase 'Those things were utterly false', that is like sticking a needle in somebody's eye and begging the question. I just didn't know what they were, but I thought that — some of them may have been true. I didn't know. I assumed they were false, but I thought that phrase . . . was too provocative, too strong.[12]

Coy wanted to take it out and replace it with 'something to the effect that the President makes a lot of decisions . . . and he made a decision that was — that deviated from publicly stated policy, but he did it for good reasons and tried to explain the reasons.' He put the change to North. 'Fine, you can sell it,' said North, understanding better than most what its chances would be; 'it is all yours.' Coy put it next to Poindexter: too large a change, too late, came the answer. He next ran into Pat Buchanan, the communications director, in the hall, 'who didn't know who the hell I was'. 'Here, if you want my opinion,' Coy said boldly — the unknown aide to the administration's chief brawler — 'we ought to change the speech to make it look more like this.' 'Sorry, kid, it's too late,' said Buchanan; 'go see Regan, if you want.' By that stage, deflated, Coy did not want. He went back to fiddling with the grammar of the thing, following the tradition set by North in McFarlane's letter to Hamilton: if you get tied into a lie, at least make it elegant.[13]

The President's words ran on.

The United States has not made concessions to those who hold our people captive in Lebanon, and we will not; the United States has not swapped boatloads or trainloads of weapons for the return of American hostages, and we will not.

Other reports have surfaced alleging US involvement: reports of a sea-lift to Iran using Danish ships to carry American arms, of vessels in Spanish ports being employed in secret US arms shipments, of Italian ports being used, of the United States sending spare parts and weapons for combat aircraft. All these reports are quite exciting, but as far as we are concerned, not one of them is true.[14]

This was cunning stuff, bearing the NSC stamp: true in the technicalities, altogether quite misleading. (Confronted at the hearings with the charge that the speech was 'absolutely . . . misleading and deceptive', Poindexter answered 'I don't think it was . . . what part are you referring to?')[15] Concessions had not been made directly to Hizbollah (this was the President's fine line, the one his staff had slightly more trouble with); and the other points were a choice collection of Aunt Sallies, silly stories that could be knocked down to leave an image of blameless behaviour. 'The bulk of the press were printing a totally erroneous story,' said Reagan later, 'and I felt that the truth was far more fair to us than what was being said.'[16]

When the speech was over, Ledeen went to North to complain. It had been 'terrible'. The President had been made to say things that could be demonstrated not to be true. He should have said, instead, 'that he had gotten emotionally involved with the hostages, that he regretted it, that he thought it was a mistake, and that he had put a stop to it when he knew it was happening.'[17] Of course, that was misleading too; but somewhat less so. Yes, said North, apparently agreeing; many people had suggested that to the President. But Reagan, and North, had appeared not to hear. When the NSC next drafted something for the President to say, as the opening statement at his press conference on the 19th, non-White House folk protested even more. Richard Armitage, reviewing the draft with a huddle of others, thought it looked 'kind of cooked . . . I mean, it was a cacophony of sounds, people saying this is crazy. It does not jibe with the facts . . . And John Moellering said, fellows, I was around during Watergate and this is a bad deal.'[18]

Certainly the line had not changed much. Reagan admitted the initiative with Iran, but it was nothing of much consequence: 'no great failure of any kind.' About 1,000 TOWs had been shipped, he said (half the actual number); in short, 'everything that we sold them could be put on one cargo plane and there would be plenty of room left over.'[19]

Where did that idea come from? Regan was asked during his testimony. He answered plainly.

> This was during a meeting where . . . we were discussing how much had been done. And the President said, well, we've only sent them a small amount.
>
> Poindexter volunteered the information. 'Oh hell, yes, a very small amount.' I said, well, you know, like that old *What's My Line* type of questioning, you know, Bigger than a breadbox? I said, 'John, how big is it? You know, can you tell me how big it is?' I have no idea, I fought a different war, what a — how big a TOW missile is, let alone spare parts for Hawks are.''
>
> And he said, 'Oh hell,' he said, 'they'd fit on a small plane, a couple of pallets.'
>
> So I said, 'Well, can you find out the answer?' And he came back a little red-faced and said, 'Well, make it a C–5.'[20]

Poindexter himself had not 'sat down and done the calculations'; he had asked North, and North had asked Secord, how best to get across to the American in the street that these were not shiploads of weapons, but small amounts. Secord had mentally squeezed the '1,000' TOWs and the 240 spare parts for Hawk batteries on to one ordinary military transport plane, but everyone had forgotten about the 18 Hawks sent in November 1985. Those were tripod-fired anti-aircraft missiles, rather large. Poindexter thought them a fair omission; they had gone to Tehran, certainly, but because they were wrong they had come right back.[21] At the hearings, he still considered the cargo-plane formulation 'effectively an accurate answer'[22], and his questioners did not push it.

By mid-November of 1986, in short, the story was becoming harder and harder to tell. At first, the players told each other — as Poindexter reassured McFarlane — that it was 'a damn good story', one they could hardly wait to make public.[23] The NSC chronology, intended as a sort of master for use by everybody in their briefings, started out as a generally truthful account of what had occurred. As Poindexter said at the hearings, rather plaintively, if they had set out wanting to mislead everyone, what would have been the point of trying to find out the facts?[24] Coy agreed: he thought the direction was 'to put all the information into it initially, and then sensitive information, classified information could be scrubbed out . . . so that . . . at some point you had a public document that you could release.'[25] Paul Thompson, on the contrary, thought the exercise was strictly controlled by necessity. If the public uproar had faded, they would have stopped it.[26] Earl, always the best assessor of these machinations, said no order came down to 'shade the facts'.

> But there is no question in my mind . . . if there were two ways to say something, that you would choose the one that emphasized the benefits the United States was getting out of this . . . That seemed to me to be a clear driving force in the exercise.[27]

On November 5th Earl, who was in charge of starting the chronology while North was away (in Europe, still talking to Iranians) had jotted down some guidelines in his notebook. Stress the objectives of the Iran operation, he noted. Proper relationship with the Gulf countries, ending the Iran-Iraq war, getting the hostages back. 'And a circle indicates putting end of war, to put it up higher.' Leave out superfluous details. (Too many details, Poindexter had warned him, might end up with the press trapping him into affirming or denying them.) Use opportunity diplomatically for benefit of United States.[28] This was rather different from the spirit in which he had started off, getting facts and dates, but North too, when he returned, seemed to have a different idea of what the chronology was meant to do. As Earl put it, apparently unconcerned that this was a factual account he was talking about, 'We had two different art forms being conceptualized here.'

It repeats, I think, other references to as little operational detail as possible ... and then there's a phrase, 'constructive ambiguity'.
*Liman.* That's a terrific phrase.
*A.* It sure is.[29]

Art apart, unexpected problems were cropping up on all sides. North was supposed to be the man who knew the story, but even he had not been involved in everything; and he had no record of what had happened except the cryptic jottings in his notebooks. The CIA, on the other hand, claimed to have records of everything, and these did not always square with North's. In Poindexter's office on the 19th, Clair George and John Gardner and North and Poindexter tried to sort it out.

And we are saying, but there was a meeting in February, and then there was a meeting on the 2nd of March. And Ollie was saying, I don't know that. And ... I said, John, you can't fight this. I mean, this is the facts of the matter. Ollie's got to go back to the drawing board and figure out why his dates don't match ours.[30]

Not until everyone put their various bits together, said Earl, did anyone realize that everything that had happened in 1985 — arms to Iran and all — had occurred before the expanded Finding of January 17th. After that, everything flowed along nicely; but 'there was some sort of problem with the 1985 period, that it was not explainable in the same way to Congress.'[31] North confidently told Gardner and George on the 19th that there was a mini-Finding to cover the November shipment, but the two CIA men had not heard of it; and their bewilderment seemed to sow doubt in North's mind, too.[32] Ledeen, who knew of that infamous shipment and was in fact quite keen to talk about it — dangerously keen, McFarlane thought — remembered a general air of mystification. McFarlane, sitting in Ledeen's den on November 21st, told North he simply could not recall the November 1985 shipment to Iran, the one he had called North about from Geneva and ordered him to deal with; North did not respond.[33] At another point, North asked Ledeen if he could remember anybody authorizing the shipment; Ledeen could not. 'Clearly it happened some way or another' was North's perplexed reply.[34] Thompson, the NSC lawyer, said he was not surprised by all the puzzlement; the national security advisors had been changing over that November, the scope of the covert action was slowly evolving (the need for a Finding perhaps not immediately apparent), and in short 'I had not yet crossed over the threshold . . . to say hey, I don't believe those things.'[35]

The chief problem with the November shipment, besides the fact that it had been done extra-legally, was that a cover story attached to it, and proved too useful to let go. According to this story, as it wove its way with increasing persistence into the NSC chronology, the Americans had not even known they were helping out with a consignment of weapons. The Israelis had told them it was oil-drilling equipment going to Iran, and the kindly Americans had been drawn, willy-nilly, into shipping Hawks. Most members of the administration had not discovered until January the true nature of the cargo. Typical of the Israelis to dissemble, to lure America in on a pretext; difficult for America, once in, to get out again.

So ran the story. 'Oil-drilling equipment' seems to have started as a proper cover, used by the Israeli defence minister, Yitzak Rabin, to talk to North on an unsecure line from London; it was also put on the pilots' manifest when they flew the missiles in, although, as we have seen, they did not believe it. No more did Charlie Allen, astute CIA man that he was, who first heard the phrase being loudly (too loudly) used by North on the telephone to McFarlane and Poindexter, both still in Geneva, as the Hawks were being shipped. North was most emphatic about it, said Allen. He himself 'had doubts as to whether Colonel North was being totally candid as to the cargo', but he did not think of telling him he ought not to be lying: 'this whole operation had been shrouded in great secrecy by the White House and there were many parts that I was totally in the dark about, and I did not know at that stage just precisely what was occurring.'[36] As with so many other players who knew only parts of the story, including even North himself at times, Allen assumed that if he heard an outright lie there was a reason for it, probably an authorization; he kept his 'serious inward doubts' inward, and did not mention them until lawyers asked him.[37] Clair George, also in at the creation of the cover story, agreed that he saw no reason why they wouldn't ship oil-drilling parts, adding smoothly: 'although certainly the coin of the realm in the Middle East is called "arms".'[38]

In Geneva, busy with the summit, McFarlane got North's

message about oil-drilling parts. North seemed, to him, uncertain what the cargo really was, and he himself, he claimed later, 'was in no position to know', despite the fact that it was he who had referred Rabin to North; but he seemed to remember having seen intelligence reports 'reflecting that Israel believed that oil-drilling equipment might have as much of an effect in Iran as weapons.'[39] Within a day, however, North 'determined . . . that it was weapons', and passed the message on to McFarlane: a fine show of uncertainty, when there had never been much doubt in either mind of what Rabin had been talking about. 'It seemed clear to me,' McFarlane said, 'that the linkage was very apparent . . . I have never felt for the past ten years that there is such a thing as deniability.'[40]

North told Cooper at his interview with Meese a year later, joking with him, that he knew it was Hawks; he also said he thought he could pass a lie-detector test to the effect that it was oil-drilling equipment.[41] This remark startled Cooper, as well it might, for even at that stage — a year after its first use by Rabin — people were still trying to lean on that thin little story. On November 20th the latest version of the NSC chronology contained the statement that, in November 1985,

> we were assured . . . that the Israelis were beginning to 'try oil-drilling parts as an incentive' since we had expressed so much displeasure over the earlier TOW shipment . . . In January, we learned that the Israelis . . . had used the proprietary aircraft to transport 18 Hawk missiles to Iran.[42]

The source of that paragraph appears to have been McFarlane. He had gone to North's office on the evening of the 18th to work on drafts of the President's statement for the next day, and he and North had begun to argue about the November Hawk shipment; McFarlane saying he could not remember it, North trying to remind him of the calls he had made from Geneva. Finally McFarlane sat down at the computer, the chronology before him, 'to write for Admiral Poindexter an account of what I could [sic] of the most egregious problems that I saw with it.'[43]

'You knew that the statements in this paragraph were false?' Nields asked North.

A. Oh, absolutely, yes.
Q. And Mr McFarlane knew that they were false.
A. Yes . . .
Q. Did you say to Mr McFarlane, 'That's not the truth?'
A. I don't have a specific recollection of that conversation.[44]

Secord, on the other hand, had spoken his mind. He dropped into the office the next day to help too; North handed him the revised chronology. Secord read it through while North watched him, intently, waiting for him to get to the lie and stop. When he did so, protesting ('this is expletive deleted'), North said that McFarlane had been through it; he was in charge; and he 'knew what the true story was.' Well, replied Secord, heading for the door, 'I will get out of you guys' hair.'[45]

As for North, 'I continued to work on this version because I believe that's what needed to be put out, because that's what Mr McFarlane had given me.' McFarlane was no longer his boss, and had not been for almost a year. But North appeared to have learned a lesson from his struggles then, over the false assurances given to Congress about the NSC and the contras: if you were told to join in with a false story by people who knew the political ropes better than you did, you joined in with the false story. He said he did not know then, nor later, all the reasons for the lies. Indeed, he maintained later that he did not know the reasons for the chronologies themselves, that nobody had ever told him what their purpose was; they sometimes seemed to be no more than a game of catch-up with what officials were disingenuously saying all around him.[46] But he was sure that his superiors had 'good and sufficient reasons' for disseminating a false story,[47] and indeed he knew the chief pretexts himself as well as the next man: safeguard the hostages, protect the boss. Although it was clear to him that 'there was a story we were going to stick with and people were digging a pretty deep hole, without me helping them, in advancing that story',[48] he got into the hole too, and helped.

The worst McFarlane could say of this effort was that it was meant to 'gild the President's motives . . . to put the best face on things and to minimize the President's role.'[49] Knowing it was that sort of exercise when he first came across it, seeing the various pieces of paper scattered round North's office and hearing 'remarks . . . devoted in loyalty to prevent the President from being damaged', he nonetheless leapt in, as North did. Parts of the chronology, to be sure, were contrary to what he knew; but 'I couldn't disprove what was on the paper, and it wasn't technically wrong. So I took it as a foundation.'[50]

To both North and McFarlane, the other man seemed more responsible for the fundamental distortions; but McFarlane, like Earl, saw no lies there, and certainly none in the parts he had written. 'Not a complete portrayal,'[51] was all he admitted later. Poindexter's deputy, Al Keel, said he never got the impression 'that anyone was not telling the facts as they were'; there were just honest mistakes, such as North thinking there were only 1,000 TOWs involved and then, after checking his records (numbers of people having been briefed in the meantime), finding that 'Oh, my God, there is 2,000.' ('That's just sloppy,' Keel told him. 'You can't have figures that are off by a factor of two. What would happen if we made a public statement?')[52] Poindexter, merely masterminding, told North to leave out the highly sensitive bits and the diversion,[53] and was confident enough in the veracity of the story until the last weekend, when everything stopped. It was still going to be a good tale, one the American people would be thrilled to hear, when at last it was all put together.

So the facts were changed, and from then on the story had to conform to them. On the 21st, when McFarlane had his interview with Meese, he told him that oil-drilling parts had been sent to Iran. He later admitted this was just hearsay, 'taking somebody's word for it'.[54] 'In November when the chronologies were being made,' he explained later, 'my own recollection of the November shipment at all of weapons or of oil parts was very very dim. I said as much to Admiral Poindexter.'[55] Poindexter said he was 'very fuzzy' on that issue too: trying to remember back a year, he said he neither believed the cover story nor had anything of substance to put in its place. So he went with the story.

On the 20th, in his office, he had sat through a meeting at which he accepted without a murmur North's contention that nobody in the government had known about the Hawks at the time they were shipped. North's presentation was dramatic, containing a graphic false description of the 'jawboning' he had had to do to get the Hawks back from Iran in November 1985; in fact, the Iranians had been only too eager to be rid of them. 'And it was tough going, you know,' Charles Cooper remembered, 'and I mean he portrayed the event as if it had happened . . . I remember he was fond of the word "dork", and he was saying "this dorked everything up." '[56] North, at his trial, said he thought that 'everybody in that room' knew that what he was saying was false,[57] but Poindexter demurred. 'I frankly at that point just didn't know what the truth was,' he said. It was 'not necessarily a false story'.[58] He suspected North was reporting something McFarlane was remembering, and not remembering right, but he did not raise it. The meeting was too big, in any case.

I had only met Mr Cooper earlier, I had no idea who he was, how close he was to Ed. His presence laid a note of caution on me. Frankly, Mr Gates's presence also . . . If it had been Ed Meese, Bill Casey and I sitting down together I would have raised it, but with the other people there I was unwilling to.[59]

But what about his own memory? Liman asked him. Wasn't it a good one? 'Fair,' the admiral said. Then how could he forget such a thing as a request to ship Hawks to Iran? 'A lot of water has passed over the dam.'[60]

The last version of the chronology (called the 'Historical') contained a number of fanciful things, especially oil-drilling parts. Poindexter, confronted with these embroideries at the hearings, protested that even that version was by no means a finished document. More and more was to be added to the chronology, and it was only the sudden events of November 25th, his resignation and North's firing, that preventing the drafting of the perfect account, 'correct in every respect'.[61] Precisely because they were unfinished, he tried to keep the different versions out of the hands of people like Regan, who wished to read them. The chief of staff, surprisingly under-informed, was desperate to know the story. He managed to get a copy of the chronology from Poindexter on the 21st, but a few hours later Poindexter asked for it back, saying it was 'incomplete'. Regan instead took the chronology home and read it, discovering that 'it did not pass my feel test.'[62] He did not, however, suggest corrections, because Meese was going to make his own inquiries. Besides, Regan had done his bit for accuracy. By his own account he had already nagged Poindexter to get the facts straight, 'so that the President can memorize them and get them in his mind':[63] assuming, tellingly, that they were nowhere in Reagan's mind to begin with.

Poindexter, however, had other pressures on him. The Israelis and the Iranians, still trying to keep lines open to the NSC, were horrified to hear that the story was being spelled out at all. Earl took a call from Nir, sometime after the 6th, in which he made a bet that there would be 'no further major revelations'. The Americans should therefore

> continue 'no comment' the way we were doing and that the Prime Minister recommended that Poindexter and the President flatly deny the operation and that any other way of dealing with it was worse than doing this.
> *Q.* He was suggesting they lie?
> *A.* Flatly deny is what I have as his words.[64]

To the bitter end — and indeed beyond it, for the Israeli government never talked in any detail about the affair, and Nir, still silent, was killed in a plane crash in 1988 — the Israelis stuck to Earl's 'phase one' and did their best to persuade the Americans to do likewise.[65] Indeed, they could not understand why the Reagan administration eventually abandoned the strategy. To offer a carefully constructed story, rather than deny the actions outright, was probably no better morally; and it was infinitely messier, as Nir had warned Earl that it would be. The Israelis could not grasp why some sort of concoction had to be fed to the press at all, and the Iranians understood it even less. As Earl fielded the ever-ringing telephone in North's office in the frantic last days of both operations, he took a message from Tehran: 'You must tell the editors of the press that they should write less about Iran because the press is read in Tehran and that isn't good. It makes the road tougher.'[66]

Indeed, by that stage, the players were beginning to feel much the same way themselves. It was plain that the story, in general and in particular, was not going over well. It kept changing; details were added in an attempt to be reassuring, but each detail opened up a new nest of worms; high officials who should have known, including Shultz, sometimes seemed genuinely in the dark. Others, too, were trying to write their versions. Casey wrote his flying back from Central America on November 19th, looking through an enormous pile of papers as he sat in a custom-built shed in the back of his aircraft, dictating from memory for five or six hours into a little hand-recorder.[67] John Gardner, who had watched him with awe and with an almost animal longing to eat the meal Casey was ignoring, reported back glumly to Poindexter after Casey had briefed Congress on the 21st: 'We didn't fix this thing.'[68]

Poindexter knew that at first hand. On the same day he had also played host to members of the Senate Intelligence Committee, sitting in hopeful cosiness at his coffee table with a list of talking points in front of him, intending to brief them on 'why we were doing this, what we had accomplished, exactly what had happened, and what our objectives were, and what the good things were, and what the problems were'. The senators were having none of that, as Gardner remembered later.

> They charged right in the room. The first thing [Chairman] Durenberger said is that — he said John, if you're not going to give us the facts, then we're gonna get the hell out of here. And I was just shocked. [69]

All this time, Reagan kept to his own story: the Iran effort had been good, and worth it, and in any case not a trade. This was a position he took right up to, and after, his retirement. Once or twice he was persuaded to admit that it was not so, that it had become a trade willy-nilly, but this was always plainly under advice and duress. During his testimony in February 1990, he maintained that his no-trade view was 'perfectly fitting'.[70] He had argued with his aides that frantic November 'that if I had a child kidnapped and held for ransom, and if I knew of someone who had perhaps the ability to get the child back, it wouldn't be dealing with the kidnappers to ask that individual to do that.'[71] Typically sentimental; and clear in the president's mind, Poindexter said, from the very beginning.[72]

Reagan's happy confidence in the story was not shared by his staff. As they fretted for him, tried to cover for him and — in Regan's notorious words — played the part of the shovel brigade following the big parade down Main Street,[73] they became convinced that the strategy was not working. In the end, as Regan complained, even the perspex-clear presidential mind became confused 'as far as what he should say and how he should and should not say it.'[74] The administration had tried phase one of Earl's primer of dissembling, no comment/deny; it had tried phase two, telling the story, in many different forums and many different contortions. Nothing appeared to work.

On November 21st, according to Earl, the scheme changed again to the final stage. The NSC staff had been told that morning that Meese was going to review their files to gather facts about the Iran operation, and Earl received a call from North on the intercom to bring his Iran file down. It did not have much in it, simply duplicates of documents of North's; but Earl dug it out as part, he supposed, of the continuing effort to get at the facts and tell the story, and took it down. North was sorting through his files, pulling out papers and stacking them on his desk; he took Earl's and added them to the pile. Possibly — though Earl was not sure — he was turning occasionally to toss papers into the burn bag or the wastepaper basket. This suddenly seemed, to Earl, to be different from anything that had happened before.

He asked his boss what was going on. The reply was alarming: 'It's time for North to be the scapegoat.' Earl supposed he must have asked what that meant; he received a rambling answer, that the Attorney General was sending people over, that the briefings of Congress had not gone well, that more questions had been raised than answered, that North had just come from a meeting in the West Wing to discuss a problem of some sort, and he had asked the Attorney General whether he might have 24 or 48 hours, presumably to resolve it; and Meese had answered that he did not know whether he could have so long. North did not explain what he meant by 'scapegoat', nor who had ordered him, nor whether he had volunteered. Purposefully, not angrily, he was sorting out papers. But Earl drew his own quick conclusions.

It seemed to me that the box, the compartment, the Iran project, was not, that phase two on that, which was the explanation to Congress, was not washing, was not going over, and that therefore the decision was taken to go to phase three, which was termination of the project, that it was politically embarrassing, and that the political mistake, if you will, of the whole Iran operation would be blamed on Oliver North . . .

Q. And termination of the compartment includ[ed] getting rid of all the documents related to the compartment?

A. All the sensitive, all the inner boxes, not the total box, that had already been briefed to the Congress, but the sensitive material within the box within the box within the box, however far it went . . . basically anything that would lead to possible loss of life.[75]

The price-list of weapons sold to Iran was one such inner box, the diversion to the contras another. Earl, back in his office, searched round in some uncertainty for anything 'that would either compromise that which I believe was being destroyed or lead to that, point to that'. He ripped some papers up, put others in the burn-bag, shredded some, erring 'on the side of destruction'. It was the Friday evening; the next morning the Attorney General's men were expected, and even on that day the shredding continued. While Reynolds and Richardson took their break for lunch, Earl noticed that North 'continued to review documents, and I think found some that were suitable for the category that we had been looking for the day before.'

Q. Termination?

A. Termination.[76]

Poindexter, too, played his part in it. On November 21st he tore up the mini-Finding, which 'would substantiate what was being alleged, that this was strictly an arms-for-hostages deal, which truly it was not intended to be.'[77] He also destroyed more than 5,000 computer messages on November 24th, logging on to the system at 4.30 in the morning and deleting them one by one.[78] Sometime before that, he remembered North coming into his office with one of his old notebooks, presumably the one that carried the note of presidential authorization for the shipment of November; he had gathered somehow, from North's manner rather than from anything he said, that he meant to destroy the notebook, and that was fine with him.[79] At the hearings, Representative Jack Brooks tried to persuade him to look differently on this destruction of records. It was an attempt to deny that the story had ever happened at all: tantamount to stealing history.

> *Q.* I wonder by any chance, did you call the archivist before ripping the Finding up and stuffing it in that burn bag?
> *A.* Absolutely not, Mr Brooks.
> *Q.* You didn't call him?
> *A.* The thought didn't cross my mind.
> *Q.* It didn't even cross your mind.
> *A.* Not at all.
> *Q.* I will bet it didn't.[80]

By the end of November 1986, all manner of drives and impulses had converged on the President and his staff. The urge to be secret; the urge to be successful, to get more hostages back, and to salvage something — anything — from the operations that were falling round their ears; the urge to be safe, uncontroversial and spared embarrassment; the impulse to tell 'stories that are very interesting' in a way that would be appreciated, maybe honoured, at least liked; the impulse to protect each other. Every one of these preoccupations led in the direction of the lie. There was plenty of deceit around already, that practised naturally in the conduct of covert operations, as North had explained. But all these particular lies, Nields asked him, these false letters and chronologies, these false bills for his security system, this shredding — were they the natural result of covert operations, too? North consulted with Sullivan, and seemed to find no answer there; he stared at his questioner. 'If you have an answer,' said Nields, in a tone that surmised he would not. He was right.[81] The tidal wave of lies had taken on a momentum of its own, and in the end had overwhelmed them all.

# Epilogue

I N lies, then, the story became public. It emerged slowly, like a sea monster casting off accretions of weed and slime; so extraordinary, so full of contradiction and deception, that the country did not have the patience to get to the end of disentangling it. In that respect, then, the artful stories and clever answers, the deniability and the wholesale shredding, achieved some of what was intended. They distorted the record to such a degree that the public investigators — many of whom, themselves, were less than eager to see the whole truth exposed — ran into the sand.

Even with the monster brought down, pegged out and eviscerated, congressmen still did not know what conclusions to draw. Watergate had inspired strong preventive legislation; in the wake of Iran-contra two measures were introduced, both frail, intended to tighten up the notification of Congress about covert actions and to stop solicitation of funds by members of the administration from foreign countries. Nobody imagined these would have much effect, and in the event George Bush, by then president, more or less laughed them away. If a president was determined on a course of action in foreign policy, even round the back of Congress, Congress could not stop him. 'I would like to think this sort of thing could not happen again,' Senator Inouye had sighed after the hearings; 'but I suppose it will.'[1]

Some greater denouement, too, was always awaited. The story, whether recounted by the players or the media, had never ended properly. The possibility of impeaching Reagan (the only constitutionally satisfying outcome) had appeared for a month or so, and gone. Perhaps there could be something else; perhaps the scandal was merely the tip of an iceberg, the first instalment of some truly portentous or horrifying tale wrapped in even less penetrable layers of deception. In February 1987, *The New Republic* dived into interplanetary speculation:

> In the early part of the 20th century, although [astronomers] could not see a planet at the edge of the solar system, they knew something was out there because of the puzzling movements of the other planets. Maybe Meese's disclosure and numerous other inexplicable developments can all be explained by the gravitational pull exerted by some still unseen force at the centre of Iranamok. What is the ninth planet of the Iranamok scandal? Entries will be judged on their plausibility and creativity.[2]

Nobody won the competition. In the end, everyone was weary. As Senator William Cohen pointed out, quoting T.S. Eliot, 'We had the experience but missed the meaning.'[3] 'I think Richard Nixon was right', mused George Bush in March 1988, 'when he said it didn't mean anything.'[4]

As time wore on, too, other elements began to dominate this uncertain world. The characters forgot what they had done; or, persuading themselves over long months that they had done something different from what they had actually done, or for different reasons, they seemed to come to believe that black was white and up was down. Reagan was the master at this; but much of the sadness of Iran-contra — human tragedy ever mixed up with the farce — came from the public spectacle of a decent man like McFarlane denying the obvious, and the gentle anxiety of those who tried to point it out to him.

Iran-contra was notable not so much for players changing their stories, although there were some notable U-turns, but for the constant repetition of stories that were implausible. With each repetition, they seemed to add to their own historical authenticity in the mind of the teller; the actor himself was persuaded that this was what he had done. And above and beyond this the years rolled on, covering with merciful forgetfulness the actual, unprompted, unmanipulated memory of actions. In 1987 the 'don't recalls' were rightly greeted with scepticism. By 1990, they were taken with a sigh. Perhaps, as R.W. Apple had said a year earlier in the *New York Times*, the country would never know the real story;[5] perhaps, too, it did not much care whether it did or not. The public drifted away, building their own rough versions of the scandal out of what the television had shown them; and each reiteration of the Iran-contra questions — at the depositions, the hearings, at North's trial, at Poindexter's — brought back an ever fainter and less satisfying answer, like the last dim echo of a shout at a mountain.

# Afterword

# The Waite Factor

BY THE end of 1991, all the American hostages had been released from Lebanon. The last to be set free was Terry Anderson, on December 4th. Surprisingly spry, articulate and without bitterness, the hostages poured out their story day after day on television and in the press. But the release that touched a nerve in Britain, opening again the whole thicket of moral questions surrounding Iran-contra, was that of Terry Waite on November 18th.

Waite had been the envoy of the Archbishop of Canterbury: a towering, bearded bear of a man, with a discomforting gaze, a ready laugh and the persistence of a Salvation Army man rattling his tin on the doorstep. His reputation was that of a miracle-worker. In 1981 he had obtained the release of British hostages from Iran; in 1984 he had persuaded Colonel Gaddhafi of Libya to release four British missionaries. Shortly after that, the American Presbyterian Church commissioned him to help free the hostages held in Beirut. As the arms deals took hold and tortuously sprang the captives, one by one, after September 1985, Waite was in the offing too: the independent churchman whose patient negotiation seemed, in the world's eyes, the only reason why hostages were being released at all.

When Iran-contra broke and the arms deals were revealed, people immediately suspected that Waite was in some way involved. As early as December 1986, the main outlines of the story were appearing in the London papers. Waite had met North at least a dozen times, usually under the auspices of the presiding Episcopal bishop of New York. North had also helped him into Beirut on American military helicopters. Both Waite and the Archbishop, Robert Runcie, were quick to scotch any rumour that Waite had been involved with the Americans. Waite added, however, with a coyness eerily similar to North's, that there was 'a whole other side to the story that could not be told.'[1] Egged on, the press soon had no chance to unearth what that story might be. On January 20th 1987, having gone back to Beirut mostly to prove his independence and his wholesomeness, Waite himself was kidnapped by members of Islamic Jihad who assumed him to be an agent of the Americans. Silence fell over his story for the next five years.

While he was away, Waite became a saint. Prayers were said for him in every church in Britain, and whatever association he had had with Iran-contra was buried or forgotten. But the press was only waiting; and when he emerged from captivity the newspapers were quick to present a different Waite, this time deluded, egotistical, naive and used. A sort of spiritual cloak-and-dagger man, he was said to have been seen leaving aircraft in Beirut with huge suitcases of money; and also to have been fitted with a bugging device concealed in a belt buckle, or perhaps in his beard, by which the Americans could track him via satellite when he went to talk to terrorists.[2] Waite later confessed that he had been offered such a thing, but had refused to wear it.[3] North called the story 'absolute hogwash'.[4] Whatever the truth, the tale seemed to carry that old Iran-contra stamp of boy-scout technology combined with foolish eagerness, and of high purposes corrupted.

Waite's release, quite by chance, coincided with the public re-emergence of North. On September 16th 1991, all charges had been dropped against him. Believing himself exonerated, 'totally, ab-solutely, completely', North had written his own account of the scandal and was out on the road promoting it. As Waite appeared in Damascus, thinner, with matted beard, but as imperiously confident as ever, North would appear by satellite — sometimes as if pulled out of bed, with rough cheeks and without a tie — to comment on him. It was the first time for almost five years that either man had been interviewed on television, a medium both had seemed made for. Indeed, up to then (or, in Waite's case, up to that January when he was seized), both had been masters of the dramatic sound-bite, North out of his car window, Waite from above some airport scrum of reporters' heads: the throwaway remarks of men completely calm in their own self-righteousness.

The two were undoubtedly useful to each other. Waite was initially referred to the White House to get help and information. He turned out to know more than the Reagan administration did about the hostages and their kidnappers, and had set up invaluable contacts. At one point, North called him 'our only access to events in Lebanon'.[5] The Americans therefore made use of him, and would have been foolish not to. In return, they helped him in and out of Beirut. The connection compromised him; but it was a compromise Waite was willing to suffer, if it worked.

He said later that he had never known about the arms deals. North, for his part, said he never told him. When people wondered why, North had a ready and familiar answer. Waite did not need to know, and would have been more at risk than ever if he had been given that secret to hide. Waite said he would have been appalled to have found out; but North, as if nothing had happened, and as if the straightforward trust of their early friendship was still in place, left messages for Waite to call him after he was released, and hoped they could still be friends.

These men's characters, and the dilemmas they faced, were remarkably similar. North's life had been military, laced with the spiritual; Waite's had been spiritual, but laced with the military. Accounts of the meetings held between them, with various priests in attendance, show both men committing their efforts to God, as if that would keep them straight.[6] Both presented themselves as servants, humble men simply doing the bidding of a master; but both treasured independence of action, the ability to skirt round problems or knock them aside, and both, at times, deliberately slipped the leash. Their superiors allowed it. Runcie knew well that he could not control what Waite got up to in the field; a highly intelligent and reflective man, he was aware that he had set a force in motion that he might regret. Waite, for his part, said he would do whatever was necessary to get the hostages out. He was willing to make himself available, confident he could draw the line where necessary. Colleagues were less certain.

In September 1985, when Benjamin Weir was released, Waite appeared at the New York press conference even though his own efforts had failed. An office, probably North's, had arranged for him to be there as 'a symbol'. He seems to have gone with alacrity. In July 1986, he got wind of the release of Lawrence Jenco and proudly telephoned North at the White House; North ordered him to go to Damascus.[7] Waite had been in Jordan, and must have known that nothing he had done had sprung Jenco; although ordered to take the credit, he had not earned it. Nonetheless, he went. By this time, the western press had come to associate Waite with the release of hostages. Their attention bolstered him, even as he distracted their eyes from what the Americans might be doing.

It is possible that Waite, like so many bit-players in the Iran-contra story, knew or inferred a little of what was happening and chose not to know more. It is probable that to call up a White House number with hot information, to be a deep source and a man willing to be sent where Americans could not go, was exciting work. The Americans seem to have played on that eagerness, just as North's was played on by the more pragmatic members of the administration. As Secord put it with characteristic bluntness, Waite was 'a convenient cover'.[8]

North had his own, more high-flown words for it. What Waite provided was 'ecclesiastical cover' and 'a spiritual presence'. He had provided a holy cloak for the exercise, a cloak North himself had toyed with. 'These were not simply political hostages,' he told the man from the *Daily Telegraph*. 'There was a strong spiritual aspect to the whole thing, that we as Anglo-Saxons miss.'[9] North went on to say that he thought the hostages would not have been released at all if Waite had not been there. Perhaps he had fed the same pablum to Waite directly; perhaps it was another way of persuading himself that the horrible bargain of arms for bodies had had a compensating side that was higher and better than that.

When he came to Britain, North was repeatedly asked whether he felt some responsibility for Waite's capture. Waite had returned to Beirut, after all, to prove that he was his own man and to scotch the rumours that he was an American agent: rumours that had taken wing because of North's contact with him. North's stock reply was to say 'I am not a terrorist' — meaning that responsibility lay simply with the men who had kept Waite in chains. In an interview for BBC's Panorama on November 11th, a week before Waite was freed, the interviewer tried to prod him further. Did he not feel guilty? North wriggled, and then came out with a memorable reply: 'Guilt? I have a problem with the word.'

The story may be summed up this way. In the cause of getting hostages out, both Waite and North did whatever they thought necessary. Waite's line of propriety, beyond which he would not go, was more limiting than North's; but both went further than they intended, took more risks than they should have, and allowed themselves to be used and bamboozled. Perhaps, in the murky webs of hostage business, that seemed necessary; perhaps, with God on their side, they really believed they could not fall into temptation.

# An Interview with Oliver North

IN LATE November 1991 North came to London to promote his book, *Under Fire*. I had felt no particular need to interview the Iran-contra characters, but the temptation to talk to North proved too strong. He had been giving public interviews for barely two months, having refused requests for five years. As I was to find, his views on the affair had shifted scarcely at all. That persistent bull-headedness was also part of the story.

The interview was carried out on November 25th, the fifth anniversary of his firing, for the *Tablet*, a Catholic weekly. As we talked, in his suite at the London Marriot hotel, North's minders stood about in coats and drank coffee. When North drank his, out of the Marriot's reproduction china, he somehow never managed to put the cup back in the saucer.

**Q.** I want to start with that moment in 1979, when you were 'born again'. You were still on active service, and General Grinalds cured you of back pain.

**A.** He didn't. God, through General Grinalds, cured me.

**Q.** Was it a sort of Damascene conversion, like Paul on the road to Damascus?

**A.** Well, in thinking about it, yes . . . of course, I'd been knocked off my horse several other times, and unlike Paul I didn't see the light quite soon enough. I think, and this is the way I've described it to others, that the Lord sometimes has to have a two-by-four that He hits some particularly stubborn people on the side of the head with. And that was the final opportunity, or it was the one I finally seized on, notwithstanding all the other things that had happened in my life in that point, where I could very clearly see that my prayers had been answered by Him, that He'd intervened in my life a number of times, and yet I'd failed to capitalize on it.

**Q.** But you had a strong faith before that, too . . .

**A.** Well, yes, I was raised in a home where I was taught to know who He was . . . but I see a difference between knowing about Him, and knowing of Him, and knowing what He wants and what He expects of us, as though you're looking at some famous figure in the movies or something like that, and knowing him personally; and that was the experience for me, coming to know Him. . . Reading the Word, and studying it, and coming to understand a lot of things I hadn't delved into before. And wanting to. This is the difference. It's like a real friendship, it's not just meeting someone on the street; you really want to know more about them. In a physical sense it's like a love affair, when you want to know someone well that you love, and that's how it changed for me.

**Q.** Now when you were born again, you understood that you were saved. Did this give you a feeling of spiritual immunity? That no matter what you did, you were all right with God?

**A.** Well, only so much as I think there's a real awareness with people who've been through that experience, who've taken that leap of faith — which I think people need to take, in a mature sense, almost a childlike sense — that you can put yourself in His hands, and acknowledge that He is in control. Romans 8.28 very clearly says, in Marine parlance if you will, "If you trust in God, it's His plan; all will be well in the end." At the same time, Romans 8.29 does not necessarily say you will understand it at the time. It's an admonishment to be faithful, and to acknowledge where you're going. And by my way of thinking, through this travail of the last five years — from this day five years ago, that's true, that's the day it was —

**Q.** So it was.

**A.** It struck me as I got up this morning — you know, I told one of the reporters as I was going in to be sentenced, something that it had never crossed my mind would happen, and he said to me something like "Colonel, you look awfully content for a man on his way to be sentenced". And being a bit of a smart-alec I shot back, "That's because I know where I'm going." And he looked a little shocked, because in our system a person going in doesn't know what the sentence is going to be until the judge delivers it, and he said, "How many years are you going to get?" and I said, "Eternity".

I suppose there is a certain sense that, whatever happens to you in this life, knowing that you are saved lifts a terrible burden: not because of what you've done or I've done, or how we've lived or how faithful *we* have been, (notwithstanding the motto of my Marine corps); but because He was faithful. He sent His son to die for you and me, and if you accept that, then it's open to you.

**Q.** But does it change your responsibility for what you do?

**A.** No, not at all. Not in the least.

**Q.** But there's a sense in which you don't earn your salvation any more —

**A.** True. There is a sense that you don't earn it. Nonetheless, we're commanded to be in this world. Not *of* this world, but *in* it, and certainly salt and light in this world, and there is a certain expectation of accountability in what we do, that we do not dishonour Him; in fact that we use our God-given talents in ways that don't bring glory to ourselves but rather glory to Him. I'm very conscious of that, and have been since then, perhaps much more so than I was before. That does not say that I don't suffer from the sin of pride. I make terrible mistakes all the time . . . it doesn't absolve us from responsibility for what we do in this life. That's a very specific charge that we are accountable, that we must act in a way that is Christian.

**Q.** But when you were going through all the arms sales and so forth, surely you were conscious that what you were doing was not Christian?

**A.** Well, of course, the great contest for a Christian in everyday life, because we are in *this* world, is to reconcile what we are doing on a day-to-day basis. I mean, if we followed Him specifically, we would do just what He charges the apostles to do, throw it all away, and come follow Me. Well, I'm not that strong; and so I've continued to try and provide for my family in a temporal sense and to put away savings for my retirement, and so forth, so clearly my faith isn't as strong as He charges me to be. And the same thing applies to my service to my country. There are those who believe that the only way to be a Christian would be to be a conscientious objector. I don't see it that way. In Matthew, He doesn't tell the centurion "Well, I don't do soldiers", or, "Lay down your sword, and *then* I'll cure your servant"; He turns to the 12 who have followed him all over Galilee, and He says, "Where have you guys been? Greater faith I have not seen in all Israel." And my understanding of that exchange is that we're charged to continue in what we're doing, to the very best of our abilities, to do it in a Christian way, and that's what I had to do. There are times in government when we have to do things that others will look at as less than Christian. I go back to the Old Testament, with what happened with Rahab and her saving two spies that Joshua had sent to Jericho. Would those two spies have been caught if she'd pointed upstairs, where she was hiding them, on the roof? Probably. And she lies, to save the spies. It was a covert operation.

**Q.** And that was a parallel, you feel, with what was going on when you were in the government?

**A.** Yes, I do. And I wrestled with those things. The greatest challenge for a Christian isn't determining between right and wrong. That's relatively easy. The real challenge is when you have to decide between good and better, and the worst and most difficult one is between bad and worse. And I had to do that on a regular basis.

**Q.** When you were making these bad and worse decisions, when you were dealing with Ghorbanifar and flying to Tehran, were you putting this consciously to God, asking Him to help?

**A.** Yes, I prayed every day, and I've prayed every day since Terry was taken, that the good Lord would soften the hearts of those who hold him. In fact, that's the prayer.

**Q.** And when you were in the middle of those dealings, did you feel you were getting answers back, about how you should proceed?

**A.** You know, I've not been one that could see clearly every single pathway to take. I can look back at places and various junctions in the road and see where I took the wrong turn. There were a lot of very difficult decisions for me, and decision points where I made the wrong call, because I'm mortal like everyone else. And I think one of the things the average inquisitors miss — whether they be part of a congressional tribunal, or the prosecutorial behemoth we were up against, or part of the day-to-day media questions — one thing they missed entirely was the spiritual dimension to all of this.

**Q.** I have only one question about Terry Waite [everywhere North had gone in Britain, he had been beseiged about him]. Were you, in a way, envious of him? Did you ever wish you could have been like him, a free humanitarian agent acting to get the hostages out?

**A.** I don't know that I felt so much envy, as enormous admiration for what he was doing. He didn't have to do it. I was in the service of my country, and duty-bound to carry out the orders of my superiors; whereas he had made a free choice to be involved in this kind of activity, well before I ever met him, and God willing will be able to return to it. He had a certain sense about him that this was something he was charged to do on a much higher plane than mine, and I admired that, and I found him to be a remarkably courageous, compassionate man; I mean that in a true Christian sense. One of the reasons that I've been so dismayed the last few days has been the way your media's treated him. They've just diminished the man. I don't understand that. I don't know what it takes to be admired by the great potentates of the press. I look at the attacks on him in the news and I say, is this some extraordinary form of punishment?

So many of the people I dealt with, day in and day out in Washington, were people who were working their own little private agenda; they were working their own little lateral arabesques from this job to that job, always upwards and onwards for their own financial gain and their own power and their own prestige, but he had none of those characteristics. And to see him being accused of being an egomaniac, things like that, it's not the Terry Waite that I came to know — know and admire. And so it wasn't a matter of wanting to be like him or him being an alter ego to me, I just had an enormous sense that this was a man who was literally selfless and has been terribly punished for it.

**Q.** You talk about Waite having orders "on a higher plane". Was there a sense in which you felt you had a dual loyalty? You had a loyalty to the president; you also say you had a duty to glorify God. Yet certainly after November 1986 you had to do things to protect the president that you knew weren't right...

**A.** Well, I go back to August of '86, when I lied to the congressional committee about what I was doing in Nicaragua... I knew right then that what I was doing was wrong. It wasn't necessarily unlawful; there's a difference. But it was wrong. And people who are simply examining life from a very secular perspective can't understand that there's a difference. There's a lot of things that are *wrong*, but are not unlawful, and there's a lot of things that are unlawful that wouldn't necessarily be morally wrong.

**Q.** Well, people have harped much more on the illegality of it.

**A.** Oh, they have. The other really remarkable thing about that is that in our system there has never been anyone charged with a violation of law for doing what I did, until me. I was the first one in 200 years of American history ever to be charged with lying in an informal inquisition; and they found out that I had by my admitting it in my testimony, and I admitted it again in my own trial. I sat right there and said I lied, that I didn't tell the truth when I should have, and the jury said not guilty.

**Q.** But as to the wrongness of it, had that troubled you before you went in?

**A.** I should have thought about it. What I should have done, with hindsight, is that we should have found some way of not having that meeting. The admiral and I thought, and deceived ourselves, that they wouldn't ask the real tough questions. And members of Congress have since stood up and admitted, "We all knew what he was doing, and we put him in a real tough spot." Perhaps it didn't apply to all 535 members of Congress, but there were men in that room, one of whom called me up on the telephone and asked me to deliver certain specific supplies, munitions, to certain groups in the Nicaraguan resistance, and he sat there and I didn't bring his name up, and he sat there when the question was asked, and he said nothing.

**Q.** On Nicaragua: you say you hate war and the taking of life, but there, with the contras, you sponsored killings when there were better alternatives. What do you say to that?

**A.** Let me be real specific about that. I was very much opposed to the idea that we would have to send American marines and soldiers to fight in that country. It seemed to be the popular answer: "Let's send in the marines!" And I was a marine.

**Q.** But it caused the deaths of a great many Nicaraguans, even if it didn't cause the deaths of any marines.

**A.** Well, if one looks at the basic political thought that was behind all that, the theory was that Communism was a terrible evil . . . and if we could encourage any one of the resistance groups that was fighting anywhere to bring down one of those regimes, if not Afghanistan, then Cambodia, or Angola, or Nicaragua, then the world would be a better place. And since they were going to fight them anyway, we ought to be in the business of helping them, and that greater good would ultimately come with a democratic outcome.

**Q.** So it was the greater good that justified the taking of those lives.

**A.** Yes. And I happen to believe that that perspective was correct. . . That doesn't mean that it was bloodless. It wasn't, and terrible things happen in all wars. But you know, I don't share the perspective that all Americans are bad people, or that all military officers or all CIA officers are bad people. I happen to believe that to the extent we were able to influence the Nicaraguan resistance, or the Afghan resistance, that we could bring about an end more quickly and more humanely, and prevent the kinds of atrocities that are inevitable in war.

**Q.** So you seem to feel that America's purpose in the world is a moral one?

**A.** I think it is. I think it is. You see, I didn't think Vietnam was immoral. The outcome was grossly immoral; to have encouraged the belief that we were really committed to an independent South Vietnam, and a democratic one, and then to abandon them in 1974–5, was grossly immoral, and that happened because of our Congress.

**Q.** What do you think now that the role of a Christian in politics should be? Your story has not been a particularly happy one. . .

**A.** Oh, I hope it's not a totally unhappy one. I mean, it's more than just a political commentary . . . first of all, there's no travail that we can face that His grace is insufficient for. There is answer to prayer, and I've seen that every day in my case.

**Q.** But you've lost your faith in man, perhaps.

**A.** No, I haven't lost it, because I think the good Lord puts within all of us — in fact it's taken from John Locke, via Thomas Jefferson — "certain inalienable rights, among them life, liberty and the pursuit of happiness"; and it's the very spark of that, which is put in every one of us at conception, that drives an awful lot of what we do, whether we're born in a free country or under a dictatorship; and that spark is something, I think, that's divinely inspired, in each one of us, in that moment when God creates us. And that gives me faith in man; that God intentionally put that there, and that's a force for good.

# Acknowledgements

THIS book was in many ways a covert enterprise itself, scribbled down in the moments I could spare between doing my job and trying to be the mother of a household; and I have many people to thank for being able to manage it at all. First, rather than last, I should thank my family for infinite patience and understanding. My husband, Malcolm, never grumbled about my long sessions immured in the bedroom upstairs, and never complained when, arriving home at eleven o'clock from a hard night backstage, he got no more than a glowering look from behind a mountain of paper. My three little boys, Simon, Tom and Pip, took it all manfully and marvellously, only occasionally asking 'Is your book *nearly* finished, Mum?'; and I am sorry for the short-temperedness they had to suffer sometimes. My parents, too, put up with it with the greatest kindness, and even let me take over the storeshed at the bottom of their garden to do my writing. To everyone my love and thanks.

Thanks must go next to those Americans who, rather than telling me to go away and mind my own business (as they might have done) were instead unfailingly kind and helpful. Walter Pincus and Haynes Johnson at the *Washington Post* both allowed me to sift through their papers from top to bottom; and I only hope I put them back in order. Malcolm Byrne and Peter Kornbluh at the National Security Archive bent over backwards to help, from providing a quiet desk to look through the North notebooks to giving me, without charge, eight volumes of depositions to make up my set; and Mr Byrne performed the extra, and considerable, kindness of looking up the references for the quotes that 'got away'. Cathy Foley at the *Washington Post* let me take over the table in the Library whenever I came to visit, and suffered me to eat my navy bean soup and crackers all over it; and my good friends Mary Jordan and Lee Hockstader provided introductions and much good fun between the reading.

Special thanks should go to Theodore Draper, who after all his careful analysis of Iran-Contra should have been allowed to keep the subject for himself; but who instead gave me time, encouragement, hospitality, many volumes of documents and some excellent lunches. My visits to him and his wife, Priscilla, always raised my morale greatly, as did the note I received from him in December 1989 and kept on my desk afterwards: 'I never understood why anyone else would be mad enough to live with this stuff. I am sure that I am being punished for something I have done in this life or some other — but you!'

Special thanks in London should go to Leslie Stone, my friend and colleague at Bush House, for gathering news-tapes of the trials; and especially for allowing me to sit in his office until 10.30, night after night, to watch the hearings live on CNN, when he might have been enjoying the baseball.

Next in line for thanks come my colleagues and superiors at *The Economist*, who, in the best traditions of Iran-Contra, knew what I was doing and turned a blind eye to my doing it. Thanks to *The Economist*, I was able to keep up daily and weekly with the American press and compile enormous scrapbooks on the affair (all that photocopying!); I was able to get documents and books from America whenever I needed them; and, most of all, I was able to make trips (increasingly under a fig-leaf of 'official business') to plunder the archives in Washington. Particular thanks are due to Doro George at the Washington office, for sending me the contemporaneous transcripts of the hearings; for always bearing me in mind when clipping the *Washington Post*; for putting up uncomplainingly with a string of special requests; and especially for trudging through the snow to collect the Tower Report. Thanks too to Muriel Davis in the New York office for sending over all those bags of depositions I couldn't carry, and for getting me each book on the affair as soon as it appeared, sometimes before; and to Rene Redford in London, for clipping and copying beyond the call of duty.

The logistics of getting the book into presentable shape were entirely the work of *Economist* staff. Thanks here to Caroline

Robinson and Tracy King, for typing in a chapter that seemed to get deleted by mistake; and especially to Pauline Cuddihy, Kay Mudge and Ginny O'Riordan in the Pre-Press Department, for continually shifting the darn thing from one computer system to another in order to get it on disk. For the next book I will be computer-friendly; I promise.

Lastly, thanks to all the staff of I.B. Tauris for help, advice and encouragement: especially to Iradj Bagherzade (whose suggestions for cuts were bold and right), and to Emma Sinclair-Webb, who dealt so calmly with all my questions. Thanks, too, to Chris Gilmore who read the proofs. The mistakes that remain are my own.

A.W.
February 1991

# Sources

THE story of Iran-contra is contained in thousands of pages of documents: notebooks, memoranda, computer notes, depositions, public testimony and records of trials. I would like to claim to have read every one, and I have tried; but I am sure some pages have escaped me. Here are the principal sources, and the abbreviations used for them in the notes that follow.

1. **Depositions** (Dep): *Report of the Congressional Committees Investigating the Iran-Contra Affair: Appendix B (100th Congress, 1st Session)*. Statements given on oath, and in private, to congressional lawyers; subsequently redacted (by the CIA and the administration) and declassified. Published in 27 volumes by the US Goverment Printing Office (Washington, 1988).

2. **Hearings**: *Joint Hearings before the Senate Select Committee on Secret Military Assistance to Iran and the Nicaraguan Opposition and the House Select Committee to Investigate Covert Arms Transactions with Iran: 100th Congress, First Session*. Published in 13 volumes (H 100–1 — 100–13) by the US Government Printing Office (Washington, 1988). North's testimony was also issued as a Pocket paperback, *Taking the Stand*, in July 1987.

3. **Exhibits** (Ex): Mostly memoranda, notes and messages bearing

on the deposition or testimony of a subject, and carrying that subject's initials. Reprinted in order in the volumes of hearings, at the end of each witness's testimony; reprinted also (but less reliably) after individual depositions.

4. **PROF notes**: Computer messages sent on the PROF system, supposedly deleted and subsequently recovered. Most of these were reproduced as exhibits in type too tiny to read; I have therefore tried, where possible, to provide references to them in the Tower Report, where they are reproduced in a readable form.

5. **Tower Report**: *Report of the President's Special Review Board*, 26.2.87 (US Government Printing Office, Washington).

6.**Final congressional report**: *Report of the Congressional Committees investigating the Iran-Contra Affair,*November 1987 final summary of all the hearings and depositions, containing both the majority and minority opinions of congressmen. The most detailed official account of the affair at the time of going to press.

7. **North notebooks**: Twenty-one spiral notebooks kept by North from the end of 1984 to November 25th 1986. Various pages, heavily blacked out by his lawyers and the government, were released during the hearings and appear in the volumes cited above, especially H 100–7, Part III, and Deps A (Source Documents). They were not released in unredacted form until May 1990, and are still unpublished. A set may be consulted at the National Security Archive, 1755 Massachusetts Ave. NW, Washington, DC; it is only through the efforts of the NSA that they have been made available to the public at all.

8. **North Trial**: Transcript of court proceedings from 31.1.89 to 4.5.89. These are unpublished, but may be consulted at the Federal District Courthouse in Washington or at the National Security Archive.

9.**Poindexter Trial**: Transcript of court proceedings from 8.3.90 to 7.4.90; unpublished, but available as above.

# Reference Notes

INTRODUCTION

1. Reagan Testimony, Poindexter Trial, 9
2. Hearings: H 100–1, 2
3. Quoted in the *Washington Post*, 21.11.86
4. Florence Gantt Deposition; Vol. 11, 693
5. Regan Test., Hearings: H 100–10, 33
6. North notebooks, undated, headed 'TCR Jan 82–Apr–83' (Classification No. AMX001928)
7. 'Why Cap [Weinberger] is Wrong'. *National Review*, 11.6.90

PART I PICTURES ON A SCREEN

*Chapter 1   The Politics of Illusion*

1. C/NE (Chief of the CIA Near East Division) Dep; Vol 5,968
2. McFarlane first cable from Tehran to Poindexter (Tower B-101)
3. *McFarlane Over the Moon*, from *The Ayatollah and I* (Readers International, 1987)
4. Langton Dep.; Vol. 15, 676
5. Howard Teicher evidence to the Tower Board, 10 (Tower B-100)
6. Interview with Ted Koppel on *Nightline*, 13.11.86
7. North Test., Hearings: H 100–7, Part III, 36 and 38; Ex OLN-14
8. George Test. of 5.8.87, at 84. McFarlane said: 'There is, in terms of Western

logic, a very good case that there ought to be moderates in Iran. That is logical. It is not, I think, the reality.' Quoted in Jane Mayer and Doyle McManus, *Landslide*, (Houghton Mifflin, 1988).

9. Langton Dep.; Vol.15, 640–641
10. Ex Allen-85 (Dep. Vol.1, 1233)
11. Ex Allen-17 (Ibid., 967)
12. Summary by Craig Fuller of Bush-Nir meeting of 29.7.86: Tower B-146
13. North PROF note to McFarlane, 27.2.86 (Tower B-78)
14. Cave Dep.; Vol.3, 836–8
15. Weinberger Dep.; Vol.27, 461–463
16. Ex CWW-1 (Dep. Vol.27, 550)
17. Ex RCM-2 (Dep. Vol.16, 711–719)
18. Ledeen Dep.; Vol.15, 1191. Wilma Hall Dep.; Vol.14, 33–34
19. North Test, Hearings: H 100–7, Part 1, 53
20. For the account that follows, see the depositions of the project officer (Vol.1, 35–167, *passim*); of the air branch officer (Vol.4, 802–975, *passim*); and of the pilot of the proprietary aircraft (Vol.21, 569–663, *passim*).
21. Regan Dep.; Vol.22, 577
22. *Ibid*, 582
23. Weinberger Dep.; Vol.27, 488
24. Taft Dep.; Vol.26, 474
25. Regan evidence to the Tower Board, 36–7; Tower B-64
26. Tower B-75n (Shultz, SRB, 50–51)
27. The *Washington Post*, 13.1.87
28. Allen Dep.; Vol.1, 603. For the 'National Timeline', see Tower, B-71-73
29. Ledeen Dep.; Vol.15, 1195
30. *Ibid.*, 1199, 1236
31. *Terms of Reference US-Iran Dialogue*, 4.4.86. Tower, B-90; Ex Allen-45 (Deps. Vol.1, 1090)
32. Cave Dep.; Vol.3, 575
33. George Dep.; Vol.12, 99
34. Tower B-53 (Chief, NESA & DCI, update)
35. Ledeen Dep.; Vol.15, 988–989
36. *Ibid.*, 1164
37. Ex Allen-24 (Deps. Vol.1, 985–988)
38. Ex Allen-32 (Ibid., 1013–1017)
39. DCI's Iran testimony for the House and Senate Intelligence Committees, 21.11.86; Ex OLN-29 (H 100–7, Part III, 199). North said exactly the same: see *Terms of Reference US-Iran Dialogue*, *op.cit.*
40. George Test. of 5.8.87, at 281
41. Ex OLN-310 (H 100–7, Part III, 1239)
42. North memorandum to McFarlane, 7.6.85 (Ex OLN-263)
43. DEA Agent 1 Dep.; Vol.8, 576–577
44. McFarlane Dep.; Vol.16, 690–691
45. See Stephen Engelberg in the *New York Times*, February 1987
46. Reagan Test., Poindexter Trial, at 19
47. McFarlane Test., Hearings: H 100–2, 21
48. North Test., Hearings: H 100–7, Part 1, 154

49. Coy Dep.; Vol.7, 1121–1122
50. George Dep.; Vol.12, 150–151; 27
51. McFarlane Test., Hearings: H 100–2, 6
52. CIA Branch 'Identity A' Dep.; Vol.4, 1323
53. Crawford Dep.; Vol.7, 1149–1163, *passim*
54. Fiers Dep. ('C/CATF'); Vol.3, 1172–1173
55. Owen Dep.; Vol.20, 869
56. Fernandez Dep. ('Thomas Castillo'); Vol.3, 317
57. *Ibid.*, 332, 482
58. Owen testimony at the North Trial: 2463. Ex RWO-9
59. *Ibid.* Reagan still remembered this story in 1990: see Reagan Test., Poindexter Trial, at 79–80.
60. Fernandez Dep.; Vol.3, 348–350
61. *Ibid.*, 337
62. For the slides themselves, see H 100–7, Part III, 1581 onwards; for the commentary, see H 100–7, Part II, 144–148.
63. Raymond Dep.; Vol.22, 146
64. Owen Dep.; Vol.20, 822
65. North Test., Hearings: H 100–7, Part 1, 168. Arcos Dep.; Vol.1, 1338. See also Secord's reservations: Secord Test., Hearings: 100–1, 231.
66. McFarlane Test., Hearings: H 100–2, 240
67. *Ibid.*, 17
68. Secord Test., Hearings: H 100–1, 56; or variations. See Bob Woodward, *Veil* (Simon & Schuster, 1987), p. 353; also McKay Dep.; Vol.16, 173.
69. Abrams Test., Hearings: H 100–5, 48–49
70. McFarlane Test., Hearings: H 100–2, 86
71. Abraham Sofaer Dep.; Voi.26, 312
72. Owen Dep.; Vol.20, 862; Ex Calero-4 (undated)
73. Calero Dep.; Vol.3, 110–111, 165–166

## Chapter 2    *Unseen, Unknown*

1. Corr Dep.; Vol.7, 852, 890
2. Arcos Dep.; Vol.1, 1329–1330
3. *Newsweek*, 26.8.85
4. *Ibid.*, 27.7.87. North apparently tipped *Newsweek* on tactics to seize the *Achille Lauro* hijackers in October 1985.
5. Fiers Dep.; Vol.3, 1096–1102
6. Watson Dep.; Vol.27, 370–371, 403
7. North Trial, 6962
8. North Test., Hearings: H 100–7, Part 1, 152, 158
9. See *Time*, 20.7.87
10. McKay Dep.; Vol.16, 763–764
11. Singlaub Test., Hearings: H 100–3, 88
12. Coors Dep.; Vol.7, 728, 740
13. Poindexter Test., Hearings: H 100–8, 348–349, 352
14. Former CIA Officer Dep.; Vol.10, 638
15. George Dep.; Vol.12, 72–73

16. Poindexter Test., Hearings: H 100–8, 71
17. Poindexter PROF note to North, 19.5.86 (Tower B-96)
18. Abrams Test., Hearings: H 100–5, 163
19. Koch Dep.; Vol.15, 157
20. Earl Dep.; Vol.9, 577–578, 761–762
21. Miller Dep.; Vol.18, 636
22. Coy Dep.; Vol.3, 953–955
23. *Ibid.*, 979, 991, 1103
24. *Ibid.*, 963–964
25. Watson Dep.; Vol.27, 398–403, *passim*
26. Tower C-13
27. North Test., Hearings: H 100–7, Part 1, 182–183
28. Abrams Test., Hearings: H 100–5, 14
29. *Ibid.*, 11–12
30. *Ibid.*, 142–143
31. C/NE Dep.; Vol.5, 923
32. Schweitzer Dep., Vol.24, 685
33. Cave Dep., Vol.3, 637
34. Poindexter Test., Hearings: H 100–8, 66
35. North Test., Hearings: H 100–7, Part 1, 274
36. Earl Dep.; Vol.9, 125–149, *passim*
37. Mason Dep., Vol.17, 611–613; Allen Dep.; Vol.1, 513
38. North Test., Hearings: H 100–7, Part 1, 300
39. *Ibid.*, 109
40. *Ibid.*, 142
41. Armitage Dep.; Vol.2, 68
42. Tower III-20
43. McFarlane Test., Hearings: H 100–2, 66
44. Allen Dep.; Vol.1, 596–597
45. *Ibid.*, 678, 802, 780–782
46. *Ibid.*, 824
47. Gates Dep., Vol.11, 994
48. North Test., Hearings: H 100–7, Part 1, 26
49. Poindexter Test., Hearings: H 100–8, 51
50. George Dep.; Vol.12, 149
51. Poindexter Dep.; Vol.20, 1066–1067
52. Poindexter Test., Hearings: H 100–8, 343–344

*Chapter 3    Secret Agents and Mystery Papers*

1. Owen Dep.; Vol.20, 676
2. *Ibid.*, 684; Owen Test., Hearings: H 100–2, 353
3. Owen Test., Hearings: H 100–2, 388–389
4. Ledeen Dep.; Vol.15, 1213
5. Hakim Dep.; Vol.13, 82, 409
6. *Ibid.*, 591–592
7. Telephone conversation between Allen and Ghorbanifar, 23.2.86: Ex Allen-39
8. Hakim Dep.; Vol.13, 591–593

9. North Trial, 2437–2438
10. Tillman Dep.; Vol.26, 1197–1200
11. *Speaking Out* (1988), p. 285
12. North Test., Hearings: H 100–7, Part 1, 281
13. See esp. Allen Dep.; Vol.1, 609–610
14. C/NE Dep.; Vol.5, 957
15. DEA Agent 1 Dep.; Vol.8, 680
16. North Trial, 7372
17. *Ibid.*, 1571–1575
18. Lawn Dep. (Jack Lawn, head of the Drug Enforcement Administration); Vol.15, 779
19. Miller Dep.; Vol.19, 7
20. *Ibid.*, 114
21. Richard Allen, quoted in *US News & World Report*, 13.7.87. Allen was Reagan's first national security advisor, and it was he who hired North (as an 'easel-carrier') to the NSC.
22. Earl Dep.; Vol.9, 726
23. Quoted in the *Sunday Times*, 5.7.87
24. Robelo Dep.; Vol.23, 481
25. DIA Major Dep.; Vol.9, 165–168
26. DEA Agent 1 Dep.; Vol.8, 620–621
27. Former CIA Officer Dep.; Vol.10, 632–633
28. North Test., Hearings: Part 1, 111
29. Calero Dep.; Vol.3, 91
30. Ex OLN-69A (H 100–7, Part III, 418–419)
31. Poindexter Dep.; Vol.20, 1064
32. *Ibid.*, 1010–1011
33. Owen Dep.; Vol.20, 675
34. Cave memo of talks with the Second Channel, 19–10.9.86; Ex-OLN-202
35. Koch Test., Hearings: H 100–6, 75–76
36. North notebooks, 15.1.86 ('Call to Ami [Nir]')
37. Secord Test., Hearings: H 100–1, 66
38. Ledeen Dep.; Vol.15, 1304
39. Ex OLN 69-A (H 100–7, Part III, 419)
40. See esp Ex Calero-4 (undated)
41. North Test., Hearings: H 100–7, Part 1, 154
42. Walker Dep.; Vol.27, 350
43. North Trial, 6320
44. Newington Dep.; Vol.20, 397, 418. Reagan Test., 135
45. Channell Dep.; Vol.4, 382, 442
46. Clifton Smith Dep.; Vol.26, 124
47. Littledale Dep.; Vol. 16, 473
48. *Ibid.*, 492
49. *Ibid.*, 436
50. *Ibid.*, 835
51. O' Boyle Dep.; Vol.20, 530–537, *passim*
52. O'Boyle Test., Hearings: H 100–3, 134–135, 154–155, 161–162

53. Tower C-9
54. North Test, Hearings: H 100–7, Part II, 16
55. O'Boyle Dep.; Vol.20, 559–570, *passim*
56. Ex OLN-1; Tower B-88. For other versions of the same memorandum, see Ex OLN-283 A,B,C and D.
57. The account that follows, up to the end of Saturday, is principally from Richardson's deposition (Vol.23, 280–305, *passim*). Other accounts are as indicated.
58. Reynolds Dep.; Vol 22, 1129
59. *Ibid.*, 1132. For memorandum discrepancies, see *Ibid.*, 1119, 1121
60. Leonard Garment at McFarlane's deposition. Vol.16, 699 ,
61. Reynolds Dep.; Vol.22, 1142
62. *Ibid.*, 1157–1158
63. *Ibid.*, 1154–1155
64. See also North Trial, 6053 (Richardson)
65. Richardson Dep.; Vol.23, 319
66. Reynolds Dep.; Vol.22, 1195
67. Richardson Dep.; Vol.23, 320
68. *Ibid.*, 321
69. Poindexter Dep.; Vol.20, 1171–1172
70. Thompson Dep.; Vol.26, 930–949, *passim*
71. Earl Dep.; Vol.9, 644–645
72. McFarlane Test., Hearings: H 100–2, 80. (Q. 'Did he say, "'I missed one"?' A. 'Something like that.')
73. Poindexter Dep.; Vol.20, 1176
74. North Test., Hearings: H 100–7, Part 1, 11
75. *Ibid.*, 149
76. McFarlane Dep.; Vol.16, 670
77. Poindexter Trial, 1223
78. Reagan Test., 39
79. Thompson Dep.; Vol.26, 1078; Poindexter Test., Hearings: H 100–8, 43
80. North Test., Hearings: H 100–7, Part 1, 145
81. Reagan Test., 157, 240. He said he realised there might truly have been a diversion for the first time as he sat in court: *ibid.*, 289
82. Poindexter Trial, 1261
83. 'The World According to Oliver North'. *Washington Post Outlook*, 21.12.86
84. North Test., Hearings: H 100–7, Part 1, 215
85. McFarlane Test., Hearings: H 100–2, 123
86. Galvin Dep.; Vol.11, at 121 (original pagination)
87. Jonathan Miller Dep., Vol.18, 837
88. The *New Yorker*, 26.1.87
89. *The New Republic*, 5/12.1.87
90. Gesell, at North's trial, acknowledged the same problem. 'Here's a case that's loaded with. . .all kinds of conduct that is very difficult to mesh with reality, and I can't be party to it. It's not my style. I try.' North Trial, 2479

*Chapter 4   The Scandal as Cinema*

1. A quote that is impossible to trace to source; apparently spread about by

North in the first days after his firing.

2. First Iran-contra article for the *New Yorker*, December 1986
3. 'Stories of Hollywood' was quoted in Paul Slansky's first Iran-contra quiz in *The New Republic*, 18.5.87; 'Raise your hand' was a presidential remark of 24.2.87.
4. The *New Yorker*, 24.11.86
5. *US News World Report*, 24.11.86
6. *Insight*, 15.12.86
7. The *New York Times*, 1.12.86
8. *Rolling Stone*, 23.4.87
9. North Test., Hearings: H 100–7, Part 1, 28
10. See Maureen Dowd in the *New York Times*, 19.12.86. Le Carre himself, talking to the author, sniffed at the idea that North might have come out of one of his books. He described him as 'a sort of tenth-rate Lawrence of Arabia'.
11. The *Spectator*, 20/27.12.86
12. Richard Cohen in the *Washington Post*, 4.8.87
13. The *Daily Express*, 25.2.87
14. For a fine inside account of the televisual manoeuvres, see Senators George Mitchell and William Cohen, *Men of Zeal*, (Viking, 1988)
15. *Time*, 11.5.87.
16. 'How Irangate Outshines the Movies'. The *Guardian*, 9.5.87
17. *Ibid.*
18. H 100–5, 383
19. *Ibid.*, 385
20. Article by Sam Howe Verhovek in the *New York Times*, 11.7.87
21. For most of these, see Tom Shales's 'On the Air' column in the *Washington Post*, 8.8.87, and subsequent days; see also the *New Yorker*, 18.7.87
22. See e.g. Haynes Johnson in the *Washington Post*, 4.6.87; Pat Buchanan in *Newsweek*, 13.7.87; Curt Sulpee in the *Washington Post Outlook*, 19.7.97; David Broder, *ibid.*, 14.7.87.
23. Hearings: H 100–7, Part II, 200
24. ABC News poll of 12.7.87
25. *The New Republic*, 3.8.87
26. As 'Waiting for the Docudrama': the *New York Times*, 4.6.87
27. 'The Con Man as Peck's Bad Boy'. *Newsweek*, 13.7.87
28. North Test., Hearings., Part II, 10–11
29. Channell Dep.; Vol.4. 89
30. Quoted in 'A Troubling Midsummer Mystery'. the *New York Times*, first Sunday of August, 1987
31. See Michael Wines in the *New York Times*, 1.2.89
32. See Henry Allen, 'The Incredible Shrinking Ollie', in the *Washington Post*, 1.2.89; Mark Tran in the *Guardian*, same day
33. Jan Krauze, 'La Montagne de l'Irangate accouche d'une souris': *Le Monde*, 31.1.89
34. Quoted in a *Wall Street Journal* editorial, 4.5.89
35. Mike Robe to David E. Rosenbaum in the *New York Times*, 28.4.89
36. *Newsweek*, 5.3.90; the *Washington Post*, 17.2.90
37. Reagan Test., 44, 100

38. *Ibid.*, 16–17
39. *Ibid.*, 25
40. *Ibid.*, 38
41. *Ibid.*, 19, 29
42. *Ibid.*, 36. Reagan later said 'I don't know how that sneaked in.' (37)
43. *Ibid.*, 137
44. *Ibid.*, 155, 207, 211–213
45. *Ibid.*, 220–221, In his memoirs, Reagan implied that he did read Tower, after a fashion: 'This diary entry [for 26.2.87] concluded: "Now I'll go on reading the Tower report till I fall asleep . . . "' *An American Life* (Simon & Schuster, 1990), p. 539
46. *Ibid.*, 9

PART II   JUST CAUSE AND HOLY WAR

## *Chapter 5   Flag, Country, Cause*

1. Owen Dep.; Vol.20, 786. See also Poindexter Dep.; *ibid.*, 1207
2. Cave Dep., Vol.3, 867
3. Fernandez Dep., Vol.3, 354–355. Tull Dep.; Vol.27, 203
4. North Trial, 3741
5. Owen Dep.; Vol.20, 693
6. North Test., Hearings: H 100–7, Part 1, 150
7. Life, January 1988
8. Insight, 13.4.87
9. North Test., Hearings: H 100–7, Part 1, 339
10. North Trial, 7620
11. 'Ollie's True Colours' by Eric Alterman; *The New Republic*, 13.3.89
12. Owen Test., Hearings: H 100–2, 439
13. North Test., Hearings: H 100–7, Part 1, 31, 36
14. Hall Test., Hearings: H 100–5, 492
15. DEA Agent 1 Dep.; Vol.8, 623
16. Ex Reynolds-2 (Deps Vol.22, 1290)
17. Woodward, *op. cit.*, p. 507. Many doubt that these words were spoken at all; if that is so, it remains interesting that it should have *seemed* plausible that they might have been.
18. Owen Test., Hearings: H 100–2, 323
19. 'Waiting for the Docudrama'. The *New York Times*, 4.6.87
20. North PROF note to McFarlane, 21.4.86 (Ex OLN-46)
21. Hakim Test., Hearings: H 100–5, 267
22. North PROF note to McFarlane, 27.2.86 (Tower B-78)
23. North PROF note to Poindexter, 16.5.86 (Tower C-10)
24. Ex JMP-9. 'It may be in our interest to . . . bury Mr Barnes.'
25. Owen Test., Hearings: H 100–2, 389–390
26. Constantine Menges, *Inside the National Security Council* (Simon & Schuster, 1988) p.196
27. North PROF note to Poindexter, 15.7.86 (Tower B-126)
28. Poindexter PROF note to North, same date (Ex OLN-295)

29. Poindexter Test., Hearings: H 100–8, 72
30. North PROF note to Poindexter, 20.9.86 (Tower B-157)
31. Armitage Dep.; Vol.2, 65
32. North Trial, 7276; *Report of the Joint Congressional Committee*, 262
33. Dutton Test., Hearings: H 100–3, 235
34. Hakim Dep.; Vol.13, 730
35. McFarlane PROF note to North, 27.2.86 (Tower B-78)
36. North Trial, 2055
37. McFarlane Test., Hearings: H 100–2, 61–62
38. North Test., Hearings: H 100–7, Part 1, 286
39. *Ibid.*, 317–318
40. Hakim Dep.; Vol.13, 140
41. Fernandez Dep.; Vol.3, 354–355
42. Poindexter Trial, 868, 878, 932
43. North Trial, 2728; Thompson Dep.; Vol.26, 423
44. North Trial, 7301
45. Calero Test., Hearings: H 100–3, 2. For contra/Sandinista statistics, see North Trial, 6398
46. Speech to the Conservative Political Action Conference dinner, 1.3.85
47. Calero Test., Hearings: H 100–3, 3
48. *Ibid.*, 2
49. Owen Test., Hearings: H 100–2, 416
50. McFarlane Test., Hearings: *ibid.*, 272
51. *Ibid.*, 159
52. *Ibid.*, 159–160
53. *Ibid.*, 270.
54. North memorandum to McFarlane of 16.3.85: *Fallback Plan for the Nicaraguan Resistance.* Ex P[aul]T[hompson]-7; Deps Vol.26, 1163
55. Ex RWO-5, RWO-6
56. North Test., Hearings: H 100–7, Part 1, 200–202; Ex OLN-260
57. Arturo Cruz Jr., *Memoirs of a Counter-Revolutionary* (Doubleday, 1989) p.181

*Chapter 6   Justifying Nicaragua*

1. H 100–7, Part III (Source Documents), 871
2. Owen Test., Hearings: H 100–2, 440. On not speaking Spanish, see Fernandez Dep.; Vol.3, 318. CIA 'Identity A' Dep.; Vol.4, 1385. Dutton Dep.; Vol.9, 523
3. 'New Ecology'. From *Nicaraguan New Time* (Journeyman Press, 1988)
4. Speech to private donors, 21.3.86; NT 2073 (Caleo Test.)
5. Owen Dep.; Vol.20, 469
6. Owen memorandum to North ('William'), 7.4.86 (Ex RWO-15)
7. Schweitzer Dep.; Vol.24, 366
8. *Ibid.*, 366, 453
9. North Test., Hearings: H 100–7, Part 1, 195
10. See Peter Meyer, *Defiant Patriot* (St Martin's Press, 1987), p.64
11. See Art Harris, *Washington Post*, 23.12.86; *Le Monde*, 7.7.87
12. Speech at Liberty University, 2.5.88

13. Channell Dep.; Vol.4, 89
14. 'The World According to Oliver North', *Washington Post Outlook*, 21.12.86
15. *Right From the Beginning* (Little Brown, 1988), p.67. For the arguments that follow see also James Fallows, 'The Conservative Mind: Partick Buchanan': The *Washington Monthly*, April 1988
16. The *Washington Post*, 13.5.87. See also the spirited debate ('Bill Casey's Reading . . . and the Bishop's Misreading') between R. Emmett Tyrell Jr and William Buckley, same day
17. Speech to the Conservative Political Action Conference dinner, 1.3.85
18. North Trial, 7648
19. Calero Dep., Vol.3, 135
20. Fernandez Dep., Vol.3, 487
21. North Test., Hearings: H 100–7, Part II, 28; Part 1, 164
22. Channell Dep.; Vol.4, 222–223
23. *Ibid.*, 495
24. Ex OLN-478 (H. 100–7, Part III, 731–732); Ex OLN-178 (*ibid.*, at 739). North was one of the principal defenders of this manual, which was more or less disowned after an uproar.
25. Cave Dep.; Vol.3, 744
26. Dowling Dep.; Vol.9, 334–335
27. *The US Congress Approves Contra Aid*. Cardenal, *op.cit.*, p.82
28. Hearings: H 100–7, Part II, 45–46
29. *The Turtles*. Cardenal, *op. cit.*, p. 63
30. North Trial, 3506
31. North Test., Hearings: H 100–7, Part II, 28
32. Minutes of National Security Planning Group meeting of 25.6.84 (Ex Reagan-2), at 2
33. Owen Memorandum to North ('BG'), 17.3.86 (Ex RWO-13)
34. Miller Dep., Vol.19, 544
35. McFarlane Test., Hearings: H 100–2, 146
36. Quoted in Ben Bradlee Jr, *Guts and Glory: The Rise and Fall of Oliver North* (Donald I. Fine, 1988), p. 128
37. 'Reagan Doctrine's Passionate Advocate' by Sidney Blumenthal: The *Washington Post*, 17.12.86.
38. *Ibid.*
39. North Trial, 2962
40. See especially Hakim Dep.; Vol.13, 561–562, 582; Ledeen, *Perilous Statecraft* (Scribner's, 1988), ps 76, 78
41. North Trial, 3694 (Conrad Test.)
42. Fernandez Dep.; Vol.3, 307
43. Gorman Dep.; Vol.12,848–849, 851
44. Owen Test., Hearings: H 100–2, 398
45. Secord Test., Hearings: H 100–1, 110–111
46. McLaughlin Dep.; Vol.16, 848
47. Garwood Test., Hearings: H 100–3, 150
48. Memorandum from North to McFarlane of 6.2.85 (Ex RCM-33); McFarlane Test., Hearings: H 100–2, 31
49. Calero Dep.; Vol.3, 152

50. North Test., Hearings: H 100–7, Part 1, 269
51. North Trial, 7546
52. North Test., Hearings: H 100–7, Part I, 158
53. See pilot's letter of complaint: Ex FIR-4 (Felix Rodriguez)
54. McFarlane Test., Hearings: H 100–2, 191
55. Secord Test., Hearings: H 100–1, 40
56. North Test., Hearings: H 100–7, Part 1, 76

## Chapter 7   Bartering for Bodies

1. Ledeen Dep.; Vol.15, 950
2. 'What Ollie North Told me Before he Took the Fifth'. The *National Review*, 30.1.87
3. Ledeen Dep.; Vol.15, 1232–1235
4. *Ibid.*, 960–961, 1158
5. *Ibid.*, 1015
6. *Ibid.*, 1028–1029
7. See Richardson's notes of the interview: Ex OLN-14, at 13
8. Mayer and McManus, *op. cit.*, 108
9. Koch Test., Hearings: H 100–6, 69–70
10. North Test., Hearings: H 100–7, Part II, 19–20
11. Television speech of 4.3.87 (*Weekly Compilation of Presidential Documents*, Vol.23, No.9, at 220)
12. *Report of the Joint Congressional Committees*, p. 262
13. North PROF note to Poindexter, 20.9.86 (Tower B-157)
14. Hakim Test., Hearings: H 100–5, 244
15. North Test., Hearings: H 100–7, Part 1, 286
16. Linda Poindexter in *People* magazine, July 1987
17. Bradlee, *op. cit.*, p. 415
18. H 100–7, Part 1, 189
19. Tape of conversation in Frankfurt: Deps A (Source Documents), at 1681
20. See *Newsweek*, 8.12.86; Bradlee, *op. cit.*, pp 160–162
21. Tape of conversation in Frankfurt: Deps A (Source Documents). at 1490–1491
22. Poindexter Test., Hearings: H 100–8, 24
23. Deps A (Source Documents), at 1524
24. *Ibid.*, 1536
25. *Ibid.*, 1533
26. *Ibid.*, 1330–1630, *passim*
27. North Test., Hearings: H 100–7, Part II, 23
28. Calero Dep.; Vol.3, 186
29. North Trial, 1989
30. Deps A (Source Documents), at 1325
31. Fernandez Dep.; Vol.3, 388
32. North Trial, 6664
33. The *New York Times*, 25.1.87
34. North PROF note to Poindexter (via Earl), 29.10.86 (Tower B-172). In one set of negotiations the hostages were referred to as 'a New Year's gift': Hakim Dep.; Vol.13, 662

35. North PROF note to Poindexter, 4.12.85 (Tower B-37)
36. McFarlane Test., Hearings: H 100–2, 50
37. Poindexter PROF to North, 16.4.86 (Tower B-91)
38. Poindexter Dep.; Vol.20, 356
39. Keel Dep.; Vol.14, 991
40. North Test., Hearings: H 100–7, Part 1, 8
41. Deps A (Source Documents), at 1593
42. *Ibid.*, 1639
43. *Ibid.*, 1617
44. *Ibid.*, 1616
45. *Ibid.*, 1318–1319
46. *Ibid.*, 1573
47. *Ibid.*, 1380
48. *Ibid.*
49. *Ibid.*, 1312
50. North PROF note to Poindexter, 4.12.85 (Tower B-36)
51. Deps A (Source Documents), at 1530
52. *Ibid.*, 1535
53. *Ibid.*, 1713
54. *Ibid.*, 1737
55. *Ibid.* 1605
56. 'Diversion memorandum', April 1986; Ex OLN-1 (Tower B-88)
57. Memorandum of Conversation, US-Iran Dialogue, 25.5.86 (Tower B-103)
58. *Playboy* interview, October 1987
59. Tower B-110
60. Cave Memorandum of the trip to Tehran: Cave Dep.; Vol.3, 1000
61. North notebooks, 27.5.86
62. North Test., Hearings: H 100–7, Part 1, 285–286
63. Coy Dep.; Vol.7, 1097
64. Deps A (Source Documents), 1375–1378, *passim*
65. Genesis 15: 7–21
66. Tower III-18
67. Shirley Napier Dep.; Vol.20, 260–261
68. North Memorandum to Poindexter of 2.10.86: attachments. Ex OLN-311
69. Tower III-18
70. Secord, *Playboy* interview, *op.cit.*
71. *Ibid.*
72. Tower B-158
73. Deps A (Source Documents), at 1608
74. North notebooks, 16.9.85
75. 'An Evangelist and North'. Bernard Weintraub in the *New York Times*, 11.7.86; North Test, Hearings: H 100–7, Part II, 163. North denied the conversation with Robertson, but said he had made the same request of others.
76. Allen Dep.; Vol.1, 963
77. North PROF note to McFarlane, 27.2.86
78. North PROF note to Poindexter, 8.5.86 (Tower B-94)
79. 'This is the damnedest operation I have ever seen. Pls let me move on to

other things.' North PROF note to Poindexter (via Earl), 29.10.86 (Tower B-172)

## Chapter 8   Bakhshish

1. Ledeen Dep.; Vol.15, 1182
2. Allen Dep.; Vol.1, 677
3. *Ibid.*, 674, 689, 1175
4. North Test., Hearings: H 100–7, Part II, 10
5. Poindexter Test., Hearings: H 100–8, 1148. Owen Dep.; Vol.20, 786
6. North Trial, 3882. For what was taken, see *Report of the Joint Congressional Committee*, p.98
7. *Report of the Joint Congressional Committee*, p. 347
8. Allen Dep.; Vol.1, 674
9. Deps A (Source Documents), at 1578
10. *Ibid.*, 1445
11. *The New Republic*, 1.6.87
12. Secord Test., Hearings: H 100–1, 296
13. *Playboy* Interview, *op. cit.*
14. *Ibid.*
15. *Ibid.* Clines was convicted in September 1990 for taking illegal profits on the arms deals.
16. *Ibid.*
17. Secord Test., Hearings: H 100–1, 60
18. Dutton Dep.; Vol.9, 497
19. Calero Dep.; Vol.3, 168–169
20. Dutton, Test., Hearings: H 100-3, 239-240
21. Deps A (Source Documents), at 1381
22. Allen interview with Ghorbanifar of 29.1.86 (Ex Allen-26)
23. Tape of conversation with Ghorbanifar of 25.1.86 (Ex Allen-32)
24. Allen Dep.; Vol.1, 966
25. 'The Iran Affair: An Insider's Account'. The *Washington Post*, 25.1.87
26. Allen Dep.; Vol.1, 957, 1033, 1043
27. Tape of conversation of 25.1.86 (Ex Allen-32)
28. Allen Dep.; Vol.1, 1159
29. Deps A (Source Documents), at 1584
30. *Ibid.*, 1586
31. *Ibid.*, 1615
32. Genesis, 15: 1–2
33. *Ibid.*, Chapter 18, *passim*
34. Hakim Dep.; Vol.13, 61, 382
35. Hakim Test., Hearings: H 100–5, 273
36. Allen Dep.; Vol.1, 693
37. *Ibid.*, 834
38. *Ibid.*, 693
39 Cave Dep.; Vol.3, 867
40. Deps A (Source Documents), at 1450
41. Hakim Dep.; Vol.13, 272; Allen Dep.; Vol.1, 1105

42. Hakim Dep.; Vol.13, 380
43. *Ibid.*, 80–81
44. *Ibid.*, 88
45. *Ibid.*, 203–207
46. *Ibid.*, 412
47. *Ibid.*, 408
48. *Ibid.*, 396
49. *Ibid.*, 390
50. *Ibid.*, 51, 524
51. *Ibid.*, 561
52. *Ibid.*, 562–567
53. *Ibid.*, 541, 548
54. *Ibid.*, 548
55. Hakim Test., Hearings: H 100–5, 218
56. Hakim Dep.; Vol.13, 29
57. *Ibid.*, 739
58. *Ibid.*, 618
59. *Ibid.*, 672
60. *Ibid.*, 428–429
61. *Ibid.*, 598–601
62. *Ibid.*, 277
63. *Ibid.*, 680
64. *Ibid.*, 613
65. Tape of Frankfurt negotiations: Deps A (Source Documents), 1536–1537
66. Hakim Test., Hearings: H 100–5, 293
67. Hakim Dep.; Vol.13, 717–718
68. Hakim Test., Hearings: H 100–5, 294
69. Hakim Dep.; Vol.13, 721–726
70. *Ibid.*, 727–728
71. Hakim Test., Hearings: H 100–5, 295
72. *Report of the Joint Congressional Committees*, page 74; Don Gregg notes of 8.8.86 (Gregg Ex-2). Secord said he sold them for $8.50 (*Playboy* Interview, *op. cit.*)
73. Allen Dep.; Vol 1, 1306–1307
74. North Trial, 3694 (Dan Conrad Test.)
75. Memorandum to BG from TC, 17.3.86 (Ex RWO-13)
76. *Ibid.*
77. Memorandum to 'The Hammer' from TC, 1.4.85 (Ex RWO-7)
78. Memorandum to BG from TC, 17.3.86 (Ex RWO-13)
79. *Ibid.*
80. Letter from Hull to Owen of 17.8.86 (Deps 20, 859)
81. Owen Dep.; Vol.20, 799
82. Memorandum of 31.1.85 (Ex RWO-2)
83. Memorandum to 'The Hammer' from TC, 1.4.85 (Ex RWO-7) 'Colonel Flacko' was a name for Jack Terrell, an American mercenary who later tried to expose the NSC operation.
84. See Leslie Cockburn, *Out of Control* (Bloomsbury, 1987), ps 168–188, *passim*
85. Used by John Singlaub and approved by Lewis Tambs, Ambassador to Costa Rica: Tambs Test., Hearings: H 100–3, 386

86.  Memorandum to BG from TC, 10.2.86 (Ex RWO-11)
87.  North Test., Hearings: H 100–7, Part II, 63


PART III   OBEDIENCE

*Chapter 9   Soldiers and servants*

1.  McFarlane Test., Hearings: H 100–2, 212
2.  Poindexter Dep.; Vol.20, 1069
3.  Poindexter Test., Hearings: H 100–8, 20
4.  McFarlane Test., Hearings: H 100–2, 37
5.  North Test., Hearings: H 100–7, Part 1, 275
6.  Hakim Dep.; Vol.13, 289
7.  *Ibid.*, 74, 280
8.  *Ibid.*, 287
9.  Secord Test., Hearings: H 100–1, 266
10.  Deps A (Source Documents), 1537–1538
11.  Tower B 120–121
12.  North Trial, Sentence (5.7.89), at 6
13.  North Test., Hearings: H 100–7, Part 1, 168, 193
14.  McFarlane Test., Hearings: H 100–2, 185
15.  Poindexter Dep.; Vol.20, 1536–1537
16.  Poindexter Test., Hearings: H 100–8, 181
17.  Walker Dep.; Vol.27, 338
18.  Secord Dep.; Vol.24, 1091
19.  North Trial, 6284
20.  Neil Livingstone and David Halevy, *The Ollie We Knew*: The *Washingtonian*, July 1987
21.  McFarlane Test., Hearings: H 100–2, 243
22.  *Ibid.*, 159
23.  North Trial, 6921–6922, 7321–7323
24.  McKay Dep.; Vol.16, 754–755
25.  North Trial, 6779
26.  Tower B-78–79
27.  McFarlane PROF note to Poindexter, 4.10.86 (Tower B-165)
28.  McFarlane PROF note to Poindexter, 4.4.86 (Tower C-9)
29.  McFarlane PROF note to North, 10.3.86 (Tower B-82n); North reply to McFarlane (an hour later), Ex RCM-45G
30.  North Trial 6289 (General PX Kelley Test.)
31.  Meyer, *op. cit.*, p.138
32.  North Test, Hearings: H 100–7, Part 1, 304. Ramsey Dep.; Vol.21, 1056
33.  Cited by Simon Hoggart in the *Observer*, 22.12.86
34.  Arturo Cruz Jr, *op cit.*, p.179
35.  *Ibid.*
36.  North Trial, 6053 (Richardson Test.)
37.  North Test., Hearings: H 100–7, Part 1, 41
38.  Poindexter Dep.; Vol.20, 1160
39.  North PROF note to McFarlane, 7.4.86 (Tower B-85)

40. The *Washington Post*, 9.12.86
41. McFarlane Test, Hearings: H 100–2, 18
42. Poindexter Dep.; Vol.20, 1248
43. *Ibid.*, 1060
44. *Ibid.*, 1061, 1215
45. Regan Dep.; Vol 22, 562–563
46. Poindexter Dep.; Vol.20, 1453, 1273
47. Watson Dep.; Vol.27, 433
48. Poindexter Dep.; Vol.20, 1067–1068
49. *Ibid.*, 1450–1455. Poindexter Test., Hearings: H 100–8, 162
50. Poindexter Test., Hearings: H 100–8, 25
51. Poindexter Dep.; Vol.20, 1052
52. *Ibid.*, 1197
53. *Ibid.*, 468
54. Hunt Dep.; Vol.14, 396–397
55. Owen Dep.; Vol.20,785
56. North Test., Hearings: H 100–7, Part 1, 181; Part II, 39
57. *Ibid.*, 26, 37
58. *Ibid.*, Part 1, 271–272
59. Quoted in David C. Martin and John Walcott, *Best Laid Plans* (Harper & Row, 1988) p. 219
60. North PROF note to Poindexter, 10.6.86 (Tower B-124)
61. Poindexter Trial, 1275. See also identical sentiments from Poindexter: Dep.; Vol.20, 1350
62. Poindexter Dep.; Vol.20, 1059
63. *Ibid.*, 1062; Reagan Test., 21
64. Poindexter Dep.; Vol.20, 1154–1155. He did, in fact, admit that it was hard not to tell him.
65. North Test., Hearings: H 100–7, Part 1, 164
66. Owen Dep.; Vol.20, 720
67. See e.g. Poindexter Test., Hearings: H 100–8, 182
68. Secord Test., Hearings: H 100–1, 136
69. 'Dogs': Ex Reynolds-2 (Reynolds Dep.; Vol.22, 1290). 'Let the phone ring': Remark to Ted Koppel on ABC's *Nightline*, 11.5.87
70. Ex OLN-69A (H 100–7, Part III, 418)
71. Quoted in Cockburn, *op.cit.*, p. 113
72. See Constantine Menges, *op. cit.*, p.195
73. Reagan Test., 139
74. *For the Record* (Harcourt, Brace Jovanovich 1988), p.25
75. North Trial 6409 (Cannistraro Test.)
76. Rodriguez Dep.; Vol.23, 783. For North's denial, see Test., Hearings: H 100–7, Part II, 88–89
77. Quoted in *Newsweek*, 13.7.87, and generally beforehand. It was sometimes 'my favourite Marine', which has a true North ring about it.
78. North Test., Hearings: H 100–7, Part 1, 99–100 (though, by then, he had forgotten it).
79. See especially Frances FitzGerald, 'Reagan's Band of True Believers': the *New York Times Magazine*, 10.5.87

80. Clifton Smith Dep.; Vol.26, 159
81. Newington Dep.; Vol.20, 397
82. Quoted in Norman Atkins, 'Oliver's Twists': *Rolling Stone*, 16/30.7.87
83. North notebooks, 16.7.85. Admiral Moreau was then assistant to the chairman of the Joint Chiefs of Staff.

## Chapter 10   Careful Orders

1. McFarlane Test., Hearings: H 100–2, 219
2. *Ibid.*, 250
3. Cave Dep.; Vol.3, 842
4. McFarlane Test., Hearings: H 100–2, 185
5. North Test., Hearings: H 100–7, Part 1, 139
6. McFarlane Test., Hearings: H 100–2, 250
7. Cited in *US News & World Report*, 'Washington Whispers', November 1987
8. Poindexter Trial, 1487
9. McFarlane Test., Hearings: H 100–2, 65
10. Secord Test., Hearings: H 100–1, 60
11. North Test., Hearings: H 100–7, Part 1, 245
12. Bradlee, *op.cit.*, pp 48–49
13. Poindexter Dep.; Vol.20, 1237. For a report of the discussions on ethics, see Richard Halloran: 'Officers Ask Themselves Troubling Questions', in the *New York Times*, 19.1.88
14. Poindexter Test., Hearings: H 100–8, 305–307
15. Quoted by Bernard E. Trainor in the *New York Times*, 12.7.87
16. Reef Points (Naval Academy Handbook), p 47 of the 1988–9 edition
17. North Test., Hearings: H 100–7, Part II. 201
18. *Trial of the Major War Criminals before the International Military Tribunal* Vol XI, pp 24–25 (Nuremberg, 1947)
19. North Trial, 6781
20. North Test., Hearings: H 100–7, Part 1, 63
21. Poindexter Test., Hearings: H 100–8, 204–205
22. *Los Angeles Times*, 15.7.87
23. *Reef Points* (pp 48–50, 1988–9 edition)
24. North Trial, 6904
25. *Ibid.*, 7315–7316
26. Poindexter Test., Hearings: H 100–8, 177
27. *Ibid.*, 178
28. *Ibid.*
29. North Test., Hearings: H 100–7, Part 1, 188
30. Poindexter Dep.; Vol.20, 1153
31. North Trial, 7511–7512. He was also asked: 'Do you think the office of the presidency would be well served by altering the documents?' and answered, 'No, and that's one of the reasons it took me as long to do it as I did.' *Ibid.*, 7500
32. *Ibid.*, 7513–7514
33. *Ibid.*, 7515–7517, 7615

34. North Test., Hearings: H 100–7, Part 1, 76

## Chapter 11    Chains of Command

1. North Trial, 4321
2. *Ibid.*, 7334. North Test., Hearings: H 100–7, Part 1, 300
3. Poindexter Dep.; Vol.20, 1473; North Trial, 4320
4. Poindexter Dep.; Vol.20, 1038
5. Profile in the *Sunday Times*, 19.7.87
6. Poindexter Test., Hearings: H 100–8, 199
7. Walker Dep.; Vol.27, 351–352
8. Poindexter Test., Hearings: H 100–8, 42
9. George Dep.; Vol.12, 118–119
10. Secord Test., Hearings: H 100–1, 75–76
11. North Test., Hearings: H 100–7, Part 1, 80
12. Calero Dep., Vol.3, 142
13. Hakim Test., Hearings: H 100–5, 308
14. Dutton Test., Hearings: H 100–3, 279
15. Poindexter Trial, 892
16. Owen Test., Hearings: H 100–2, 372
17. North Test., Hearings: H 100–7, Part 1, 68
18. Livingstone and Halevy, 'The Ollie we Knew': The *Washingtonian*, July 1987
19. See Seymour Hersh: Article on the Libyan bombing in the *New York Times Magazine*, March 1987
20. Taft Dep.; Vol.26, 513
21. Russo Dep.; Vol 24, 101
22. Tambs Test., Hearings: H 100–3, 371. Tambs later said he did not mean to imply that the President was a king: 'obviously, we have a system in which we have popular sovereignty.' Obviously. *Ibid.*, 416
23. *Ibid.*, 421
24. *Ibid.*, 422–425, *passim.* Tambs said: 'The orders we were given were not manifestly illegal.'
25. North Trial, 2711
26. Poindexter Dep.; Vol.20, 1149
27. George Dep.; Vol.12, 150
28. McMahon Dep.; Vol.17, 28–29
29. Jonathan Hirtle Dep.; Vol.14, 251
30. Poindexter Test., Hearings: H 100–8, 170
31. McFarlane Test., Hearings: H 100–7, Part II, 231
32. McFarlane Test., Hearings: H 100–2, 157–157, 242
33. Poindexter Dep.; Vol.20, 1199
34. Poindexter PROF note to North: 'Be Cautious', 15.5.86 (Tower C-10)
35. North Trial, 6947
36. North Test., Hearings: H 100–7, Part I, 42, 247
37. *Ibid.*
38. DEA Agent 1 Dep.; Vol.8, 709–710
39. North Test., Hearings: H 100–7, Part 1, 247
40. North trial, 6774–6775

41. Poindexter Trial, 1288
42. North Trial, 6842. North Test., Hearings: H 100–7, Part 1, 137
43. North Test., Hearings: H 100–7, Part II, 3
44. North trial, 7268
45. North Test., Hearings: H 100–7, Part II, 178
46. McFarlane Test., Hearings: H 100–2, 80
47. Owen Dep.; Vol.20, 694
48. North Trial, 7354
49. Poindexter Trial, 1275
50. Sullivan proved this with a photograph at the hearings. Altogether North left 80 boxes of papers and 737 PROF notes in his computer. North Trial, 5687
51. Bradlee, *op. cit.*, p.276
52. Cave Dep.; Vol.3, 717
53. Earl Dep.; Vol.9, 1004
54. North Test., Hearings: H 100–7, Part 1, 57
55. North Trial, 4008
56. McFarlane Rebuttal, Hearings: H 100–7, Part II, 215
57. McFarlane Test., Hearings: H 100–2, 138, 31
58. McFarlane Rebuttal, Hearings: H 100–7, Part II, 228
59. McFarlane Test., Hearings: H 100–2, 37
60. *Ibid.*, 45
61. Tower B-19–20
62. McFarlane Rebuttal, Hearings: H 100–7, Part II, 225–226
63. Poindexter Test., Hearings: H 100–8, 99–100
64. *Ibid.*, 47
65. Poindexter Dep.; Vol.20, 1325
66. *Ibid.*, 1324
67. *Ibid.*, 1325
68. Poindexter Dep.; Vol.20, 1473
69. Poindexter PROF note to North, 16.4.86 (Tower B-91)
70. North Test., Hearings: H 100–7, Part 1, 229
71. Poindexter Test., Hearings: H 100–8, 1528
72. Florence Gantt Dep.; Vol.11, 691–692
73. North Test., Hearings: H 100–7, Part II, 87
74. Poindexter Test., hearings: H 100–8, 183
75. McFarlane Dep.; Vol.16, 669–670
76. Meese Dep.; Vol.18, 135–137
77. Hall Test., Hearings: H 100–5, 541. The disapproved memorandum was North's to McFarlane of 2.9.84 (Ex RCM-30B). North had suggested approaching a private donor for a helicopter for the contras; McFarlane wrote on the memo 'Let's wait a week or two. I don't think this is legal.'
78. Armitage Dep.; Vol.2, 53, 181
79. George Dep.; Vol.12, 150
80. Gesell Instructions to Jury, North Trial, 8456
81. See the *New York Times*, 21.7.90
82. Meese Test., Hearings: H 100–9, 257
83. Regan Test., Hearings: H 100–10, 52

84. Reagan television address of 4.3.87
85. Mentioned during Poindexter Test., Hearings: H 100–8, 208
86. Tower III-24
87. North Test., Hearings: H 100–7, Part 1, 268

*Chapter 12    The Men Responsible*

1. McFarlane Test., Hearings: H 100–2, 263
2. *Ibid.*, 5
3. Koch Dep.; Vol.15, 26, 28
4. Poindexter Test., Hearings: H 100–8, 71
5. Weinberger Dep.; Vol.27, 481
6. A point emphasized by Keker at North's trial: 7999–8000
7. News reports of 5.12.86
8. 'Overcome by Ribbons'. The *Washington Post*, 11.12.86. See also *Congressional Quarterly*, 13.12.86
9. Reported by Susan F. Rasky in the *New York Times*, 22.3.87
10. The *Washington Post*, 10.12.86
11. *Congressional Quarterly*, 13.12.86
12. *Ibid.*; also quoted by Suzanne Garment in the *Wall Street Journal*, 15.12.86
13. *Ibid.*
14. See the *New York Times*, 19.12.86
15. 'Face Down in the Mud'. *The New York Times*, 22.12.86
16. The *Washington Post*, 17.12.86
17. Reported by Joel Brinkley in the *New York Times*, 20.12.86
18. The *New York Times*, 19.12.86
19. *Ibid.*
20. 'Charging up Capitol Hill'. *Time*, 20.7.87
21. Remark to a group of southern journalists, cited in *Newsweek*, 25.5.87
22. North Test., Hearings: H 100–7, Part 1, 184, 237
23. North Trial, 8277
24. North Trial, Sentence, ps 36–37
25. McFarlane Dep.; Vol.16, 667
26. Poindexter Test., Hearings: H 100–8, 120
27. Poindexter Dep.; Vol.20, 1238–1239
28. Poindexter Test., Hearings: H 100–8, 38–40, *passim*
29. Owen Dep.; Vol.20, 694–695
30. Newington Dep.; Vol.20, 458
31. Coy Dep.; Vol.7, 1094
32. North Trial, 7706
33. *Ibid.*, 7110
34. *Ibid.*, 7669–7670
35. North notebooks, 25.11.86
36. Ledeen Dep.; Vol.15, 1142. McFarlane Dep.; Vol.16, 677
37. Hall Test., Hearings: H 100–5, 502
38. North Test., Hearings: H 100–7, Part 1, 10
39. Earl Dep.; Vol.9, 1071
40. Coy Dep.; Vol.7, 1095

41. North Dep.; Vol. 20, 480, 489
42. North notebooks, 25.11.86
43. North Test., Hearings: H 100–7, Part 1, 275
44. Poindexter Test., Hearings: H 100–8, 229
45. Thompson Dep.; Vo;.26, 1098–1099. Poindexter Test., Hearings: H 100–8, 167
46. Poindexter Test., Hearings: H 100–8, 120
47. Poindexter Dep.; Vol.20, 1066–1071
48. *Ibid.*, 1067, 1071, 1068
49. Poindexter Test., Hearings: H 100–8, 119
50. Quoted in Mayer and McManus, *op. cit.*, p 361
51. Regan Test., Hearings: H 100–10, 33–34
52. Regan Dep.; Vol.22, 656
53. 'JR [John Richardson] notes of Cong'l brfng on Tues am'. Ex EM-53
54. Poindexter Dep.; Vol.20, 1439–1440
55. The same story was also given to Thompson: 'I wasn't aware. . .but I had some suspicion.' Deps Vol. 26, 917
56. Poindexter trial, 1831
57. Poindexter Test., Hearings: H 100–8, 38
58. *Time*, 16.4.90
59. Poindexter Test., Hearings: H 100–8, 298
60. Regan Dep.; Vol.22, 531
61. Poindexter Test., Hearings: H 100–8, 209
62. Reagan Test., 243–244
63. Poindexter Dep.; Vol.20, 1235–1236, 1443
64. *Time*, 25.5.87
65. McFarlane Test., Hearings: H 100–2, 219. Ledeen Dep.; Vol.15, 1020
66. North Trial, 8144
67. McFarlane Dep.; Vol.16, 613; McFarlane Test., Hearings: H 100–2, 71
68. McFarlane Test., Hearings: H 100–2, 7
69. *Ibid.*, 239
70. *Ibid.*, 160
71. *Ibid.*, 283
72. *Ibid.*, 236. He went on. 'I am sorry. I don't mean to be frivolous about it.'
73. *Ibid.*, 277
74. Seymour Hersh, 'Did the Iran-Contra Committees Protect Reagan?' The *New York Times Magazine*, 29.4.90
75. Mcfarlane Test., Hearings: H 100–2, 59. See also Allen Dep.; Vol.1, 974
76. See State of the Union Address, 27.1.87; radio address, 6.12.86
77. Hakim Test., Hearings: H 100–5, 379
78. Secord Test., Hearings: H 100–1, 135
79. The *Washington Post*, 11.8.85
80. Poindexter Test., Hearings: H 100–8, 689. McFarlane PROF note to Poindexter of 1.11.86 (Ex JMP-71)
81. Thompson Dep.; Vol.26, 1107
82. Owen Test., Hearings: H 100–2, 415
83. North Test., Hearings: H 100–7, Part 1, 235
84. North Trial, Sentence, 8–9

85. Cave Dep.; Vol.3, 754
86. *Caveat: Realism, Reagan and Foreign Policy* (Macmillan, 1984) p. 85

PART V WHAT'S RIGHT AND WHAT'S LEGAL

*Chapter 13   On the Edge of the Law*

1. Poindexter Trial, 2271
2. Owen Dep., Vol.20, 692, 713
3. Hakim Dep., Vol.13, 730
4. North Trial, 6493 (Cannistraro Test.)
5. *Time*, 13.7.87
6. North Test., Hearings: H 100–7, Part II, 89
7. North Trial, 3636–3637
8. Weinberger Dep., Vol.27, 491
9. McFarlane Test., Hearings: H 100–2, 219–220
10. Owen Dep., Vol.20, 492
11. Channell Dep.; Vol.4, 460
12. Calero Dep.; Vol3, 142–143
13. Poindexter Test., Hearings: H 100–8, 186
14. Poindexter Dep.; Vol.20, 1125
15. Regan Dep.; Vol.22, 632
16. Channell Dep.; Vol.4, 460
17. Reagan Test., 72
18. Sigur Test., Hearings: H 100–2, 296
19. McFarlane Test, Hearings: H 100–2, 30
20. North Test., Hearings: H 100–7, Part II, 120
21. Abrams Test., Hearings: H 100–5, 141
22. North Test, Hearings: H 100–7, Part 1, 250
23. *Ibid.*, 166
24. *Ibid.*, 142
25. George Test., 6.8.87, 52–53
26. Poindexter Test., Hearings: H 100–8, 35
27. North Test., Hearings: H 100–7, Part 1, 148–149
28. Ex OLN-40 (H 100–7, Part III, 254)
29. Poindexter Trial, 756
30. *Ibid.*, 803
31. Sporkin Test., Hearings: H 100–6, 185
32. McFarlane Test., Hearings: H 100–2, 261
33. *Ibid.*, 181
34. *Ibid.*, 266
35. *Henry V*, Act IV Sc 1
36. Second Test., Hearings: H. 100–1, 196
37. Stephen Trott Dep.; Vol.27, 148
38. Meese Dep.; Vol.18, 164
39. Answer to a student's question about pardons, 25.3.88
40. Reagan Test., 53
41. Mentioned in a joking aside to Simon Peres, prime minister of Israel, c.

14.3.88. After realizing that the microphone had picked it up, Reagan went on: 'Oh boy, now they'll say that Reagan wants to lie to Congress or something.'

42.  Koch Dep.; Vol.15, 161. Koch said this was the general Pentagon feeling, Weinberger included.

43.  Weinberger Dep.; Vol.27, 467, 490. 'It wasn't on a legal basis that I opposed it. It was on a policy basis with the strongest possible views.'

44.  Koch Dep.; Vol.15, 18

45.  *Ibid.*, 56, 162–164

46.  Koch Test., Hearings: H 100–6, 76

47.  Miller Dep.; Vol 18, 859

48.  Regan Dep.; Vol.22, 583

49.  *Ibid.*, 636

50.  George Dep.; Vol.12, 79

51.  *Ibid.*, 65–66

52.  Deps A (Source Documents), at 1103

53.  Sporkin Test., Hearings: H 100–6, 118–183, *passim*

54.  George Dep.; Vol.12, 95, 97

55.  Poindexter Dep.; Vol.20, 1025

56.  Poindexter Test., Hearings: H 100–8, 144. Thompson Dep.; Vol. 26, 1069-70

57.  Poindexter Dep.; Vol.20, 1109

58.  Armitage Dep.; Vol.2, 233

59.  Poindexter Test., Hearings: H 100–8, 158

60.  George Dep.; Vol.12, 117–118

61.  McFarlane Test., Hearings: H 100–2, 208

62.  North Trial, 7301

63.  North PROF note to Poindexter, 17.9.86 (Tower B-157); Ex OLN-164

64.  George Dep.; Vol.12, 121–122

65.  McMahon Dep.; Vol.17, 19, 193

66.  Woodward, *op. cit.*, p. 501

67.  Motley Dep.; Vol.20, 19

68.  Poindexter Trial, 2236

69.  Reagan Test., 53

70.  *Ibid.*, 74

71.  North Trial, 6780–6781, 6831; North Test., Hearings: H 100–7, Part 1, 166–167

72.  *Ibid.*

73.  Motley Dep.; Vol.20, 28

74.  McFarlane Test., Hearings: H 100–2, 189

75.  *Ibid.*, 22

76.  North Trial, 3975

77.  Thompson Dep.; Vol.26, 1056

78.  North trial, 3954

79.  North Trial, 4583

80.  McFarlane Test., Hearings: H 100–2, 25

81.  *Ibid.*, 187, 260–1

82.  George Dep.; Vol.12, 23

83.  North Trial, **4584**

84.  McFarlane Test., Hearings: H 100–2, 31
85.  Secord Test., Hearings: H 100–1, 72
86.  Fiers Dep.; Vol.3, 1207
87.  *Ibid.*, 1158–1162
88.  George Test., 38
89.  Fier Dep.; Vol. 3, 1205
90.  *Ibid.*, 1209
91.  *Ibid.*, 1135–1136
92.  *Ibid.* 1226
93.  See Joe Pichirallo and Walter Pincus: 'What Did Bush Know and When Did he Know it?' *Washington Post National Weekly Edition*, 29.5–4.6.89
94.  Fiers Dep.; Vol.3, 1203
95.  *Ibid.*, 1247
96.  *Ibid.*, 1196–1196
97.  *Ibid.*, 1207, 1249
98.  Fiers Dep.; Vol.3, 1093
99.  Abrams Test., Hearings: H 100–5, 35–36
100. Poindexter Dep.; Vol.20, 1266. Similarly, the whole NHAO operation was described by Ambassador Duemling as 'overt, but in many ways covert'. Deps.9, 12
101. Fiers Dep.; Vol.3, 1172
102. CIA Identity A Dep.; Vol.4, 1377–1378
103. Fernandez Dep.; Vol.3, 312
104. Ferdandez Test., Hearings: H.100-4, 3
105. *Ibid.*, 359–360
106. Ex TC ('Thomas Castillo')-6
107. Fernandez Dep.; Vol.3, 507–508
108. Ferdandez Test., Hearings: H.100-4, 37
109. Fernandez Dep.; Vol.3, 1133–1134
110. Ex C/CATF (Fiers)-33
111. Ferdandez Test., Hearings: H.100-4, 40
112. Fernandez Dep.; Vol.3, 535
113. North notebooks, 13.1.85

## Chapter 14    Right and Wrong

1.  North Trial, 6927. Questions about the lying letters to Congress produced another variant: 'I didn't think it was a violation of law. I knew it wasn't the right thing to do.' *Ibid.*, 7446
2.  Hearings: H 100–7 Part II,100. *Report of the Congressional Committees*, p.667
3.  Ex JMP-108
4.  Weinberger Dep.; Vol.27, 492
5.  Koch Dep.; Vol.15, 97, 92
6.  North Test., Hearings: H 100–7, Part II, 11
7.  McFarlane Test., Hearings: H 100–2, 206 (though he later called this 'a poor choice of words.') Poindexter Dep.; Vol.20, 1052; Ex OLN-260 (H 100–7, Part III, 1029)
8.  McFarlane Test., Hearings: H 100–2, 146

9.  North Trial, 7403–7404
10. *Report of the Joint Congressional Committees*, p. 411
11. Buchanan, *op. cit.*, p.227
12. The *Washington Post*, 9.12.86
13. *Life*, December 1988
14. Galatians, 2: 16–21
15. North Trial, 7999
16. *Ibid.*, 8262
17. *Ibid.*, 7431
18. *Ibid.*, 7430–7431
19. Hall Test., Hearings: H 100–5, 552
20. *Ibid.*
21. *Ibid.*, 557
22. *Ibid.*, 461
23. *Ibid.*, 539–540
24. *Ibid.*, 565
25. Bradlee, *op. cit.*, p.280
26. Hall Test., Hearings: H 100–5, 516
27. *Ibid.*, 493
28. *Ibid.*, 514, 492
29. Earl Dep.; Vol.9, 889
30. Owen Test., Hearings: H 100–2, 387
31. *Ibid.*, 392
32. North Test., Hearings: H 100–7, Part 1, 3
33. *Ibid.*, 276
34. Ledeen Dep.; Vol.15, 1140
35. Koch Test., Hearings: H 100–6, 106
36. Ephesians, 5: 12
37. Owen Dep.; Vol.20, 723
38. McFarlane Test., Hearings: H 100–2, 132
39. *Ibid.*, 129. He then said: 'I apologize. I don't mean to be silly.'
40. Richard A. Petrino, 'Ollie North, the Misdirected Midshipman': The *Los Angeles Times*, 30.12.86
41. North Test., Hearings: H 100–7, Part 1, 132 ·
42. North trial, 7717–7722, *passim*
43. *Ibid.*, 7301
44. 'The Victorian Defendant': the *Washington Post*, c. 12.4.89
45. North Trial, 7221–7222
46. Poindexter Dep.; Vol.20, 1125
47. North Trial, 7307–7309
48. Poindexter Dep.; Vol.20, 1146
49. Ledeen Dep.; Vol.15, 1186
50. McFarlane Test., Hearings: H 100–2, 51
51. Cave's report of the Tehran meetings: Tower B-119
52. McFarlane Test., Hearings: H 100–2, 268
53. North Test., Hearings: H 100–7, Part 1, 220
54. DIA Major Dep.; Vol.9, 205–207
55. Koch Test., Hearings: H 100–6, 96–97

56. *Ibid.*, 102
57. Owen Dep.; Vol.20, 690
58. North Test., Hearings: H 100–7, Part II, 117
59. North Trial, 2292, 2768
60. Earl Dep.; Vol.9, 921. Poindexter described them as 'people that you might not want to go to dinner with'. Test., Hearings: H 100–8, 295
61. Gregg Dep.; Vol.12, 1078–1080
62. Schweitzer Dep.; Vol.24, 337, 350–351, 557
63. Bradlee, *op. cit.*, p. 421
64. Regan Dep.; Vol.22, 540
65. Quoted in the *Washington Post*, August 1987
66. Gallup Poll of 4–7.5.89
67. 'Ollie and Aristotle': the *Washington Post*, 8.8.87; Ginder's reply, 11.8.87
68. North Trial, 7647
69. *Reef Points*, ps 34 and 37 of the 1988–9 edition
70. *Ibid.*
71. North Trial, 7372
72. The *Los Angeles Times*, 14.7.87
73. North Test., Hearings: H 100–7, Part 1, 90
74. North Trial, 7243
75. Poindexter Dep.; Vol.20, 1320
76. North Trial, 8154
77. Abrams Test., Hearings: H 100–5, 115
78. Poindexter Dep.; Vol.20, 1204, 252
79. North Trial, 6286–6287
80. Owen Dep.; Vol.20, 660
81. Owen Test., Hearings: H 100–2, 348; North Test., Hearings: H 100–7, Part 1, 136–137
82. North Test., Hearings: H 100–7, Part 1, 137
83. Hearings: H 100–3, 55–57
84. Calero Test., *ibid.*, at 57
85. North Test., Hearings: H 100–7, Part 1, 136. DEA Agent 1 Dep.; Vol.8, 868
86. North Trial, 7887
87. *Ibid.*, 7211
88. *Ibid.*, 7145–7159, *passim*
89. See Richard Cohen in the *Washington Post*, 5.5.89
90. Keker summation, North trial
91. George Dep.; Vol.12, 118
92. Hirtle Dep.; *Ibid.*, 253–270
93. North Trial, 6835
94. See Coors Dep. (Vol.3), *passim*; North Trial 7332
95. North Trial, 3689 (Conrad Test.). Of putting down weapons lists, Abrams said: 'Oh God, I mean, it is an absolute, direct, violation of the Boland Amendment, of course.' Test., Hearings: H 100–5, 99
96. Conrad Dep.; Vol.6, 347
97. North Trial, 5441 (Hall Test.)
98. Secord Dep.; Vol.24, 1045, 1051

!

99. North Trial, 3742
100. Conrad Dep.; Vol.6, 653–657
101. Channell Dep.; Vol.4, 150
102. Miller Dep., Vol.19, 254–255
103. North Test., Hearings: H 100–7, Part 1, 122
104. *Ibid.*, 120
105. *Ibid.*, 121
106. DEA Agent 1 Dep.; Vol.8, 479–481
107. *Ibid.*, 392–395, 504–524, 618–623, *passim*
108. DEA Agent 2 Dep.; *ibid.*, 849(it)

*Chapter 15   Criminal Inquiries*

1. Cooper Dep.; Vol.7, 9–11; Meese Dep.; Vol.18, 56
2. Cooper Dep.; Vol.7, 30, 51
3. *Ibid.*, 13
4. *Ibid.*, 291–292
5. *Ibid.*, 19–24
6. *Ibid.*, 66–67
7. *Ibid.*, 30
8. *Ibid.*, 38
9. Richardson Dep.; Vol.23, 224
10. Meese Dep.; Vol.18, 214
11. *Ibid.*, 38
12. Quoted in the *Wall Street Journal*, 8.4.87
13. Meese Dep.; Vol.18, 53
14. Cooper Dep.; Vol.7, 59–64
15. *Ibid.*, 183
16. Meese Dep.; Vol.18, 67–69
17. Cooper Dep.; Vol.7, 483
18. *Ibid.*, 73–84, *passim*
19. Meese Test., Hearings: H 100–9, 263
20. Meese Dep.; Vol.18, 84
21. Meese Test., Hearings: H 100–9, 384
22. Meese Dep.; Vol.18, 80, 199
23. Cooper Dep.; Vol.7, 127
24. Meese Dep.; Vol.18, 95
25. *Ibid.*, 106
26. *Ibid.*, 121
27. *Ibid.*, 184–185, 233–234
28. *Ibid.*, 99–101
29. Cooper Dep.; Vol.7, 132
30. *Ibid.*, 340
31. *Ibid.*, 448
32. *Ibid.*, 167, 181
33. The occasion was when Meese realized that no action had been taken to seal North's office after his firing. *Ibid.*, 391–392
34. *Ibid.*, 159–160

35. *Ibid.*, 209
36. Meese Dep.; Vol.18, 125–126
37. Meese Test., Hearings: H 100–9, 348. Meese Dep.; Vol.18, 237, 126
38. *Washington Post* interview, 19.4.87
39. Cooper Dep.; Vol.7, 390–394
40. *Ibid.*, 205
41. Reynolds Dep.; Vol.22, 1179
42. Cooper Dep.; Vol.7, 207–208
43. *Ibid.*, 202–204. Meese Dep.; Vol.18, 15, 155
44. Meese Dep.; Vol.18, 141
45. McFarlane Test., Hearings: H 100–2, 69. McFarlane Dep.; Vol.16, 670. 'I think it was his own conclusion that he had drawn on his own that surely using this money. . .for another program wasn't right.'
46. *Ibid.*, 142
47. Regan Dep.; Vol.22, 659
48. Meese Dep.; Vol.18, 148
49. Regan Dep.; Vol.22, 663
50. Keel Dep.; Vol.14, 920. Meese agreed that this was a case of 'reading each other's feelings rather than expressed words'. Test., Hearings: H 100–9, 382
51. Meese Dep.; Vol. 18, 154
52. Meese Test., Hearings: H 100–9, 335
53. Meese Dep.; Vol.18, 155
54. Cooper Dep.; Vol.7, 211
55. Ex CJC-36 (Deps Vol.7, 712)
56. Meese Press Conference of 25.11.86; *Weekly Compilation of Presidential Documents*, Vol.22, No 48, at 1604
57. Press Conference, *passim*
58. Meese Dep.; Vol.18, 203
59. Weld Dep.; Vol.27, 602–606
60. Richardson Dep.; Vol.23, 351
61. Meese Dep.; Vol.18, 155–156
62. *Catch-22*, pp 487–488
63. Stephen Trott Dep.; Vol.27, 112
64. *Ibid.*, 615
65. See excerpts from indictment in the *New York Times*, 17.3.88
66. See the *New York Times* and the *Washington Post*, 8.12.88
67. North Trial, 2870
68. The *Washington Post*, 10.1.89
69. Cooper Dep.; Vol.7, 204, 420
70. Meese Test., Hearings: H 100–9, 338
71. North Test., Hearings: H 100–7, Part 1, 15
72. *Ibid.*, 257
73. *Ibid.*, 14
74. *El Financiero* (Mexico City), 29.9.1987. Picked up by The *New Republic* in early October
75. McFarlane Test., Hearings: H 100–2, 213–214
76. *Ibid.*, 236
77. *Ibid.*, 214

78. See the *New York Times*, 10.11.88
79. Cooper Dep.; Vol.7, 1009–1010

PART V   LIVES AND LIES

*Chapter 16   The Realm of the Lie*

1. Hearings: H 100–7, Part II, 196
2. North Test., Hearings: *ibid.*, Part 1, 9–10
3. Owen Dep.; Vol.20, 787
4. Cave Dep.; Vol.3, 810
5. *Ibid.*, 945
6. North Test., Hearings: H 100–7, Part II, 7
7. Memorandum of meeting between North, Earl, George and Cave, 9.5.86 (Deps A (Source Documents)), at 1222
8. Cave Dep.; Vol.3, 999
9. Cave's *Account of US Mission to Tehran*: Tower B-118
10. North Test., Hearings: H 100–7, Part 1, 8–9; 233
11. Allen Dep.; VOl.1, 985–988
12. *Ibid.*, 810–818, *passim*
13. North Test., Hearings: H 100–7, Part 1, 8, 333
14. North PROF note to Poindexter, 9.9.86 (Tower C-13)
15. See William Greider, 'The Tower of Babel', in *Rolling Stone*, 23.4.87
16. North Dep.; Vol.20, 483
17. George Dep.; George Test, 6.8.87, at 36 Vol.12, 151–152
18. George Test., at 198
19. Quoted in the *New York Times*, c. 25.11.87
20. Poindexter Dep.; Vol.20, 1048
21. McFarlane Test., Hearings: H 100–2, 123
22. Quoted in Bradlee, *op. cit.*, p. 319
23. McFarlane Test., Hearings: H 100–2, 2
24. George Test., 6.8.87, at 40, 78–79
25. *Ibid.*, 192; Fiers Test., Hearings: H 100–11, 217
26. Fiers Dep.; Vol.3, 1255. He also said: 'My frame of mind was to protect, to be a member of the team.' Test., Hearings: H 100–11, 122
27. Fiers Test., Hearings: H 100–11, 121–122
28. Abrams Test., Hearings: H 100–5, 65
29. North trial, 4799
30. Poindexter Dep.; Vol.20, 1086–1087
31. McFarlane Test., Hearings: H 100–2, 80
32. *Ibid.*, 67
33. North Trial, 5642
34. *Ibid.*, 4129–4130
35. Secord Test., Hearings: H 100–1, 293
36. North Test., Hearings: H 100–7, Part 1, 7
37. *Ibid.*, 88
38. Earl Dep.; Vol.9, 853–854
39. North Trial, 5636

40.  Reef Points (p 37 of the 1988–9 edition)
41.  North Trial, 7314
42.  North Test., Hearings: H 100–7, Part II, 201
43.  Poindexter Test., Hearings: H 100–8, 265
44.  *Ibid.*, 333–334
45.  North Test., Hearings: H 100–7, Part 1, 183
46.  'The Culture of Lying': *The New Republic*, 13–20.7.87
47.  North Trial, 7426
48.  The *New York Times*, 11.7.87
49.  North Trial, 6289
50.  Richard Halloran, *op. cit.*, in the *New York Times*, 19.1.88
51.  'Retired Officers Split on Ethics Questions': Bill McAllister in the *Washington Pos* mid-July 1987
52.  Halloran, *op.cit.*
53.  See Poindexter Test., Hearings: H 100–8, 265
54.  McFarlane Rebuttal: H 100–7, Part III, 241
55.  McFarlane Test., Hearings: H 100–2, 68
56.  McFarlane Rebuttal: H 100–7, Part III, 240
57.  North Trial, 5641–5642
58.  Hall Test, Hearings: H 100–5, 521
59.  *Ibid.*, 529
60.  North Trial, 5362
61.  Hall Test., Hearings: H 100–5, 505–506
62.  Allen Dep.; Vol.1, 1177
63.  North Test., Hearings: H 100–7, Part 1, 35
64.  *Ibid.*, 339
65.  Poindexter Test., Hearings: H 100–8, 158
66.  Earl Dep.; Vol.9, 627
67.  Ex JMP-43, at 43; Poindexter Test., Hearings: H 100–8, 71, 561, 567
68.  Poindexter Test., Hearings: H 100–8, 253–254
69.  *Ibid.*, 99–100, 344
70.  *De Officiis*, III, xii
71.  Poindexter Trial, 1174–1175
72.  *Ibid.*, 1565
73.  *Ibid.*, 993–994, 1033–1034, 1496–1497, 1572

## Chapter 17    Questions and Answers

1.  Earl Dep.; Vol.9, 627
2.  Poindexter Dep.; Vol.20, 1130–1131
3.  Ex OLN-69A; H 100–7, Part III, 403
4.  'JR[ichardson] notes of Cong'l brfng on Tues am'. Ex EM-53
5.  Minutes of NSPG meeting of 25.6.84 (Ex Reagan-2)
6.  North Trial 3947, 3983–3984
7.  *Ibid.*, 7437, 6782
8.  McFarlane Test., Hearings: H 100–2, 18
9.  Poindexter Dep.; Vol.20, 1167; Poindexter Test., Hearings: H 100–8, 157, 250
10.  Poindexter Test., Hearings: H 100–8, 169–185, *passim*

11. *Ibid.*, 172
12. North Trial, 1511
13. *Ibid.*, 7369
14. For this whole section, see North Trial 6869–6900, *passim*
15. Earl Dep.; Vol.9, 732
16. Regan Dep.; Vol.22, 579
17. McFarlane Test., Hearings: H 100–2, 155
18. Earl Dep.; Vol.9, 281–282
19. A correction had to be rushed out after his press conference of 19.11.86.
20. Earl Dep.; Vol.9, 732–733
21. North notebooks, 25.11.86
22. McFarlane Test., Hearings: H 100–2, 39
23. Ex JMP-94
24. Abrams Test., Hearings: H 100–5, 71–75
25. *Ibid.*, 72
26. McFarlane Test., Hearings: H 100–2, 71
27. *Ibid.*, 85
28. *Ibid.*, 86
29. *Ibid.*, 127
30. North Trial, 6884
31. McFarlane Test., Hearings: H 100–2, 115
32. North notebooks, 4.3.85
33. The *New York Times*, 11.3.88
34. Poindexter Trial, 1036
35. For this whole section of cross-examination, see North Trial, 7357–7430, *passim*.
36. Ex JMP-12 (Hearings: H 100–8, 441)
37. See *ibid.*, 443
38. North Trial, 7402
39. *Ibid.*, 7430
40. *Ibid.*, 7402–7403
41. *Ibid.*, 7405
42. Reagan Test., 146–147. Reagan appeared to believe the letter himself: 'Look, it says he is just helping ... ')
43. North trial, 7405
44. For North's account, see North Trial 6902–6907; for McFarlane's, see *ibid.*, 4110–4114
45. *Ibid.*, 7439, 6894
46. *Ibid.*, 7447
47. *Ibid.*, 4829
48. *Ibid.*, 6488–6489
49. *Ibid.*, 6548–6549
50. *Ibid.*, 1519
51. Letter from Charlotte Eldridge Sutter, dated 13.7.87
52. Thompson Dep.; Vol.26, 976, 1044
53. North Test., Hearings: H 100–7, Part 1, 180
54. North Trial, 6927
55. *Ibid.*, 8021

56. Poindexter Trial, 2159
57. Poindexter Dep.; Vol.20, 1478–1479
58. Poindexter Test., Hearings: H 100–8, 153–155
59. *Ibid.*, 152–154
60. North Trial, 6926–6927
61. Owen Dep.; Vol.20, 783
62. North Trial, 6927
63. *Ibid.*, 2777 (Owen Test.) Owen subsequently refused to answer the trickier questions.
64. Earl Dep.; Vol.9, 855
65. Poindexter Dep.; Vol.20, 1512
66. Earl Dep.; Vol.9, 856
67. *Ibid.*, 853
68. Poindexter Trial, 1975
69. *Ibid.*, 2262
70. *Ibid.*, 1549
71. See Memorandum of the Meeting by Steven K. Berry, 3.9.86 (Ex OLN-127; H 100–7, Part III, 553); see also Pearson's summary, Ex JMP-15 (H 100–8, 103)
72. Owen Test., Hearings: H 100–2, 363
73. *Ibid.*, 384
74. Poindexter Dep.; Vol.20, 1481, 1487–1488
75. Poindexter Trial, 1552

## *Chapter 18 'A Damn Good Story'*

1. Regan Dep.; Vol.22, 645, 667–668
2. Regan Test., Hearings: H 100–10, 21–22
3. Regan Dep.; Vol.22, 630
4. Earl Dep.; Vol.9, 987
5. *Weekly Compilation of Presidential Documents*: Vol.22, No. 45, at 1534
6. Keel Dep.; Vol.14, at 75
7. See Keel's notes of 10.11.86; the *Washington Post*, 26.7.87, and Regan's notes of the same meeting, *ibid.*, 31.7.87
8. North notebooks, 5.11.86
9. Thompson Dep.; Vol.26, 763
10. *Comp. Pres. Docs*, Vol.22, No. 45, at 1559
11. Coy Dep.; Vol.7, 1027, 1043
12. *Ibid.*, 1042–1043
13. *Ibid.*, 1041–1042
14. *Comp. Pres. Docs*, *ibid.*
15. Poindexter test., Hearings: H 100–8, 281
16. Reagan Test., 31
17. Ledeen Dep.; Vol.15, 1056
18. Armitage Dep.; Vol.2, 63, 235
19. *Comp. Pres. Docs*, Vol.22, No.45, at 1583
20. Regan Test., Hearings: H 100–10, 25
21. Poindexter Test., Hearings: H 100–8, 239

22.  *Ibid.*, 240
23.  PROF note of 7.11.86: Ex RCM-48. See also Ex GPS-36 (note from Poindexter to Shultz): 'When we do lay out the facts it will be well received, since it is a good story.')
24.  Poindexter Test., Hearings: H 100–8, 148
25.  Coy Dep.; Vol.7, 1024–1025
26.  Thompson Dep.; Vol.26, 911
27.  Earl Dep.; Vol.9, 62
28.  *Ibid.*, 989–994
29.  *Ibid.*, 1038
30.  George Dep.; Vol.12, 126–127
31.  Earl Dep.; Vol.9, 984–985
32.  Poindexter trial, 2649–2650
33.  Ledeen Dep.; Vol.15, 1053
34.  *Ibid.*, 1136
35.  Thompson Dep.; Vol.26, 1122
36.  Allen Dep.; Vol.1, 399–411, *passim*
37.  *Ibid.*, 856
38.  George Test. of 6.8.87, at 5
39.  McFarlane Test., Hearings: H 100–2, 53–54
40.  *Ibid.*, 49
41.  Cooper Dep.; Vol.7, 193. Cooper Test., Hearings: H 100–6, 330–331
42.  McFarlane Test., Hearings: H 100–2, 92
43.  Ex RCM-58 (H 100–2, 665)
44.  North Test., Hearings: H 100–7, Part 1, 30–31
45.  Secord Test., Hearings: H 100–1, 126
46.  North Trial, 7032
47.  North Test., Hearings: H 100–7, Part 1, 15
48.  North Trial, 7039
49.  McFarlane Test., Hearings: H 100–2, 78
50.  *Ibid.*, 68
51.  McFarlane Test., Hearings: H 100–2, 90
52.  Keel Dep.; Vol.14, 904–905, 987
53.  Poindexter Test., Hearings: H 100–8, 338
54.  McFarlane Dep.; Vol.16, 684
55.  McFarlane Test., Hearings: H 100–2, 93; Ex RCM-59
56.  Cooper Dep.; Vol.7, 99,194
57.  North Trial, 7631
58.  Poindexter Test., Hearings: H 100–8, 113
59.  Poindexter Dep.; Vol.20, 1540
60.  *Ibid.*, 1075–1076
61.  Poindexter Test., Hearings: H 100–8, 149
62.  Regan Dep.; Vol.22, 536
63.  *Ibid.*, 645
64.  Earl Dep.; Vol.9, 1011
65.  *Ibid.*, 1040
66.  *Ibid.*, 1057

67. North Trial, 6614–6630, *passim*
68. Poindexter Trial, 2696
69. *Ibid.*, 2665
70. Reagan Test., 19
71. *Ibid.*
72. Poindexter Test., Hearings: H 100–8, 186, 282. Poindexter Dep.; Vol.20, 1393–1394
73. Regan to the *New York Times*, 16.11.86
74. Regan Dep.; Vol.22, 640
75. Earl Dep.; Vol.9, 901–902, 623–627, *passim*
76. *Ibid.*, 631–639, *passim*
77. *Ibid.*, 1110
78. Poindexter Trial, 1836
79. Poindexter Dep.; Vol.20, 790
80. Poindexter Test., Hearings: H 100–8, 296–297
81. North Test., Hearings: H 100–7, Part 1, 184

## EPILOGUE

1. PBS interview with Judy Woodruff, 29.7.87
2. *The New Republic*, 16.2.87
3. Hearings: H 100–7, Part II, 93
4. First interview after the indictments, c. 18.3.88
5. The *New York Times*, 8.1.89

## AFTERWORD

1. See *The Sunday Times*, 21.12.86
2. See for example the *New York Times*: 'Ex-Reagan aides ask if North equipped Waite', 27.11.91
3. Interview with James Buerk, BBC 1, 22.12.91
4. Interview on BBC Newsnight, 18.11.91
5. North memorandum to Poindexter, 9.12.85
6. See Gavin Hewitt, *Terry Waite: Why was he Kidnapped?* (London: Bloomsbury, 1991)
7. Interview with James Buerk, 22.12.91
8. See the *New York Times*, op cit
9. Interview with Eric Bailey, 26.11.91

# Index